THE YAHWIST

The Bible's First Theologian

PETER F. ELLIS, C.SS.R.

THE YAHWIST

The Bible's First Theologian

WITH THE JERUSALEM BIBLE TEXT OF THE YAHWIST SAGA

Fides Publishers, Inc.
Notre Dame, Indiana

To—Jack and Rosemary, Anne and Tom
Peggy and Joan, Mary and Frank

PREFACE

There are certain convictions which take hold of an individual and eventually compel him to write. The first and foremost of those underlying the present work is the conviction, long apparent to many, that the immense labors of biblical scholars in the last century and particularly in the last forty years have led inevitably to a peak from which the whole study of the Sacred Scriptures must henceforth be viewed. The peak is what authors have often called—sometimes with misgivings because of terminology but always with conviction—biblical theology.

The second of these convictions is that the human authors of the inspired books of both the OT and the NT must, as a general rule, be considered theologians and their writings the works of theologians. If it is barbaric to read poetry as if it were prose, then it is at least philistinish to read theology as if it were history—the fate for too long of many OT theologians.

The epithet is perhaps too harsh; the reality however is harsher. And the injustice it inflicts upon the inspired theologians is harsher yet. They are misunderstood; and this is the lesser injustice. The greater injustice inflicted upon them is that their message, which they labored to conceive and toiled to communicate as only writers can, has gone largely unheard. As Antony said with neater rhetoric, "This was the most unkindest cut of all."

In recent years there has been redress for the theologians of the NT, especially St. Paul and St. John. For the Synoptics redress has taken longer, but the process is well along the way. OT theologians have been less fortunate. Their literary personalities have yet to be limned with a sure hand. Their psychology, methodology, and respective audiences still await identification. And their works, shrouded in anonymity and concealed in many cases in larger theological works for which they provided both source material and inspiration, have yet to be decisively delineated.

The present work aims to redress on however small a scale this patent injustice. It is not meant to be an introduction to OT theology except in the widest sense. Too many introductions tend to be as detached and casual as a passing handshake. It is the writer's hope that this book will be for the reader no passing handshake but the beginning of a warm theological friendship with the OT theologian who composed the first great theological opus in the history of theology.

The book deals with the Yahwist's saga, the theological opus of an ancient genius who could be called—and with equal justice—the Hebrew Homer, "the father of theology," the earliest monumental theologian in history. As Israel's earliest *great* theologian he is the first in a line that runs eventually to a St. Paul, a St. Augustine, a St. Thomas Aquinas. Coming at the beginning, and with all the disadvantages of a pioneer, he nevertheless launched the writing of theology, gave to the Israel founded by Moses the thrust and momentum given later by St. Paul to the New Israel founded by Christ, and provided for theologians down the centuries seminal theological insights of such depth and vitality that they have not ceased to this day to contribute to the continual development of theology. Like St. Paul, the Yahwist is a theologian for the ages.

The author presents *The Yahwist—The Bible's First Theologian* as a pioneer, in-depth study of an OT theologian *as a theologian.* The book projects the Yahwist as the first of those who have performed the major functions of the well-rounded theologian: the function of the positive theologian—searching out and evaluating the major contributions of revelation and inspired theologizing up to his own time; the function of the speculative theologian—reflecting upon and deepening his understanding of the truths of revelation taken both individually and in relation to the totality of the existing deposit of revelation; and the function of the practical, pastoral theologian—synthesizing the results of his reflections and presenting them to his contemporaries in a language they could understand and in a form that reflected and responded to their needs, their problems, and their challenges. The key words in the book are: theologian, theologizing, theology. The book attempts to justify these words in relation to the Yahwist.

However poorly the author succeeds in this justification, he is convinced that the Yahwist himself will succeed where he has failed. It is for this reason, for the convenience of the reader, and in the belief that an author always speaks best for himself, that the full text of the Yahwist's saga has been appended to the book. The translation is the translation of the Jerusalem Bible.

With regard to bibliography the reader will notice that only the barest details are given in the footnotes and in the suggested readings following each chapter. Full particulars concerning all works referred to in the footnotes and the suggested readings will be found in the bibliography given at the end of the book.

There remains the happy task of acknowledging the help received from others. The writing of a book is a lonely work, but it is never done alone. This book is no exception. Without the aid of the authors mentioned in the footnotes, especially Gerhard von Rad, Edmond Jacob, and John L. McKenzie, it could never have been written. Gratitude to all of them is not the least of the sentiments with which the author is filled as he comes to the end of his work. In a special way the author wishes to thank the following: the Dominican Fathers of the École Biblique in Jerusalem in whose library and under whose benign influence the first sketch of the book was written; Doubleday and Company for permission to use the Jerusalem Bible translation of the Yahwist's saga; his students at Mount Saint Alphonsus, Esopus, and at Fordham University, whose enthusiastic response to the Yahwist was a sorely needed encouragement in the dark moments of many a *"cui bono"* period; his confreres, the Rev. Louis Hartman, the Rev. William Biffar, and the Rev. Robert Menth, whose interest and enthusiasm for matters biblical have been no small source of wonder and encouragement over the years; and finally Mrs. Joseph Woods, whose unflagging attention to detail has saved the author many an error and whose kindness and care in typing the manuscript have brought to completion the finished work.

Peter F. Ellis, C.SS.R.

Mount Saint Alphonsus
The feast of Saint Alphonsus
August 2, 1968

CONTENTS

Chapter I

INTRODUCTION

In almost every field there comes a time when the subsidiary sciences become so well-honed and the materials amassed so abundant that scholars in the field begin to sense the moment when a new science will be born. Physicists in the early nineteen forties sensed the birth of the atomic age. Missile experts in the late fifties sensed the arrival of space-age science.

In the biblical field it has been the same. Material knowledge concerning the Bible has quadrupled since the turn of the century. And the subsidiary sciences of exegesis, archeology, philology, linguistics, anthropology, history, form criticism and redaction criticism, and literary form studies have progressed at such a pace in the last forty years that biblical scholars feel confident that they have seen the birth of the ultimate biblical science—biblical theology.

The birthday of biblical theology as a science will always be disputed, but with the publication of Walter Eichrodt's *Theology of the Old Testament* in 1933 and Gerhard von Rad's *Old Testament Theology* in 1957 the feeling grows that the critical breakthroughs have been made and that biblical scholars have entered the bright new world of biblical theology.

The glow of achievement, however, does not dim the fact that the bright new world has its problems. One need only read R. C. Dentan's *Preface to Old Testament Theology* or K. Stendahl's article on biblical theology in the *Interpreter's Dictionary of the Bible* or E. Schillebeeckx' *Revelation and Theology* or any of a multitude of less ambitious studies of the subject to become increasingly and uncomfortably conscious of a singular lack of

1

agreement not only on terminology but even on concepts and definitions.[1]

Concepts of what biblical theology is, of course, depend inevitably upon what one understands by theology itself. And concepts of what a biblical theologian is depend very much upon what one understands by the word theologian. Practically everyone would accept such men as Barth, Rahner, Tillich, Schillebeeckx, Häring and others of equal stature as theologians. And no one would hesitate to accept as theologians such greats of the past as St. Thomas, St. Anselm, St. John Damascene, and St. Augustine. But how many would accept as theologians St. Paul, John the Evangelist, Matthew, Mark, Luke, Our Lord himself? And if the authors of the NT books are accepted as theologians why not such OT writers as the author of Daniel, the author of Job, the Priestly author-editor of the Pentateuch, the prophets Deutero-Isaiah and Ezechiel, the authors of the Deuteronomist's History, of Ur-Deuteronomy, of the Elohist's saga, and of the Yahwist's saga?

The question is not as simple as it sounds. Many are ready to admit that St. Paul and St. John were theologians but only because they have "heard" of the theology of St. Paul and they have "heard" St. John called "the Theologian." Matthew, Mark, and Luke were not in the past spoken about as theologians. Is it right then to say they are not theologians or were we mistaken about them in the past? Our Lord never wrote anything, not even a Gospel. Does that mean we cannot speak of him as a theologian? But then Socrates never wrote anything either. And yet no one hesitates to call Socrates a philosopher. What is the answer? The answer is they were all theologians in some sense because they not only sought to understand the things of faith but sought as well to explain them in a coherent manner to others. This is true of the NT authors. It is equally true of the OT authors.

Why then do we tend to swallow hard on the word "theologian" and the verb "theologizing" when it is applied to biblical authors? Two reasons may be suggested. First, the overemphasis in the past on direct revelation has worked to the detriment of indirect reve-

---

[1] Cf. R. C. Dentan, *op. cit.*, pp. 87-95; J. Bright, *The Authority of the Old Testament*, pp. 112-145; G. Vos, *Biblical Theology*, pp. 11-27; H. Vorgrimler, *Dogmatic versus Biblical Theology.*

lation acquired through the human function of inspired theologizing. This overemphasis can be traced to a faulty understanding of inspiration—as if the word of God were handed down to its human authors by a quasi dictation so that they had nothing more to do than record what they heard.

Such a concept has long since died. But not its consequences. Until very recently there has been a decided reluctance to recognize the fact that biblical authors, for all that they enjoyed the charisma of inspiration, had nevertheless the mundane task of carrying through like any other author all the complex activities involved in the thinking out, organizing, composing and communicating their inspired message.[2] Proximately the overemphasis on direct revelation can be traced to St. Thomas's tract on prophetic inspiration. Aquinas concentrated on the direct revelation made to the prophets under the influence of oral inspiration. His failure to treat the indirect revelation made to the biblical authors under the influence of what may be termed literary or book inspiration led his followers to ignore for the most part the influence of literary inspiration and its natural consequence—indirect revelation.

The analysis made by P. Benoit of the different forms of inspiration has redressed this imbalance in the understanding of inspiration and revelation and opened the way to a new view of the inspired writers. This view sees them as theologians moved by inspiration to write and, while writing under inspiration, to come to new revelation (in the wide sense of the term) through their understanding and penetration of earlier revelation and through the new insights arrived at by the normal human activity of theologizing.[3]

The second reason is the overemphasis on form criticism prior to World War II which led to an atomization of biblical writings and a consequent failure to look at the whole context and framework of the biblical theologian's work. In this period the form critics oriented themselves to the individual pericopes to such an

---

[2] St. Luke in the prologue to his Gospel (1:1-4) comments briefly on his "work" as an author. The author of 2 Machabees in his preface (2:19-32) and epilogue (15:37-39) describes at length and with some humor the trials and torments of an author.

[3] *Aspects of Biblical Inspiration*, pp. 88-101.

extent that they allowed the inspired work as a literary unit to recede into the background. They saw the trees but missed the view of the park as a whole.

Since World War II the emphasis on redaction-criticism, the science which studies source materials according to the integration given them by the theological aims of the author, has swung the pendulum of attention from the individual pericopes to the aims of the work as a whole and to the framework and unity of the inspired books as literary works. As a consequence redaction-criticism, or *Redaktionsgeschichte* as it is called, has shifted attention from the inspired writers as collectors and historians to a new view of them as creative theological writers. This has been the case especially with the Gospels and their authors.[4] It is now the case also with the OT books and their authors. Gerhard von Rad, perhaps more than anyone else, has made use of the best insights of *Redaktionsgeschichte* to study the OT theologians *as theologians* producing works of inspired theology.[5]

The happiest result of the new view of literary inspiration and the new insights provided by *Redaktionsgeschichte* has been the demise of the idea that the inspired theologians were principally historians. As a consequence the Gospels are no longer studied primarily as biographies but as Christologies; and the OT salvation history works (e.g. the Yahwist's saga, the Deuteronomist's History, and the Pentateuch as a whole) are no longer studied as primarily historical but as primarily theological and only secondarily historical. Another happy result has been the growing realization that the primary approach to the works of the biblical theologians must be literary. Alonzo Schökel in his book *The Inspired Word* has made a brilliant and persuasive presentation of this new approach.

Are we then justified in speaking of the inspired authors as theologians and their books as theology? As a matter of fact we do not bestow the accolade of "theologian" on just anyone who ex-

---

[4] Most recent works on the Gospels reflect this change. R. Brown's Anchor Bible commentary, *The Gospel According to John*, is a particularly brilliant example.

[5] The salutary influence of redaction criticism in resurrecting the great, creative theologians whose theologizing accounts for the major portion of the OT is nowhere so persuasively demonstrated as in G. von Rad's *Old Testament Theology; The Problem of the Hexateuch;* and *Genesis.*

plains to others in a coherent manner the things he believes. We tend to stratify and to give the title "theologian" only to those in the top stratum. But we not only stratify those who theologize, we stratify as well the end products of theologizing. Thus the end product of one man's theologizing we accept as "theology" in the best sense of the word; the end product of another man's theologizing we ignore.

Granting that the principle of stratification is based upon something more than the "popular" estimation concerning who deserves the title "theologian," it is this elusive something we must discover if we are to distinguish the true theologian from the multitude of those who theologize but do not theologize in a professional manner nor produce what is commonly referred to as "theology" or "a theology."

E. Schillebeeckx speaks of two levels of reflecting on the data of faith. "The reflection," he says, "that is inherent in the life of faith can take two forms. The first of these forms can be encountered in all the faithful: it is the spontaneous, undeliberate reflection on faith which all Christians pursue. But it can be extended to a deliberate, methodical, and systematic reflection, and this is precisely theology."[6]

Can we say of the inspired writers, if not of all of them at least of many of them, that their reflection on faith was "deliberate, methodical, and systematic," and that consequently the books they produced may be labelled precisely "theology"? Obviously these norms will have to be vindicated for each particular inspired author before we can classify him as a professional theologian. But what does it mean to engage in reflection on faith that is "deliberate, methodical, and systematic"?

Before we attempt to answer this question, let us run down the history of revelation and theology from the beginning to the present time. In the earliest centuries certain direct, seminal revelations were made to the Patriarchs, to Moses, and to the prophets. From the 10th to the 6th centuries B.C. a series of inspired authors reflected upon these direct revelations and the interventions of God that accompanied or followed them and produced works

---

[6] *Revelation and Theology*, p. 99.

which contained at least limited syntheses of the revelation, direct and indirect, in possession of the community of the people of God in their time. The Yahwist, in the 10th century B.C., was the first to do this. He was followed by the Elohist in the 9th century, the "D" author of Ur-Deuteronomy in the 8th century, the Deuteronomist author of the complex that runs from Deuteronomy through Joshua to 2 Kings in the 6th century, and the Priestly author-editor of the Pentateuch in the 6th or 5th century. These works were for the most part what have come to be called Salvation Histories in one form or another.

In the same centuries the prophets developed from simple messengers of the Covenant in the era of preclassical prophecy to messenger-theologians in the era of classical prophecy. Isaiah, Jeremiah, Ezechiel, and Deutero-Isaiah not only passed on their message as messengers from the Covenant God, they reflected on the message and developed what may be called theological presentations of the message fortified with new insights on revelation and limited syntheses. This was particularly true of Ezechiel and Deutero-Isaiah.[7]

In the centuries following the exile the Chronicler wrote a new type of Salvation History and the sages produced in the wisdom tradition such profoundly theological works as Job, Proverbs, and Ecclesiastes. Daniel was written as apocalyptic theology in the second century and the book of Wisdom as wisdom theology in the first century.

In the fullness of time Christ came with new seminal revelation; Paul developed a limited synthesis of revelation between 50 and 65 A.D.; and the Synoptic and Johannine limited syntheses were produced between 65 and 90 A.D. No NT author would appear to have attempted a full synthesis of revelation.

There followed the work of the early Church Fathers and the beginning of systematic theology with the theologizing of Irenaeus, Augustine, and John Damascene. In the 12th and 13th centuries with the work of Hugh of St. Victor, Abelard, Peter Lombard, St. Albert, St. Bonaventure, Alexander of Hales and St. Thomas, the golden age of the Summas began. Since the age of

---

[7] Cf. G. von Rad, *Old Testament Theology*, vol. II, pp. 220-262. See also R. E. Clements, *Prophecy and Covenant*, pp. 119-129.

the Summas we have had for the most part only commentaries on the Summas followed by the age of the manuals.[8] The present age is an age of specialization with some few theologians, such as Barth, Tillich, and Rahner attempting to surpass the Summas, but with what success is not yet known.

Throughout all these ages from the Patriarchs to the Evangelists to the Fathers to the theologians of the high middle ages down to the theologians of the modern age, the development of revelation has progressed in a twofold manner: first, by an accretion that resulted from certain direct seminal revelations made by God to a few privileged individuals; second, by an accretion that resulted from centuries of reflection upon revealed data by innumerable theologians, issuing during the ages of inspired theologizing in new, but indirectly attained, revelation, and in the period that followed the close of the NT down to the present in new insights and new explicitations of the revealed data, but not in new revelation.

It would appear clear that to receive and to pass on a direct revelation as, for example, the prophets did, does not require any degree of reflection that could properly be called theologizing. It would also appear, however, that the fundamentally critical giving of direct revelation was rare. It is difficult to make a headcount of these seminal direct revelations, but if one leaves out the prophets (and by no means all that they said stems from direct revelation), the number is relatively small. In the NT, for instance, the Gospels of Matthew and Luke are certainly theologies based on revelation given to others. Neither Luke nor the author of Greek Matthew (our canonical Gospel) was an eyewitness of the life of Christ. In the main Mark falls in this category also, unless we predicate his presence as witness to many of the events of Christ's life, and this is most difficult to predicate. John perhaps received direct revelation. Paul testifies explicitly to receiving direct revelation but gives no indication of its extent and makes it more than clear that a large part of his teaching is reducible to what we would call simple theologizing, even if theologizing under inspiration.[9] This is certainly true for most of the material in Paul's Epistles and for the Epistle to the Hebrews as a whole.

[8] Cf. *Introduction to Theology*, Theology Library, vol. I, pp. 260-277.

[9] Cf. J. A. Fitzmyer, *Pauline Theology—A Brief Sketch*, pp. 11-15.

Practically all modern interpreters of St. John's Apocalypse would consider it a theological work in apocalyptic form containing little if any direct revelation.

In the OT it is difficult to find a single author who writes as the recipient of direct revelation. If Amos or Ezechiel should turn out to be the inspired authors of their books as we have them now (a most unlikely happening), we would have clear examples. But even in Amos and especially in Ezechiel we already find the directly revealed prophetic word "theologized." In the rest of the OT it is difficult to find a single author who writes as a recipient of direct revelation.

We may conclude then that the major portion of the Bible, OT and NT, represents what we would today call deduced theological teaching derived from reflection upon direct revelation and the development of that direct revelation both by the tradition of the community and by the theologizing of earlier inspired theologians. *This means, for all practical purposes, that the OT and NT inspired writers as a group did the same thing theologians down the centuries have done—they theologized on the given data of revelation (both direct and indirect revelation) and passed it on to their contemporaries in writings whose principal aim was to expound this data of revelation.*

Is this sufficient to categorize the inspired writers as theologians? Is the reflection on faith presented in the works of the inspired writers sufficiently "deliberate, methodical, and systematic" to earn for them the title "theologian" and for their works the title "theology?" It would appear it does. But it remains to be seen whether the inspired writers performed substantially the same functions as modern theologians.

We have seen that the inspired biblical theologians, like their later uninspired colleagues—the Fathers of the Church and theologians down the centuries—theologized on the revelation they received from others and with the help of reason or intelligence illuminated by faith effected a new understanding of the already given revelation. They did this, however, with the accompanying influence of the charisma of inspiration. Did this special influence of inspiration which the inspired authors enjoyed alter the *way* in which they theologized? It seems not. Inspiration altered the *authority* but not the *way* the inspired writers theologized. It altered the intrinsic authority of their teaching, since their theology, unlike the theologies of uninspired theologians, became itself revelation with the same authority as the revelation upon which they based their theologizing. It is for this reason, for example, that we can speak of the different Christologies of St. John and the Synoptics. Each is a theologian whose mind, illuminated by faith in the same manner as an uninspired theologian, reflects on the revelation in words and deeds given by the Son of God and with the assistance of inspiration effects a new understanding of this fullness of revelation given by Christ. The new understanding has the authority of God behind it. It is the Word of God. It is properly revelation in the same way as any of the inspired books of the Old Testament. But—the *human activity* that went into the production of each of these Gospels is the same as that human activity which we commonly speak of as theologizing, i.e. effecting a deeper understanding and explicitation of revelation by the activity of a mind illuminated by faith.

The mental activity, therefore, of an inspired theologian is no different from that of an uninspired theologian, and we can with justice say that the inspired writers engaged in "deliberate" reflection on revelation. Can we, however, speak of this reflection as "methodical" and "systematic?"[10] Again, this will have to be demonstrated in every particular case. But can we speak of *any* inspired writer as a "methodical" theologian?

In the *Instruction of the Pontifical Biblical Commission Concerning the Historical Truth of the Gospels* (par. 9), speaking about the formation of the Gospels, it is stated concerning the preaching of the Apostles: "This primitive instruction was committed to writing by the sacred authors in Four Gospels for the benefit of the churches, with a method suited to the peculiar purpose which each (author) set for himself." In relation to theologizing and theology the significant words in this statement are: "method suited to . . . purpose." The evangelists' purpose in each

---

[10] Cf. J. Macquarrie, *Principles of Christian Theology*, p. 35: "The word 'systematic' should not be taken too strictly. It is the traditional word, and there are no good reasons for dropping it, but it should not be taken to mean something like a metaphysical system in which everything from God to the electron is given its place."

case is to make known to the audience the reality of Christ, the fullness of revelation. An analysis of the literary form of the Gospels indicates that the evangelists proceeded methodically and that the basic method each used was to so arrange the traditional data dealing with the Christ event that doctrines considered important by the author were expressed by the pattern of the book as a whole.

It is the same basic method used by many of the Old Testament theologians, especially the Yahwist, the Elohist, and the Priestly author of the Pentateuch. The question we must ask is whether such a method is sufficiently methodical to establish the inspired writers as professional theologians? It would appear it does. It is a methodical arrangement of material to achieve a specific new understanding of the events, and the methodical arrangement is a necessary element in the presentation of this new revelation.

Such a method is assuredly not scientific in the strictest sense of the term. It does not constitute a demonstration of the truth of conclusions drawn by rigorously logical deduction from established principles. But it is a demonstration and it does proceed from principles, derived either from earlier revelation or from new revelation, to establish new conclusions based upon new insights which are at least reductively the product either of rational intuition or rational deduction however imperfect the logical process by which the authors arrived at their conclusions. It can be shown, therefore, that inspired theologians reflected deliberately upon divine revelation and passed on to others in a methodical and coherent manner the fruits of their reflections.

Can we say, however, that this reflection on revelation was not only deliberate and methodical but systematic as well? Here certainly we enter the area of greatest difficulty.

The systematic theologian as we know him performs three interconnected functions. He performs as positive theologian, as speculative theologian, and as pastoral theologian. He cannot do the third well without the second, and he cannot do the second at all without the first.

1. As positive theologian he studies first the living Word of God in its normative expression in the Sacred Scriptures; then the explication of the living Word of God in the teaching of the Fathers;

in the teaching of the councils, especially the dogmatic teaching of the councils; in the teaching of the infallible and the ordinary magisteria; and finally in the explicitation of the Word of God achieved by theologians and theological systems down the centuries.

2. In his function as speculative theologian he strives to penetrate the truths of faith in order to achieve a deeper insight into the intelligibility of each separate truth; he searches out the mutual connections and the inner divisions of the mysteries of faith; and he attempts to form a synthesis of the totality of revelation.[11]

3. Finally, in his function as practical theologian he attempts to elucidate for his contemporaries in contemporary thought forms and language the totality of revelation or at least some part of it. He studies the needs, the ills, the challenges of contemporary society and ministers to them as a good doctor to his patients—fortifying what is weak, healing what is sick, and propounding ceaselessly what is necessary for ongoing religious good health. Lastly, he is conscious always that man does not live by bread alone but by his vision of the future, and consequently he attempts with whatever evocative powers of communication he possesses to present to his contemporaries a synthesis of revelation that will enable them to integrate the truths of the faith for the present and at the same time provide an illuminating vision for the future. His function, in a word, is to make God's living word of revelation fully living for this generation and so elicit from this generation that vital response of faith and works that constitutes the essence of religion.

It would seem clear, then, that without the work of the positive theologian the work of the speculative theologian could not be initiated and if initiated would be fruitless. Without the work of the speculative theologian the practical theologian for all his knowledge of the ills, the needs, and the challenges of his contemporaries would have nothing to offer. But without the work of the practical theologian the "living word" would die, however valid the work of the positive theologian and however sound the work of the speculative theologian.

---

[11] Cf. E. Schillebeeckx, *Theology and Revelation*, pp. 130-160.

It is precisely because the Word of God is a "living word" and, as such, as valid and necessary now as when it was first uttered or written that both then and now practical or functional theologians have been called upon to express its meaning to their contemporaries. The inspired theologians, therefore, like their modern counterparts, had to function not only as positive and speculative theologians but as practical theologians as well. It is because they did this that we have the Bible at all.

In either case, whether we deal with an ancient inspired theologian or a modern uninspired theologian, the "word" must correspond to the same revealed reality whether the reality is expressed in the ancient thought forms and language of the inspired theologian or by the modern thought forms and language of the contemporary theologian. The difference between the inspired word and the word of the modern theologian cannot be in the reality expressed since each must speak of the same reality if the word is to "live." The differences can only be extrinsic; first, the difference of audience, since each must speak the same revealed message but to a different audience and consequently in the different thought forms required by the condition of the audience if the word-message is to be a living word-message to this audience; second, the difference in authority of the inspired author's word and the word of the modern theologian. The inspired theologian's expression of the word-message to his contemporaries is guaranteed by inspiration. The contemporary theologian's expression is not inspired and is guaranteed to be the "living word" of God only to the degree that it corresponds to the normative reality expressed by the inspired theologian.[12]

Does this mean that the exegete and the biblical theologian have the last word? By no means. The exegete deals inductively with the word of God establishing the meaning of the individual words, sentences and paragraphs or parts of the inspired work. The function of the biblical theologian as positive theologian is to understand the inspired work as a whole, to go to the dynamic life center of the inspired work by going back to the mind of the inspired theologian and thus in part at least to the mind of God revealing.

---

[12] Cf. E. Schillebeeckx, *op. cit.* pp. 175-194.

The biblical theologian does this by retracing the work of the inspired theologian in such a way that he arrives at the original intuitions of the inspired theologian. Since the inspired writer's opus is the effective expression of his theological intuitions, the biblical theologian or student of biblical theology studies the opus as a whole and from its structure and methodology, particularly the inspired author's use of source materials to express his basic intuitions, comes to the life center of the work.[13]

This life center or pool of basic intuitions is precisely what constitutes the "living word." Since this living word is addressed to and calls for a response from every generation, it will be necessary in every generation not only to penetrate this "living word" but to hand it on to those to whom it has been addressed by God. This, however, is not the work of the biblical theologian whose function is positive, but the work of the speculative and practical theologian. Thus neither the exegete nor the biblical theologian has the last word, precisely because the "living word" he deals with as positive theologian is the living word as expressed to a past generation. And it matters not that the past generation had the privilege of hearing the "living word" from an inspired theologian. If it is to remain the "living word" it must not only correspond to the original revealed reality, it must also be rethought, resynthesized, and reexpressed in living forms of communication to each new generation. This is not the work of the biblical theologian, who is essentially a positive theologian, but the work of the speculative and practical theologian.

In relation to the inspired biblical theologians we have seen that they performed the functions of positive and practical theologizing. They evaluated, however uncritically by modern standards, the content of revelation such as it was in their times, and passed it on in language and thought forms that made it the "living word" of God to their contemporaries.

We are left, however, with that function which is most proper to a theologian as a theologian—the function of speculative and systematic theologizing.[14] Can we say that the inspired theolo-

---

[13] Cf. A. Schökel, op. cit. pp. 269-277.

[14] E. Schillebeeckx, op. cit., p. 141, says: "Scientific study implies unity and synthesis. In the science of theology, the many different partial insights develop into

gians speculated on the content of revelation and systematized it before passing it on in their inspired works to their contemporaries?

We shall have to begin with two distinctions. First, as far as we can ascertain (and some may question this in regard to St. Paul and the OT theologian-author of the book of Wisdom) the inspired theologians did not utilize any particular philosophical system as a tool for penetrating the content of revelation and as a framework for communicating their speculative understanding and synthesis of the living word.

Secondly, the inspired theologians did not attempt or at least did not achieve a synthesis of the totality of revelation. It may be argued that St. Paul in the thirty years of his theologizing gives evidence, in the progression of his thought from the Early Letters to the Great Letters to the Captivity Letters, of attempting a synthesis of the totality of revelation. There is no evidence, however, that he achieved such a synthesis. Nor is there any evidence to indicate that he attempted in any one work to present such a systematic presentation of the totality of revelation. It may happen of course that we shall someday find ourselves in the position of the man who does a jigsaw puzzle. When we have completed the puzzle by putting all the pieces in the correct place, we may find that the picture we have put together corresponds to the picture we find in one of Paul's Captivity Epistles. It is not likely, but we shall only know for certain when we have ourselves achieved a satisfactory synthesis of the totality of revelation.

Unlike the inspired theologians, modern theologians not only use philosophy (and the philosophic systems differ from age to age) as a tool for theologizing and as a framework for their theology, but they take the further step, never as far as we know attempted by their inspired colleagues, of attempting to discern the inner divisions and interconnections of the totality of revealed truth and express them in grand and structured syntheses. That no theologian, with the possible exception of St. Thomas, has come close to achieving such a synthesis does not affect the dis-

---

a single all-embracing fundamental view from which the whole content of revelation can be surveyed. The search for the mutual connection between the mysteries of faith eventually gives rise to a theological system."

tinction. The fact remains that no inspired biblical theologian as far as we can ascertain even attempted such a synthesis; whereas no professional theologian today would not at least *hope* to make such a synthesis. As E. Schillebeeckx says:

> The provision of a scientific synthesis of what is offered by a broadly based positive theology is regarded as the most important function of speculative theology. . . . Although God's free will has no cause, he has nonetheless established an organic and structural connection in all that he has freely brought about. The history of salvation and the content of revelation form a single whole, in which the one fact of salvation or the one truth of faith is based on another datum, with the result that the mutual connection of these mysteries of salvation and their synthesis provide us with a deeper insight into revelation.[15]

No OT theologian attempted a synthesis of the totality of revelation; nor did any NT theologian, with the possible exception of St. Paul in the Captivity Epistles. But both OT and NT theologians attempted limited syntheses of revelation. The trend of St. Paul's thought is certainly toward synthesis; and the four Gospels unquestionably represent limited syntheses, each dealing with the same revelation given by the Christ event, but each giving a different though not contradictory theology or Christology.

In the OT it is the same. A series of theologians in different periods of Israel's history attempt to synthesize the current revelation. The Yahwist in the 10th century outlines a basic synthesis which for all practical purposes becomes normative for the rest of the OT and for a good part of the NT. He interrelates and unifies in his saga the revelation given up to his time dealing with Yahweh, the Lord of History, election, covenant, the kingdom of God and Messianism. He is followed by the Elohist a century later and by the author of Deuteronomy in the 7th century. In the 6th century the most ambitious of all the OT limited syntheses is produced by the Priestly author-editor of the Pentateuch.[16] Even more restricted syntheses are produced by the Deuteronomist

---

[15] *Revelation and Theology*, p. 130.

[16] R. E. Clements, *Abraham and David*, p. 82, says: "The Priestly interpretation, which ascribes a central position to the covenant with Abraham, represents the latest and more elaborate of these (Yahwist's, Elohist's, and Deuteronomist's) covenant theologies."

author of the great history that runs from Deuteronomy to 2 Kings and by the Chronicler. What is important about all these OT theologies (and several others could be mentioned) is that they represent genuine attempts at theological synthesis however restricted and unfinished.

The contention can be sustained, therefore, that the inspired theologians exercised, in addition to the functions of positive and practical theologizing, the function of speculative theologizing as well. They did not attempt to synthesize the totality of revelation, but they did synthesize. They did not use any philosophical system as a tool to work with or as a background for their syntheses, but they did not work without tools and independent of all system. In place of philosophical systems they used traditional forms and methods of procedure. The wisdom theologians theologized in the tradition of wisdom writers. The Yahwist, the Elohist, the Priestly author, the Deuteronomist, and the Chronicler theologized in the age old tradition of Salvation History writers. The author of Daniel theologized in the apocalyptic tradition. In the NT the evangelists theologize in the Salvation History tradition and St. Paul in the tradition of rabbinical argumentation.

If the charisma of biblical inspiration had continued to the time of a theologian like St. Augustine, we might have less difficulty distinguishing theology in the Bible from theology outside the Bible. Hypothetically, Augustine would have worked under inspiration and with the help of philosophy would have worked toward that synthesis of the totality of revelation which today we consider the most important task of speculative theology. Inspiration unfortunately ceased before theologians, with the help of philosophy and philosophic systems, began to reach for this higher synthesis of the totality of revelation. But the attempt at synthesis, not the actual synthesis, is what is characteristic of the speculative theologian. And this was present almost from the beginning, and certainly with the Yahwist.

Theology, therefore, runs from the beginning to the present essentially the same. What differs from age to age is not the act of theologizing but the methods used and the scope of the syntheses attempted. Thus in the OT the methods used are for the most part the method of Salvation History presentation. In the NT the same method is continued but a little philosophy is thrown in by St. Paul plus the method of rabbinical argumentation. Philosophy from Paul to the present has been the principal methodical tool in theologizing. The aim also remains essentially the same both in the Bible and in the ages of theologizing that have followed the Bible with the difference, already noted, that the inspired theologians appear to have aimed only at restricted syntheses; whereas, after the Bible, theologians have made the more ambitious attempt, with the aid of philosophy, to synthesize the totality of revelation.

CONCLUSIONS

When the terminology of a science has been battered for two centuries by successive waves of scholarly dispute and debate,[17] it must—if it is to be used with any kind of precision—be either retired completely and newly formulated or defined anew by each author before he attempts to use it. In the light of what has been said above, the latter would seem the only reasonable alternative. The following represents the author's understanding of the common terminology.

Taken in its strictest sense the term biblical theology should refer to that theology contained in the Bible and in the Bible alone. Biblical theologians, as a consequence, would be those theologians and those only who, writing under inspiration, composed theological works which found their way into the Bible either directly as finished works or indirectly as source works taken up by other inspired theologians. An example of the former would be St. Paul whose theological works entered directly into the NT. An example of the latter would be the Yahwist's saga whose theological work entered the Bible via its amalgamation with the other traditions contained in the Pentateuchal theology of the Priestly author.

Taken in a wider sense—the sense it is usually given today—biblical theology is one area of the study of positive theology. It aims to discover the basic theological insights and the limited theological syntheses achieved by the inspired theologians and elaborated

---

[17] Cf. R. Dentan, *op. cit.*, pp. 15-86.

by them in their inspired writings. Again—in a wider sense—the biblical theologian is the positive theologian who engages in this study of the theology of the inspired theologians. His work is similar to the work of a positive theologian in any other area of positive theology; for example, in the area of patristic theology, conciliar theology, or the theology of Augustine, St. John Damascene and the great scholastics. He must first establish the authenticity of the theological works he sets out to analyze. He must then date the works, study the theologian's audience, identify the precise theological questions and theses taken up by the theologian, ascertain his response to these questions or the conclusions of his theses, and finally establish by demonstration the synthesis achieved by the author or at least attempted. The biblical theologian who studies the positive theology of the inspired theologians as found in the Bible will do all this for every inspired writer from the Yahwist to St. Paul. He will in addition attempt to do this in biblical categories. And he will as far as possible attempt to show the line of dependence and development from one biblical theologian to another.

Since, as far as can be ascertained, the inspired theologians did not aim at syntheses of the totality of revelation—an aim realistically possible only for NT theologians at any event—it would follow that the province of the biblical theologian as positive theologian would not go beyond the limited syntheses of the inspired theologians.

Speculative biblical theology, however, can go further. The aim of speculative biblical theology as a science is to discover and reconstruct from the revelation contained in the Bible the basic pattern of ideas dealing with man's salvation and existing, organically and hierarchically structured, in the mind of God. Since this pattern of ideas was revealed progressively and to different authors, the positive biblical theologian sees it in the Scriptures but only "as through a glass darkly." He does not see it as a whole, however sure he may be that all the elements of the pattern are to be found in the Scriptures. The attempt to reconstruct this pattern—as it exists in the mind of God—and to express it in biblical categories is the ultimate aim of the speculative biblical theologian.

How this reconstruction is to be achieved and how it is to be presented in biblical categories is difficult to say. When the work of the positive biblical theologian has been completed and the contributions of all the inspired theologians have been analyzed and arranged in their correct doctrinal relationships, the speculative biblical theologian will take over and look for some central theme around which or through which it will be possible to recognize the unity and interrelationship of all the limited syntheses of the inspired theologians.[18] Whether this ideal, central, synthesizing theme is to be the Kingdom of God, or election, or vocation, or promise-fulfillment, or the person of Christ, or the Church, or covenant is still a matter of debate. It is probably too early to say and certainly too early to judge.[19]

Someday—and there is reason to believe the day is not too far off—definitive studies will be completed dealing with the theological works of the major OT and NT theologians: the Yahwist, the Elohist, the author of Ur-Deuteronomy, the Deuteronomist, Ezechiel, Deutero-Isaiah, the Priestly author of the Pentateuch, the Chronicler, the evangelists, and St. Paul. The present work is far from definitive. But hopefully—it is a beginning.

SUGGESTED READINGS

R. C. Dentan, *Preface to Old Testament Theology.*
G. Vos, *Biblical Theology.*
G. E. Wright, *God Who Acts.*
J. Barr, *Old and New in Interpretation*, 15-102.
E. Schillebeeckx, *Revelation and Theology*, 87-195.
K. Stendahl, "Biblical Theology," in *The Interpreter's Dictionary of the Bible*, vol. I, 418-432.
G. von Rad, *Old Testament Theology*, vol. II, 410-429.
J. M. Robinson, & J. B. Cobb (eds.), *The New Hermeneutic.*
H. Vorgrimler (ed.), *Dogmatic versus Biblical Theology.*
P. Watson, "The Nature and Function of Biblical Theology," *ET* 73 (1962), 195-200.
N. W. Porteous, "The Present State of Old Testament Theology," *ET* 75 (1963), 70-74.

---

[18] Cf. A. Schökel, *op. cit.*, p. 270f.
[19] Cf. G. von Rad, *Old Testament Theology*, vol. II, p. 427f.

R. A. F. MacKenzie, "The Concept of Biblical Theology," *Proceedings: CTSA 10* (1955), 48-73.

O. A. Piper, "Biblical Theology and Systematic Theology," *JBR* 25 (1957), 106-111.

J. Blenkinsopp, "Biblical and Dogmatic Theology: the Present Situation," *CBQ* 26 (1964), 70-85.

A. Schökel, "Argument d'écriture et théologie biblique dans l'enseignement théologique," *NRT* 81 (1959), 337-354.

P. Benoit, *Aspects of Biblical Inspiration*, 64-127.

J. Bright, *The Authority of the Old Testament*, 112-160.

D. McCarthy & W. Callen (eds.), *Modern Biblical Studies*, 9-48.

J. Macquarrie, *Principles of Christian Theology*, 1-36.

Chapter II

THE YAHWIST

THE YAHWIST AND THE CRITICS

He was Israel's earliest great theologian. He gave to his nation a national epic and to the world its first major theological opus. His paradise account alone launched a thousand books. The names of his characters in Genesis have been household words for more than two millennia. He has exerted a major influence upon Jewish and Christian theologians of all ages and his influence upon his own nation and upon the world have made him more than comparable to Homer.

Yet for all his skill as a storyteller and for all his magnitude as a theologian, not even his name has come down to us. We call him the Yahwist or J author because the critics long ago noticed that he alone among the authors whose works are amalgamated in the Pentateuch used the name Yahweh (spelled by German authors Jahweh) for God from the beginning of his saga. Emmanuel Lewy is convinced that the prophet Nathan is the unknown Yahwist.[1] Others have identified Abiathar, the High Priest under David, as the Yahwist. But we shall never identify him unequivocally; and perhaps it is just as well. No more fitting name than "Yahwist" could be found for the theologian who made Yahweh the protagonist not only of the history of Israel but of all history.

---

[1] *The Growth of the Pentateuch*, p. 186ff.

21

The critics have always praised him for his style.[2] More recently they have begun to praise him not only for his style but for his theological profundity. G. von Rad is unstinted in his praise of the Yahwist as a theologian: "As regards the creative genius of the Yahwist's narrative there is only admiration. Someone has justly called the artistic mastery in this narrative one of the greatest accomplishments of all times in the history of thought.[3]

Unlike earlier critics, who considered the Yahwist a mere compiler and even spoke of a "school of Yahwists," present-day critics, without denying the existence of a school of Yahwistic disciples and continuators, tend to agree with the judgment of E. Speiser when he says: "It goes without saying that a work with such distinctive personal traits could stem only from an individual author."[4]

The Yahwist is an individual, but the question of one or many authors is misunderstood if by individual is understood an author who composed in complete independence more or less after the manner of a modern novelist. The Yahwist was never independent

style

---

[2] As far back as 1896, S. R. Driver said of him: "His touch is singularly light: with a few strokes he paints a scene which, before he has finished, is impressed indelibly upon his reader's memory. In ease and grace his narratives are unsurpassed; everything is told with precisely the amount of detail that is required; the narrative never lingers, and the reader's interest is sustained to the end" (*An Introduction to the Literature of the Old Testament*, p. 119). E. Speiser expresses the prevailing opinion today: "What is truly distinctive about this writer is his incisive style, his economy and boldness of presentation, his insight into human nature, and the recognition that a higher order and purpose may lie behind seemingly incomprehensible human events. There is common agreement that we have in J—or alternatively, in those portions of Genesis that critical consensus attributes to J—not only the most gifted biblical writer, but one of the greatest figures in world literature" (Anchor Bible *Genesis*, p. xxvii). See also Martin Buber, *The Prophetic Faith*, pp. 87-95.

[3] Cf. *Genesis*, p. 24. E. Jacob says of him: "The Old Testament counts among its authors several real theologians, of whom the most ancient, the one called the Yahwist by the critics, portrays the history of humanity and of Israel's earliest days as a succession of events according to the principle of grace (God's initiative), of punishment (man's disobedience) and of faith (God's requirement and man's normal attitude towards him) . . ." (*Theology of the Old Testament*, p. 11).

[4] E. Speiser, *ibid*, p. xxviii. To those who would deny the individuality of the Yahwist and explain the saga as the result of an accretion of traditional materials stratified by the efforts of many generations, G. von Rad poses the following problem: "One plan alone governs the whole, and a gigantic structure such as this, the whole conforming to one single plan, does not grow up naturally of its own accord. How could such heterogeneous materials as those embraced by the Yahwist have cast themselves in this form of their own accord?" (*The Problem of the Hexateuch*, p. 52).

of his sources. Nor was he independent of his predecessors, the earlier bards and minstrels, who for generations recited in tribal gatherings and around the campfire the accumulated traditions of Israel's patriarchal and exodus periods. "The oral epic," as G. Kirk says of Homer's *Iliad* and *Odyssey*, "develops gradually and almost imperceptibly from one performance to another, and from one singer to the next, from generation to generation."[5]

In the course of the centuries unusually gifted storytellers arise who not only repeat the old stories with verve and gusto and new insights, but organize and synthesize chains of earlier recitals, weaving them into a single opus combining exceptional range and profundity with recognizable organic unity. These works are so admired and respected by the ordinary bards and minstrels that eventually they become models to be repeated rather than outlines to be continued and developed. They become literary monuments, first frozen, at least substantially, in oral form, and eventually in writing.[6] The storytellers whose productions achieve such distinction are the monumental composers. Homer was one. The Yahwist was another.[7]

Too much has been said by authors, however, about the Yahwist as stylist, storytelling genius, Hebrew Homer. The epithets are probably justified but they can be misleading. The Yahwist's greatness is not in his unique style. In all probability many of the narrative gems credited to him should be credited instead to his predecessors, the bards and the minstrels who shaped, reshaped and passed on from generation to generation the traditional tribal and national legends. The genius of the Yahwist resides in his gift for creative theologizing.

Authors who considered him a mere compiler neglected to analyze the saga as a whole and as a consequence failed to recognize

[5] Cf. *The Homeric Poems as History*, fasc. 22 of the revised *Cambridge Ancient History*, p. 10f.

[6] Cf. the remark of B. W. Anderson: "The Yahwist's composition of an epic in literary form was a completely new thing in Israel" (*Understanding the Old Testament*, p. 165).

[7] J. L. McKenzie does not exaggerate when he says: "To this document is attributed one of the most substantial contributions not only to biblical thought, but to the whole history of human thought" ("The Theologies of the Old Testament," in the *Leblond Lectures*, St. Mary's Seminary, Norwood, Cincinnati, Ohio, 1960-1961, p. 2).

the creative personality of the author. They did not realize that the Yahwist not only compiled existing traditions but welded them into a well-knit and artfully structured theological unity. They missed completely that unity of outlook of the Yahwist that could see in all the complexity of Israel's traditions a thread of continuity and a singleness of purpose that gave evidence of a divine design and plan.[8]

Modern authors, especially Hempel, Hölscher, Noth, Eissfeldt, Weiser, von Rad and Speiser, while not neglecting the Yahwist's sources, have shifted the focus of critical attention from the sources of the saga to the creative personality of the author who was able to bring together so many and so varied traditions and make of them a unity testifying to his own point of view and his own theology of history. This view—that Yahweh is the Lord of History and that Israel's history testifies to the working out of Yahweh's plan of salvation for Israel and for all mankind—dominates the saga and gives it that unity in complexity characteristic of theologizing and theology at its best.[9]

The steps have been gradual and progressive—the stylist, the storyteller, the theologian. Study of the Yahwist now centers on

---

[8] As E. Jacob puts it: "The Yahwist . . . seeks to write a work of synthesis. Having at his disposal much written or orally transmitted material, he makes a selection and retains only what serves his fundamental theme, which is to show that history is the fulfilling of a promise . . . The promise is that of a land to possess, a promise made formerly to Abraham and renewed to Moses. It is at the moment when this promise seemed to have been fully carried out, probably in the reign of Solomon, that the Yahwist undertakes the composition of his work; he reviews the road travelled, in order to find in the march of events towards the goal of the promise, reasons for thankfulness and faith" (*Theology of the Old Testament*, p. 195).

[9] Speaking of Hebrew historical writing, H. F. Hahn says: "This recognition of the religious motivation of Hebrew historiography is the most important development in biblical criticism of the last two decades. It has brought about a new appreciation of the purposeful character of the Yahwistic history, the oldest example of historical composition in Hebrew literature, and of the literary achievement of its author. As Rudolf Smend had once described the Yahwist as an easily identifiable literary personality, who was the most important historical writer in the Old Testament, others now began to give him great importance as a creative writer. Gerhard von Rad, in a detailed study of the manner in which the Hexateuch had been composed, showed how the Yahwist had taken previously existing materials and welded them together into a unified whole by supplying the basic viewpoint from which the history of Israel's beginnings was to be regarded by loyal Israelites . . ." (*The Old Testament in Modern Research*, p. 153).

his theology. But to appreciate his theology, one must first study his saga.

THE SAGA AND THE CRITICS

The saga like the Yahwist himself has been the discovery of the higher critics. The history of Pentateuchal criticism has been many times told and need not be repeated.[10] Although some authors contest the documentary theory, especially the Scandinavian school and a few outstanding Jewish scholars,[11] the majority of scholars agree that the Pentateuch contains four basic sources, each of which gives its own peculiarly nuanced theological interpretation of Israel's salvation history: two narrative sources—the Yahwist's saga from Judah around 950 B.C. and the Elohist's saga from Israel around 850 B.C.; and two partly narrative and partly legal and liturgical sources—the Deuteronomic source from Israel around 700 B.C. and the Priestly source from Judah around 550 or 500 B.C.

The Yahwist's saga is now combined with these three other sources in the grand theological opus of the priestly school, popularly known as the Pentateuch. To detach it and lift it in its essentials from the Pentateuch is the work of the higher critics. Fortunately the work has been practically completed and the reader will find the results in any of the larger introductions.

It is possible, therefore, to give a fairly complete text of the saga, based upon the critical consensus of what belongs to the Yahwist (see pp. 33-40).[12] Where a departure is made from this consensus or where a passage credited to some other author is

---

[10] For extensive summaries of pentateuchal research, see H. F. Hahn, *The Old Testament in Modern Research*, pp. 1-43; A. Weiser, *The Old Testament: Its Formation and Development*, pp. 74-142; and O. Eissfeldt, *The Old Testament: An Introduction*, pp. 155-245. For a more popular explanation, see the author's *The Men and the Message of the Old Testament*, pp. 51-98.

[11] See E. Nielsen, *Oral Tradition*, for an explanation of the traditio-historical method. For a criticism of this method, see C. R. North, "The Place of Oral Tradition in the Growth of the Old Testament," *Expository Times*, LXI (1949-50), pp. 292-296. See also U. Cassuto, *La Questione della Genesi*, and Y. Kaufmann, *The Religion of Israel*, p. 153ff.

[12] See also the running text of the saga, taken from the Jerusalem Bible translation, in the appendix.

credited instead to the Yahwist, the fact is noted and some justification given. Where the Yahwistic and Elohistic sagas have been so fused together that it is virtually impossible to separate them without losing the continuity of the narrative, the joint accounts are given. The importance of studying the inspired author's actual opus, however difficult it is to establish every part of it with critical certainty, can hardly be underestimated. The author's work is the main thing. It provides the indispensable internal evidence. Everything else—background, biographical detail, archeological evidence, etc.—belongs to external evidence. It is important. But ancillary.

The structure of the saga follows in general the structure given to Israel's history by the events themselves. With the exception of the primeval history which is peculiar to the Yahwist's version of Israel's history, the saga follows the structure framed by tradition and reduced to schematic form in the earliest of Israel's confessional credos (Dt 6:20-23; 26:5-9; Jos 24:2-18). A comparison of the two shows the similarities and the differences.

The Yahwist's sequence of events from the patriarchal history to the exodus and the march to the promised land is the same as

Dt 26:5-9	*The Yahwist's Saga*
5b. My father was a wandering Aramaean. He went down into Egypt to find refuge there, few in numbers; but there he became a nation, great, mighty and strong. 6. The Egyptians ill-treated us, they gave us no peace and inflicted harsh slavery on us. 7. But we called on Yahweh the God of our fathers. Yahweh heard our voice and saw our misery, our toil and our oppression; 8. and Yahweh brought us out of Egypt with mighty hand and outstretched arm, with great terror and with signs and wonders. 9. He brought us here and gave us this land, a land where milk and honey flow.	Gn 2-11 The Primeval History Gn 12-50 The Patriarchal History which is developed at great length by the Yahwist. Ex 1-5 The oppression in Egypt. Ex 6-15 The plagues and the exodus under Moses. The Yahwist includes the Sinai event which is not mentioned in the Deuteronomic credo. Nm 10-24 The march from Sinai to the plains of Moab. The conquest, alluded to in Dt 26:9, is not described in the saga, either because lost or never included.

illustrate

the sequence in Dt 6:20-23; 26:5-9; Jos 24:2-18, and in the Elohist's saga. Bernard Anderson observes that the Yahwist wrote his epic backward, beginning with an expansion of the Mosaic tradition, then unifying and rearranging the patriarchal traditions so that they were governed by the theme of the promise given to Abraham and fulfilled on Sinai, and finally prefixing the primeval history.[13] The observation is apt in so far as the Yahwist undoubtedly has structured the patriarchal history in such a way that it anticipates the exodus and the covenant at Sinai. It is misleading, however, if it is interpreted to imply the imposition of the promises on the patriarchal history.

There is indeed a backward movement in the saga, but it would seem better to say that the Yahwist begins with the combined patriarchal promises-exodus fulfillment corpus and then moves backward to the beginning of time to show the relevance of this promise fulfillment story to all history.[14] It is noteworthy in this regard that while the Yahwist certainly climaxed his history with the exodus-covenant account, it is not the longest part of his saga. The patriarchal traditions in sheer bulk come to almost twice the length of the exodus-covenant account.

Structural similarities between the credos and the saga need no explanation. They are founded for the most part on the actual sequence of events. The differences are another matter. There are three major differences; the Yahwist's addition of the primeval history, the omission of the Sinai covenant in the credos, and the apparent lack of a conquest story in the saga.

No time need be taken explaining the first difference. The primeval history, it is generally agreed, had no part in Israel's national traditions prior to the Yahwist and must be credited to him as a creative theological construct.

The omission of the covenant at Sinai in the credos requires

---

[13] Cf. *Understanding the Old Testament*, p. 168.

[14] G. von Rad, *The Problem of the Hexateuch*, p. 66 sees the backward movement of the saga from the already combined patriarchal and exodus-settlement tradition to the non-existent primeval history. He says: "The Settlement tradition started out from the patriarchal history, and at no time contained a statement of the early history of the world in any form. But precisely at the point where it failed the Yahwist, it set him free to develop his own highly personal presentation on his own terms."

some explanation. G. von Rad explained it in the simplest manner possible. He claimed that the tradition behind these credos originated in tribes which had experienced the exodus but not the Sinai covenant and that it was the Yahwist who first united the hitherto separate traditions of the exodus and the covenant at Sinai.[15]

The simplicity of the solution, however, has always seemed contrived in view of the fact that almost three hundred years elapsed between the time of the Yahwist and the time of the conquest and the Sinai experience. Even if it were true that the exodus and the covenant were experiences of different tribal groups, and this is far from proved, it is difficult to see how the traditions would not have been amalgamated long before the time of the Yahwist. They are at least implicitly associated in the admittedly ancient tradition contained in Jos 24.

Artur Weiser explains the omission far more satisfactorily on the basis of the distinction between the salvific *interventions* of God (the proper content of an historical credo) and events such as the covenant at Sinai which deal not so much with a salvific intervention as with an encounter between God and his people and their acceptance of his will. "The reason," Weiser says, "why certain texts do not mention the Sinai tradition . . . is due to the fact that they *restrict* themselves to the recital of the saving acts in history on grounds which make it clear that their silence concerning the Sinai tradition cannot be used as an *argumentum e silentio* for the reconstruction of the whole contents of the festival cult, as is done by von Rad."[16]

The apparent omission of a conquest account in the saga is more difficult to explain. The simplest explanation, which may very well be the correct one, has always been that there was indeed a Yahwistic account of the conquest but that it was not taken up by the redactors of the Pentateuchal sources.[17] The many authors who have seen fragments of the last part of the saga in Nm 25:1-5;

---

[15] Cf. *The Problem of the Hexateuch*, p. 53f.

[16] Cf. *The Old Testament: Its Formation and Development*, p. 86.

[17] Cf. B. L. Goff, "The Lost Yahwistic Account of the Conquest of Canaan," *JBL* 53 (1934), pp. 241-249.

32; Dt 34; Jgs 1, and even in the books of Samuel and Kings are firmly convinced there was a conquest account.[18]

The alternative, that the Yahwist never wrote or never included a conquest or settlement account and that the saga ended with the Balaam incident in Nm 24, would account quite simply for the lack of what one would otherwise naturally expect. The absence of a conquest account, however, cannot be presumed. The whole of the saga and especially the tension created between promise and fulfillment would seem to be directed to and find its fulfillment in the taking possession of the land promised so long before to the patriarchs.[19] The Yahwist himself clearly speaks of an attempted but unsuccessful conquest in Nm 14 and of the successful conquest of the king of Arad (Nm 21:1-3) and other kings of Transjordan (Nm 21:21-35). There was, therefore, a conquest of some sort and the Yahwist was by no means ignorant of a conquest tradition. References to the conquest or settlement in the credos of Dt 6 and 26 and in a number of psalms (cf. Pss 105, 106, 135, 78, 68) indicate, moreover, that a conquest or settlement tradition was a normal and constituent part of Israel's salvation history accounts.

The possibility, however, that the Yahwist purposely omitted a conquest account of Palestine or Canaan proper can be entertained; especially in view of G. E. Mendenhall's theory concerning

---

[18] G. von Rad, for example, takes it for granted that the saga included an account of the conquest (cf. *Old Testament Theology* I, p. 121). J. L. McKenzie says that the Yahwist's history ". . . very probably carried the history of Israel up to the reign of David, but the latter part of the document has been so dismembered by compilers that it can no longer be clearly discerned" (cf. "Theologies of the Old Testament," *Leblond Lectures*, St. Mary's Seminary, Norwood, Cincinnati, Ohio, p. 2). H. Cazelles, in Robert-Feuillet's *Introduction à la Bible* I, p. 361, attributes to the Yahwist or at least to his school sections in Joshua and Judges and suggests the possibility that the saga ended with the succession history of Solomon. H. Wolff, on the other hand, terminates the saga at Nm 25 and believes the intent of the Yahwist's proclamation demonstrates "a striking decline of interest in the conquest" (cf. "The Kerygma of the Yahwist," *Interpretation* 20, 1966, p. 133). Although Judges 1 is frequently said to be a fragment of the Yahwist's conquest story, G. E. Wright contests the view and claims that Judges 1 is not a single document from the lost Yahwistic account of the conquest but a collection of different material (cf. "The Literary and Historical Problem of Joshua 10 and Judges 1," *JNES* V, 1946, pp. 105-114).

[19] Cf. G. von Rad, *Old Testament Theology* I, pp. 296-305.

the nature of the conquest.[20] Mendenhall claims the terms "conquest" and "settlement" are misnomers. He admits no large immigration of "Israelites," no radical displacement or extermination of the Canaanites. He believes that instead of a conquest by invaders there was a revolution by the people of the land against their kings and the political system they represented. This "revolution" preceded and accompanied the entrance of the Yahwistic immigrants. Yahweh, the patron of the Israelites released from bondage in Egypt, became the patron of the oppressed Canaanites when the immigrant group rallied the support of the rebelling people of the land. Jos 24 probably recounts one ceremony among many of amalgamation of the Canaanites to the immigrants' faith.

Such an amalgamation with the Canaanites, in the sense that early Israel was made up of the four Rachel tribes who entered from the desert and combined with the other tribes who were predominantly Canaanites who rallied to the new religion, would explain many things in Israel's subsequent history. It would explain the frequency of Canaanite names in early Israel; the considerable cultural borrowing of Israel from Canaan, perhaps even the language Israel used; the Gabaonite covenant with Joshua in Joshua 9 and the Jael-Sisera incident in Judges 4; much of the information in the tribal blessing of Gn 49; and especially the strangely limited and almost "Benjaminite" account of the "conquest" in Joshua 1-10.[21] There seems little doubt the conquest accounts were composed long after the events and preserved only the haziest memory of the actual events.[22]

Most of all, such an explanation of the "conquest" would help to explain why the Yahwist might well have intentionally omitted an account of the conquest from his saga. His saga, as Wolff, von Rad, and Speiser have pointed out, propounded as central to Israel's "Kerygma" the bountiful blessing of Yahweh that Israel was

---

[20] Cf. "The Hebrew Conquest of Palestine," *BA* 25 (1962), pp. 66-87.

[21] Cf. J. L. McKenzie, *The World of the Judges,* pp. 45-120; M. Noth, *The History of Israel,* pp. 53-108; H. H. Rowley, *From Joseph to Joshua;* B. Anderson, *Understanding the Old Testament,* pp. 70-91.

[22] G. von Rad says: ". . . no clear memory was retained of the fact that, in reality, the entry of the clans was to a large extent accomplished without recourse to war, that is, it took place in the course of changing pasture-ground" (*Old Testament Theology* I, p. 298).

destined to bring to the nations.[23] A "conquest" story would ill accord with such a kerygmatic message.

Such an explanation would account for the lack of a conquest story in another way. If the immigrant tribes were the Rachel tribes, that is, the northern tribes, it seems not improbable that the tribe of Judah and even David himself were originally Canaanites who in the course of the two centuries before the Yahwist had been converted to Yahwism. Thus David's immediate subjects in Palestine proper might well have been ninety percent Canaanite. The stories that deal with David's ancestors—his origin from Tamar, the Canaanite, in Gn 38; his relation to Rahab, the Canaanite from Jericho in Jos 2; and his relation to Ruth, the Moabitess, in what might well be the core of truth in the Ruth legend —lend some foundation for the possibility that David and the whole tribe of Judah had been totally Canaanite in an earlier stage of Israel's history.

While it is true that an anti-Canaanite polemic runs through the saga,[24] it is equally true that the Yahwist's specific polemic is religious not national. His animus is against the fertility cult of the Canaanites not against the Canaanites as a people.[25] The land promise, moreover, which is so frequently repeated in the saga, emphasizes most often, not the conquest of the land, but the "giving" of the land to the descendants of the patriarchs. And while it is true that the Yahwist speaks in Gn 27:39-40 of the conquest of the Edomites and in Nm 24:17-19 of the conquest of the Moabites and other nations, it is equally true that these peoples were for the most part outside of Palestine proper and were only conquered as late as the time of David.

The possibility cannot be discounted, therefore, that the Yah-

---

[23] Cf. H. W. Wolff, "The Kerygma of the Yahwist," *Interpretation* 20 (1966), pp. 129-158.

[24] See below, pp. 169ff.

[25] Granting that Mendenhall and McKenzie have rightly reconstructed the "conquest" story as a revolt of the Canaanites against their kings and against an oppressive feudal system, one can understand how the Yahwist would oppose the Canaanite system and particularly its religion without being against the Canaanites as a people, just as postrevolutionary Americans were against the English system though not against the English people of whom they were in many cases the direct descendants.

wist terminated his saga with the Balaam episode and purposely omitted any account of the conquest. At a time when the triumphant Yahwism of the Davidic empire was perhaps again making converts, or hoping to make converts, as it had in the heyday of its appearance in Canaan, a conquest account would hardly have served as a *captatio benevolentiae*. It is not improbable, as a consequence, that the existing conquest narratives came into being at a later date when Israel was on the defensive against a resurgent Canaanite fertility cult. These later accounts testify to a true but severely limited conquest—one which the Yahwist might with impunity have neglected in proclaiming his kerygmatic message about Israel the source of blessing for all mankind.

Whatever the solution to the problem of the missing conquest account, the basic structure remains the same. The saga has three parts: a primeval history in Gn 2-11; a patriarchal history in Gn 12-50; and a national history in Ex 1-24 and Nm 10-24; or, if one visualizes the structure in accord with the mind of the Yahwist: a part dealing with the interventions of Yahweh in the prehistory of mankind and Israel; a part dealing with the interventions of Yahweh in the patriarchal era of Israel; and a final part dealing with the interventions of Yahweh in the national history of Israel.

The following structural arrangement shows the contents of the saga with the approximate number of verses belonging to the Yahwist in each section of Genesis, Exodus, and Numbers as we have those books now. The numbers can be only relative guides for two reasons. First, it is impossible to tell how much of the original saga the final editor of the Pentateuch did not include at all. It would seem certain that at least small portions of his Joseph story and Exodus story have been eliminated. Second, where the editor found a parallel in the Elohist's saga and preferred it to the Yahwist's account, it becomes impossible to determine exactly the original length of the Yahwist's account. Authors generally agree, however, that the redactors of the Pentateuch did not exclude much that was available in the Yahwist's saga. Their inclusion of so many parallel accounts and so many duplicated narratives indicates an almost scrupulous attachment to tradition. It is likely, therefore, that the redactors omitted little that was available to them, and as a consequence the relative amount of material in each section should correspond with some accuracy to the dimensions of the original saga.

If the Priestly author, as the critics agree, has included the major part of the Yahwist saga in the final amalgamation of his sources to form the Pentateuch, then the amount of material contained in each section of the original saga would be apportioned as follows: roughly 150 verses in the primeval history; 800 verses in the patriarchal history; 600 verses in the national history.

Structurally viewed the saga bulges in the center. Even if there had been an account of the conquest joined to the Exodus and Numbers sections of the national history, the 800 verses given to the patriarchal history would still seem long. Any analysis of the saga as a whole, therefore, must take this imbalance into account.[26]

PART I—THE PRIMEVAL HISTORY

The Yahwist's primeval history has been amalgamated in Gn 1-11 with the Priestly source by the final editor of the Pentateuch. Out of approximately 300 verses in Gn 1-11, roughly 150 belong to the Yahwist and 150 to the Priestly source. The following pericopes are generally credited to the Yahwist:

Paradise	Gn 2:4b-25
The Fall	3:1-24
Cain and Abel	4:1-16
The descendants of Cain	4:17-24
The descendants of Seth	4:25-26
Sons of god and the daughters of men	6:1-4
The corruption of mankind	6:5-8
Preparations for the flood	7:1-10, 12, 16b
The flood	7:17a, 22-23
The flood subsides	8:3, 6, 8-13, 20-22
Noah and his sons	9:18-27
Genealogies	10:8-19, 21, 24-30
The tower of Babel	11:1-9
The descendants of Terah	11:28-30

[26] See pp. 203f.

PART II—THE PATRIARCHAL HISTORY

The patriarchal history in Gn 12-50 contains materials from three sources: the Yahwist's saga, the Elohist's saga, and the Priestly source. Out of approximately 1300 verses in Gn 12-50, roughly 800 belong to the Yahwist; 300 to the Elohist; and 200 to the Priestly source. The following pericopes are generally credited to the Yahwist:

THE STORY OF ABRAHAM

The call of Abraham	12:1-3, 4a, 6-9
Abraham in Egypt	12:10-20
Abraham and Lot separate	13:1-5, 7-11, 13-18
The campaign of the four great kings	14:1-16[27]
Melchizedek	14:17-24
The divine promises and covenant	15:1-4, 6-12, 17-21[28]
The birth of Ishmael	16:1-2, 3b-14
The apparition at Mamre	18:1-33
The destruction of Sodom	19:1-29
The origin of the Moabites and Ammonites	19:30-38
The birth of Isaac	21:1-2a, 6-7, 33
The sacrifice of Isaac	22:1-19[29]
The descendants of Nahor	22:20-24
The tomb of the patriarchs	23:2-20[30]
The marriage of Isaac	24:1-67
The descendants of Keturah	25:1-6, 11b

---

[27] Although an independent tradition, there is good reason (see pp. 70f) to believe the Yahwist incorporated this ancient tradition into his saga.

[28] Possibly vv 2b-3a,5,13-16 come from the Elohist.

[29] Although frequently credited to the Elohist, there are good reasons, as Speiser shows (Anchor *Genesis*, p. 166) for attributing the story to the Yahwist.

[30] Generally credited to the Priestly source, there are nevertheless indications, as Speiser shows (*ibid*, p. 173), pointing to the Yahwist.

THE STORY OF ISAAC AND JACOB

---

[31] Vv 12,17-18,20-22 should probably be credited to the Elohist.

[32] 30:1-2,6,17-20,21-23 should probably be credited to the Elohist.

[33] Probably Elohistic in part but the distribution is unclear.

[34] Perhaps vv 4-11 should be credited to the Elohist.

THE STORY OF JOSEPH

Joseph and his brothers	37:2b-11
Joseph sold by his brothers	37:12-20, 25-27, 28b
The story of Judah and Tamar	38:1-30
Joseph's early days in Egypt	39:1-6
The attempt to seduce Joseph	39:7-20
Joseph in gaol	39:21-23
Jacob's sons return to Canaan	42:26-28
Jacob's sons leave again with Benjamin	43:1-14
The meeting with Joseph	43:15-34
Joseph's cup in Benjamin's sack	44:1-17
Judah intervenes	44:18-34
Joseph makes himself known	45:1-15
Pharaoh's invitation	45:16-20
The return to Canaan	45:21-28
Jacob leaves for Egypt	46:1
Joseph welcomes them	46:28-34
Pharaoh grants an audience	47:1-6
Joseph's agrarian policy	47:13-26
Jacob's last wishes	47:27a, 29-31
Jacob adopts Joseph's two sons and blesses them	48:8-22[35]
Jacob's blessings	49:2-28[36]
Jacob's funeral	50:1-11, 14

PART III—THE NATIONAL HISTORY

The national history, relating the events that went into the birth of Israel as God's chosen nation, is broken up into two sections by extensive interpolations of Priestly material. The first sec-

---

[35] The text probably contains Elohistic elements.

[36] The material in ch. 49 is obviously from the period of the Judges but it has been adapted (especially 49:8-12) and incorporated into his saga by the Yahwist.

tion in Ex 1-24; 32-34 is separated from the last section in Nm 10-24 by the huge liturgical corpus of the Priestly source interpolated after Ex 24.

Both in Ex 1-24; 32-33 and Nm 10-24 there is an admixture of material from the Yahwist, the Elohist, and the Priestly source. Out of approximately 1200 verses in both sections, roughly 600 come from the Yahwist. The distribution of source material is more difficult and more debatable than the distribution in Genesis, principally because so much of the Exodus story has been taken from liturgical complexes. Nevertheless, the following pericopes in Exodus and Numbers can be attributed with good probability to the Yahwist:

THE LIBERATION FROM EGYPT

The Hebrews oppressed	Ex 1:8-12, 22
The birth of Moses	2:1-10[37]
Moses escapes to Midian	2:11-22
The burning bush	3:2-4, 7-8
Moses instructed for his mission	3:16-20
Moses granted miraculous powers	4:1, 5-7
Aaron, the mouthpiece of Moses	4:10-14
Moses returns to Egypt. He leaves Midian	4:18-20a
The son of Moses circumcised	4:24-26
Moses meets Aaron	4:27-31
The first audience with Pharaoh	5:1-5
Instructions to the slave-drivers	5:6-14
The Hebrew foremen complain	5:15-18
The dilemma of the foremen. Moses prays	5:19—6:1
The water turns to blood	7:14-17, 21, 23-25
The frogs	7:26-29; 8:1-15

---

[37] Ch. 2-4 contain carefully redacted Yahwistic and Elohistic material. The disengagement of the sources is extremely problematical.

The gadflies	8:16-32
Death of the Egyptians' livestock	9:1-7
The hail	9:13, 17-18, 23b, 24b, 25b-26, 28-29, 33-35
The locusts	10:3-7, 12a, 13b, 14b, 16a, 17-19
The darkness	10:21-29
Moses proclaims the death of the first-born	11:4-8
Injunctions relating to the Passover	12:21-23
Death of the firstborn	12:29-31
Israel's departure	12:27a, 28-39; 13:20-22
The Egyptians pursue the Israelites	14:5-7, 10, 13-14
The crossing	14:19b-21, 24-25, 27, 30-31
Song of victory	15:1-19

ISRAEL IN THE DESERT

Marah	15:22-25
The manna	16:4-5, 28-31, 35
The water from the rock	17:1-7
A battle against the Amalekites	17:8-16

THE COVENANT AT SINAI

The Israelites come to Sinai	19:2b
Preparing for the Covenant	19:10-11, 13b, 14-15
The theophany on Sinai	19:16-20a
Moses on the mountain	24:12-15
The golden calf	32:1-6[38]
Moses forewarned by Yahweh	32:7a, 8-10
The prayer of Moses	32:11-14

---

[38] The close redaction of Yahwistic and Elohistic materials in ch. 32-33 makes precise reconstruction of the Yahwist's account extremely difficult.

THE HALTS IN THE WILDERNESS

From Kadesh to Moab

Edom refuses right of way	20:1b, 14-21
The capture of Hormah	21:1-3
The bronze serpent	21:5-9
By stages to Transjordania	21:12-20
The conquest of Transjordania	21:21—22:1
The king of Moab appeals to Balaam	22:5-8, 13-19, 21
Balaam's donkey	22:22-35
Balaam and Balak	22:36-38; 24:2-25

THE DATE OF THE SAGA

The principal purpose of determining as nearly as possible the date when the saga was written is to establish the immediate and remote historical background of the Yahwist's audience and thus help to recreate the precise *Sitz im Leben* of the saga.

Determining the date of the saga helps the reader in other ways. In an era when revelation was developing by the addition of revealed truths as well as by simple theologizing, it helps the reader to judge the Yahwist on the basis of the limited revelation in the possession of Israel up to his time.

It helps the reader judge the Yahwist's literary and methodological approach by comparing it with the literary forms of communication before and up to his time; e.g. the use of foreshadowing techniques in the David and Solomon histories (1 Sm 16ff and 2 Sm 9ff) and the use of parables in the wisdom tradition to teach moral truths in 2 Sm 12.

It helps to determine the time between the Yahwist and his sources (e.g. the 800 years between the Yahwist and his earliest patriarchal traditions) and forces the reader as a consequence to consider more critically the historicity of these sources.[39]

Finally and most important it helps to put the reader in the precise life-situation of the Yahwist and his audience and thus understand better their needs, problems, and challenges.

---

[39] See below, pp. 88-96.

It is the general opinion of authors (e.g. Weiser, von Rad, Anderson, Speiser, Noth, Lewy, de Vaux, Wright, Jacob, and others) that the Yahwist wrote his saga sometime in the reign of Solomon (965-926). Some of the reasons for this opinion may be stated as follows.

First, it was in the era of David and Solomon that two of the concepts dominating the Yahwist's saga—the concept of a greater Israel and the concept of a universal God-given mission to rule the nations—pervaded the thinking of Israelite intellectuals. It was an era when hopes were high and optimism unbounded.[40]

Second, the Davidic history in 1 Sm 16-31 and the Succession History of Solomon in 2 Sm 9-20; 1 Kgs 1-2, both of which are dated to the Davidic-Solomonic period, betray similarities in mentality, interests, and psychological approach to the Yahwist's saga.

Third, the texts foreshadowing the rise of the Davidic dynasty (Gn 49:8-12 and Nm 24:7-9, 17-19) appear to have an *ad hoc* motivation which would be cogent at the time of Solomon, when the fate of the dynasty and the succession were still in question, but much less cogent in later centuries when the dynasty was taken for granted as fully established.

Fourth, Gn 27:39-40, which speaks of the subjection of Edom to Israel followed by an attempt to throw off that subjection, presumes the author knows about David's conquest of Edom (cf. 2 Sm 8:12-14) and the later revolt of Edom in the time of Solomon (cf. 1 Kgs 11:14ff). This would indicate a *terminus a quo* sometime in the reign of Solomon.[41]

Fifth, nowhere in the Yahwist's saga is there any allusion to the division of Solomon's kingdom after his death in 926. Nor is there any allusion to animosity between Judah and the northern tribes led by the sons of Joseph. In fact, in the blessing of Joseph (Gn

---

[40] Cf. G. von Rad, *The Problem of the Hexateuch*, p. 70.

[41] H. W. Wolff, "The Kerygma of the Yahwist," *Interpretation* 20 (1966) pp. 134-135, says: "If one ask in which peoples besides Israel the narrator is interested, the answer is the very peoples which, according to 2 Samuel 8, were incorporated into David's empire: the Philistines (Gn 26:1-8; compare 10:14), the Moabites (Nm 22; 24:17) and Ammonites (Gn 19:37-38), the Arameans (Gn 24:10; 31:20), the Edomites (Gn 25:23,30; compare 27:39f.; Nm 24:18), and the Amelekites (Ex 17:8-16), in addition to the Canaanites who were conquered and incorporated into David's empire (Gn 9:25)."

49), which has a prominent place in the Yahwist's saga, both Judah and Joseph are singled out for praise. This would indicate a *terminus ad quem* no later than 926 B.C.[42]

Finally, the time was ripe and the period was conducive to the writing of a history with a theological purpose and a pastoral orientation. As E. Jacob says:

> In the life of a people, all periods are not equally favorable to historical composition; in a general way history is written under the dominion of striking events which by their creative nature constitute a turning point and which are the opportunity for reflection and exhortation. These notable events may be of two kinds: a people which has reached the peak of its power feels the need of looking back over the way it has come to reach it; on the other hand national disasters are also appropriate times, for the trial opens the people's eyes to the causes which have occasioned it and the reflection which it suggests may be the cause of a salutary re-awakening.[43]

Israel in the time of Solomon had reached "the peak of its power." In the Yahwist she had a thinker who could look back over the way she had come to reach that peak.

AN OUTLINE OF THE SAGA

An appreciation of the Yahwist's theological and artistic achievement requires some knowledge of his purpose and the means he used to realize his purpose. When these have been adequately analyzed the reader will be able to evaluate for himself the author's theological accomplishment. He may also, perhaps,

---

[42] There are some who extend the saga as far as 1 Kgs 12:19 and date it to the 9th century. Others go even further and bring its date down to the late 8th century. The complete absence of even an allusion to the catastrophic division of Solomon's empire is the strongest argument against the latter opinion. The impartiality of the author in his treatment of the northern tribes would militate against the former. The argument of E. Lipinski, "Nimrod et Assur," *RB* 73 (1966), p. 89, against a 10th century dating of the Yahwist is more difficult to explain. Lipinski claims that Gn 10:8-12, on archeological grounds, can be dated no earlier than 883, the foundation date of Chale as capital of the Assyrian Empire under Asshurbanipal II. Since Gn 10:8-12 is generally considered a Yahwistic text, this dating would place the Yahwist somewhere in the reign of King Jehoshaphat of Judah (870-848). Possibly the text is a later addition or the archeological evidence has been misinterpreted.

[43] *Theology of the Old Testament*, p. 194.

be able to experience for himself the aesthetic satisfaction of evaluating the degree to which the author achieved his purpose by
utilizing the limited means at his disposal.

The general purpose of the author may be deduced from the
literary form and from the subject matter of the saga. It is a form
of interpretative narrative of the acts of God in Israel's history.[44]
From form and content the reader may conclude that the Yahwist
aimed to teach his audience about Yahweh, the Lord of History,
about the meaning of Israel's history, and about themselves as
individuals and as God's covenanted people.

The narrower purpose of the author—the particular teaching or
doctrine he hoped to impart—is more difficult to determine. To
discover precisely what it was the Yahwist aimed to teach, it will
be necessary to gain an acquaintance with his audience, analyze
his sources and use of sources, ascertain his literary techniques
and in the light of these pinpoint as far as possible the precise theological interpretations he proposed to set forth for the instruction
of his audience. His audience, sources, techniques, and theology
will be the burden of the remaining chapters. The following outline, however, will give the reader some idea of what to expect in
the saga.

Since the saga is composed by the juxtaposition and connection
of numerous originally independent narrative sources, the outline
will attempt to indicate the Yahwist's *functional* use of his sources
and at the same time some of the literary techniques he utilized
to interconnect and interpret them.

Where a story or narrative unit serves more than one purpose
and as a consequence must be read on more than one level, the
outline will attempt to indicate the different levels by pointing out
not only the theme of the story as a whole but also the underlying
motifs that help connect it with other parts of the saga. The Fall
Story in Gn 3, for example, is the first in a series of "sin-punishment-forgiveness" stories whose purpose is to show the "progress
of sin," a motif that dominates the whole of the primeval history
in Gn 2-11. At the same time, the Fall Story has the "promise"
motif in Gn 3:15, a motif that runs through the saga from begin-

---

44 Cf. G. E. Wright, *The God Who Acts: Biblical Theology as Recital.*

ning to end, and the "fertility" motif, a motif that recurs frequently and is sometimes used to show that Yahweh is the true Lord of fertility and at other times to show that the fertility cult religion of Canaan is the enemy both of God and Israel.

The outline attempts, therefore, by indicating themes, motifs, foreshadowing texts, and key words to turn the reader's attention to some of the different levels of meaning intended by the author and certainly recognizable by his original audience. The literary techniques will be explained in ch. V; the themes and motifs in ch. VI. Key words, where they occur in foreshadowing texts, will be italicized. Elsewhere, they will be given under the heading—key words.

Part One

THE PRIMEVAL HISTORY

1) THE PARADISE STORY (Gn 2:4b-25)
    Motifs: a) Yahweh's love for mankind.
                b) Yahweh is Lord of fertility.
                c) Yahweh covenants with Adam.
2) THE FALL STORY (3:1-24)
    Motifs: a) Sin, punishment, forgiveness.
                b) Yahweh, not the "serpent," is Lord of fertility.
                c) Yahweh promises man's conquest of the serpent.
    Foreshadowing: "I will make you *enemies* of each other: you and the woman, your *offspring* and her *offspring*. It will *crush* your head and you will strike its heel" (3:15).
3) THE CAIN AND ABEL STORY (4:1-16)
    Motifs: a) The progress of sin.
                b) Sin, punishment, forgiveness.
                c) Yahweh is Lord of fertility.
    Key word: "accursed" (Cain: 4:11).
4) SIN OF SONS OF GOD AND DAUGHTERS OF MEN BRINGS THE FLOOD (6:1—9:29)
    Motifs: a) Sin, punishment, forgiveness.
                b) Yahweh is Lord of fertility.
                c) The progress of sin.
                d) Yahweh covenants with Noah.

✓ Foreshadowing: "*Accursed* be *Canaan*. He shall be his brothers' meanest *slave*." He added: "*Blessed* be Yahweh, God of Shem, let *Canaan* be his *slave!* May God extend Japheth, may he live in the tents of Shem, and may *Canaan* be his *slave!*" (Gn 9:25-27).

5) GENEALOGICAL FOCUS ON SHEM (10:8-19, 21, 24-30; 11:28-30)
   Key names: Shem and Eber (10:21); Terah, Abram, Nahor, Haran (11:28-30).

6) THE TOWER OF BABEL AND THE CALL OF ABRAM (11:1-9; 12:1-3)[45]
   Motifs: a) Sin, punishment, forgiveness.
           b) Promise to Abraham.
           c) Election of the seed of Abraham.
✓ Foreshadowing: "I will make you a *great nation;* I will *bless* you and make your *name* so famous that it will be used as a *blessing.* I will *bless* those who bless you: I will *curse* those who slight you. All the tribes of the earth shall *bless* themselves by you" (12:2-3).

Part Two

THE PATRIARCHAL HISTORY   *Foreshadowings are most important.*

1) ABRAM ENDANGERS THE PROMISE (12:4a, 6-20)
   Motif: Yahweh overcomes all obstacles to his plan.
   ✓ Foreshadowing: "It is to your *descendants* that I will give this *land*" (12:7).

2) ABRAM ENDANGERS THE PROMISE BY ALLOWING LOT CHOICE OF TERRITORY (13:1-5, 7-10, 13-18)
   Motif: Yahweh overcomes all obstacles to his plan.
   Foreshadowing: "All the *land* within sight I will give to you and your *descendants* forever . . ." (13:14-17).

3) ABRAM IS BLESSED BY MELCHIZEDEK (14:1-24)
   Motif: Legitimation of Jerusalem as city of God.
   Key word: "blessed" (14:20).

---

[45] The primeval history ends with the promise of deliverance through Abram. Without the call of Abram the sin-punishment-deliverance pattern of the Tower of Babel story is incomplete. Here, presumably, with the call of Abram, which provides the deliverance element in the pattern of sin-punishment-forgiveness, the oral reciter of the saga would pause before going on to the second part of his narrative.

4) THE COVENANT WITH ABRAM (15:1-2a, 3b-4, 6-12, 17-21)
   Motif: Yahweh seals his promises with covenants.
   Foreshadowing: "To your *descendants* I give this *land* . . ."
   (15:18).

5) ISHMAEL BY HAGAR IS NOT THE CHILD OF PROMISE (16:1-2,
   4-14)
   Motif: Yahweh overcomes all obstacles to his plan.
   Foreshadowing: 16:11-12.

6) SARAH's OLD AGE IS NO OBSTACLE TO THE PROMISE (18:1-15)
   Motif: Yahweh overcomes all obstacles to his plan.

7) ABRAHAM's INTERCESSION CANNOT HELP THE FERTILITY CULT
   SODOMITES (18:16—19:29)
   Motif: Anti-fertility cult polemic: Abraham is a source of
   blessing to the nations but not to the devotees of the fertility cult.
   Foreshadowing: "Shall I conceal from Abraham what I am
   going to do, seeing that Abraham will become a *great nation* with all the nations of the earth *blessing* themselves
   by him?" (18:18)

8) ORIGIN OF THE MOABITES AND THE AMMONITES (19:20-38)
   Motif: Anti-fertility cult polemic.

9) SACRIFICE OF ISAAC, THE CHILD OF PROMISE (22:1-19)
   Motif: Test of Abraham's faith in Yahweh's ability to overcome all obstacles to his plan.
   ✓ Foreshadowing: ". . . I will shower *blessings* on you, I will
   make your *descendants* as many as the stars of heaven. . . .
   All the *nations* of the earth shall *bless* themselves by your
   descendants, as a reward for your obedience" (22:17-18).

10) THE MARRIAGE OF ISAAC AND REBECCA (24:1-67)
    Motif: Antifertility cult polemic: Isaac must not marry a Ca-
    naanite.

11) JACOB, THE CHILD OF PROMISE (25:1-6, 11b, 18, 21-34)
    Motifs: a) Yahweh overcomes obstacle of Rebecca's barren-
    ness.
    b) Choice of second-born.
    ✓ Foreshadowing: "There are two nations in your womb, your
    issue will be two *rival* peoples. One nation shall have the

mastery of the other, and the *elder* shall *serve* the *younger*"
(25:23).

12) Isaac Endangers Rebecca and the Promise (26:1-14)
Motif: Yahweh overcomes all obstacles to his plan.
Foreshadowing: ". . . to you and your *descendants* . . . I will
give all these *lands* . . . ; and all the *nations* in the world
shall *bless* themselves by your *descendants* . . ." (26:2-5).

13) Renewal of Promise to Isaac at Beersheba (26:15-33)
Motif: Election of the seed of Isaac.
Foreshadowing: ". . . I will *bless* you and make your *descend-
ants* many . . ." (26:24).

14) Isaac Receives the Blessing (27:1-45)
Motifs: a) Choice of second-born.
        b) Blessing and curse.
Foreshadowing: "May nations *serve* you . . . Be *master* of your
brothers . . . *Cursed* be he who curses you; *blessed* be he
who *blesses* you!" (27:29). "You shall live by your sword,
and you shall *serve* your brother. But when you win your
freedom, you shall shake his yoke from your neck" (27:40).

15) Renewal of Promise to Jacob at Bethel (28:10-22)
Motif: Election of the seed of Jacob.
Foreshadowing: ". . . I will give to you and your *descendants*
the *land* . . ." (28:13-14).

16) Wives and Twelve Sons of Jacob in Haran (29:1–31:54)
Motifs: a) Yahweh is the Lord of fertility.
        b) Yahweh fulfills his promises.

17) Jacob, Despite Esau's Animosity, Returns to the Land of
Promise (32:4–33:18a)
Motif: Yahweh overcomes all obstacles to his plan.
Foreshadowing: "Your name shall no longer be Jacob, but
Israel, because you have been strong against God, you shall
prevail against men" (32:28-29).

18) The Rape of Dinah and the Crimes of Simeon, Levi, and
Reuben (34:1-31; 35:21-22)
Motif: Preparatory to the election of fourth-born Judah over
first-, second-, and third-born Reuben, Simeon, and Levi in
Gn 49:2-12.

19) JUDAH AND TAMAR (38:1-30)
    Motifs: a) Antifertility cult polemic.
           b) Genealogical legitimation of David's claim to the throne.
           c) Choice of second-born son of Judah by Tamar.
20) THE JOSEPH LEGEND (37—50)
    Motifs: a) Sin, punishment, forgiveness (Joseph's brothers).
           b) Yahweh is Lord of History (passim but especially 45:5-8).
           c) Blessing on the nations (Egypt—47:13-26).
           d) Election of second-born (48:8-22; 49:2-12).
           e) Genealogical legitimation of David's claim to the throne (49:8-12).

Foreshadowing: ". . . I saw your sheaves gather round and bow to my sheaf . . . I thought I saw the sun, the moon and eleven stars bowing to me" (37:5-11). "Therefore God sent me ahead of you to ensure for you a remnant on earth and to *save your lives in an extraordinary manner*" (45:7). "Then Israel said to Joseph, 'Now I am about to die. But God will be with you and *take you back* to the country of your fathers'" (48:21). "Judah, your brothers shall praise you: . . . The *sceptre shall not pass from Judah* . . . until he come to whom it belongs, to whom the *peoples shall render obedience* . . ." (49:8-12).

Part Three

THE NATIONAL HISTORY

1) OPPRESSION IN EGYPT (Ex 1:8-12, 22)
2) EARLY HISTORY OF MOSES, THE LIBERATOR (2:1-23)
3) THE CALL OF MOSES (3:1—4:31)
    Motif: God fulfills his promises.
    Foreshadowing: "I mean to *deliver them* out of the hands of the Egyptians and *bring them up* out of that land to a *land* . . ." (3:8, 17ff).
4) MOSES BEFORE PHARAOH (5:1—6:1)
    Motif: Yahweh overcomes all obstacles to his plan.

5) THE PLAGUES (7:14—11:8 passim)
Motif: Yahweh is Lord of History.
6) THE PASSOVER SACRIFICE (12:21-23)
7) THE TENTH PLAGUE, THE EXODUS, THE CROSSING OF THE SEA
(12:29-39; 13:20-22; 14:5-7, 10-14, 19-21, 24-25, 27, 30-31;
15:1-8)
Motifs: a) Yahweh is Lord of History.
b) Yahweh fulfills his promises.
8) FROM THE SEA TO MOUNT SINAI (15:22-25a; 16:4-5, 28-31, 35;
17:1-16; 19:2)
Motif: Yahweh overcomes all obstacles to his plan.
9) YAHWEH COVENANTS WITH ISRAEL ON SINAI (19:10-20; 24:12-
15a; 34:1-5, 10, 14-28)
Motifs: a) The election of Israel.
b) Yahweh fulfills his promises.
10) FROM MOUNT SINAI TO THE OASIS AT KADESH (Nm 10:29—
16:34 passim)
Motifs: a) Israel a source of blessing (the Hobab story—
10:29-32).
b) Sin, punishment, forgiveness—motif of the stories
testifying to Israel's lack of trust in Yahweh: the
revolt at Taberah (11:1-3); the revolt at Kibroth-
hattaavah (11:4-34); the revolt of Miriam and
Aaron against Moses (12:1-16); the revolt on the
borders of the promised land (13:17-33; 14:1, 4,
11-25, 39-45); the revolt of Dathan and Abiram
against Moses (16:1b-2, 12-15, 25-34).
11) FROM KADESH TO THE PLAINS OF MOAB (20:1b, 14-21; 21:1-3,
4b-9, 12-35)
Motifs: a) Sin, punishment, forgiveness—revolt on the road
to the Sea of Suph (21:4b-9).
b) Yahweh overcomes all obstacles to his plan—conquest of the king of Arad (21:1-3) and of the
kings of Transjordan (21:12-35).
12) THE BALAAM ORACLES (22:1-3; 24:1-25)
Motifs: a) Yahweh overcomes all obstacles to his plan.
b) Israel cannot be cursed but must be blessed.
c) Legitimation of the Davidic dynasty.

Foreshadowing: "A hero arises from their stock, he *reigns* over countless peoples. His *king* is greater than Agag, his majesty is exalted . . . He has crouched, he has lain down, *like a lion*, like a lioness; who dare rouse him? *Blessed* be those who bless you, and *accursed* be those who curse you" (24:7-9). "I see him—but not in the present, I behold him —but not close at hand: a *star* from Jacob takes the leadership, a *sceptre* arises from Israel . . . " (24:17-19).

SUGGESTED READINGS

H. W. Wolff, "The Kerygma of the Yahwist," *Interpretation* 20 (1966), 129-158.

B. W. Anderson, *Understanding the Old Testament*, 2nd ed., 165-187.

E. Speiser, *The Anchor Bible: Genesis.*

G. von Rad, *The Problem of the Hexateuch*, 1-93.

———, *Genesis*, 13-43.

H. Cazelles, "Pentateuque," in *Dict. de la Bible Suppl.*, col. 770-803.

M. Noth, *Exodus.*

H. F. Hahn, *The Old Testament in Modern Research*, 1-43.

A. Weiser, *The Old Testament: Its Formation and Development*, 74-142.

O. Eissfeldt, *The Old Testament: An Introduction*, 155-245.

E. Nielsen, *Oral Tradition.*

C. R. North, "The Place of Oral Tradition in the Growth of the Old Testament," *Expository Times*, LXI (1949-50), 292-296.

W. Beyerlin, *Origins and History of the Oldest Sinaitic Traditions*, 145-170.

Chapter III

THE YAHWIST'S AUDIENCE

Authors ordinarily do not write in a vacuum. Nor do they, as a rule, write simply for the sake of clarifying their own thought. They write for an audience. And their audience influences not only how they write but what they write. It can be assumed, as a consequence, that an acquaintance with the audience for whom an author wrote will provide no small clue to the interpretation of what he has written.

It can be assumed also that what a religious author writes will, as a general rule, be directed to some need of his audience. It will aim to serve the audience, either positively—if the work informs the audience about something it needs to know or interprets what is already known but not understood in the correct manner; or negatively—if it refutes outright errors, dangerous attitudes, or pernicious compromises.

To the degree that a religious author truly grasps the genuine needs of his audience and supplies for them, his word and insights will be accepted—at least intellectually—and provide the measure of thought-guidance required by the audience for its religious well-being. It is here that the insights and influence of a great theologian are decisive; for, having laid down the correct interpretation of the past or the present, he at the same time lays a foundation upon which future theologians can build.[1]

---

[1] The value of a great author's insights is incalculable. As Oliver Wendell Holmes said: "A valid idea is worth a regiment any day." It is the appreciation of this fact of experience that induces so many at all times to read the great authors. That great insights like great ideas can be born out of time and lie fallow is implicit in the dictum of Victor Hugo: "An idea when its time is ripe is irresistible."

51

In dealing with the Yahwist's tenth century B.C. audience, we shall find that an acquaintance with their background, their needs, and their challenges provides many clues to the interpretation of the Yahwist's saga. We shall study first, therefore, the political, social, and religious background of the reign of Solomon. We shall then consider briefly three works written for this same general audience by contemporaries of the Yahwist. We shall try to determine the teaching purpose and literary techniques of the three works and then compare them with the teaching purpose and literary techniques of the Yahwist.

With these works as guides and the political, social, and religious background of the period as the *Sitz im Leben* of Israel in the reign of Solomon, we shall attempt to determine the needs of the Yahwist's audience and phrase the questions that audience might have posed to the Yahwist for his theological answers.

In all of this of course it will be necessary to beware tailoring the needs of the audience to the teaching of the Yahwist's saga. This can be done with some security by using the testimony of Judges, 1 & 2 Samuel, and 1 & 2 Kings, in addition to extrabiblical documents, as the primary sources for the political, social, and religious background of the Yahwist's audience. To the degree that the saga fits into this background and responds to this audience we shall be on safe grounds in our interpretation of the Yahwist's mind. To the degree that it does not fit in, we shall be in the area of conjecture and probability.

THE POLITICAL BACKGROUND

At the close of David's reign and as a consequence of the conquests of David, Solomon ruled the Middle East from the borders of Egypt to the banks of the Euphrates. Philistia, Edom, Moab, Ammon, and the Aramaean kingdom centered around Damascus has become satellite states subject to Israelite control and Israelite taxation. As the court recorder put it ". . . the Lord gave victory to David wherever he went" (2 Sm 8:6; 2 Sm 8:1-18; 10:1-19; 12:26-31).

It would seem that David ruled directly over Israel, Judah, and Ammon. The provinces of Damascus and Edom were controlled by his troops and ruled by his appointed governors. Moab, Philistia, the kingdom of Hamath and certain city states of Upper Syria conceded his hegemony. And Hiram, the King of Tyre, was his close ally (2 Sm 5:11). As B. W. Anderson says, "Never before or after the time of David did Israel exceed this zenith of political power."[2]

The rise of Israel, however, from a dependency of Philistia at the death of Saul (1 Sm 31:1) to third ranking power of the Middle East by the end of David's life, was not accomplished without severe restrictions on the independence of the Tribal Confederacy. By making Jerusalem his capital, David centralized his seat of power and administration in a neutral site which was neither Israelite nor Judean but Davidic. Administration of law was taken over by the king (2 Sm 14:4-17; 15:1-6) and a bureaucracy, patterned on the Egyptian model, was set up (2 Sm 8:15-18). The Ark was brought to Jerusalem, and hence forth Israelites who wished to worship before the Ark were obliged to come to David's capital city. Military conscription, annual levies, and perhaps even forced labor after the manner of the Egyptian *corvée* followed upon a census taken of all the tribes (2 Sm 24 and 20:24).

These measures affected the independence of all the tribes but were undoubtedly accepted, and for the most part gladly, as the price that must be paid for power, prestige, and wealth. There persisted, however, the old enmity between the Joseph tribes and the tribe of Judah. And there was in addition the fateful and explosive issue of the Saul dynasty. The support of the northern tribes and particularly of the Benjaminites for Ishbaal and the Benjaminite line of Saul introduced political factions that did not soon die out. The "long war between the house of Saul and the house of David" (2 Sm 3:1) and the enmities it cemented led to acts that scarred the new nation's soul. Abner, general of the northern armies after the defeat of Saul, was murdered by Joab in blood revenge for the death of Asahel (2 Sm 3:26-30). Not long after, would-be supporters of David assassinated Ishbaal, Saul's son and successor (2 Sm 4:5-8). David's further decimation of the Saul line by delivering to the Gibeonites seven sons of Saul to be

---

[2] B. W. Anderson, *Understanding the Old Testament*, p. 144.

crucified (2 Sm 21:1-9), however justified, was bound to enrage the Benjaminites as a tribe and embitter all Israelite supporters of the Saul dynasty.

It was not purely out of friendship, therefore, that David brought Jonathan's son, Meribbaal—the grandson of King Saul—to be near him in Jerusalem (2 Sm 9:1-12). Nor would David have been unduly surprised when his guest-hostage went over to Absalom (2 Sm 16:1-3) at the time of the latter's revolt against his father. The remark attributed to Meribbaal by Ziba: "The House of Israel will give me back my father's kingdom today" (2 Sm 16:3) could well have expressed Meribbaal's feelings and expectations if not his actual words.

Shimei's curse of David "Be off, be off, man of blood, scoundrel! Yahweh has brought on you all the blood of the House of Saul, whose sovereignty you have usurped. . . ." (2 Sm 16:7), and the later revolt of Sheba, a Benjaminite, can be reckoned as part of the same political blood legacy (2 Sm 20:1ff).

Blood feuds were not David's only problem. There was always the animosity of the antimonarchists (1 Sm 8-12 passim), for whom the very idea of a human king was anathema. And there were those others who would resent the idea of an hereditary monarchy—Israelites for whom leadership of the tribal amphictyony had to be a matter of the spirit and for whom the very model of an Israelite leader was the charismatic Judge, a man moved by the Spirit of God to save his people at a particular time, but only at a particular time and not continually as a king. For these Israelites the ideal was the tribal confederacy, the amphictyony. Whatever their attitude toward Saul, he had not really jeopardized the amphictyony. With David, however, the very idea of the amphictyony was beginning to die out. In Solomon's time it had become a memory.[3]

---

[3] See J. L. McKenzie, *The World of the Judges*, p. 118 ff.; also J. Bright, *Early Israel in Recent History Writing*, pp. 111-126; and the remarks of B. W. Anderson, *Understanding the Old Testament*, p. 166: "This radical change (the organization of Israel around a new center: the royal city of Jerusalem, by David and Solomon), which met with the protest of conservative religious circles, must have had far reaching implications for Israel's oral traditions . . . Were the Israelite traditions to go out of date in this new situation? Or could they be adapted to the new way of life?"

The institution of the monarchy, it would seem, was firmly entrenched by the time of Solomon; nevertheless, it was still suspect in some quarters and perhaps hated in others, particularly in conservative religious quarters. It was an institution that needed to be legitimated by more than David's victories in the field and Solomon's prestigious building projects at home.

Solomon himself was firmly established as king, thanks to the *coup d'etat* of Nathan and Bathsheba (1 Kgs 1:1ff) and his own efficiency in removing enemies and suspected enemies (1 Kgs 2:1ff). He still had enemies and there were revolts, but they failed to shake the iron grip of the golden king on his sometimes rebellious subjects. Jeroboam, an Ephraemite, led an internal revolt that never got off the ground and had to flee to Egypt for refuge (1 Kgs 11:26-40). Hadad, an Edomite, rebelled, but, as far as can be seen, without notable success (1 Kgs 11:14-22 and Gn 27:40). Rezon, an Aramaean, was more successful (1 Kgs 11:23-25). He took over Damascus and nullified Israelite influence in the northeast section of the empire, but the extent of his influence is debatable. As far as is known these were small clouds in a reign that lasted almost forty years and faced few external threats.

Internally, however, the situation was different. Solomon was the youngest of David's sons and had by intrigue vaulted to the throne of Israel over the head of his older brother, Adonijah (1 Kgs 1-2). In the eyes of those for whom the traditional right of primogeniture was sacred, Solomon could be looked upon and probably was looked upon as a usurper. He was even more suspect in the eyes of those for whom the very idea of the monarchy was an arrogant, godless innovation and in the eyes of those for whom charismatic designation was a *sine qua non*. There was nothing "charismatic" about Solomon.

Likewise, there must have been those, at least in religious circles, who looked with dismay and misgiving at Solomon's numerous pagan wives and the religious toleration and even encouragement Solomon accorded them (1 Kgs 11:1ff).

And finally there was the opposition of those who quite naturally feared that Israel was becoming like all the other nations. Under David, and as a result of his conquests, Israel had absorbed thousands of Canaanites, very many of whom did not become converts of Yahwism. For all practical purposes, indeed, the monarchical system in Israel was similar, at least in externals, to Canaanite monarchies of the time. It had a standing army, spearheaded by chariot divisions. It had a system of taxation. It had a bureaucracy modeled upon that of Egypt (cf. 2 Sm 8:16-18; 1 Kgs 4).[4]

In view of these political events and in view of the rapid rise of Israel from a petty satellite of Philistia in the early days of Saul and David to the third ranking power in the Middle East in the time of Solomon, many and particularly the conservative religious element among the people, may have wondered and even asked *"Quo vadis, Israel?"*

Was it indeed the will of God that the monarchy should succeed to the place of the earlier, desert-based, covenanted amphictyony? Was David and his dynasty really designated by God to lead Israel to the fulfillment of her God-given destiny? Was Israel's destiny to rule the nations as a political power or did she have, in God's far-seeing design, a higher spiritual mission?[5] What should Israel's attitude be to the Canaanites and to the surrounding nations? Was Solomon, in view of his dubious route to the throne in place of his older brother, Adonijah, and in view of his lacking any apparent charismatic designation, truly the elect of Yahweh, as David had been before him? This was the situation at the beginning of Solomon's reign; and it was in this period that the Yahwist grew to maturity and began his theologizing.

THE SOCIAL BACKGROUND

It is difficult to conceive the changes that took place in Israel in the four score years that separated the little mountain kingdom of Saul from the middle east empire of Solomon. At the height of Solomon's career wealth poured into Israel's coffers from at least a half-dozen subject states, adding to the already considerable booty amassed by David in the course of his continuous military conquests.

To these sources of burgeoning wealth was added in time the

---

[4] R. de Vaux, *Ancient Israel*, p. 129ff.
[5] See pp. 205-211.

income from Solomon's far-flung commercial enterprises—his horse and chariot trading with Cilicia and Egypt (1 Kgs 10:28-29) and his fleet of Tarshish ships, manned by Phoenician sailors, which opened the Arabian peninsula, the eastern coast of Africa, and perhaps even parts of India to Israelite traders (1 Kgs 9:26-28; 10:22). Solomon's control of the caravan routes running through Ezion-geber in the South, Damascus and Palmyra in the Northeast, and Megiddo and Hazor in the North gave him a stranglehold with lucrative returns on trade with Arabia, Mesopotamia and Syria respectively. His control of the Mediterranean coast assured him all the fat dividends of a middleman between Egypt in the South and Phoenicia, Syria, and Anatolia to the North.

The Queen of Sheba came to hear and admire Solomon's wisdom, but it seems quite certain she went back to Arabia with trading agreements in her purse (1 Kgs 10:1-13). And if the Queen of Sheba learned from Solomon, there is little doubt but that Israelite traders brought back not only foreign products but the invigorating and broadening influence of extensive foreign cultural contacts. It was not without reason that Otto Eissfeldt dubbed Solomon "the enthroned merchant."

With the wealth came a building boom. Israelites who as children remembered the rustic palace of Saul at Gibeah now gaped wide-eyed at the magnificent new Temple built by Solomon in Jerusalem (1 Kgs 5-8) and at the still more magnificent palace complex constructed to house the king, his wives, his concubines, and his proliferating courtiers (1 Kgs 7:1-12; 10:16-21).

We know little about private building projects but affluent Israelites no doubt put their new found wealth into the "winter houses" and "summer houses" mentioned at a later date by the prophet Amos.

Outside of Jerusalem Solomon took care to construct chariot cities at Gezer, Megiddo, and Hazor, where chariot troops were garrisoned ready to protect the homeland and patrol the outposts of the empire. Like his father before him Solomon could not call upon Israelite architects and technicians for his building projects but had to call upon Hiram of Phoenicia (2 Sm 5:11; 1 Kgs 5:1-18; 7:13-46). His buildings as a result, and especially the Temple, were thoroughly Canaanite in style and structure.

Throughout the "empire", meanwhile, Israelite public officials learned the art of governing, and Israelite diplomats the art of bargaining; while at home an Egyptian-trained and perhaps Egyptian-staffed bureaucracy (1 Kgs 4:1ff) kept the books and provided the matrix for the kingdom's intellectual class.[6]

A long peace, a rapid rise in the general living standard, the building of better homes, and the creation of a leisure class, not to mention the numerous challenges to stir the imagination and kindle the genius of a have-not people finally given its place in the sun—all of these gave rise to a cultural revolution.[7]

Leading the revolution was the king whose reputation for wisdom even during his lifetime elicited the praise of the Queen of Sheba. The better part of 1 Kgs 3-11 is dedicated to the theme of Solomon's wisdom and abounds with material testifying to the popular belief that Solomon was indeed the wisest of kings (1 Kgs 3:3-28; 4:29-34; 10:1-10, 23-24). Later ages attributed to him the books of Proverbs, Ecclesiastes, Wisdom, and the Canticle of Canticles.

It is disputed how much if any of what was attributed to Solomon in later ages was truly written by him and with good reason. One senses easily the exaggeration of such statements as 1 Kgs 4:32-33: "He composed three thousand proverbs, and his songs numbered a thousand and five. He could talk about plants from the cedar in Lebanon to the hyssop growing on the wall; and he could talk of animals, and birds and reptiles and fish." And there is reasonable doubt that Solomon truly authored the collections of maxims and wisdom sayings attributed to him by the compiler of Proverbs (Pr 1:1; 10:1; 25:1).

But, exaggerations aside and later attributions of wisdom words understood in the spirit in which they were made, the legend of Solomon as the wisdom teacher *par excellence* can hardly be without some foundation.

Nor was the cultural revolution restricted to Solomon. Israel's alliance with Egypt and Tyre, two seats of ancient learning and culture, in addition to the contacts that went hand in glove with

---

[6] R. de Vaux, *Ancient Israel*, p. 129ff.

[7] O. Eissfeldt, *op. cit.* 49; 65-66.

Israel's new international status, could not but enkindle interest
and perhaps even fascination with the secular learning of the time.
Egypt's millenium-old tradition of wisdom literature[8] and Canaan's
ancient mythology—so dramatically resurrected in the excavation
of Ras Shamra[9]—not to mention the traditions and literature of the
indigenous, cultivated Canaanites, whose history in Jerusalem
alone went back well before the 14th century B.C., could hardly
have failed to interest and influence the affluent leisure class of
Solomon's court and capital.

The genius of the Israelite authors who composed the Rise of
David History (1 Sm 16–2 Sm 5), the Succession History of Solomon (2 Sm 6-20; 1 Kgs 1-2), and perhaps the Joseph story in Genesis (Gn 37-50) have not without reason suggested a golden age
of literature in the reign of Solomon. As G. von Rad says: "Unquestionably, we have here to do with the traces of an enlightenment on a broad basis, an emancipation of the spirit and a step-
ping out from antiquated ideas."[10]

How broad the basis of this enlightenment is difficult to determine. The average Israelite became acquainted with the national
and religious traditions of his people through the oral teaching of
his father, through the sagas and songs of the minstrels, through
the teaching of the elders at the gates, and through the chanting
of psalms and the recital of religious traditions at the Temple and
at the local sanctuaries. Undoubtedly much of the lore preserved
in the later wisdom collections (especially Proverbs) was passed
down to the young by the elders, the sages, and the itinerant
storytellers.

How much of this material was in written form is impossible to
say. It is certain, however, that writing had been in use in Palestine, and particularly in Phoenicia, since at least the 14th century.[11] Inscriptions dating from between 1700 and 1200 B.C. have

---

[8] Cf. ANET, passim.

[9] J. Finegan, Light from the Ancient Past, pp. 171-174.

[10] G. von Rad, Old Testament Theology I, p. 53.

[11] In the story of Wen-Amon's journey to Phoenicia (ca. 1100 B. C.) the art of
writing is taken for granted as the following words indicate: ". . . and he (the
King of Byblos) had the journal rolls of his fathers brought, and he had them read
out in my presence, and they found a thousand deben of silver and all kinds of
things in the scrolls" (ANET, p. 27).

been found in Palestine, and about twenty-five of the inscriptions found in Serabit-el-Khadim in the southwestern part of the Sinai peninsula are in Canaanite or Phoenician script and date to about 1500 B.C.[12] Since these latter are almost certainly the work of slave-laborers in the Egyptian mines, they testify to the early and relatively widespread use of the art of writing. It is certain that David and Solomon had scribes (2 Sm 8:16; 1 Kgs 4:3) and since the Israelites in general took so much from the cultured Canaanites who preceded them, there is little doubt they took the art of writing as well. 1 Kgs 11:41 speaks of the Acts of Solomon which is undoubtedly a literary work of some sort dating from the period of Solomon or shortly thereafter.[13]

In addition to Israel's own traditions, there is good reason to believe that at least the more educated Israelites would have been acquainted with the wisdom lore of Egypt and the mythology of Canaan and Mesopotamia. The Yahwist's use of mythological motifs in Gn 2-11 is otherwise inexplicable. His acquaintance with the Gilgamesh epic in one form or another is reflected in the flood story and probably also in the paradise story. His acquaintance with Mesopotamian creation stories either through residual tradition from the ancient past or more likely through Canaanite or Hurrian intermediaries would seem certain from his description of man's beginnings in Gn 2. It might even be conjectured that the Yahwist utilized these myths, mediated through Canaanite writings, in order not only to demythologize them but to appeal to those enlightened Canaanites in the kingdom who were well disposed to Yahwism.

Obviously, then, the cultural climate was ripe and even propitious for literary work. It was a time of peace, prosperity, leisure, inquiry, and even intellectual sophistication. It was a time as well when a new nation, savoring its wealth, relishing its power, looking out on the world and contemplating its own newfound prestige and influence, might have asked itself in all seriousness: "Why this dramatic change?" "Whence the roots of this phenomenon?" "Whither away for the future?" And in answering—produced a literature!

---

[12] The dating ca. 1500 is Albright's.

[13] O. Eissfeldt, *The Old Testament: An Introduction*, p. 48ff.

For whom was the Yahwist writing?[14] The scope of his work is such that only the educated could properly appreciate it. On the other hand so much of his saga is popular in nature, traditional in content, and pertinent to all that there is no good reason why it should not have found a ready audience also among the uneducated.

THE RELIGIOUS BACKGROUND

The religious background in the time of Solomon was far from homogeneous. Yahwism had entered Canaan with the Israelites as the religion of the conquerors. Of the conquered peoples of the land many no doubt became converts to Yahwism. Many however did not. And between those who did not join the new religion and those who did, bringing with them their Canaanite customs, laws, and religious attitudes, the influence of Canaanite religion on Yahwism was extensive. One may compare in this respect the centuries long preaching of the Gospel in the lands around the Mediterranean before those lands became thoroughly Christian. J. Bright summarizes the situation as follows:

> Some of those absorbed into Israel were Canaanites, while others were at least partly Canaanite in culture. Though as members of Israel all became worshippers of Yahweh, many of them, we may not doubt, remained pagans at heart. We may suppose, too, that local shrines perpetuated pre-Mosaic practices many of which accorded ill with Yahwism. Moreover, since Canaan was immeasurably ahead of Israel in material culture, cultural borrowing naturally took place in all areas. It was inevitable that some Israelites should view the agrarian religion as a necessary part of the agrarian life and begin to propitiate the gods of fertility. Others, no doubt, accommodated the worship of Yahweh to that of Baal, and even began to confuse the two. The Book of Judges is undoubtedly correct in recording the period as one of theological irregularity.[15]

What is known about Canaanite religion is known for the most part from the Old Testament itself and from extrabiblical docu-

---

[14] E. Lewy is of the opinion that Nathan the prophet was the Yahwist and that he wrote the saga as a primer for Solomon and his sons (*The Growth of the Pentateuch*, pp. 177-241).

[15] J. Bright, *A History of Israel*, p. 156.

mentary evidence unearthed in recent decades by archeologists. The biblical testimony is generally and naturally prejudiced as a result of the continual warfare between monotheistic Yahwism and polytheistic Baalism, the religion of the land. The principal evidence comes from documents such as the Egyptian Execration texts (ca. 1850 B.C.), the Ras Shamra Texts (ca. 1400 B.C.), and from artifacts, particularly figurines and plaques, unearthed by the archeologists.

These sources show that Canaanite religion was essentially a nature worship, directed to the fertility gods, from whom the worshipers sought, by prayer, sacrifice, and other cult practices, fertility for field, flock and family.

The principal god of the Canaanite pantheon was El, with his consort Ashera; but Canaanite religion in Israelite times was centered upon Baal and his consort, the goddess Anath. Baal, who was known as the storm-god, had many titles. He was called Baal-Saphon, Baal-Hadad, Baal-Zebul; or depending upon where he was worshiped, Baal-peor, Baal-Sidon, Baalbek, etc. Anath was his wife and sister and in the documents is frequently referred to as the virgin, Anath.

In the Ugaritic myths,[16] which were reenacted in the Canaanite cult, Baal dies and struggles with Mot, the god of the underworld. Eventually with the help of Anath he rises, and with his resurrection fertility returns to the land. His period in the underworld represents the dry hot summer, his resurrection, the coming of the rains and the ingathering of the crops.

The following lines from "The Descent of Ishtar to the Nether World," a Mesopotamian myth, but belonging to the same fertility cult religion as that celebrated in Canaan, are illustrative of the average Canaanite's belief in relation to fertility and the death of Baal followed by his long struggle in the underworld with the god, Mot. During this time which corresponds to the long dry summer, the poet says:

> Since Ishtar has gone down to the land of no return,
> The bull springs not upon the cow, the ass impregnates not the jenny,
> In the street the man impregnates not the maiden.

---

[16] *ANET*, pp. 129-158.

The man lies down in his (own) chamber, the maiden lies down on
her side.[17]

After the victory and resurrection of Baal, who is identified with
the new vegetation, the goddess Anath agrees to "effect unions
in the earth, diffuse love in the land, pour out well-being into the
midst of the earth, increase love amidst the fields."[18]

Soon after the resurrection of Baal, a house is built for Baal and
his consort Anath. The two gods consummate the *hieros gamos*,
or sacred marriage, which in the cult is reenacted by the king and
a sacred prostitute and in many cases by the individual worshipers
and the temple personnel known as hierodules or sacred prostitutes. The purpose of these unions was based upon a belief in
imitative magic (cf. Dt 23:18-19; Nm 25:1ff; and Amos 2:7). Thus
Canaan's liturgy was based upon a reenactment of these myths
with the purpose of persuading the gods to return fertility to the
field, the flock, and the family for another year.

Because the cult centered upon the fertility of the land, the
major feasts were agrarian feasts celebrated at the time of the fall
and spring harvests, which usually coincided with the beginning
of the rainy season on the one hand and the end of the rainy season on the other. Israel baptized these feasts and at least one of
them, the spring harvest feast, was later baptized by the Church
—the feast of Pentecost.[19] The fall festival became the Israelite
New Year feast and was baptized by making it the Covenant renewal feast.[20]

The most degrading elements in the Canaanite cult were the
practices of infant sacrifice and sacred prostitution. Infant sacrifice
was never adopted by Yahwism, though sometimes practiced, and
was regularly reprobated by the inspired writers (cf. Gn 22; Ex
13:1-16; Jer 7:31; 2 Kgs 3:27; 21:6-7).

Sacred prostitution and the licentious practices it led to (cf. Dt
23:18; Nm 25:1ff)[21] penetrated Israel in times of religious relaxa-

---

[17] *ANET*, p. 108.

[18] J. Gray, *The Legacy of Canaan*, p. 40.

[19] T. Maertens, *A Feast in Honor of Yahweh.*

[20] R. de Vaux, *Ancient Israel*, pp. 484-506.

[21] Herodotus, *Persian Wars* I, n. 199.

tion and syncretism (cf. 1 Kgs 18-19; Jer 2-3; 7; 19). But at all times Israel reacted against these practices (cf. Gn 19; Ex 23:19, 24; Lv 18; Jgs 19; Ho 1-2). Figurines and plaques of serpents (sometimes in bronze) and of the nude female figure (which almost certainly represent Qadesh, the goddess of fertility) have been unearthed in almost every major Palestinian excavation.[22] In a number of plaques, the goddess Qadesh is represented nude standing upon a bull-calf and holding a serpent in her hand or around her body.[23] J. Gray concludes as follows concerning the influence of Canaanite religion on Israel in the time of Solomon:[24]

> As we study the attributes and functions of Baal, especially in his hypostasis as Hadad, the god of storm and rain-cloud who utters his voice in the heavens, who mounts the clouds, and whose temple is completed at the same season as, and with rites recalling, the dedication of Solomon's Temple in Jerusalem, we conclude that the cult of the Syrian Baal must have been well established in Palestine and have left its impress upon the cult of Yahweh when the Israelites settled the land. No doubt much of this assimilation was due to Solomon and his Phoenician craftsmen and allies, but most probably this phase of the cultural development of Israel in Palestine was but the crystallization of a tendency to conform to the Baal-cult which was almost inevitable when the tribes of Israel crossed over from the desert to the sown.

This was the state of religion in the time of Solomon. The old amphictyonic order had broken down. In the monarchy Church and state were united; and there was question—at least in conservative religious circles—whether the state had not swallowed up the Church.

The conquests of David introduced many Canaanite subjects into the kingdom. And Solomon's influential Canaanite wives eventually turned the king to the worship of the Baal fertility cult gods (cf. 1 Kgs 11:1ff).

The old priesthood under Abiathar had been deposed and a

---

[22] Cf. *ANEP*, p. 162, nn. 469ff.

[23] Cf. *ANEP*, p. 163, nn. 471-474; and L. Hartman, "Serpent," in *The Encyclopedic Dictionary of the Bible* col. 2174ff; also L. Hartman, "Sin in Paradise," *CBQ* 20, 1958, 26-40.

[24] J. Gray, *The Legacy of Canaan*, p. 121.

new high priest, Zadok (who may well have been originally the high priest of Canaanite Jerusalem) was in control.[25] His conversion may have been genuine, but his antecedents were suspect.

Solomon's Temple had been built by Canaanites. The Canaanite sacrificial system had been baptized. Likewise Canaanite feasts.[26] The Baal fertility cult was practiced in the countryside and in Jerusalem itself. Yahwists in general and conservative Yahwists in particular may well have wondered if the enemy was not already within the gates.[27]

In Samuel's time the people had said: ". . . there shall be a king over us. And we also will be like all nations. . . ." (1 Sm 8:19-20). In many a Yahwist's eyes, Israel had indeed become "like all nations." She was in grave danger of forgetting that her vocation at Sinai had made her different. The question was not, did an enemy exist, but did all recognize the enemy?

SUGGESTED READINGS

E. Maly, *The World of David and Solomon.*

J. Bright, *A History of Israel*, 163-208 but especially 202-208.

M. Noth, *The History of Israel*, 141-224.

O. Eissfeldt, "The Hebrew Kingdom," in the *Cambridge Ancient History*, vol. II, ch. xxxiv, fasc. 32, 24-33, 49-69.

E. Lewy, *The Growth of the Pentateuch*, 177-217.

R. de Vaux, *Ancient Israel*, 91-142.

G. von Rad, *Old Testament Theology* I, 36-68.

W. Eichrodt, *Theology of the Old Testament*, 436-456.

J. M. Myers, "Solomon" in *The Interpreter's Dictionary of the Bible*, vol. IV, 399-408; "David," *ibid.* vol. I, 771-782.

J. Gray, *The Legacy of Canaan*, especially 26-72; 121-130.

A. Malamat, "The Kingdom of David and Solomon in its Contact with Egypt and Aram Naharaim," *Biblical Archeologist* XXI (Dec. '58) 96-102; and "Aspects of the Foreign Policies of David and Solomon," *JNES*, vol. XXII (1963) 1-17.

---

[25] H. Ringgren, *Israelite Religion*, p. 61.

[26] Cf. H. H. Kraus, *Worship in Israel*, pp. 36-45.

[27] On Israel's opposition to the Baal fertility cult, cf. M. Buber, *The Prophetic Faith*, p. 73.

L. Hartman, Articles on Baal, Canaanites, Serpent in *The Ency-clopedic Dictionary of the Bible*.

E. Jacob, *Ras Shamra et L'Ancien Testament*, Cahiers d'Arch. Bib.

R. A. F. MacKenzie, *Faith and History in the Old Testament*.

R. Maisler, "Canaan and the Canaanites," *BASOR*, 102 (1946), 7-12.

A. Kapelrud, *The Ras Shamra Discoveries and the Old Testament*.

Y. Kaufman, *The Religion of Israel*, 21-152.

J. Gray, *1 and 2 Kings*, 23f; 222-277, especially 251-277.

J. M. Fenasse, "Baalism et Yahwisme" in *Bible et Terre Sainte*, 69 (Nov., 1964).

CONTEMPORARY LITERARY WORKS

The background of the 10th century Israelites—political, social, and religious—is important because it can suggest areas of thought and interest which might well have been of concern to the Yahwist in the writing of his saga. Literary works from this same period, however, are far more important because they do not merely suggest but tell in no uncertain terms what was of paramount importance to their authors and presumably to their audience.

We shall be concerned, therefore, in the first place with the teaching purpose of these narratives. In addition, we shall study the form, the style, the tone, the literary techniques, and the psychological insights of the authors. All of these will testify to the intellectual and literary achievements of the period—achievements it may be assumed the Yahwist shared. If it is true, as is generally held, that the Yahwist's saga was written in the same general period as these documents, affinities in some or all of these areas will hardly be surprising.

Three works, composed in the period of David and Solomon, are of particular interest in relation to the Yahwist's saga: the History of the Ark in 1 Sm 4-6 and 2 Sm 6; the History of David's rise to the throne of Israel in 1 Sm 16—2 Sm 5; and the Succession History, also called the Court History, in 2 Sm 6-20; 1 Kgs 1-2.

In the History of the Ark it is the legitimation of Jerusalem, David's new city, as the city chosen by God to be his "resting place" that commands attention. In the Rise of David History and in the History of Solomon's Succession David and his dynasty loom large; larger still, however, as in the Yahwist's Saga, looms the Lord of History leading David to his throne and his dynasty into a future fraught with messianic portent.

THE HISTORY OF THE ARK

Before dealing with the teaching purpose and the literary characteristics of the Ark History, it will be necessary to say something about the present position of the History and its dismemberment by the editor in 1 and 2 Samuel.

Authors are agreed that 1 and 2 Samuel, as we have them, represent one part of a great historical work—called the Deuteronomist's History—written toward the middle of the 6th century and consisting of Joshua, Judges, 1 and 2 Samuel, and 1 and 2 Kings. It is also agreed that the work as a whole is made up mosaic-fashion of many different sources connected by the Deuteronomist in a consistent and purposeful pattern designed to testify to certain basic theological teachings relevant to the situation of Judah and the exiles in the period of the Babylonian captivity.

In the Books of Samuel, in which several chapters from the History of the Ark are distributed by the author-editor, the presence of different sources is indicated in a number of ways. There are apparent contradictions in the text which testify to different versions of the same story (cf. 1 Sm 7:12 with 9:16; 13—14; 28; 31; also 15:35 with 19:22-24). There are extremely brusque transitions (e.g. between 1 Sm 1-3 and 4:1-7:1). There are frequent doublets (e.g. the twofold anointing of Saul, the twofold account of David's meeting with Saul, the twofold attempt of Saul to spear David, etc.). And there are clear differences in tone, style, and theological bent (passim).

While distinguishing sources is not easy, the following would appear to be distinct sources: a source related to Judges (1 Sm 1-3; 7:2-14); a source dealing with the Ark—The History of the Ark—(1 Sm 4-6 and 2 Sm 6); two sources dealing with the origin of the monarchy (an antimonarchical source in 1 Sm 8; 10:17-24; 12; 13:8-14; 15; and a promonarchical source in 1 Sm 9-10:16;

continued in 13—14 minus 13:8-14); two parallel sources dealing with David's rise from shepherd boy to king (1 Sm 16—2 Sm 5); the source dealing with the succession of Solomon to the throne of David—The Succession History—(2 Sm 6-20; 1 Kgs 1-2); and finally a collection of pieces dealing with David (2 Sm 21-24).

In the books of Samuel these sources are so arranged that the reader's attention is drawn to David and his dynasty. Samuel is introduced as prophet (1 Sm 1-3) and judge (7:2-14) to so establish his authority that the reader will have no hesitation in accepting as legitimate the monarchy founded by him (1 Sm 8-12). Saul is introduced as the first legitimate king of Israel (1 Sm 10:24 and 11:1-15), anointed by Samuel but soon rejected by him in place of another who is to come (13:8-14; 15:1ff). Finally David is introduced (1 Sm 16:1-13) and the history continues to the end with David and his dynasty as the focal point of the narrative (1 Sm 16—2 Sm 24).

The purpose of the Ark History, in view of its dismemberment by the Deuteronomist who put one part (1 Sm 4-6) early in his history of the monarchy and the other late (2 Sm 6), is obscured. One must first take the history as a whole and explain its purpose in its original state. One must then explain why the Deuteronomist dismembered it to make it serve his own different purpose.

The history begins, almost ex abrupto, in 1 Sm 4:1b. The only connection with part I of 1 Samuel (ch. 1:1-4:1a) is the place, Shiloh, and Eli's old age. Otherwise, there is a complete shift of scene and emphasis. Samuel is not mentioned at all. Eli appears not only as priest but as Judge as well (4:18). Nothing is said about the heinous crimes of Eli's sons. And the situation is one of war not peace as in ch. 1-3. Moreover, the center of interest is the Ark itself, not Samuel, nor Eli, nor the war with the Philistines, nor even the destruction of Shiloh. Thus the narrative is designed in a way completely different from the parts before and after it. It is designed to point away from Shiloh, the place where the Ark was lodged in the time of the Judges, to some new resting place for "Yahweh, the Lord of Hosts, who is enthroned upon the Cherubim."

The narrative in 1 Sm 4-6, however, does not designate the new resting place. It recounts the opening of war between Israel and

the Philistines (1-4), the bringing of the Ark to the battlefield
(5-9), the capture of the Ark (10-11), the effect of this capture on
Eli and his daughter-in-law (12-21), the 'adventures' of the Ark
in the land of the Philistines (5:1-12), and finally the return of
the Ark to the land of Israel (6:1-7:1).

In 7:1 the Ark is brought to the house of Abinadab on the hill,
and on that note—a sad note when one realizes that the Ark had
been the central shrine of the amphictyony for the better part of
two hundred years—the account apparently ends. It is only apparently the end, however, for the story continues in 2 Sm 6.

In 2 Sm 6 the Ark is again the center of interest. David goes
down to the house of Abinadab on the hill (cf. 1 Sm 7:1) and
brings the Ark in procession to Jerusalem, his newly conquered
capital. Thus by the hand of God the Ark eventually finds its way
to a new and lasting resting place in the City of David, and the
account itself rests.

All signs indicate, as Hertzberg says, that 2 Sm 6:1-15, "is unquestionably a continuation of the ark narrative of I. 4-6."[28] The
original source, which embraced both parts, was used by the Deuteronomist because he was intent on showing how God had been
"with David" even to the extent of taking up his abode with him
in his new capital, Jerusalem.

As it stood, however, the early part of the Ark History (1 Sm
4-6) dealt with a period prior not only to David and his capture of
Jerusalem but prior even to Saul and the institution of the monarchy. For chronological reasons, therefore, the Deuteronomist
placed it early in his history of the institution of the monarchy.
For the same reasons he reserved the ending of the Ark History
(2 Sm 6) until he had recounted David's capture of Jerusalem
(2 Sm 5:6-12). At that point all was ready for the account of the
triumphal entry of the Ark into the City of David.

The account is dated to the time of David rather than to the
time of Solomon for two reasons: first, because the references to
Eli and his sons in 1 Sm 4 betray no undertones of the disgrace
that overtook the priestly line of Eli in the time of Solomon (1 Kgs
2); and second, because the need for an account legitimating

---

[28] H. W. Hertzberg, *1 and 2 Samuel*, p. 277; also pp. 62-63.

Jerusalem as a cultic place for Yahweh was obviously of prime importance early in the history of the new sanctuary.

If this analysis is correct, one may safely conclude that the Ark History was originally written as an explanation of how—through the coming of the Ark—Jerusalem came to be a true "holy place" of Yahweh in Israel. "In type," as G. von Rad says, "this extended narrative is a cult legend, the purpose of which was to show that thenceforth Jerusalem was a legitimate cultic place for Israel."[29] A similar etiological cult legend, dating to a later period and written for the purpose of legitimating the area north of the City of David where the Temple was built during the reign of Solomon, is found in 2 Sm 24.

The significance of the Ark History for understanding the Yahwist's audience lies in the need it evinces to legitimate the new capital of David as a cultic place for Israel. David's act of bringing the Ark to Jerusalem and attaching to his court the priests of the house of Eli, of whom Abiathar was the chief, made Jerusalem the religious center of Israel. Prescinding from David's religious zeal, the move was a stroke of political genius. Perhaps no other act could have been so influential in uniting the tribes around their new king and in calming the fears and blunting the opposition of the antimonarchists.

There must have remained, however, a feeling of distrust and perhaps even of repugnance for the place David had chosen to bring the Ark. Throughout all of Israel's prior history in Palestine Jerusalem had been a thoroughly Canaanite city. David, moreover, if the conjectures of authors are correct, took over not only the city itself but the ancient shrine of the Canaanite god worshiped there. Authors conjecture likewise that Zadok, who replaced Abiathar as high priest in the time of Solomon (1 Kgs 2) was originally the high priest of the earlier Canaanite sanctuary.[30]

For any or all of these reasons any Yahwist author in the period of David and Solomon might well have felt it incumbent upon himself to justify or legitimate to the best of his historical ability

[29] G. von Rad, The Problem of the Hexateuch, p. 177.

[30] R. de Vaux, Ancient Israel, pp. 373 f.

the choice of Jerusalem as the new "resting place" of Yahweh in the midst of his people.[31]

It is this aspect of the situation in 10th century Israel that certainly explains the Ark History and the etiological legend of the Temple area in 2 Sm 24. Might it not as well explain the inclusion in the Yahwist's saga of Abraham's meeting with Melchizedek? No adequate explanation of the Genesis 14 account has been forthcoming. It is admittedly an ancient source, certainly lacking any of the touches that would attach it stylistically to the established sources of the Pentateuch and capable of having been attached to the Abraham story at almost any time in its transmission. Nevertheless, no other source for the material is so likely as Jerusalem itself in the time of David and no other time would have been so propitious and so judicious for its inclusion in the traditions of Israel.[32] At one stroke it lends the respectability of tradition in the link with Abraham and the perspective of salvation history in that event of long ago that nevertheless looked so far into the future.[33]

Less probable but not to be dismissed is the possibility of an etiological motif, carried along with the obedience motif, of Gn 22, in the reference to the "land of Moriah" (vv 2-4) and the "mountain of vision" in v 14. E. Speiser rightly questions the too ready attribution of Gn 22 to the Elohist and adduces good reasons on internal evidence to credit it to the Yahwist.[34]

Only 2 Chronicles 3:1 directly associates Mount Moriah with the site of Solomon's Temple and identifies it as the place chosen by David in 2 Sm 24. Whether the association is late, based upon the desire of later authors to link the Gn 22 story with Solomon's Temple, or early, based upon a genuine more ancient tradition

[31] On the Ark History as justification for Jerusalem as the site of the Temple, see V. W. Rabe, "Israelite Opposition to the Temple," CBQ 29 (1967), pp. 228-233; and H. J. Kraus, Worship in Israel, pp. 181-183; T. E. Fretheim, "Psalm 132: A Form Critical Study," JBL 86 (1967), p. 298.

[32] M. Buber, The Prophetic Faith, p. 69 sees the purpose of the Melchizedek story in Gn 14 as legitimation of Jerusalem.

[33] This is substantially the opinion held by G. von Rad in his commentary on Genesis 14 (Genesis, p. 173 f). See also B. W. Anderson, Creation versus Chaos, pp. 69-70.

[34] E. Speiser, Genesis, p. 166.

dating at least to the time of David, is impossible to tell. If the latter, then the Gn 22 story, like the Gn 14 story, may contain an early Yahwistic attempt to legitimate Jerusalem as the place chosen by God for his "resting place."

One literary technique may be mentioned as an affinity of the Ark History with the Yahwist's saga—the propensity of the author for putting speeches into the mouths of his characters. In the short span of his narrative speeches are put into the mouths of the ancients of Israel (1 Sm 4:3), the Philistines (1 Sm 4:6-9; 5:7-8, 11; 6:2-9); and others (1 Sm 4:16-17, 21-22; 2 Sm 6:9).

DAVID'S RISE TO KINGSHIP

Affinities between the Yahwist's saga and the Ark History, as demonstrated above, are tenuous at the best. The same may be thought for the Rise of David story and the Succession History of Solomon, but for these the foundation is at least stronger. G. von Rad, in discussing the "New Spirit" at large in Solomon's court in the 10th century, gives good reason to expect affinities between the Yahwist's saga and the above mentioned contemporary documents:

> Though it was still beset with internal problems, David's empire was, after the union of North and South, a state with immense possibilities of expansion. As far as foreign relations went, it was pretty well established; the cultic life was attached to a new centre and with new forms; there was a brilliant court which, for its time, stood at the zenith in the cultivation of things of the mind. All these were factors which could not but have their effect on the innermost center of a people's life—indeed, they compelled Israel to come to a completely new understanding by way of reflection on her historical origin. It is amazing that we can name three major historical works which must have followed upon one another at relatively short intervals in this era—the history of David's rise to power (1 Sm 16:14—2 Sm 5:12), the history of the succession after David (2 Sm 6:12—1 Kgs 2), and the Yahwist's history.[35]

In the History of David's Rise to Kingship at least two ancient

---

[35] *Old Testament Theology* I, pp. 48f.

accounts have been fused. The Deuteronomist editor has rearranged the ancient sources to suit his own purposes, making it difficult to determine exactly where the ancient sources began and
ended. The substance of the story is found between 1 Sm 16 and
2 Sm 5, but the original may have begun before 1 Sm 16 and may
have ended either in 2 Sm 7 or 2 Sm 8.

Since the early history of David was bound up with the history
of King Saul, the Deuteronomist combined the Saul and David
sources to contrast the downfall of Saul, abandoned and rejected
by God, with the rise of David, the man chosen by God as "a man
after his own heart" (cf. 1 Sm 13:14 and 16:7).

The purpose of the history as we have it now and as it was in
the beginning is to show that David was indeed the divinely ordained successor of Saul. This is so much the theme and intent of
the story that Hertzberg with good reason entitles it "David must
increase, Saul must decrease."[36]

The account begins, following the rejection of Saul in 1 Sm 15,
with the secret anointing of David by Samuel at Bethlehem (1
Sm 16). From that point on everything is arranged by the hand of
God to ensure David's rise.

Saul needs a musician and thus David is introduced to court circles in which his future lay. David's father sends him to bring provisions to his brothers, but this only serves as an opportunity to
pit the young Bethlehemite against Goliath and thus precipitate
him into a military life that leads to the kingdom. He becomes
friend of Jonathan, the crown prince. He marries Saul's daughter,
Michal. Sent to the front by Saul (in the hope that he might perhaps be killed and thus eliminated) he wins new renown by his
exploits on the battlefield.

Even his exile wins him a following. And while in Ziklag his
raiding parties are always against the enemies of Israel. In the
eventual showdown between Saul and the Philistines, David is
saved from having to fight on the side of the Philistines. When
Saul dies in battle on Mt. Gilboa, David is left without a serious
rival for the kingship.

In addition to showing the hand of God at work in David's rise

---

[36] H. W. Hertzberg, *1 and 2 Samuel*, p. 241.

to the throne, the author goes out of his way to show that David did not usurp the throne, that he respected Saul and did nothing to dethrone him, and that he came to the throne not through his own conniving efforts but by the will and design of God.

The theological interpretation of events is given by the author in remarks interspersed throughout the narrative highlighting the hand of God in the rise of David to the throne. Three series of texts are particularly significant.

(1) The first series shows that God is "with" David, protecting him and guiding him. In 1 Sm 16:18 a report on David's credentials ends up with the words: ". . . and Yahweh is with him." In 17:37 Saul sends David into battle against Goliath with the words: "Go, and Yahweh be with you!" In 18:12 the author remarks: "Saul feared David, for Yahweh was with him but had turned away from Saul." And in 18:28: "Saul now realized that Yahweh was with David. . . ."

In 2 Sm 5:10 the author gives his clearest expression of the "Yahweh with him" theme in the theological comment: "David grew greater and greater, and Yahweh, God of Sabaoth, was with him." And in 2 Sm 7:9, God says to David in Nathan's dynastic oracle: ". . . I have been with you on all your expeditions. . . ."

The consistent use of a phrase such as "God with him" would appear to be so deliberate and so telling in effect that it must be considered a true "technique" utilized by the author to insinuate his theological teaching.

(2) A second series of texts, in which the ascendency of David to the throne of Israel is either implicitly or explicitly taken for granted as the will and design of God, betrays the conscious use by the author of a technique known as foreshadowing—a storyteller's device, whereby knowledge of the future is given in order to arouse anticipation and suspense and at the same time prepare the audience to look for an interconnection of the parts of the story with the whole (cf. p. 115-127).

These texts occur regularly in 1 Sm (cf. 13:14; 15:28; 16:13; 18:8; 20:31; 23:17; 24:21; 25:30; 26:25; 28:17). A few may be quoted as examples; thus: Samuel in 13:14 tells Saul ". . . Yahweh has searched out a man for himself after his own heart and designated him leader of his people." David's name has not even been mentioned, nor will it until ch. 16 yet the foreshadowing already points unmistakably not only to his coming but to his ultimate destiny to be "prince."

In 23:17 Jonathan foretells David's rise to the throne in his words: "Have no fear; for the hand of my father Saul will not reach you; you are the one who is to reign over Israel, and I shall be second to you." And in 25:30 Abigail takes for granted that David will be king in her words: "When Yahweh has done for my lord all the good he has promised you, when he has made you prince over Israel. . . ."

The technique of the foreshadowing text is significant not only for its use as a theological device but also for its testimony to the use of this technique in the time of the Yahwist. The Yahwist will use it extensively (cf. pp. 123-127).

(3) A third series of texts consistently portrays David as a man of piety who seeks counsel from the Lord and is submissive to his will (cf. 1 Sm 16:7; 17:37, 45-47; 23:2, 4, 10-12; 24:6, 18-20; 26:9-11; 30:6-8). These texts not only demonstrate that David is indeed the man God seeks "after his own heart," they show as well the deliberate choice of incidents and events which testify to the theological teaching of the author. The Yahwist too will make a deliberate choice of certain incidents rather than others in order to put across his theological teaching.

Along with the general tenor of the story which shows Saul decreasing and David increasing these texts testify in a subtle but unmistakable way to the unwavering conviction of the inspired author that David was truly the king sought by God and destined by God to rule his people. If 2 Sm 7 was the climax of this story, as some authors believe, then these texts may rightly be considered the inspired author's buildup toward the great dynastic promise made by Nathan to David.[37] As Hertzberg rightly observes: "The rise of David is represented not as having been a piece of chance good fortune or a wise piece of policy, but as a miraculous event

---

[37] In his critical analysis of 2 Sm 7, M. Noth comes to the conclusion, based on internal evidence, that the original form of 2 Sm 7 is pre-Solomonic (*The Laws in the Pentateuch and Other Essays*, p. 259). If this is true, and Noth's reasoning is cogent, then it enhances the possibility that 2 Sm 7 was the conclusion of the Rise of David History.

disposed by a higher hand. In this way the material is brought into the larger context of all Scripture and becomes an episode in the history of God's guidance."[38]

The Rise of David History manifests several affinities with the Yahwist's saga—one of pivotal importance, the others incidental. Of pivotal importance is the author's concern to highlight and for all practical purposes legitimate the rise of David to the throne of Israel. His apologia for David is central to the history as a whole and testifies to the need for an apologia in the time of David and probably also in the time of Solomon, when there were still factions in the kingdom tending to view with skepticism the 'new' institution of the monarchy and the even more audacious claim of a 'perpetual' dynasty.

The Yahwist, who cannot be said to be deeply concerned with the rise of David as a phenomenon to be apologetically explained or defended, is nevertheless deeply concerned with the necessity of integrating the new facts of history—the institution of the monarchy and the perpetuity of the Davidic dynasty—into the ongoing flow of Israel's Salvation History.

This concern is testified to in the Yahwist's foreshadowing of David's rise to kingship in such texts as Gn 49:8-12 and Nm 24:9, 17-19. The Yahwist's deeper theologizing on the meaning of David and his dynasty for Israel's Salvation History and for the future of God's plan for the redemption of mankind will be treated later (cf. pp. 189-204). For the present it is enough to note that the Yahwist shares with his contemporary fellow author a deep interest in the theological implications of David's position.

Less important, but not to be ignored, are the literary techniques shared by the Yahwist with the author of the David History. The latter's use of the foreshadowing technique, the repetition of a significant phrase, and the use of selected incidents designed to create a theological impression will all be utilized by the Yahwist in his saga.

---

[38] H. W. Hertzberg, *1 and 2 Samuel*, p. 244. Cf. also P. J. Calderone, *Dynastic Oracle and Suzerainty Treaty*, p. 60: "It appears evident, then, that in this oracle Yahweh is promising, in fact bestowing, a kingship with its full implications of hereditary possession through a dynasty. Theologically, this divine grant is tantamount to legitimation."

THE SUCCESSION HISTORY OF SOLOMON

The heart of the Succession History is found in 2 Sm 9-20 and 1 Kgs 1-2.[39] There is no reasonable doubt that the history ended in 1 Kgs 2, but the same cannot be said for the beginning. Some authors begin the history with the Michal incident in 2 Sm 6:16-23. Others begin with the genealogy of David's sons in 2 Sm 3:2-5. But nothing certain can be said for the beginning.

Like the Rise of David History, the Succession History has not only been incorporated by the Deuteronomist into his monumental history, which begins with Joshua and ends with 2 Kings, but has been rearranged as well.

The clearest evidence of this is the separation of the material in 1 Kgs 1-2 from the narrative of 2 Sm 9-20. These chapters which originally brought the Succession History to a climax are now used by the Deuteronomist as the introduction to his Solomon story in 1 Kgs 1-11.

Another more difficult example of rearrangement is the position of the Michal episode in 2 Sm 6:16-23. It is not clear what position this episode had in the Succession History. It may have been the opening scene. In its present position it has been appended to the Ark History.[40]

The theme of the Succession History is succinctly stated in the words of Bathsheba to David in 1 Kgs 1:20: "Yet you are the man, my lord king, to whom all Israel looks, to name for them the successor of my lord the king." Directly or indirectly almost every

---

[39] "History is another area in which we can see Israel's intellectual growth. The first real history found anywhere in the ancient Near East is in the book of Samuel, especially the famous court history, extending from David's succession to the throne in 2 Samuel to his death at the beginning of 1 Kings. The latter is an extraordinary document; it is almost history in the modern sense, and quite similar to the kind of history that Herodotus wrote, though Herodotus had a speculative and philosophical approach that is quite absent from the Hebrew Bible. But historical Hebrew narrative also lacks the speculations and dubious analogies with which Herodotus abounds, coming after a century and a half of speculative thought. Here early Israel's empirical logic has produced something unique in its way. Her best historical writing far outshines Herodotus in sobriety and realism" (W. F. Albright, *New Horizons in Biblical Research*, p. 31).

[40] G. von Rad, *The Problem of the Hexateuch and Other Essays*, p. 176ff.

incident in the history can be seen to relate to the question of the succession.

The Michal incident in 2 Sm 6:16-23 relates to the succession in that it terminates with the observation that ". . . to the day of her death Michal, the daughter of Saul, had no children." A successor to the throne from the house of Saul would seem then to be eliminated from the very beginning of the history.

In 2 Sm 7 the promise to David of an eternal dynasty introduces immediate tension, since the queen mother is known to be barren and yet the dynasty has been assured perpetuity. In 2 Sm 9 the spectre of Saul's dynasty rises again. Meribbaal, the grandson of Saul, is brought to the court of David and the reader is not only plagued by the suspicion that perhaps through Meribbaal the kingdom will revert to the dynasty of Saul, but is caught up in the tension that existed between such a suspicion and the certainty of the promise made by Nathan that David's, not Saul's, dynasty will be eternal (cf. 2 Sm 7:15).

The unsavory details of David's liaison with Bathsheba are given in 2 Sm 10-12 in the context of the war with the Ammonites. Their first child dies, and again the question of the succession comes to the surface. A second child is born and named Solomon (12:24). Almost nothing is said about him except the tantalizing statement, apparently made in passing, that ". . . Yahweh loved him and made this known through the prophet Nathan who named him Jedidiah in accordance with the word of Yahweh" (12:24-25).

Adding to the tension the author has introduced an unvarnished account of David's crimes and thus raised the question: "Have David's crimes nullified the promise and prophecy of Nathan?" This would appear to be the insinuation of the comment: "But what David had done displeased Yahweh" (2 Sm 11:27).

In the remaining chapters the expected successors of David by primogeniture are successively eliminated. Amnon, the first-born (cf. 2 Sm 3:2-5; 5:13-15) is assassinated by his brother Absalom (2 Sm 13). Absalom, who now has the right of succession by primogeniture, is in turn assassinated by Joab (2 Sm 18:14).

With the deaths of Amnon and Absalom leaving the question of the succession still unresolved, the author further enhances the tension of his narrative by recounting the revolt of Sheba, the Benjaminite—a revolt which threatens not only the succession but the dynasty itself (2 Sm 20).

The history reaches its climax in 1 Kgs 1-2 when Adonijah, the last of David's sons to have the right of succession by primogeniture, is eliminated by a *coup d'etat* and the question of the succession is resolved in favor of Solomon.

The theme of the Succession History is clear. Solomon is indeed "by the grace of God" king! He is not king by reason of primogeniture but by the will of God made manifest in the working out of events in the Succession History. Of those who might have claimed the throne by right of primogeniture, Amnon has been eliminated by Absalom in revenge for his crime against Tamar; and Absalom has been eliminated by the will of God manifest in the turn of events that brought his well conceived revolt to an ignominious end (cf. 2 Sm 17:14). Finally, Adonijah has been by-passed, before being executed, by a *coup d'etat* based upon a dubious promise made by David that Solomon would be the son to succeed him (1 Kgs 1:27).

So singleminded a concentration on the subject of succession warrants without demur the title given this work—the Succession History. The subtle foreshadowing of Solomon's eventual success (2 Sm 12:24-25), the equally subtle indication that the working out of the succession has been in the hands of God maneuvering events behind the scenes (2 Sm 17:14), and the skillful selection of events that shows Solomon coming unsullied to the throne suggest that the author's purpose was to provide an apologia for Solomon. But was it more than that?

Certain elements of the history suggest something deeper than the succession of Solomon as the overall intent of the historian. The history in other words does more than justify the succession of Solomon. It provides as well a demonstration or elaboration of the meaning of Nathan's oracle in 2 Sm 7:11-16.

In the oracle the promise had been made that David's dynasty would be established forever. To emphasize and remove all ambiguity from the promise the oracle introduces the question of a possible revocation of the promise because of the infidelity of the Davidic kings and—rejects it: "If he does evil, I will punish him with the rod such as men use, with strokes such as mankind gives. Yet I will not withdraw my favor from him, as I withdrew it from your predecessor" (2 Sm 7:14-15).

A closer analysis of the Succession History reveals an interest in sin and its effects which would seem to be both unnecessary and out of place if all the author was interested in was the succession of Solomon.[41]

Thus the author takes considerable pains to recount the "iniquities" of David. He introduces a long description of the war with Ammon (2 Sm 10; 12:26-37) to serve as a frame for his detailed description of David's sins back in Jerusalem and, lest the reader fail to get the point, steps in himself and declares, "But what David had done displeased Yahweh" (2 Sm 11:27).

In 2 Sm 12 the words of Nathan make explicit what is already implicit in the remainder of the Succession History—there is a hidden chain of cause and effect binding together the sins of David and the successive disasters that overtake his family and his dynasty: "So now the sword will never be far from your House, since you have shown contempt for me and taken the wife of Uriah the Hittite to be your wife." 'Thus Yahweh speaks, "I will stir up evil for you out of your own House. Before your very eyes I will take your wives and give them to your neighbor, and he shall lie with your wives in the sight of this sun. You worked in secret, I will work this in the face of all Israel and in the face of the sun" ' (2 Sm 12:10-12).

The "sword" not only does not depart from the house of David, it devours successively Amnon, Absalom, and Adonijah. In addition it threatens the very dynasty of David in the revolt of Sheba. If, as seems probable, the "sword" prophecy of Nathan in 2 Sm 12:10-12 is not a genuine prediction but a foreshadowing text put in his mouth by the author (compare 12:11-12 and 16:20-22), then the sin-punishment motif of these chapters can be shown to be central to the history, since foreshadowing texts come directly from the author and indicate the intent of his account (see p. 122).

Another element of Nathan's oracle—the element found in the

---

[41] Cf. P. J. Calderone, *op. cit.* p. 64.

words, "Yet I will not withdraw my favor from him, as I withdrew it from your predecessor"—also comes in for considerable attention in the history. Thus, David's words to Michal, "I was dancing for Yahweh, not for them. As Yahweh lives, who chose me in preference to your father and his whole house . . ." and the author's own comment about Michal, "And to the day of her death Michal, the daughter of Saul, had no children" (2 Sm 6:21-23) suggest from the very beginning of the history that there will be no revival of the Saul dynasty. It has, as the oracle of Nathan makes clear, been definitively rejected.

This conclusion is further confirmed by the defeat of the hopes ascribed to Meribbaal by Ziba during the dark days of Absalom's rebellion, "Why, he has stayed in Jerusalem because, he says, 'The House of Israel will give me back my father's kingdom today'" (2 Sm 16:3). The final defeat of any hopes entertained for the Saul dynasty is described in the hapless outcome of the revolt led by the Benjaminite, Sheba (2 Sm 20).

The history would appear to make clear that where Saul and his dynasty had been rejected *because of his sins*, David and his dynasty had been preserved *despite his sins!* It seems then, unless we have overinterpreted the author's intentions, that the Succession History was written not only to legitimate the succession of Solomon but to provide a demonstration from history of the working out of Nathan's dynastic oracle.

Thus the author shows David committing "iniquity" and being chastened with "the rod of men," but despite his sins and the sins of his sons God's "steadfast love" is not taken away from him as it was taken from Saul who went before him (2 Sm 7:14-15). The promise, therefore, is unconditional, and neither the crimes of David himself nor the iniquities of his sons can nullify it.

If this is indeed the thought of the author and the intent of his history, then it is fair to say that for him and for his audience the institution of the monarchy and the perpetuity of the Davidic dynasty were theological facts of the first importance.

Of the affinities that seem to be discernible between the Succession History and the Yahwist's saga, some are thematic, some literary, and some psychological.

The most obvious of the thematic affinities is the interest of both authors in the David dynasty. Less obvious is the theme of election which passes over the firstborn to choose one who does not have the ordinary right of primogeniture. In the Succession History the author seems to be saying that God who maneuvers events behind the scenes has passed over those who had the right to the throne of David by primogeniture and thus made clear his election of Solomon. The subtle foreshadowing in 2 Sm 12:24 "Yahweh loved him . . ." would seem to confirm a thesis of election which is independent of the rights of primogeniture.

In the Yahwist's saga the firstborn (e.g. Ishmael, Esau, Reuben, and Manasseh) is regularly passed over and the choice of God falls upon one who does not have the right of primogeniture (e.g. Isaac, Jacob, Judah, Ephraim). In the Succession History the rejection of the firstborn seems to be mentioned by design by the author in order to bring out the divine election of Solomon. In the Yahwist's saga it is not clear whether the rejection of the firstborn is a matter of simple historical fact, a theological technique for inculcating the absolute freedom of God's choice, or an apologia in advance for Solomon. If the latter, the Yahwist would appear to be suggesting that as God had rejected the firstborn in the past, so might he do in the future.

Literary affinities, as in the Ark History and the Rise of David History, can be found in the frequent use of direct, invented, discourse; in the use of the foreshadowing technique;[42] and in the use of obstacle stories[43] to heighten the suspense and focus the attention of the reader on the central theme.

In the Succession History obstacles are constantly raised threatening the fulfillment of the Nathan oracle, e.g. the barrenness of Michal, the death of Amnon and Absalom, the threat of Meribbaal, the revolt of Sheba, and the *coup d'etat* of Adonijah.

In the Yahwist's saga the fulfillment of the promise to the Patriarchs seems constantly on the verge of frustration due either to the sterility of the patriarchal wives, the taking of the patriarchal wives into a foreign court, or the ultimate obstacle—the command of God to Abraham to offer in sacrifice the child of promise.

---

[42] See pp. 115-127.
[43] See pp. 136-138.

Psychological affinities between the Succession History and the Yahwist's saga, while readily discernible, are not so easily—because of their nature—demonstrable. That two gifted authors might share a similar, sophisticated world-view of Israel's history, is by no means inherently improbable. It is another matter, however, to demonstrate this similarity when the one is writing about Israel's ancient history and the other about her modern, contemporary history; and when the one is bound by tradition to use and incorporate ancient sources in his work while the other writes freely, bound only to the memory of recently acted out history.

Nor is it easy to show the affinity in the attitude of both to women, to sin, to the human heart, and to the presence of God in Israel's history when the fields in which the authors do their work are so disparate in time. Much will depend upon the perceptiveness of the reader himself.

We will begin with the demythologized, apparently totally secular, world-view of the two authors. In the writing of the Solomonic period of enlightenment, as G. von Rad says, ". . . a radical change had come over the conception of Yahweh's action in history; for people were beginning to see that, in addition to activity by means of miracles or dramatic, catastrophic events, Yahweh had another quite different field in which he worked, one which was much more hidden from men's view and lay rather in their daily lives."[44]

The writers of this period no longer see God only in the isolated, momentous interventions of God in Israel's history. They see him now behind the scenes working through the human which is not necessarily interrupted by the miraculous. They see him in the ordinary, purely secular events of life. He is no longer only in the heavens or in the storm; he is in the heart, in the welter of passions that govern the often misguided actions of struggling men.

And his action is no less sure than it was in the heroic days of the past. He guides from within, though unknown to characters caught up in the maelstrom of power politics, court intrigue, family quarrels, and the ever varying vicissitudes of passion-swept private lives. All is done freely, spontaneously, almost as if God

---

[44] G. von Rad, *Old Testament Theology* I, p. 51.

and his designs were irrelevant. The story is thoroughly secular, totally divorced from the mythological, almost dispassionate in the telling.

It is, however, a demythologized, not a detheologized, world. Beneath the ordinary and above the secular and throughout all is the guiding hand of the Lord of History. And so adroit is the theologian, so expressive his restraint, and so deft his theological touch that he can, with the barest minimum of theological comment (cf. 2 Sm 11:27; 12:24; 17:14), limn with a sure hand the abiding, guiding presence of God shining through the mundane screen of his narrative.

In the Yahwist's saga the nature of the source materials and the lack of freedom to tamper with them preclude the imposition of such a world-view on most of the history. Occasionally, however, where the Yahwist had a relatively free hand, as in Gn 24, it comes through. The Yahwist's Laban story and Joseph story in Genesis smack strongly of this same world-view of history.

In addition to the sophisticated world-view affinity, some would see affinities in the depth of psychological insight shared by the two authors—the wonderful insight into the hearts of David, Amnon, and Absalom in the Succession History and the masterful insight of the Yahwist in the paradise story, the Jacob-Laban story, and the Joseph story.

Another affinity in the field of psychology would be the two writers' insight into women and their influence on the men in their lives—in the Succession History the author's perceptiveness in his depiction of Michal, Bathsheba, and Tamar (the sister of Absalom); and in the Yahwist's saga the author's masterful depiction of the perennial woman, Eve, and of the patriarchal wives, Sarah, Rebecca, Rachel, and Tamar (the daughter-in-law of Judah), and the official's wife in the Joseph story.

Lesser affinities, which may be purely adventitious, might be found in the "blessing" concept in Gn 12:1-3 and 2 Sm 7:29; the "seed" concept in Gn 3:15 and 2 Sm 7:12; the "barren mother" theme as an obstacle story in the Sarah, Rebecca, and Rachel stories in Genesis and in the Michal story in 2 Sm 6; the overall buildup of tension in each of the works—in the fulfillment of the patriarchal promises in the Yahwist's saga and in the fulfillment of the promise to David in the Succession History; the place of Eve as an occasion of sin in Gn 3 and the place of Bathsheba and Tamar as an occasion of sin in 2 Sm 11 and 13.

Perhaps even more adventitious affinities could be found in such small stylistic similarities as the following: "to make a name for" in Gn 11:4; 12:2 and 2 Sm 7:9; "good and evil" in Gn 3:5 and 2 Sm 14:17; "in that day you shall die" in Gn 2:17 and 1 Kgs 2:37; and "deep sleep" (which comes from the Lord) in Gn 2:21 and 1 Sm 26:12.

Taken individually these lesser affinities are meaningless. Taken globatim and together with the larger, thematic, methodological, and psychological affinities, they vastly enhance the basic impression the reader receives that, in the two works, we are dealing with contemporary theologians responding theologically to the needs of the same audience.

SUGGESTED READINGS

G. von Rad, *Old Testament Theology* I, 42-46; 48-56; 308-318.
— —. *The Problem of the Hexateuch and Other Essays*, 18-78; 176-204; 292-300.
— —. *Genesis*, 169-176; 342ff.
H. W. Hertzberg, *1 and 2 Samuel*, especially 45-63; 275-281; 292-297.
J. Gray, *1 and 2 Kings*, 75-111.
A. Robert, & A. Feuillet (eds.), *Introduction à la Bible* I, 417-427.
E. Speiser, *Genesis*, 101-109; 162-166.
O. Eissfeldt, *The Old Testament: an Introduction*, 137-143; 271-281.
R. de Vaux, *Ancient Israel*, 259ff; 297-302; 304.
J. L. McKenzie, *The World of the Judges*, 76-120; 169-175.
P. J. Calderone, *Dynastic Oracle and Suzerainty Treaty*.

Chapter IV

THE YAHWIST'S SOURCES

THE NATURE OF THE SOURCES

An analysis of the component parts of the Yahwist's saga reveals a rich variety of source materials, running from a few demythologized myths in the primitive history to an abundant store of early ethnological and cultic sagas in the patriarchal history through hero legends and liturgical legends in the national history. The nature of these sources is such that it is impossible to say whether any of them (with the exception of the mythological sources) were ever in written form prior to the Yahwist.

In the primitive history the creation story and the paradise story in Gn 2-3 and the flood story with its antediluvian and postdiluvian genealogies in Gn 5-10 all presume some acquaintance, either directly or through the medium of Canaanite versions of the originals, with the Mesopotamian classics—"Enuma Elis" and the "Gilgamesh epic."

In the patriarchal history the stories about Abraham, Isaac, and Jacob testify to the existence of many etiological sagas dealing with the origins of the different tribes, the origins of the different Israelite sanctuaries, and the origins of many place names in Canaan. The Joseph story is at best a tribal saga.

In the national history there are preserved a number of hero legends about Moses, particularly in the early chapters of Exodus and in Nm 11-22; some liturgical traditions, especially the passover tradition in Ex 7-14 and the Sinai tradition in Ex 32-34; and the Balaam legend in Nm 22-24.

Although the cultic credos in Dt 6:20-23; 26:5-9; and Jos 24:2ff probably antedate the Yahwist, they are too brief to be considered sources. Nor is it likely that the Yahwist had to depend upon them for the main outline of his saga since the major portion of his source material came from a living tradition that was already well acquainted with the basic outline—patriarchal period, exodus period, conquest. It would appear that both the Yahwist and the credo authors depended upon these traditions; the credos representing a short, and the Yahwist's saga a long, form of the same.

Since the Yahwist depended upon Israel's traditions as the basic material for his saga, and since these traditions are not only legendary in nature but separated in time from the Yahwist by at least seven or eight centuries (from the time of Abraham in the 19th-18th century, to take the earliest, to the time of the Yahwist in the 10th century), the questions that arise immediately and naturally are the following: 1) how authentic is the material in these traditions?[1] 2) Granting that the patriarchal traditions are substantially historical, what do they tell us (and the Yahwist) concerning theology in the period of the Patriarchs? 3) How can we be sure that these truths contained in the theology of the patriarchs are anterior to the Yahwist and were not retrojected by him back into the period of the patriarchs? To answer these questions we shall study first the historical milieu of the patriarchal period and then the theology of the patriarchs as testified to in these traditions.

THE HISTORICAL VALUE

It has become fashionable in recent years to speak about the different books of the Bible, even the historical books, as primarily didactic and theological and only secondarily historical. This position is, on the whole, both sound and defensible. If one gets the impression, however, that history was unimportant to the biblical writers, that it was only a matter of "means," a "handy way" for teaching theology, a method in itself unimportant and perhaps

---

[1] O. Eissfeldt rightly observes, "The biblical sources for the time of the Patriarchs . . . can be used for an historical account only when subjected to exact study and criticism" ("The Hebrew Kingdom," C.A.H. II, ch. 24, pp. 6-8).

even replaceable with another method, then such a position does not do justice to the biblical writers' attitude toward history.

Actually, it is far closer to the truth to say that Israel's theologians learned the major part of their theology through history—that is, through the acts of God intervening in Israel's life and through the acts of Israel in response to those divine interventions. There was no question, therefore, of ever separating history and theology. As far as Israel's theologians were concerned, the marriage of history and theology in the life of the nation was a marriage made in heaven and in their writings they were determined that what God had joined together no man should put asunder. History, in the Bible, as a consequence, is subordinate to theology, but it is never unnecessary, unimportant, or dispensable.[2]

For the biblical writer the interpretation of an event was far more important than a detailed chronicle or a rounded description of the event. Nor was he minded to give all the events, all the facts. He made a choice because for him the significance of events, even one event, was far more important than heaping up a quantity of unimportant facts or detailing a chronicle of meaningless events. He was interested in the meaningful event and his major preoccupation was to show the theological meaning or significance of the event for his audience.

One should not, therefore, berate a biblical author for not telling the name of the Pharaoh of the exodus or the date of David's capture of Jerusalem. The inspired authors had more important matters on their minds.

As E. Jacob says:

> To speak of history and revelation through history, two realities must be brought together: raw facts and their interpretation. The latter is even more important than the facts, for it is one's idea of an event which assures for it its quality as an historical fact, that is as a decisive fact in the course of events. . . . The Old Testament is a clear example of the priority of the interpretation of history over its presentation, for the narration of history implies for the Israelite an

---

[2] As E. Jacob says: ". . . the special characteristic of biblical revelation is that God binds himself to historical events to make them the vehicle of the manifestation of his purpose" (*Theology of the Old Testament*, p. 188).

interpretation of it, because he views God's action through faith and not by the methods of the archivist or the archaeologist.[3]

Theological interpretation, important as it was, did not blind the biblical writers to the facts. Indeed, it is true to say that the biblical historians achieved standards of reliability and excellence which were, in their day, considerably higher than the standards of historical writing in other contemporary cultures.

They did not, and for obvious reasons, follow the detailed rules devised by moderns for the writing of scientific history. Nevertheless, as a general rule, they had respect for the basic norm of historical writing; namely, to set down the facts objectively and not to let partiality interfere unduly with their recording of those facts.

There is nothing that testifies more to the general objectivity of the biblical historians than the fact that so many readers are scandalized by the stories told in the Bible. Biblical authors tell such things as the mystical experiences of Abraham, David, and Jeremiah. But they also tell how Abraham tried to palm his wife off as his sister so that he would not be killed by strangers desiring his wife; how David not only took Bathsheba from bath to bed but callously had her husband killed so he could keep her there; and how Jeremiah, for all his depth of spiritual communion with God, nevertheless turned in revolt and almost abandoned his mission.

The biblical historians, moreover, generally abhor myth. In an age in which the writing of myths was part and parcel of the literature of Mesopotamia, Egypt, and Ugarit, Israel's writers alone never indulged in anything that could properly be called myth in the older understanding of the word.[4]

The balance of historicity and theology is, in the last analysis, a matter of emphasis. Moderns emphasize the scientific history. They look down on the biblical historians. In biblical times, the shoe was on the other foot. The emphasis was on theology, on the acts of the gods. In biblical times the complaint of the intellectuals probably was that Israel's historians were too historical!

---

[3] *Op. cit.*, p. 184.

[4] *Humani Generis*, par 39. But see below, pp. 141-145. Also J. Barr, *Old and New in Interpretation*, pp. 15-33.

In a world that swarmed with mythological writings, biblical writers were the exception precisely because they placed so much emphasis on history. The myths attempted to explain reality by rehearsing the acts of deities in the misty past. Man meant nothing to them. The Israelite writers, on the other hand, did not neglect God; but they knew history was a two-way street on which both God and man walked, never just God alone. The idea was revolutionary.[5]

In dealing with the historical value of the Yahwist's sources, one must admit, with the professional historians, that history can be written with confidence and security only when contemporary records testifying to the facts are available. Confidence in testimony tends to diminish, and with good reason, with the distance of the testimony in time from the facts attested to.

The nature of the evidence is also important. Direct testimony is more important than indirect testimony. And where indirect testimony is the only testimony, then the quantity of the evidence will be an important factor in itself.

Depending upon the nature and the quantity of the evidence, especially indirect evidence or testimony, it is possible to arrive at a "nuanced" historical judgment. Defining a nuance as a shade of difference or a delicate gradation, the situation may be summarized by saying that the delicate gradation in the size of the 'h' with which the word "historical" is spelled can vary, depending upon the nature and extent of the evidence, all the way from a very large capital "H" to a tiny but nevertheless distinctly visible small "h."

On this basis we shall have to admit that the sources of the Yahwist are not historical with a capital "H." Taking as a test case the Yahwist's patriarchal sources—by far the oldest sources in his saga —one must admit that to the present day no contemporary docu-

---

[5] "For the first time, we find affirmed the idea that historical events have a value in themselves insofar as they are determined by the will of God. This God of the Jewish people is no longer an oriental divinity, creator of archetypal gestures, but a personality who ceaselessly intervenes in history, who reveals his will through events. Historical facts thus become 'situations' of man in respect to God, and as such they acquire a religious value that nothing had previously been able to confer on them. The Hebrews were the first to discover the meaning of history as the epiphany of God, and this conception was taken up and amplified by Christianity" (M. Eliade, *Cosmos and History*, p. 104).

ments testifying to the existence of a single patriarch have ever been discovered. Even if one were to go on the impossible assumption that the Pentateuch as we have it now was the written testimony of Moses in the 13th century B.C., one would be, on the basis of the Pentateuch itself, at least five centuries away from the time of Abraham.

The Bible, therefore, contains no contemporary written witness to the patriarchs; nor do contemporary extrabiblical documents. Of the thousands of extrabiblical documents in our museums from the patriarchal period, not a single document has been found that testifies directly to any single fact in the saga of the patriarchs. They are not mentioned by name. Nor is there any allusion to them either as individuals or as a group. As far as the contemporary records are concerned, the patriarchs did not exist.

Lacking contemporary testimony to the facts, the best one can do is evaluate the traditions of Israel about the facts *as tradition*, i.e., as the living memory of a nation concerning its past, passed down from generation to generation by word of mouth.

The problem, then, is to assay the value and accuracy of this living memory at the time when it passed from the oral to the written page and became part of the book we now know as the Pentateuch. Was this living memory of Israel concerning her forefathers a faithful memory? Did it preserve the basic facts? Did it preserve also the details? Did it, in the seven to nine centuries of its existence before being frozen in written form, suffer any total loss of recall and thus lose the basic facts and have to re-create them on the basis of "what must have been"?

It is important to note that in such an evaluation, we are not directly concerned with the literary forms in which Israel's traditions were transmitted. Nor are we concerned with the selection of facts about the patriarchs which Israel's living memory made, preserving what was important to her, sloughing off what was unimportant. We are concerned for the present with nothing more than the basic content of what Israel remembered and kept alive in her living tradition. Did it correspond to fact or not? Is there any way we can test and prove the reliability of this tradition?

The surest test of historicity—confrontation with contemporary documents testifying to the facts—cannot help us with the answer to our question. There is, however, another scientific test that will give reasonable certitude concerning the historicity of the patriarchal traditions. The certitude is based not on contemporaneous documents testifying to the same facts but on contemporaneous documents testifying to the authentic tone of the traditions and to their general agreement with the historical milieu they purport to portray.

In other words, we do have contemporary extrabiblical documents which deal with the period of the patriarchs and give good reason to hold that the data about the patriarchs found in the Yahwist's saga goes back to a well-founded tradition authentic in its essentials and faithfully conserved by Israel's living memory. John Bright puts it this way: "We may, therefore, assume that, between the Pentateuchal documents as we read them and the events of which they tell, there lies an unbroken and living, if complex, stream of tradition."[6]

The evidence for the authenticity of the patriarchal stories as stories that fit into the milieu of the early second millennium is based upon patriarchal nomenclature, customs, travels and mode of life, evaluated for authenticity against the background of the early second millennium.

The names of two of the patriarchs are found in texts of the period: Jacob and Abraham. Jacob occurs in three forms: as the name Jacob-el in an 18th century text; as the name of a Hyksos chieftain named Jacob-har, and as the place-name Jacob-el in a 15th century Egyptian list of Thutmosis III.

Abraham's name in the form Abamram is found in Babylonian texts of the 16th century. Names of men associated with Abraham such as Nahor, Terah, and Serug (Gn 11:22-26) are found in texts from Mari and from Assyria.

Of the twelve sons of Jacob, the name Benjamin is found in a Mari text as the name of a tribe. Zabulon occurs in the Execration texts of Egypt. Levi and Ishmael occur at Mari and names similar to Asher and Issachar are found in an 18th century Egyptian list.

None of the names mentioned in these extrabiblical texts refers to any biblical character. The names, however, show that with

---

[6] *A History of Israel*, p. 64.

respect to nomenclature the patriarchal narratives are perfectly in
accord with the nomenclature of the period they purport to
describe.

With regard to patriarchal customs evaluated against the background of the early second millennium in Mesopotamia the results
are the same. In the Genesis stories concerning the patriarchs a
number of incidents used to be completely inexplicable to biblical
commentators. These incidents dealing for the most part with
marriage customs and inheritance laws could not be explained
from any later biblical laws or customs. They have now been
proved to be customs thoroughly at home in early second millennium Mesopotamia, testified to explicitly by extrabiblical texts
from the excavated archives of Nuzi, a town in the East-Tigris
region of Mesopotamia.[7]

When Sarah, Abraham's wife, cannot have a child, she offers to
her husband as concubine her slave Hagar. It is now confirmed by
legal texts from Nuzi that at Nuzi a childless wife was obligated
to provide her husband with a substitute who could bear a child.
The same texts forbid the expulsion of the slave wife and her child
—a law which explains, if a legal explanation is necessary, why
Abraham was so reluctant to send Hagar and Ishmael away when
Sarah, angered by Hagar, demanded it (Gn 16).

Nuzi texts also explain the enigmatic position of Eliezer in Gn
15. Abraham is sad because he has no heir and Eliezer will inherit
his property. In 15th century Nuzi, if a man was in debt or needed
money, he could adopt a money lender as his heir. The adoption
had to be made because by law a man could not alienate his ancestral property. By adopting the money lender the borrower got
around the law. If, however, the debtor had a son, the son would
by law become the legal heir instead of the adopted heir. The custom has no known parallel in later law and is entirely peculiar to
the patriarchal story.

Another situation in the patriarchal stories illustrated by Nuzian
customs is the adoption of Jacob into the household of Laban.

---

[7] The significance of the Nuzi excavations is evident in the tenor of E. Speiser's
Anchor Genesis passim. On the excavations, cf. J. Finegan, *Light from the Ancient
Past*, pp. 65-67.

Jacob is obliged by Laban to take only Laban's daughters as wives. This is paralleled by a Nuzian custom.

Also, Rachel steals Laban's household gods, the well-known teraphim. The reason for this is now clear from Nuzian texts. Whoever had the teraphim had the title to inheritance. Rachel's thievery, therefore, had nothing to do with religion. She was stimulated by the more prosaic maternal compulsion to provide a nest-egg for her children.[8]

With regard to the mode of life and travels of the patriarchs evaluated against the background of the early second millennium the results are again the same. W. F. Albright, for example, suggests the following interpretation of the elusive name 'Apiru: "During the past fifteen years it has become possible to pinpoint the background of the stories of Abraham with a precision wholly undreamed of when the first edition of this survey was written. The meaning of the term 'Apiru-'abiru, later 'Ibri, "Hebrew," has now been established; it meant something like "donkey-man, donkey driver, huckster, caravaneer."[9]

It is remarkable how much of the patriarchal narrative about Abraham fits together when it is realized that the great patriarch was a trader who led donkey-caravans. It explains his extensive travels. It explains his association with Ur of the Chaldees and with Haran. Ur was the greatest trading city of the early second millennium in Mesopotamia. Haran in Syria was perfectly situated as a trading city and its name meant "Caravan City."

In addition, the cities in Syria and Palestine with which Abraham was associated are now known to have been important caravan cities. All of these cities, moreover, have been shown by archeologists to have been in existence in the early second millennium. Some, like Ur of the Chaldees which was destroyed in

---

[8] R. O'Callaghan, *Aram Nakaraium: A Contribution to the History of Upper Mesopotamia in the Second Millennium B. C.*, p. 403, sums up the evidence as follows: "Thus the resemblance between biblical and Nuzian practices of inheritance in regard to illegitimate sons, the rights of the *errebu* and adopted son, of the slave and finally of daughters appears so striking that to infer from it a social milieu, fairly common . . . as the original source of such usage is in no wise rash and is strongly confirmatory of the evidence given in Genesis as to the local and cultural provenience of the patriarchs."

[9] *The Biblical Period from Abraham to Ezra*, p. 5.

the 17th century and not reoccupied for centuries, existed before and during but not after the period in which the Genesis narratives place Abraham. Gerar, a stopping place used by Abraham, has only recently been identified; and it is no surprise to find that Gerar was occupied in precisely the period in which the Genesis narratives place Abraham (Gn 20). We might hope for more evidence, but the evidence such as it is would appear sufficient to establish the substantial historicity of the patriarchal narratives. As Albright says:

> Until recently it was the fashion among biblical historians to treat the patriarchal sagas of Genesis as though they were artificial creations of Israelite scribes of the divided monarchy or tales told by imaginative rhapsodists around Israelite campfires during the centuries following the occupation of the country. . . . Archeological discoveries since 1925 have changed all this. Aside from a few diehards among older scholars, there is scarcely a single biblical historian who has not been impressed by the rapid accumulation of data supporting the substantial historicity of patriarchal tradition.[10]

THE THEOLOGICAL VALUE

In an evaluation of the theological content of the Yahwist's sources it is evident that extrabiblical sources can afford no direct assistance. On the other hand, it should be remembered that by helping to establish the substantial historicity of Israel's most ancient traditions, extrabiblical sources help indirectly to establish the substantial historicity of patriarchal religion. If one can accept with confidence the nomenclature, customs, travels, and mode of life of the patriarchs because the tradition which transmitted them was substantially faithful, there is no good reason why one should not accept with equal confidence the picture of patriarchal religion transmitted by the same tradition.

It must be admitted, nonetheless, that in both the events of patriarchal times and in the theology of the patriarchs there is evidence of retrojection on the part of later authors. As a result, it is not always easy to distinguish the theology of the patriarchs from

---

[10] *Op. cit.*, p. 1f. See also by the same author, *Yahweh and the Gods of Canaan*, passim, but especially pp. 53-109.

the theology of later theologians such as the Yahwist. It can be done, however, with reasonable certainty.

Before attempting to isolate and evaluate the theology of the patriarchs, two questions must be answered briefly. The first is simple. In talking about a theology of the patriarchs are we talking about an organized body of theological truths possessed by the patriarchs? The answer can only be that the patriarchs were certainly not theologians. They could not be said to have had "a theology" except in the rudimentary sense of living according to the tenets of whatever natural religious truth they were able to grasp and believing those few undeveloped truths they had received by revelation with a strong but theologically naive faith. The phrase, therefore, "theology of the patriarchs," must be taken in the widest possible sense. The patriarchs as individuals and as a group probably knew less theology in the strict sense of the term than the average child in Sunday school.

A second question which deserves attention before entering into the content of the patriarchal theology and the question of possible retrojection of that theology by later authors is the question of prehistoric tradition. Did the religious truths known by the patriarchs derive from prehistoric tradition going back to the first man or are they totally independent of any such tradition, presuming (what cannot be proved) that such a tradition truly existed in the first place?

Three reasons militate against the existence of any tradition going back to the first man in paradise. First, the antiquity of man, which by liberal estimates is pushed back to one-half million years at least; by conservative estimates to at least 50,000 years. If one follows only the conservative estimates, it is difficult to see how an oral tradition could have passed substantially intact down the interminable stretch of so many millennia.

Secondly, even if one presumes the well nigh impossible, namely, that such a tradition could exist and pass inviolate down so many thousands of years, one must still face the fact, attested to by the Bible itself, that Abraham's ancestors were polytheists. In the book of Joshua (24:2), in the account of the renewal of the covenant at Shechem, Joshua clearly states what every Israelite must have known: "Yahweh the God of Israel says this, 'In ancient days your ancestors lived beyond the River—such was Terah the father of Abraham and of Nahor—and they served other gods . . .' " It is extremely difficult, as a consequence, to see how Abraham's polytheistic ancestors would have been the vehicle for a substantially incorrupt primitive tradition going back to paradise, especially since the substance of that tradition would have consisted in the revelation of the existence of the one God.

Thirdly, it has been the common belief for centuries that the teachings contained in the first eleven chapters of Genesis go back to a primordial revelation. This, however, can hardly be correct and must be considered the natural conclusion of an uncritical reading of the chapters in question. Without in any way denying that some primordial revelation was made to the first man and woman, it is the opinion of modern scholars that the theology of Gn 1-11 comes from the pen of the Yahwist and Priestly authors respectively—authors who lived, the one in the 10th and the other in the 6th century before Christ, a minimum, therefore, of eight to nine centuries after Abraham and untold millennia after Adam.

The major portion of the theology in Gn 1-11 comes from the Yahwist who wrote at a relatively late period in the development of Israel's theology. These chapters, therefore, should not be considered as belonging to the inherited theological knowledge of the patriarchs. They are rather the result of the Yahwist's theologizing on the content of the revelation made to the patriarchs, to Moses, and the early prophets, and represent a reconstruction on the basis of that later revelation of what the earlier revelation "must have been" or "would have been." This is a thesis which is adequately defended by a number of authors.[11]

Granting the patriarchs were not theologians themselves, that they had no proper "theology" to speak of, and were not the inheritors of a primitive revelation, the question arises: what precise theological truths were revealed to the patriarchs? Before looking into these truths, however, it will be well to begin with some cautions.

First, the interpreter should beware of reading into the minds and faith of the patriarchs in the early second millennium B.C.

---

[11] B. Vawter, "Understanding Genesis," in *Studies in Salvation History*, ed. L. Salm, p. 68 ff.

doctrines revealed only in later ages. When we deal with the patriarchs we are at the beginning of revelation, down at the bedrock upon which God is just beginning to build.

Secondly, the interpreter should not make the mistake of imagining that the patriarchs received certain revealed truths as so many distinct capsules of divine truth to be treasured by them and handed down like the family silver to each succeeding generation. If the Bible teaches anything about God's way of revealing and teaching, it is that he does not teach as we are accustomed to teach in our classrooms. He teaches by his actions, by the existential impact of his encounters with men; in short, he lets certain men meet him and experience him vividly as a Person.

Lastly, it is impossible to adequately analyze the experience of Abraham and his successors in their encounters with the God of revelation. Mystical experiences (even the most ordinary) must of necessity be explained in mundane language. If even a St. Teresa of Avila and a St. John of the Cross experienced great difficulty in adequately describing their mystical experiences, surely little can be expected from the earliest recipients of revelation, whose theological background was infinitely inferior and whose words of explanation, if such there ever were, have not been recorded anyway.

To scrutinize realistically the religious beliefs of the patriarchs, the interpreter must go back to Ur of the Chaldees in southern Mesopotamia in the 19th-18th century B.C. and begin with Abraham in a pagan world, which as far as is known had never received revelation up to this time.

Abraham himself before his call is presumably a pagan and polytheist. His people and the people of his country worship the many gods of Mesopotamia—nature gods for the most part, worshiped through their symbols: the rivers, the mountains, the sun, the moon, the stars, and sometimes animals.

These gods are considered by them to be the powers behind the forces of nature. They are invoked for the salvation they can bring: health and wealth and natural increase. They are especially invoked in time of calamity because calamities caused by the forces of nature are considered the effects of the anger of the gods.

Much could be said about these gods; they may be categorized

briefly, however, in the following manner. They are not very interested in men, whose only function is to be servants of the gods.
They are arbitrary in their behavior toward men, acting on whim,
independently of any norms of genuine love or justice. Amongst
themselves they are equally arbitrary. They and their goddess
consorts are not bound by any particular moral law and often their
lives as described in the myths would embarrass any decent man
or woman. It is believed that certain acts of the gods in the ageless
past have determined for all future time the recurring, cyclic order
of nature. This order is kept functioning by acting out the primeval myths in the cult, thus keeping present by a sort of sympa-
thetic magic the ancient acts of the gods. The gods themselves
have no plan for the world, no designs for man's future, no final
purpose for history.[12]

The God who speaks to Abraham in the patriarchal traditions
is different. He is not described as a nature god, as a creator-god,
or as any of the gods of the Mesopotamian pantheon. Nothing is
said about his relationship to other gods. No goddess is ever associated with him. Nor is he associated with any cult or cult cycle
of myths. He is, one might say, a "new" God. He manifests himself
many times to Abraham, beginning in Mesopotamia, continuing
with manifestations of himself in Syria, Palestine, and Egypt, at
Bethel, Shechem, at Mambre and other places.

He is a God who is interested in Abraham. He speaks to him as
a person, using the "I-Thou" person-to-person form of address. He
promises him a salvation beyond his dreams. He who is childless
will be the father of a nation. To this nation will be given as homeland the land of Palestine. Isaac and Jacob encounter this same
God and receive the same promises. His interest in the patriarchs
is continued from generation to generation and his promises of salvation are the same.

The theological notions the patriarchs formed about this God,
can be known only from what they themselves tell us about him
in his actions. He is personal in his dealings with them. He is not

---

[12] Cf. H. F. Hahn, *The Old Testament in Modern Research*, p. 216: "In the natu-
ralistic religions of the ancient world, the chief emphasis was on the continuity of
deity, nature and man, and on the necessity for maintaining a natural harmony
among them in order to preserve the prosperity and well-being of human society."

restricted to place or time. He is consistent in his attitude. He is eminently benevolent. He appears, from the promises he makes, to have a design for men based upon a plan which in due time will be fulfilled.[13]

Thus, the God of the patriarchs, as he is revealed through the patriarchal traditions in Genesis, is personal, unrestricted, unassociated with other gods, all powerful, provident, and benevolent. The question, however, may be raised as to whether the patriarchs themselves realized the God they worshiped was indeed the "only" God.

It is truly difficult to say whether the patriarchs' belief in God should be labeled monotheism or monolatry. Monotheism properly speaking is the explicit acknowledgment of the existence of one God and one God only with the explicit denial of existence to any other god or gods. Monolatry properly speaking is the explicit acknowledgment and worship of one God but not explicitly denying the existence of other gods. What the patriarchs thought about the gods worshiped throughout the ancient Near East is not clear.

In the modern world polytheism is for all practical purposes dead. Those who believe, believe in one God. They are monotheists in the strict sense of the word. In the world of Abraham, polytheism was the common and universal belief. Those who believed at all were polytheists. Monotheists were unknown.

Abraham, if he was a monotheist, was the lone exception in a world of polytheists. He certainly worshiped one God, the true God, and to this extent he was at least a monolatrist. But he nowhere denies the existence of other gods. He does not, as later Israelites do, heap ridicule on the idols of the polytheists. In the traditions of Israel about Abraham and the patriarchs, strangers speak of the God of Abraham as being the special God of Abraham, or Isaac, or Jacob (Gn 26:28; 20:27). In one text, which is ambiguous and may be a gloss, there is even a distinction made between the God of Abraham and the god of Nahor, the brother of Abraham (Gn 31:53). It must be admitted the evidence is inconclusive. As Pere de Vaux says:

---

[13] R. F. MacKenzie, *Faith and History in the Old Testament*, pp. 8-39.

This God is unique. He is not surrounded by a numerous pan-theon, nor does he have a consort. Since he is unique and alone, He demands of his faithful an undivided veneration and the house of Jacob must do away with the strange gods which it brought from beyond the River (Gn 35:2). All the consequences of this doctrine, however, are not sharply delineated, and revelation in this first stage is much more precise in what it affirms than in what it denies.[14]

In view of the generally accepted opinion of scholars that the theology contained in Gn 1-11 was not known to the patriarchs but was the work of later theologians (the Yahwist and the Priestly author), who reconstructed what must have been in the beginning from what they knew about theology in their own time, a final question must be asked about the patriarchal theology. Is it possible that later authors have attributed to the patriarchs revelations the patriarchs never really received? Is it possible, for instance, that such truths as the existence of one, personal, all-powerful, benevolent God, the making of a promise by this God to the patriarchs that from them would come a nation, and that to this nation would be given the land of Palestine were never known by the patriarchs but were the result of retrojection by later theologians?

The answer is not easy, and the fact of retrojection in the primeval history and in the patriarchal history itself does not ameliorate the difficulty. Without attempting to speak for everything in the patriarchal history, it can be said that the historical evaluation of the patriarchal traditions as substantially historical is valid not only for the mundane content of the traditions but for the testimony the traditions present for the theology of the patriarchs. The evidence indicates that the "tradition" as tradition is faithful and as "tradition" it contains both.[15]

---

[14] A. Robert and A. Tricot, *Guide to the Bible*, Vol. II, p. 399.

[15] "If the customary law of Genesis is a faithful reflection of contemporary law, and if the social and legal practices recorded in Genesis are correct for the Patriarchal Age but not for the post-Mosaic period, it follows that we cannot *a priori* dismiss the religious content of the Patriarchal narratives as late. These narratives are not retrojections from the age of the Prophets, but actual oral tradition, modified only slightly in the course of time—modified, that is, by the omission of mythical elements, by the heightening of certain elements regarded as important, etc.—but still generally valid as records of early periods" (W. F. Albright, *New Horizons in Biblical Research*, pp. 10-11).

Against the hypothesis that the theology of the patriarchs is a substantial retrojection of later beliefs into the past there are three arguments. First, it is generally true that traditions are preserved because of their importance to a particular people. Nothing, however, was more important to Israel than the revelations and promises made to the patriarchs. It is reasonably doubtful, therefore, that the patriarchal traditions would have been preserved at all if it were not for these revelations and promises.

Secondly, the revelations and promises made to the patriarchs are found in both the Yahwist tradition and the Elohist tradition. In each there is substantial agreement on the theology of the patriarchs. Where there is retrojection in either of them, it is not retrojection of the substance, but explicitation of the substance of the patriarchal theology. In addition, it is most significant that both traditions present the work of Moses not as *a beginning* but as *a continuation and fulfillment* of the promises made to the patriarchs (cf. Ex 3:15ff; Jos 24:2ff).

Thirdly, the patriarchal traditions present a brief, incomplete, and sometimes ambiguous description of the religion of the patriarchs. If later authors were writing up the religion of the patriarchs according to their own advanced ideas, it is reasonably doubtful that they would have left so many ambiguities in the traditions. Psychologically, the soundest argument for the authenticity and antiquity of the patriarchal theology is precisely its very primitiveness, paucity, and naiveté.[16]

THE YAHWIST'S USE OF HIS SOURCES

To assert that the basic historical and theological message of the patriarchal traditions is authentic does not mean that every-

---

[16] Martin Buber expresses the present attitude toward these traditions: "In our own times critical investigation is once again beginning to recognize that the element of the promising of the land in the legends of the Fathers is not in itself a free creation of the Yahwist, a predating, perchance, of the needs of the tradition of the occupation of the land, but belongs to old and indeed to the oldest traditions. In other words: it will not do to view the stories of the Fathers as no more than a pseudo-historical justification of the claim to Canaan. It has been emphatically pointed out that the Fathers owed their position in the Israelite traditional sagas primarily to their function as recipients of revelation . . ." (*Moses: The Revelation and the Covenant*, p. 173).

thing in the traditions corresponds to historical truth. Oft-told tales add and subtract details in the course of time. Generally only the authentic core of the traditions withstands complete change. The details come and go like leaves on a tree. How the tradition will fare from generation to generation depends on the audience. The bard or minstrel or teaching elder must make the tradition relevant to his audience, always attempting to conserve what is essential while at the same time adapting what is un-essential to the ways of thinking of the new generation. His work is very much the reminting of old coins, retaining their basic value and content, but giving them perhaps a new form and a new edge.[17]

The Yahwist's use of his sources is much the same. Of the 62 stories in Genesis some 50 come from the pen of the Yahwist. Before analyzing his use of these stories in the elaboration of his theology, it will be necessary to ask how strictly he felt bound to accept the traditions and conserve them. When it is established that he felt so bound to the traditions that he did not generally feel free either to ignore them or to radically change them, we shall then have to ask what freedom he allowed himself (and what freedom was allowed him by his audience) in interpreting these traditions and submitting them to that enlargement of meaning they would gain by inclusion in the overall pattern of his saga.[18]

It is perhaps important to explain that freedom means not only the adding or subtracting of details but especially the freedom

---

[17] G. von Rad, *Genesis*, pp. 36-42. Von Rad views the process as follows: ". . . the presentation of events in the major source-documents J and E is, it seems to us, itself the conclusion and the internal balancing up of a long process of transmission; each of the individual narrative units which are now joined together in the main sources has a long history behind it, in the course of which it has been subjected to a variety of processes of reminting, and so reinterpreted as to be made relevant in up-to-date preaching. The units were, to begin with, completely independent. Then, as a general rule, they were absorbed into one of the larger blocks of traditions, e.g. those dealing with the patriarchal history, the events at Sinai, the wandering in the wilderness, etc., and were adapted to them. Then these blocks were themselves coordinated, although this again was not determined by the actual historical course of events, since that had long passed out of memory; its basis was rather a preconceived theological picture of the saving history already long established in the form of a cultic confession" (*Old Testament Theology* I, p. 4).

[18] J. Barr, *Old and New in Interpretation*, pp. 65-102.

exercised by the storyteller in making the individual stories submit to the exigencies of his overall pattern. The meaning of a story
as intended by its original narrator may well differ from the meaning of the same story included in the overall pattern of a theological or historical complex. One may cite as example the
original meaning of the flood story and the new meaning it received in the Yahwist's primeval history.[19] Again, a story's relation to the pattern as a whole and even its relation to other stories
included in the overall pattern of the theological complex may
easily give it not only an additional meaning but sometimes even
a totally different meaning. One may cite as example here the
use of the Abraham-Isaac sacrifice story in Gn 22.

The truth of this observation can perhaps best be exemplified
from the New Testament by examining Matthew's Sermon on the
Mount where sayings of Our Lord spoken at different times
and to different audiences are amalgamated in an overall literary
pattern which comes more from Matthew than from Our Lord.
In Matthew's pattern some of the sayings have a meaning, given
to them by their position in the pattern, different from the original
meaning of the isolated sayings as originally intended by Our
Lord. Matthew preserved the saying because it had the sacrosanct
quality that came from belonging to the tradition. But at the same
time he felt free to give it the added or different meaning it gets
from being included in his overall pattern because he felt free
to use this traditional material in his theological interpretation of
Our Lord's basic message.

The basic steps in the formation of the Gospels provide an enlightening analogy for the literary activity of the Yahwist. They
help in particular to explain his twofold and apparently opposed
attitude toward his sources, namely: his respect for, and con-
servation of, the individual sayings and stories made sacrosanct
by tradition; and at the same time his assurance of literary freedom in making these individual units of tradition part of a larger
whole, thus giving them a different meaning, which in some

---

[19] As A. Heidel says: "The skeleton is the same in both cases, but the flesh and
blood, and above all the animating spirit are different" (*The Gilgamesh Epic and
Old Testament Parallels*, p. 268).

cases ignores or at least is ignorant of the original meaning of the story.

In this analogy a Gospel is understood to be an arrangement of the traditional preaching about Christ in such a way that doctrines considered important by the author are expressed by the pattern of the book as a whole. Thus, the material in the Gospels is generally considered to have gone through three stages.

In the first stage, Our Lord announced the Good News (Gospel) which was Himself. He did this both by his acts and by his words. In preaching the good news he followed the basic law of communication which demands that a preacher adapt himself to the situation in life of his audience. Thus what he did and what he said during the years of his public life constitute the *ipsissima facta* and *ipsissima dicta* which became the fundamental message later preached by the Apostles and put in written form by the Evangelists.

In the second stage, the Apostles preached the Good News throughout the Roman Empire. Since they too had to adapt to the situation in life of their different audiences, the sayings of Our Lord and the events of his life came to be expressed in different terminology and in different contexts. Over the course of some 30 or 40 years (the period between Pentecost and the writing of the first Gospels) the constant repetition of these sayings and events resulted in more or less stereotyped forms of expression.

In the third and final stage,[20] each of the Evangelists made a selection of these stereotyped sayings and stories and arranged them in a comprehensive written work (Gospel) directed to the situation in life of the Church at large in their particular area. In this pattern or arrangement (which we call a Gospel) the individual stories and sayings acquired a meaning from the pattern which they perhaps did not have as used by the Apostles in their preaching over the course of 30 years nor perhaps even in the original preaching and setting of Our Lord's life. In all three stages, how-

---

[20] An individual Gospel may have gone through even more redactional stages. R. Brown opts for as many as five redactions of the material in the Johannine gospel (See *The Anchor Bible: The Gospel according to John* (1-XII), pp. XXXIV-XXXIX).

ever, the Word and the way it was preached was always the servant of the message as a whole, and it is this that constituted the basic control at each stage.

In the formation of the Yahwist's saga a similar process took place. In the first stage there were the *ipsissima facta* and the *ipsissima dicta* of the different patriarchs. In the second stage these sayings of the patriarchs and the events of their lives were passed on from generation to generation by the bards and the minstrels who accommodated the telling of the now traditional stories to the life situations of their particular audiences. In the final stage the Yahwist, after a period of some eight or nine centuries, gathered the stereotyped stories made sacrosanct by tradition and arranged them in a pattern in such a way that doctrines he considered important for his audience were expressed by the pattern of his saga as a whole.[21]

In the formation of the patriarchal traditions as in the formation of the Gospels there was adaptation to the situation in life of the audience. And just as in the second and third stages of the Gospel formation, this adaptation too brought with it changes. The changes, however, were not so much in the basic message as in the way the basic message was expressed. As in the Gospels the message as a whole provided a control. The way in which it was expressed was subject to variation but not the basic message, however intangible the basic message itself may sometimes seem to be.

Both of the questions asked earlier—namely, how strictly did the Yahwist feel bound to accept these traditions and what freedom did he allow himself in interpreting them?—may now be answered by pursuing the evolution of a particular unit of patriarchal tradition from its initial stage in the time of the patriarchs through its intermediate stage of transmission down the centuries by the bards and storytellers to its present position in the Yahwist's saga. A particularly cogent example is the story about Abraham and Sarah in Gn 12:10-20.[22] Six points may be considered.

---

[21] G. von Rad says: "As we now have them, these separate traditions are no longer independent as once they were, but have been amalgamated into larger literary compositions. . . . Ignoring the initial stages, such sketches lie before us in the final form in the work of the Jahwist and the Elohist, and in the history of David's rise to power" (*Old Testament Theology*, II, p. 425).

[22] G. von Rad in his *Genesis* gives many more examples.

1. The story (like the stories in Gn 20 and Gn 26 on the same motif) pivots around the wife-sister deception theme.

2. From documents that have come down from the early second millennium in Mesopotamia it is now known that in Hurrian society of that period (and in no other that we know), certain juridical rights and privileges were enjoyed by a woman who was not only a wife but also a sister either by blood or by adoption.[23]

3. In Gn 12:10-20 the wife-sister theme is the element in the story which proves its basic historicity, since the privileged wife-sister status is attested to by contemporary documents from the time of the patriarchs and from the Hurrian society in which they lived.

4. The element in the story that accounts for its sacrosanct position in Israel's tradition (and which was the basic reason for telling the story in the first place) is its testimony to the privileged status of the patriarch's wife who became in due course the fore-mother of the chosen nation. (The concern of Israel's theologians with genealogies is evident at all stages of Israel's history but never more so than in Genesis.)

5. When the story came to be told in later centuries in social conditions which knew nothing about the unusual custom in Hurrian society of adopting a wife as sister to enhance her prestige and in which the idea of a man marrying his own sister was reprobated, storytellers, who on the one hand were bound by sacrosanct tradition to recount the story, were, on the other hand, compelled by the odium of the custom to either tone it down or explain it away. In the Elohist's version it is toned down by saying Sarah was indeed Abraham's sister—but by another mother (Gn 26:11-13). In the Yahwist's version, it had been explained away, probably by an earlier storyteller, by attributing to Abraham an astute deception which today would be called an outright lie (Gn 12:11-13).

6. In its final stage the episode is incorporated by the Yahwist in his theological pattern. He does not change it or discard it even though it must have embarrassed him (though less than we might think). He cannot change or discard it because tradition has made

---

[23] E. Speiser, *Genesis*, pp. 91-94, 184-185.

it sacrosanct. He uses it; but he does not use it for the precise reason for which the story was initially told, because he no longer understands that reason any more than the early storytellers who had passed it down the centuries and given the face-saving explanation they thought necessary. In his saga, then, the story is not recounted for its basic reason which was to express the privileged wife-sister status of the foremother of the chosen nation, but for the false explanation given by the embarrassed storytellers, namely, that despite the little faith of Abraham at this time, God himself had stepped in to protect the foremother of the chosen people.

As a consequence of this analysis one can say that Gn 12:10-20 exemplifies the following points: a) the common concern of the Yahwist and the original storyteller for the purity of the chosen line; b) the power of the original reason—the purity of the chosen line—to establish and keep the story sacrosanct in Israel's tradition; c) the storyteller's respect for and retention of the tradition despite his adaptation of the story to the social requirements of his milieu; d) the Yahwist's respect for tradition in that he felt obliged to retain the story despite its perhaps odious picture of Abraham; e) the Yahwist's use of the story in his theological pattern for a reason other than the precise reason that gave it birth.

Thus, the Yahwist does not necessarily use a traditional story because of its historical value. In many cases he makes no particular judgment about the historicity of an incident—though we may presume he generally considered the stories historical—because his interest is not so much in the precise fact or event portrayed as in the place the story will serve in his overall pattern. In other words, it is the functional value of the story that is primary for the Yahwist. The historical value is important, but less so. And this is not untypical of theologians.

In conclusion it may be said that the Yahwist in his predilection for the functional value of his material is not unlike the New Testament theologians who made a selection from the many sayings and deeds of Our Lord passed down by tradition and then used these selected stories according to their own theological patterns—even when, in some cases, the pattern required a position for the stories which was either chronologically or topographically at variance with the original time and place of the event or saying.

In the Yahwist's saga, as in the Gospels, it is to the functional use of the story that there is given the first importance. And this in the last analysis can be justified by the subservience of the individual units of tradition to the basic message of which they are a means of expression. Or to put it more bluntly, the Yahwist, though conscious of the importance of historicity, will nevertheless not allow himself as a theologian to be hamstrung by the merely historical.[24]

SUGGESTED READINGS

G. von Rad, *Old Testament Theology* I, 17ff; 121ff; 168; 297; II, 420ff.

―――. *The Problem of the Hexateuch and Other Essays*, 57ff; 168ff.

―――. *Genesis* 13-42.

E. Speiser, *Genesis*, xxxvii-lii.

O. Eissfeldt, *The Old Testament: An Introduction*, 9-56; 132-143.

A. Bentzen, *Introduction to the Old Testament* I, 44ff; 74ff; 235ff.

B. Childs, *Myth and Reality in the Old Testament*.

B. Vawter, "Understanding Genesis" in *Studies in Salvation History*, ed. by L. Salm.

R. A. F. MacKenzie, *Faith and History in the Old Testament*.

W. F. Albright, *The Biblical Period from Abraham to Ezra*.

―――. *Yahweh and the Gods of Canaan*.

―――. *From the Stone Age to Christianity*.

C. North, *The Old Testament Interpretation of History*.

J. Bright, *A History of Israel*, 41-93.

G. Mendenhall, "Biblical History in Transition" in *The Bible and the Ancient Near East*, 32-53.

M. Eliade, *Cosmos and History*.

J. L. McKenzie, *Myths and Realities*, 146-206.

M. Marty, "The Bible and Tradition," *The Critic*, Aug.-Sept. 1965, 28-37.

―――――

[24] G. von Rad, *Genesis*, pp. 21-22; and E. Jacob, *Theology of the Old Testament*, p. 184.

G. S. Kirk, "The Homeric Poems as History," *C.A.H.*, rev. ed.,
   fasc. 22.

G. E. Wright, *The Old Testament against its Environment.*

E. Cassirer, *The Philosophy of Symbolic Forms*, Vol. 2: *Mythical
   Thought.*

C. Gordon, "The Story of Jacob and Laban in the Light of the
   Nuzi Tablets," *BASOR* 66, 1937, 25ff.

H. Frankfort, *The Intellectual Adventure of Ancient Man.*

I. Hunt, *The World of the Patriarchs.*

Chapter V

THE YAHWIST'S
LITERARY TECHNIQUES

The production of a unified, organically structured literary work is no small feat. It demands deep thought, elaborate planning, and a considerable grasp of literary technique. The true "opus" is never an accident.

A study of the theme, the structure, and the literary techniques of the Yahwist's saga will show, we believe, that the saga is a true "opus." We will begin with the literary techniques and devices used by the Yahwist. They will contribute to a clear picture of the structure, which in turn will help considerably to a grasp of the central themes and their subsidiary motifs.

In dealing with the sources of the Yahwist it has been stated that he drew the major portion of his narrative material from Israel's oral traditions, which consisted for the most part of etiological stories, liturgical recitals, assorted pagan myths, and some few poetic works. As in the formation of the Gospels, these source materials went through three stages. In their earliest preliterary stage the majority of the traditions subsisted for a time in relative isolation at their place of origin. In a second stage they began to be grouped in continuous narratives either through a natural and gradual coalescence based on similarity of material content in the traditions or as a result of the more deliberate efforts of the bards and the minstrels who gathered the material and arranged it in narrative cycles.

Just how far this coalescence and grouping had progressed in the second stage before the Yahwist took up the traditions as the raw material for his saga it is difficult to determine. Certain narrative sequences, for instance the Abraham-Lot cycle, the Jacob-

Esau and Jacob-Laban cycles, and the Joseph story, were perhaps already well established stories by the time of the Yahwist.

Whatever the condition of the material in the second stage of its transmission, the problem that faced the Yahwist was how to fuse these sequences into a continuous narrative which would not only have unity and cohesion but would in addition testify, through the sequence and arrangement of the material in an over-all pattern, to the basic theological teachings he had set out to inculcate by means of the saga as a whole.

Two things in particular made the Yahwist's task more difficult than the task of the ordinary storyteller—the expanse of his saga, stretching from the creation of the world to the entrance of Israel into the Promised Land in the 13th century, and the recalcitrance of some of the material which, though it may not have fitted into his plan, he was nevertheless bound to include because of its sac-rosanct nature as tradition. His problem, therefore, was: to unify the different, and sometimes recalcitrant, traditions; arrange them in such a way that the thread of continuity would be clearly per-ceptible between one part and another; and so link the different parts of the saga internally that each would contribute in its own way to the central and subsidiary themes of the work as a whole.

At his disposal the Yahwist had a number of techniques and de-vices developed down the centuries by the bards and the minstrels in order to hold the attention and sustain the interest of their audi-ences throughout the length and breadth of long oral narratives. If it is remembered that Homeric bards declaimed the Iliad and the Odyssey for twenty or more hours over the course of a number of evenings to unlettered audiences, the need for such devices will be readily appreciated.

Without going into all the techniques and devices used by the Yahwist, some appreciation of the following will contribute signif-icantly to the reader's interpretation of the saga; story patterns, patterns of stories, obstacle stories, genealogies, dialogues, solilo-quies, theological comments, foreshadowing texts, demythologiz-ing and retheologizing.

Since the technique of putting one's own words in the mouth of another is found in many forms in ancient literature and since it is the most difficult to accept because of its apparent dishonesty, it will be best to begin with an explanation of the origin, the use, and the benefits of this technique. Later and more briefly something will be said about the different forms this technique takes in the Yahwist's saga.

LITERARY VENTRILOQUISM

As long ago as 1907, Samuel Driver proclaimed as one of the principles which, once recognized, would "be found to solve nearly all the difficulties which, upon the traditional view of the historical books of the Old Testament, are insuperable," the principle that "some freedom was used by ancient historians in placing speeches or discourses in the mouths of historical characters."[1]

If this freedom is accepted and recognized, it will hardly solve "nearly all the difficulties . . . ," but it will go a long way toward opening a path that leads directly to the mind of the inspired theologian. This can be said because if it is the sacred author who composes the speeches or discourses, it can be presumed, more often than not, that the speeches or discourses express his theological interpretation, or at very least, the bent of his mind and the direction of his thought.

This we shall find to be especially true of such techniques as foreshadowing texts, divine soliloquies, and divine dialogues which differ significantly from the more ordinary literary techniques of using direct instead of indirect discourse in the telling of stories and of attributing words to an individual to express the intention behind his deeds instead of giving a long description of what he had actually done (cf. Nm 20:18-20; Ex 1:9).

The placing of speeches in the mouths of historical characters is admitted by all in later books of the Bible, e.g. Deuteronomy, which is made up almost from beginning to end of speeches put in the mouth of Moses;[2] the didactic books, especially Tobit, Es-

---

[1] *An Introduction to the Literature of the Old Testament*, p. 11.

[2] It has not escaped notice that Israel's inspired writers put into God's mouth the expression of Israelite laws whose similarity to laws in the Code of Hammurabi and other Middle Eastern law codes might, in a more copyright-minded society, have subjected God Himself to a charge of plagiarism. A. Jones, in his engaging essay "And God said . . ." (*Unless Some Man Show Me*, pp. 125ff), discusses the problem.

ther, and Judith; the book of Daniel, which contains a series of pseudonymous prophecies attributed to Daniel; and even in the Gospels, particularly in the Gospel of John. That this is a technique invented by storytellers and does not correspond to "what actually happened" is not immediately obvious to all. We shall begin, therefore, with a demonstration.

In the Aeneid, in the Odyssey, in the Ugaritic legend of Aqhat, and in the Akkadian epic of Gilgamesh, there is a type of text that bears a startling resemblance to certain texts in the Yahwist's saga. In these texts, which are placed by the author in the mouth of a god or goddess, a shade, a seer, or some famous person, a prediction is made concerning the near or distant future. The prediction is sometimes clear, sometimes vague, but always calculated to arouse in the reader either anticipation or suspense or both. In some cases, depending upon the amount and detail of the knowledge given concerning the future, the prediction serves as well to outline the story as a whole or at least some part of the story.

The following texts from the Aeneid and from Genesis will indicate the similarity of the biblical and the extrabiblical storyteller's technique. In the text from the Aeneid, written at the height of the Augustan age when Rome ruled the world, Latinus, the pre-Roman king of Italy and the father of the maid Lavinia who will eventually marry the Trojan hero, Aeneas, is lying in a woodland glade. He hears a voice from the forest make the following prediction concerning Rome's future greatness:

> Seek not, Latinus, to marry your daughter to a man of the Latin race. From abroad shall sons-in-law come to wed our women and make our name illustrious: to their descendants the whole spinning globe shall be a footstool and an empire—all that the sun looks down on, even to the ends of the earth (Book VII, 160-165).

The text from Genesis has God foretelling the following events in Israel's history to the patriarch, Abraham:

> Know this for certain, that your descendants will be exiles in a land not their own, where they will be slaves and oppressed for four hundred years. But I will pass judgment also on the nation that enslaves them and after that they will leave, with many possessions. For your part, you shall go to your fathers in peace; you shall be

buried at a ripe old age. In the fourth generation they will come back here, for the wickedness of the Amorites is not yet ended. (Gn 15:13-16)[3]

In the text from the Aeneid, Vergil's Roman audience knows exactly what he is talking about when he uses these pseudopredictions to arouse anticipation and suspense and to connect such early events as the marriage of Lavinia and Aeneas with the eventual glory and world rule of Rome.

In the Genesis text, the inspired author's audience knows, as Vergil's audience knows, what the storyteller is cryptically predicting. The "land not their own" is Egypt. The slavery and oppression for "four hundred years" signifies the enslavement by the Pharaohs. The judgment on "the nation" is a reference to the ten plagues. The going free "with many possessions" refers to the exodus from Egypt under Moses. And the return, when the "wickedness of the Amorites" is complete, refers to the conquest of the Promised Land in the time of Joshua.

The similarity of these texts suggests that what is a literary technique in the time of Vergil may well be a literary technique in the Bible. Since one may rightly dispute the cogency of literary analogies based upon works so widely separated in time, one cannot use Vergil as the basis for a literary comparison with the Bible. Fortunately earlier texts are available. What these earlier texts testify to is the existence and use of the literary technique which is called "foreshadowing," a technique which is common to both biblical and extrabiblical literature.[4]

Since foreshadowing is the most dramatic form of literary ventriloquism, we shall presume that a justification of foreshadowing

---

[3] G. von Rad suggests Gn 15:13-16 is an insertion "from E?" (*Genesis*, p. 182). But only the use of *Elohim* rather than *Yahweh* distinguishes it as "E" (see E. Speiser, *Genesis*, p. 113).

[4] The importance of such literary comparisons is more than obvious. A recent author with whom I am in full agreement expresses it as follows: "Old Testament literature from its earliest to its latest documents had its connections with the cultural environment of its day, and no matter how unique we may consider its religious message to be, that message was set forth to be intelligible to the people of its day, so that the more accurately we understand the thought world of that day the better we shall understand the Old Testament message." M. Ellenbogen, *Foreign Words in the Old Testament* (London, 1961) p. 1. See also J. L. McKenzie, *Myths and Realities*, pp. 146ff.

will serve equally as a justification of divine soliloquies, divine dialogues, and theological comments.

We shall begin with a definition of a foreshadowing text. We shall then attempt to establish foreshadowing as a biblical literary technique by means of analogies drawn from Homeric, Ugaritic, and Akkadian literature. Lastly, we shall suggest some dividends the exegete may reap from a study of foreshadowing as a literary technique.

Foreshadowing may be defined as a storyteller's technique or device, whereby knowledge of the future is given in order to arouse anticipation and suspense and at the same time prepare the audience to look for an interconnection of the parts of the story with the whole.[5]

The term "foreshadowing" means "to give information in a more or less vague manner, but in a way to arouse curiosity, as to what *may* happen in the future."[6] When the information is controlled by the storyteller to achieve specific effects such as anticipation or suspense, we may properly consider it a technique.

Thus when the storyteller wishes to arouse anticipation, he gives clear knowledge about the future. When he wishes to arouse in the reader that combination of hope, fear, and uncertainty which gives rise to suspense, he gives knowledge about the future that is vague, general, and uncertain. The arousal of such emotions helps sustain the reader's interest and attention; and where the anticipation and suspense reach high levels of intensity, the storyteller by their resolution at the end of the story can achieve for the reader a genuine catharsis.

In addition to the initial suspense aroused by the foreshadowing of future events, the storyteller very often continues to build up

---

[5] "In folk literature strict unity is one of the basic laws of composition, and definite techniques were evolved to unify a work and organize its parts. The study of these techniques has been carried on mainly by classical scholars in connection with the growth of the Homeric poems in oral tradition. They consist of devices such as prologue and epilogue, recurring lines, foreshadowings, retrospections, themes, and over-all structures, whereby the essentially disparate parts are stitched together to form a unity. These devices of continuity and interconnection seem to have grown up with the tradition and out of the experience of the reciter in handling large masses of material." (C. H. Lohr, "Oral Techniques in the Gospel of Matthew," *CBQ* 23, 1961, p. 404.)

[6] D. C. Stuart, "Foreshadowing and Suspense in the Euripidean Prolog," *Studies in Philology*, XV, 1918, 295.

suspense.[7] He accomplishes this in many ways but principally by repetition of foreshadowing texts, by introducing delays and digressions which retard the fulfillment of the predictions made (see pp. 136ff), and by a gradual development from vague foreshadowing to clear foreshadowing.[8]

Besides arousing anticipation and suspense, foreshadowing permits the author to prepare the audience to look for an interconnection of the parts of his story with the whole. Where there is a short space of time between the foreshadowing and the fulfillment, events interconnect naturally and easily for the reader. Where the period between foreshadowing and fulfillment covers a long time, the foreshadowing texts help to keep particular incidents in perspective and at the same time provide for the reader a clue to the meaning of events which might otherwise seem irrelevant or digressive. The importance of such a technique for writers like Vergil, Homer, and the Yahwist, whose narrative content runs to some length, is considerable.[9]

Turning now to foreshadowing as an established literary technique, common to both biblical and extrabiblical literature of the ancient world, we are faced with the problem of comparative literary study. For the sake of brevity we shall examine only a few examples. Anyone who investigates the literature will find many more.[10]

We can begin with an example from the Odyssey. The date of

---

[7] That foreshadowing and even outright foretelling do not necessarily destroy suspense is obvious to anyone who has ever read a good story a second time. "When the reader of an ancient epic knows beforehand the outcome either of the main plot or of the separate episodes, he usually feels no uncertainty about the events that have been foretold; his interest in the story, however, is by no means at an end; he remains in a state of emotional tension and is on the lookout for something which he either wishes or dreads to see happen" (G. E. Duckworth, *Foreshadowing and Suspense in the Epics of Homer, Apollonius, and Vergil*, p. 37f).

[8] G. E. Duckworth, *op. cit.* pp. 53ff; also C. H. Lohr, *op. cit.*, pp. 403ff; and J. Gray, *1 and 2 Kings*, pp. 23f.

[9] It should be noted that the use of foreshadowing texts as a technique is not affected directly by the debate between proponents of literary criticism and oral tradition. The debate deals with an approach to criticism and would not involve a technique which is equally at home in literary and oral spheres of communication. See E. Nielsen, *Oral Tradition*, p. 11f.

[10] See G. E. Duckworth, *op. cit.* See also *ANET*, pp. 72-97; 129-150; and R. G. Collingwood, *The Idea of History*, p. 44.

the Odyssey is disputed, but it is generally placed somewhere in the 8th century, approximately two hundred years after the Yahwist.[11] In the text, the shade of the seer, Teiresias, foretells to Odysseus his return home, his vengeance on the suitors of Penelope, and Odysseus' later fate.

> My Lord Odysseus, you will find trouble in your house—a set of scoundrels eating up your stores, making love to your royal consort and offering wedding gifts. It is true that you will pay out these men for their misdeeds . . . but whichever way you choose to kill them . . . when you have cleared your palace of these suitors, you must then set out once more upon your travels (XI, 100-107).

If we move back now from the 8th to the 14th century B.C. and from the Ionian coast of Asia Minor to the coastland of ancient Phoenicia, we find the foreshadowing technique used in Ugaritic literature but with considerably less sophistication than in Homer. In the Tale of Aqhat, for example, Baal foretells to Daniel that a son will be born to him. In due course, Aqhat is born. The same foreshadowing technique is used at least five times in the one story.[12]

If we move from the 14th to the 20th century B.C., the probable date for the monumental composition of the Gilgamesh epic[13] we find foreshadowing used regularly even at that early date. Three times it is foretold that Enkidu will embrace a harlot and then the wild beasts will reject him. In a dream Gilgamesh learns beforehand that Enkidu will come to Uruk. Again in a dream, interpreted for him by Enkidu, Gilgamesh learns that Enlil has destined him for kingship but not for everlasting life. Still again in a dream, Enkidu learns that the gods have sat in council and that Enlil has decreed his, Enkidu's, death.[14]

As a transition from extrabiblical to biblical foreshadowing texts and as an example of how a biblical author takes over a myth and utilizes its foreshadowing texts for his own purposes, the reader

---

[11] See G. S. Kirk, "The Homeric Poems as History," in *The Cambridge Ancient History*, rev. ed., II, pp. 9-11.

[12] *ANET*, pp. 130-131; 143; 146; 148; 150.

[13] See N. K. Sandars, *The Epic of Gilgamesh*, p. 8.

[14] See N. K. Sandars, *op. cit.*, pp. 62, 64, 65, 68, 87, 105. Also *ANET*, pp. 72-97.

may compare the following passage from the Gilgamesh epic with its demythologized version in the Priestly author's flood story. In the Gilgamesh epic, Utnapishtim is speaking to Gilgamesh about the flood. In the biblical version the story is demythologized and the subjects are God and Noah, but the storyteller's foreshadowing technique is retained.[15]

Epic of Gilgamesh

In those days (Utnapishtim says) the world teemed, the people multiplied, the world bellowed like a wild bull, and the great god was aroused by the clamor. Enlil heard the clamor and said to the gods in council. "The uproar of mankind is intolerable and sleep is no longer possible by reason of the babble." So the gods in their hearts were moved to let loose the deluge; but my lord Ea warned me in a dream. He whispered their words to my house of reeds, ". . . O man of Shurrupak . . . tear down your house and build a boat, abandon possessions and look for life, despise worldly goods and save your soul alive. Tear down your house, I say, and build a boat. These are the measurements of the barque as you shall build her; let her beam equal her length, let her deck be roofed like the vault that covers the abyss; then take up into the boat the seed of all living creatures."

Priestly Author

The earth (says the Priestly author) grew corrupt in God's sight, and filled with violence. God contemplated the earth: it was corrupt, for corrupt were the ways of all flesh on the earth. God said to Noah, 'The end has come for all things of flesh; I have decided this, because the earth is full of violence of man's making, and I will efface them from the earth. Make yourself an ark out of resinous wood. Make it with reeds and line it with pitch inside and out. This is how to make it: the length of the ark is to be three hundred cubits, its breadth fifty cubits, and its height thirty cubits . . . For my part I mean to bring a flood, and send the waters over the earth, to destroy all flesh on it, every living creature under heaven; everything on earth shall perish . . . From all living creatures, from all flesh, you must take two of each kind aboard the ark, to save their lives with yours; they must be a male and a female . . .'

A parade example of foreshadowing is the dream of Joseph in Gn 37:6-8; the sequel and fulfillment of this foreshadowing text is well known:[16]

Now Joseph had a dream, and he repeated it to his brothers. 'Listen' he said 'to this dream I have had. We were binding sheaves in the countryside; and my sheaf, it seemed, rose up and stood upright;

---

[15] See N. K. Sandars, *op. cit.*, p. 105f.

[16] E. Speiser attributes Gn 37:2-20 to the Yahwist (*Genesis*, p. 287ff).

then I saw your sheaves gather round and bow to my sheaf.' 'So you want to be king over us,' his brothers retorted 'or to lord it over us?'

For the reader of the Yahwist's saga (and many other books in the Bible), a recognition of the fact that biblical storytellers knew and utilized the foreshadowing technique can pay significant dividends. Some of these dividends may be indicated.

Since it is of the nature of foreshadowing to draw upon the knowledge of events known by the author's audience, the date of the latest event foreshadowed should supply at least a *terminus ante quem* for the composition of the story or saga. In passing, it should be noted that the storyteller often foreshadows events far beyond the end of his story. The last event foreshadowed, therefore, gives no certain clue to where the story or saga originally ended. Thus foreshadowings of the Davidic dynasty in no way proves that the Yahwist's saga carried Israel's history up to David.[17]

Since the storyteller uses foreshadowing texts to give the reader a broad outline of how the story will develop, the reader should be able to use them as clues to the basic plan envisioned by the author. This is particularly true of such texts as Gn 12:1-3 and 15:13-16 and it may be true of Gn 3:15.

Since the storyteller uses foreshadowing texts to prepare the audience to look for the interconnection of parts of his story with the whole, the foreshadowing texts may well supply a key to the author's selection of traditions to be incorporated in his story. As authors have pointed out, the Yahwist and the Elohist drew for their raw material upon the accumulated traditions of their people as formulated by earlier storytellers.[18] Very often, however, the final composer utilizes a tradition for a purpose other than that for which it was formulated by the earlier storyteller. The foreshadowing texts should help to reveal the new label placed by the final composer on the old story.

Since foreshadowing texts link early events with later events, they supply a valuable clue to the author's philosophy or theology

---

[17] See Duckworth, *op. cit.*, p. 28f.

[18] G. von Rad, *op. cit.*, pp. 30-42; J. L. McKenzie, *Myths and Realities*, pp. 169-174.

of history. For an understanding of the theology of history of an author such as the Yahwist, who connects primeval history with patriarchal history and patriarchal history with the history of Israel's heroic and royal periods, such texts should be of no small value.[19] G. von Rad, for instance, speaks of Gn 15:13-16 as "a cabinet piece of Old Testament theology of history."[20]

Since foreshadowing texts sometimes proceed in series from obscure to clear and from the general to the specific, it should be possible, where the exegete succeeds in establishing a series, to explain the early, obscure texts in the series by the later, clear texts. This procedure should provide assistance for the exegesis of the primeval history as a whole and for the interpretation of Gn 3:15 in particular (see pp. 196-202).

Lastly, from the pedagogical standpoint an explanation of literary "ventriloquism" and particularly of the foreshadowing technique and the use of the terms "foreshadowing" and "foreshadowing text" should help considerably in explaining why so many apparently trivial and unnecessary prophecies appear in the historical books of the Bible. If these terms could be substituted for such odious terms as "pseudoprophecy" and "prophecy after the event," the semantic breakthrough alone would be of considerable value.

FORESHADOWING

In the Yahwist's saga the foreshadowing technique is used with great artistry. The Yahwist utilizes foreshadowing texts to show the direction of his narrative, to link part with part, and to emphasize the basic doctrinal points of his saga. He uses series of texts as refrains and for the purpose of highlighting key words and key phrases.[21] He sometimes uses foreshadowing texts as anticipatory

---

[19] The terminology is loose. For a discussion of the terms "religious prehistory," "primitive history," and "mythopoeic," see J. L. McKenzie, op. cit., pp. 199f.

[20] Op. cit., p. 183.

[21] The value of a foreshadowing text as a refrain consists principally in its value as a repetitive device. What J. Muilenburg observes about repetition in Hebrew poetry applies as well to describe its function in narrative forms: "Repetition . . . serves . . . to center the thought . . . , to focus the richness of varied predication upon the poet's prevailing concern . . . , to give continuity to the writer's thought;

summaries and, if the saga concludes as some authors think at Nm 24, then it is not improbable that he has used the foreshadowing texts in Gn 3:15 and Nm 24 to provide "inclusio-conclusio" boundaries to his story.[22]

The following would appear to be recognizable series of foreshadowing texts in the Yahwist's saga: a) a series dealing with the rise of Israel: Gn 12:1-3, 7; 13:14-17; 15:4-5; 26:3-4; 28:13-15; 49:8-12; Nm 24:7, 17-18; b) a series dealing with the exodus events: Gn 15:13-16 (?); 45:7; 48:21; Ex 3:8; c) a series dealing with Israel's conquest of Edom: Gn 25:23; 27:29, 40; Nm 24:7-9, 17-19); d) a final series, more difficult to establish than the others, which would appear to deal with the very heart of the saga—the triumph of Yahwism over the false religion of Canaan and the rise of the Davidic dynasty—probably begins with Gn 3:15 and runs through Gn 9:26-27; 12:1-3 (cf. also 26:3-4; 27:29; 28:14-15); 49:8-12, ending with the disputed allusions to a future Israelite king in Nm 24:7, 17-18.[23]

While Gn 3:15 is the most obscure of the foreshadowing texts in the Yahwist's saga, its basic ideas and its key words (particularly "seed," "curse," and "enmities") would appear to place it in the series beginning with Gn 3:14 and ending with Nm 24:17-18. The

---

the repeated word or phrase is often strategically located, thus providing a clue to the movement and stress of the poem. . . . This iterative propensity of ancient Israel extends beyond its expression in poetry. In narrative, the literary genre most characteristic of her life and thought, repetition appears as a major stylistic device" ("A Study in Hebrew Rhetoric: Repetition and Style," *Supplements to VT 1* (1953), p. 99f).

[22] *Inclusio*, known among classical scholars as ring composition, is a Semitic stylistic device in which what is said in the beginning of a piece is repeated at the end. The repetition forces the attention of the reader back to the beginning and thus not only serves as a frame for the piece as a whole but sometimes interconnects intervening parts with the beginning and end. The antiquity of *inclusio* as a stylistic device in the time of the Yahwist can be shown from its use in the Nikkal poem from Ras-Shamra (cf. A. Goetze, "The Nikkal Poem from Ras-Shamra," *JBL* 60 (1941), p. 354). The key words "blessing," "curse" recur regularly in the saga and especially in Gn 12:2-3 and Nm 24. With the theme of blessing implicit in Gn 2 and the theme of curse explicit in Gn 3:14-19, it is quite possible that Nm 24 represents an *inclusio* that returns the reader's attention to Gn 2-3. Cf. N. W. Lund, *Chiasmus in the New Testament: A Study in Formgeschichte*, pp. 130-136. Lund gives a number of examples showing the antiquity of chiasma as a stylistic device as early as the second millennium B.C.

[23] W. F. Albright translates this text: "When the stars of Jacob shall prevail, and the tribes of Israel shall arise," and denies any reference to an Israelite king (*JBL* 63, 1944, pp. 219; 226f).

last two texts in this series (Gn 49:8-12 and Nm 24:17-18), which are generally interpreted to refer to the "seed" of Judah (i.e. the Davidic dynasty), would appear to clarify the more obscure terms of Gn 3:15.[24]

An analysis of the Yahwist's use of foreshadowing texts reveals five characteristics.[25] a) The foreshadowing texts tend to recur in series after the manner of a refrain. b) They are usually placed in the mouth of God, a prophet, or some important person. c) They frequently repeat the same basic ideas and sometimes even the same key words. d) They tend to outline the storyline to be followed in the saga. e) The foreshadowing usually proceeds from obscure to clear, from the general to the specific.

The first two characteristics, recurrence in series after the manner of a refrain and putting the foreshadowing text in the mouth of God, a prophet, or some important person, are clear in the texts foreshadowing the exodus:

> Then *Yahweh* said to Abram, 'Know this for certain, that your descendants will be exiles in a land not their own, where they will be slaves and oppressed for four hundred years. But I will pass judgment also on the nation that enslaves them and after that *they will leave*, with many possessions' (Gn 15:13-14).
> Then *Joseph* said to his brothers. . . . God sent me before you to make sure that your race would have survivors in the land and *to save your lives*, many lives at that' (Gn 45:7).
> Then *Israel* said to Joseph, 'Now I am about to die. But God will be with you and *take you back* to the country of your fathers' (Gn 48:21).
> And *Yahweh* said: 'I have seen the miserable state of my people . . . I mean to *deliver them out of the hands of the Egyptians and bring them up* out of that land to a land rich and broad, a land where milk and honey flow . . .' (Ex 3:7-8).

The third characteristic, the repetition of the same basic ideas and sometimes even the same key words or their synonyms, can

---

[24] See pp. 196-202.

[25] The observant reader will discover many other foreshadowing texts not only in the Yahwist's saga but in the Elohist's saga and in the Priestly author's narrative. A few examples will suffice: Gn. 35:7-12; 46:3-4; 50:24. Later authors may be dependent on the Yahwist for some of these texts, but the technique was so common that it was more likely used without any conscious dependence on the Yahwist's narrative.

be illustrated from the Edom texts. The basic idea is Israel's conquest of Edom and the key words are "master" and "serve." In the more difficult and debatable series beginning with Gn 3:15, the key words would appear to be "seed," "enmities," and "curse." The Edom texts will serve as an example:

> So she went to consult Yahweh, and he said to her:
> 'There are two nations in your womb,
> your issue will be *two rival peoples.*
> One nation shall have the mastery of the other,
> and the *elder shall serve the younger*' (Gn 25:23).
> Esau said to his father, 'Was that your only
> blessing, Father? . . .'
> Then his father Isaac gave him this answer:
> 'Far from the richness of the earth
> shall be your dwelling-place . . .
> and you shall *serve your brother.*
> But when you win your freedom, you shall shake
> his yoke from your neck' (Gn 27:38-40).
> (Gn 27:26-29 should be read in conjunction with
> Gn 27:38-40.)
> I see him—but not in the present . . .
> *a star from Jacob takes the leadership* . . .
> It crushes the brows of Moab
> the skulls of all the sons of Sheth.
> *Edom becomes a conquered land;*
> a conquered land is Seir (Nm 24:17-19).

The fourth characteristic, the tendency of the foreshadowing texts to outline the storyline to be followed in the saga, can best be illustrated from Gn 15:13-16. In the text, God foretells to Abraham that his posterity will be "exiles in a land not their own," that they will be "slaves and oppressed for four hundred years," that they will "leave, with many possessions," and that "in the fourth generation they will come back here," when "the wickedness of the Amorites" is complete.

The events foreshadowed here might be given as chapter head-

ings for the remainder of the Yahwist's saga: the sojourn and oppression in Egypt, the Exodus, and the conquest.[26]

If Gn 3:15 can be established as a foreshadowing text, its basic
ideas—the enmities between the seed of the woman and the seed
of the serpent and the eventual conquest of the seed of the serpent
by the seed of woman—would appear to give the broad, theological outline of the saga as a whole: namely, the rise of chosen, covenanted Israel and the covenanted Davidic dynasty and their conquest of the forces of anti-God in the world, represented by the
fertility religion of the Canaanites in the time of the Yahwist.

The fifth characteristic, the progressive clarification of the foreshadowed knowledge, from vague to clear, and from general to
specific, is best illustrated from the exodus texts where the land
of Israel's sojourn and oppression is spoken of obscurely as "a land
not their own" in Gn 15:13, the first foreshadowing text in the
series, and quite clearly as Egypt in Ex 3:8, the last text in the
series.

DIVINE SOLILOQUIES

The divine soliloquy as a literary technique is similar to the
foreshadowing technique in that the author puts his own words
on the lips of another, but different in that it has a different form
and purpose. It has a much greater theological density than the
foreshadowing technique.

In the divine soliloquy, which may very well be the literary in-
vention of the Yahwist, the author has God mull over a theological
problem and express his decision or solution. Since the words and
the thought come from the Yahwist himself, the soliloquies represent for the reader a view of the Yahwist's theological thinking.[27]

The divine soliloquy as a literary technique is treated at some

---

[26] It is disputed whether the Yahwist concluded his saga with the story of the
conquest. More likely the saga ended in Nm 24. This, however, would not prevent
him from making allusions in his foreshadowing texts to the conquest and even
much later events such as the dynastic promise to David.

[27] The divine soliloquy is not peculiar to the Yahwist. It is found also in Dt
32:26-35; Ho 6:4; 11:8f (see G. von Rad, *Deuteronomy*, pp. 198f).

length by R. MacKenzie.[28] In the soliloquies (the following are listed: Gn 2:18; 3:22; 6:3; 6:7; 8:21f; 11:6f; 18:20f), as MacKenzie points out, the Yahwist uses a fairly stereotyped construction consisting of two parts: a) the motivation; b) the proposition (cf. Gn 12:11f; 16:2; 19:31f; 25:30 etc.).

Although the pattern is so common that it may be considered a specific literary form when used elsewhere, the Yahwist is compelled, since God does not speak with anyone else in these speeches, to have God "speaking in his heart,"[29] and thus the "proposition takes the form of a resolution or self-exhortation." The theological interpretation of God's mind expressed by the Yahwist in these soliloquies is developed briefly by MacKenzie.[30] The author's summary of his position on the soliloquies as a literary technique is expressed very happily in the introductory section of his article:

> Speech, traditionally regarded as one of the noblest faculties of man, is an obvious and natural choice for expressing the sentiments, will, judgments, etc., of the divinity. The myths of all peoples attribute speech to gods and goddesses (not to mention animals and the elements); but a special situation is created for the Israelite religious teacher (in this as in all other things) by the nature of his doctrine. Only the one God enters into consideration; there can be no dialogue between divinities. If Yahweh is to speak, it must be either to His inferiors—elements, animals, heavenly ministers, men—or to Himself. The Yahwist, wishing to relate the religious prehistory of Yahweh's dealings with mankind, and confident in his understanding of the ways of God, is not satisfied with recording external actions, and the interventions—better, the constant control—of Yahweh in the development of mankind. With a sublime simplicity, he reads God's mind, and interprets for us, plainly and directly, the motives and springs of action in that mind. Thus, in several key passages, he *boldly undertakes the artistic creation of divine speeches*, not addressed to any lesser beings but uttered in majestic self-communion by his unique and self-sufficient God. In this way he makes known to us the heart of that God, and *conveys the essence of his own lofty theological doctrine*.[31]

[28] See R. MacKenzie, "*The Divine Soliloquies in Genesis*," CBQ 17, 1955, pp. 277ff.

[29] *Genesis* 8:21.

[30] See R. MacKenzie, *op. cit.*, pp. 281ff.

[31] See R. MacKenzie, *op. cit.*, p. 277.

DIVINE DIALOGUES

A third form of theological development by means of putting words into the mouth of God is the Yahwist's use of divine dialogues. Similar to foreshadowing texts and the divine soliloquies in the basic ploy of putting his own words into the mouths of others, the dialogues differ in form from both. In the dialogues, the Yahwist has God engage a human in conversation and thus expounds through the dialogue some matter of theological import.

The dialogues differ from ordinary conversational dialogue, such as that between Abraham, Sarah, and Pharaoh,[32] in that the latter is used for simple narrative purposes, while the former is addressed to the exposition of a theological matter and uses God as the principal and definitive speaker.

The clearest examples of such dialogues are found in Gn 3:1-5; 3:8-19; 4:6-16; 15:1-20; 18:23-33; Nm 14:11-25.[33] Each of these dialogues must be studied as a whole if the reader is to understand its theological content. As G. von Rad points out in his exegesis of God's dialogue with Abraham in Gn 18:23-33, "the conversation with Abraham is thus heavily burdened with a problem of belief; it has a 'theological spirit' (Pr.)." Von Rad goes on to say:

> But though one must struggle greatly for a clean exposition of the whole, one may not assume that the conversation has only one meaning and one thesis toward which it is driving, like a modern philosophical treatise. Texts like this always have somewhat wide meshes; they are open toward many sides and have room for more than one single interpretation. It was not, of course, the primary intention of the text to extol Abraham as the paradigmatic, prophetic intercessor. But the narrator would scarcely feel himself badly misunderstood if we were to read this text from the viewpoint of intercession and its power.[34]

Much more could be said for the Yahwist's proclivity for putting his words into the mouths of others. From what has been said

---

[32] Gn 13:10-20.

[33] The Yahwist uses dialogue for theological purposes in a number of places (cf. Ex 32:21-24; 32:30-35). It had become a theological technique quite early (cf. 2 Sm 12:7-15).

[34] G. von Rad, *Genesis*, p. 209.

above about foreshadowing, divine soliloquies, and divine dialogues it would seem warranted to at least suspect that wherever God is represented as speaking, the reader may prudently question whether it is not God speaking but rather the author expounding his theology by putting it in God's mouth. How much of this theology comes from the pen of the Yahwist and how much he found already expressed by earlier storytellers in their theological development of the traditions can only be ascertained from a close critical study of the text. The examples cited above would seem for the most part to come directly from the Yahwist.[35]

THEOLOGICAL COMMENTS

In a general way it can be said of almost all the literary devices used by the Yahwist that they are used to serve his theological purposes. This is especially clear in a "programmatic" text such as Gn 12:1-3. The same can be said for the divine soliloquies and the divine dialogues in Gn 2-11. When these are taken in conjunction with the tradition or mythological story they accompany, they serve as a general rule to provide commentary, so that story and dialogue or soliloquy constitute a sort of diptych.

In addition to these sometimes lengthier theological commentary devices, the Yahwist used another more simple device for putting his theological stamp on the traditions he inherited and the mythological motifs he adapted. We can best entitle this device the theological comment, since it is usually brief and always theological.[36] It consists of a brief statement expressing the author's theological viewpoint on an event or series of events.

Sometimes put into the mouth of others and sometimes standing alone as the obvious personal comment of the author, the theological comment is used in several different ways. It is sometimes used to give a new theological twist to an old tradition as, for example,

---

[35] H. M. Dion, "The Patriarchal Traditions and the Literary Form of the Oracle of Salvation," (*CBQ* 29, 1967, pp. 198-205) discusses a technique closely associated with the Yahwist's foreshadowing technique.

[36] The theological comment is not restricted to the Yahwist. A New Testament example would be the words of the Evangelist: "He only said this to test Philip; he himself knew exactly what he was going to do" (Jn 6:5).

in the introductory comment to the Abraham-Isaac story in Gn 22:1: "After these events God put Abraham to the test."[37]

In other contexts the author uses the theological comment to give his theological interpretation of an event or series of events which might otherwise have been thought fortuitous in nature by his audience. The author's comment in Gn 45:5, 8 is a good example: "Do not grieve, do not reproach yourselves for having sold me here, since God sent me before you to preserve your lives . . . So it was not you who sent me here but God, and he has made me father to Pharaoh, lord of all his household and administrator of the whole land of Egypt." Understood in the light of this theological comment which is put by the author in the mouth of Joseph, the whole Joseph story is seen as part of God's plan for Israel and the world—a far cry from simple happy chance or a rags-to-riches story. The technique in this context is obviously the same as the technique used in the Succession History (cf. 2 Sm 11:27b and 17:14b).

More difficult to determine exactly, but ultimately of crucial importance, is the Yahwist's use of the theological comment in recasting mythological stories and motifs to serve his didactic purpose. Sometimes, as in the flood story, he simply demythologizes by means of theological comments, e.g. Gn 6:5-6. In other cases the theological comment serves to bring out precisely that aspect of the onetime myth which the author wishes to emphasize for his theological purposes. A probable example is the comment in Gn 2:25: "Now both of them were naked, the man and his wife, but they felt no shame in front of each other." Other examples are found in Gn 2:18, 24; 3:7; 4:26; 6:8.

GENEALOGIES

The Yahwist's use of genealogies as a literary device is difficult to evaluate fully—particularly in the primitive history—because so much of his genealogical material has been supplanted by the more detailed and elaborate Priestly genealogies. It is also difficult to determine how much of the arrangement of names found in the

---

[37] Gn 22 is usually attributed to the Elohist. E. Speiser, however, with good reason attributes it to the Yahwist (see *Genesis*, p. 166).

genealogies came down to the Yahwist through tradition and how much change or rearranging is due to his own proper, theological initiative. Despite these difficulties, it seems possible to recover the basic plan and purpose of the Yahwist's genealogies and give a fair indication of their literary character and theological purpose.

The Yahwist's genealogical pattern in the primitive history is not perfectly clear. From Adam and Eve three sons are born—Abel, Cain, and Seth. Abel is eliminated by Cain (Gn 4:8). Cain's genealogy is followed for six generations, then no more is said about it (4:17-24).[38] Seth's line is pursued only one generation, as far as Enos (4:26), and is then abandoned in favor of the Priestly genealogies.

In the Priestly genealogies nothing is said about Abel and Cain as the first sons of Adam. Seth is given as the first son and, agreeing with the Yahwist's truncated genealogy, Seth's son is given as Enos (5:6 and 4:26). But unaccountably Seth's priestly genealogical table includes most of the descendants attributed to Cain by the Yahwist,[39] and Noah is the son of Lamech, who is the last of Cain's line in the Yahwist's genealogy. The "P" author's genealogy terminates Seth's genealogy at Noah.

On the assumption that the Yahwist and the "P" author would not have disagreed on the relation between Seth and Noah, the Yahwist's genealogy, despite the lacuna after the mention of Enos in 4:26, must have run from Adam to Seth to Noah. Some confirmation for this conclusion can be found in 5:29 which says of Noah: "Here is one who will give us, in the midst of our toil and the labouring of our hands, a consolation derived from the ground that Yahweh cursed." The reference in the text to Yahweh and the motif of working a soil that has been cursed (Gn 3:17-19) suffice to attach the verse to the Yahwist's genealogy. They do not, however, prove that in the Yahwist's genealogy Noah was the descendant of Seth rather than Cain. The only clear indication that

---

[38] Gn 5:28-29 in all probability contains the continuation of the Yahwist's genealogy, but it is not clear whether it is a continuation of 4:24 or 4:26 and whatever at one time followed 4:26 (see J. Chaine, *Le Livre de Genese*, pp. 90ff; also O. Eissfeldt, *The Old Testament: An Introduction*, pp. 191f; and E. Speiser, *Genesis*, p. 41).

[39] Compare 5:6-31 and 4:17-19.

Noah descended from Seth rather than Cain in the Yahwist's genealogy comes from the comment of the Yahwist in 4:26: "This man was the first to invoke the name of Yahweh" and his later comment in a similar vein about Noah in 6:8: "But Noah had found favour with Yahweh."

Two other considerations lead to the probability that in the Yahwist's genealogies Noah must have descended from Seth rather than Cain. First, the fact that Cain is cursed by God and sent out as a wanderer across the face of the earth—a consideration that renders it antecedently improbable that the Yahwist would have gone on to derive the righteous Noah from such a cursed progenitor.[40]

And second, the at least implicit links supplied between Cain and the builders of the Tower of Babel, two stories taken by the Yahwist from a tradition that seems to have known nothing about the flood. First, the Yahwist's remark in 4:16 that "Cain left the presence of Yahweh and settled in the land of Nod, east of Eden" seems to be taken up in the Tower of Babel story in 11:2 with the words: "Now as they moved eastwards they found a plain in the land of Shinar where they settled." And second, the Yahwist's remark in 4:17 that "He became builder of a town . . ." which would make him the ancestor of city builders, and the remark in 11:4 where the men who had migrated eastward say: "Let us build ourselves a town and a tower. . . ."[41] It should be added that the builders of the Tower are punished in a way that reminds one of the punishment of Cain—they are "scattered" by the Lord all over the earth.

However incoherent the Yahwist's genealogical line appears before the flood, it is clear enough after the flood. Noah has three sons (Gn 9:18-19), Shem, Ham, and Japheth, from whom the whole earth is once more populated as it was before the flood. Quickly eliminating the descendants of Ham and Japheth from his narrative the Yahwist focuses his attention on Shem.[42] From Shem descend eventually Abram, Nahor, and Haran (11:28-30).

---

[40] On the Cain-Seth genealogy, see O. Eissfeldt: *The Old Testament: An Introduction,* p. 191.

[41] G. von Rad, *Genesis,* pp. 107ff.

[42] Gn 10:8-19, 21, 24-30.

From Abraham two sons are born: Ishmael (16:1-15) and Isaac (21:1-2). The narrative disposes of Ishmael and concentrates on Isaac. From Isaac two sons are born: Esau and Jacob (25:21-26). Esau is eliminated and the saga continues with the twelve sons of Jacob.[43]

In the Judah-Tamar story in Gn 38, the Yahwist ends up with a genealogy almost identical in form with the Esau-Jacob genealogy in Gn 25:21-26. Two sons are born to Tamar, but the firstborn, Zerah, gives place to the secondborn, Perez.[44] From Perez according to Nm 26:21; Ruth 4:18ff; 1 Chr 2:3ff there eventually descends David.

Studying the overall pattern of the genealogies,[45] the Yahwist's procedure can be seen to be a narrowing of the focus from many to one. Thus, the Yahwist's genealogies seem by design to have continually narrowed in the primeval history from all men to one man—Abraham; in the patriarchal history from all of Abraham's descendants to Jacob and the twelve tribes; and in the tribal history from all the descendants of Judah to David; although the genealogy leading from Perez to David is left open.

Whether emphasis on the secondborn instead of the firstborn (e.g. Isaac instead of Ishmael, Jacob instead of Esau, Perez instead of Zerah, and Judah in Gn 49 instead of Reuben, Simeon, or Levi) is by accident or design is debatable.

The studied story pattern common to the birth narratives of Esau and Jacob (Gn 25:21-26) and Zerah and Perez (Gn 38: 27-30) would seem to indicate design. What the purpose of such a design would be is not clear. It could be the Yahwist's way of inculcating God's freedom of choice in making his election. It might also have something to do with an antecedent apologia for Solomon who was God's choice over Adonijah, the crown prince of Judah at the time of Solomon's succession to the throne (1 Kgs 1-2).

---

[43] Gn 29:31-35; 30:3, 7-16, 20, 24.

[44] Gn 38:27-30.

[45] It is to be noted that the genealogy as a literary and didactic device is used extensively throughout the Bible, both Old Testament (e.g. the Priestly author and the Chronicler use it) and New Testament (Matthew and Luke each use genealogies in their own didactic manner).

With regard to the Yahwist's text, it is not impossible that the birth of Seth preceded that of Cain and Abel in one of the sources used by the Yahwist just as it does in the "P" source. The brothers, Jubal and Tubal-cain—the former mentioned as the "ancestor of the tent-dwellers and owners of livestock" and the latter "the ancestor of all who play the lyre and the flute"—have obvious contacts with Cain and Abel. It is not impossible that the Yahwist's Cain and Abel story represents another tradition about these same sons, and that the Yahwist made use of both traditions without bothering to harmonize them. In such a case, the question of the Sethite genealogy in the Yahwist's saga is not settled, but the possibility of the Yahwist's using a trilogy of descendants from the first man, from whom Cain is eliminated, remains open.

If, on the other hand, the Yahwist included Cain among the descendants of Seth, then it would appear that the whole of his narrative down to Noah was concerned only with the increase of sin motif; and the election motif with its elimination-of-peoples process in the genealogies would start only after the flood in the new beginning vouchsafed to Noah and his descendants.[46]

In the theological plan of the Yahwist the genealogies would appear to have served several purposes. They established a connection between the recipients of God's initial, salvific acts and the Yahwist's audience—10th century Israel. They served in the preflood narrative to show that Adam's revolt was not a onetime thing but continued in his descendants, who without God's special help brought greater and greater evils upon mankind (thus, the sin of Cain, the vengeful code of Lamech, the sin of the daughters and the sons of God).

After the flood (and before the flood as well if it can be established that Noah descended from Seth rather than Cain) the genealogies serve to show that God has deliberately and for his own good reasons elected Israel from amongst all the nations descended from Noah and Adam to be his key human agent in the work of restoring mankind. They show also that in his choice of those through whom he will effect his salvific plan he is not limited by any human law, such as that pertaining to the firstborn,

---

[46] J. Chaine, *op. cit.*, pp. 82ff.

but is sovereignly free to choose as he wills. Whether the regular choice of one who did not enjoy the primacy of primogeniture has any connection with an apologia for Solomon is, as mentioned above, debatable. If it does, it would at the most be only a minor motif.[47]

THE OBSTACLE STORY

Few literary techniques have enjoyed so universal and perennial a vogue as the obstacle story. It is found in ancient and modern literature from the Gilgamesh epic and the Odyssey to the Perils of Pauline and the latest novel. Its character is episodal in that it is not self-contained but finds its *raison d'être* in its relation to the larger story or narrative of which it is a part. Its purpose is to arouse suspense and sustain interest by recounting episodes which threaten or retard the fulfillment of what the reader either suspects or hopes or knows to be the ending of the story.

In the Yahwist's saga where the end of the story—the birth of a great nation from Abraham, possession by this nation of the land of Canaan, and a prospect of world influence for the new nation—is known from the beginning by the audience and regularly and unequivocally foretold or foreshadowed for greater emphasis,[48] the need for obstacle stories, if only to arouse suspense and sustain interest by retarding the fulfillment of what had been foretold, is self-evident.

It is not by accident, therefore, that between the making of the promise to Abraham in Gn 12 and the partial fulfillment of the promise by the making of the nation on Sinai in Exodus 19-24, the storyteller interposes a series of episodes which threaten to negate at almost every step along the way the fulfillment of the promise.

---

[47] It is by no means clear that the succession in Israel's monarchy was determined by primogeniture. The principle of primogeniture was observed in tribal, amphictyonic Israel, and both Absalom and Adonijah, David's sons, seem to have expected to profit from this principle; but it is noteworthy that David bypassed the principle of primogeniture in designating as his successor the younger son, Solomon.

[48] Gn 12:1-2, 7; 13:14-17; 15:7-8, 17; 18:18-19; 22:15-18; 24:7; 26:2-4; 28:13-15.

Thus, immediately following the promise in Gn 12, Abraham not only leaves the land of promise to go down to Egypt but lets Sarah, the mother of the promised nation, be taken into an Egyptian harem. To further compound the problem of fulfillment of the promise it is found that Sarah, the promised mother of the nation, is barren (Gn 16)! Abraham's taking the solution of this impasse into his own hands by having a child through Hagar, Sarah's maid, casts further doubt on the promise since Ishmael is a child of unbelief (Gn 16). The obstacle of Sarah's and Abraham's old age in Gn 18 further threatens the fulfillment of the promise. Finally, when the child has at long last been born, God commands Abraham to offer him in sacrifice (Gn 22)!

As each obstacle is overcome, however, still another arises. Isaac's wife, Rebecca, like Sarah before her, is barren (Gn 24:21). When Jacob is born and the promise is renewed to him, new obstacles bar the way to fulfillment. Esau's animosity forces Jacob to flee the land of promise (Gn 27). In Mesopotamia Jacob marries Rachel, but like Sarah and Rebecca, Rachel is temporarily barren (Gn 29:31). To further complicate matters, Laban threatens to keep Jacob from the land of promise by binding him to service in Mesopotamia (Gn 29-30). Finally, when Jacob breaks away from Laban and returns to Canaan he is threatened once more by his brother Esau's animosity (Gn 32).

In the Joseph story[49] and the Exodus account[50] the same technique is used. Indeed, if the Yahwist's saga is considered as a whole it will be seen that from beginning to end the author so structures his narrative and so intersperses his obstacle stories as to create a continual tension between the elements of promise and fulfillment.

Inevitably the literary aspect of the obstacle story raises the question of historicity, if not with regard to the substance of the story at least with regard to the sequence of events. With regard to the substance one can only repeat what has already been said about the substantial historicity of the traditions taken as a whole (see pp. 88-96). With regard to the sequence of events and even

---

[49] Gn 37:4, 8, 11; 39; 42:29-38; 43-44.
[50] Ex 1-2; 5-11; 14; Nm 13-14; 16; 20:14-21; 22-24.

the selection of events—in this case obstacle stories—there seems no good reason why the author should not be allowed that expansive liberty generously and usually willingly allowed to storytellers. No one seriously faults the evangelists, who dealt in a similar manner with substantially historical traditional stories, for their use of conscious literary techniques to evoke by their individual gospels different theological aspects of the total message of Christ.[51] Such liberty should not be denied the Yahwist or any other theologian.

In the Yahwist's saga, above and beyond the storytellers' elementary use of such techniques to arouse interest and sustain suspense, the obstacle stories are used for definite theological purposes. They serve to focus attention on the reliability of the word of God. They point up the need for faith, all obstacles to the contrary notwithstanding. They underline the inevitable fulfillment of God's plan and the pains he takes to have his designs brought to fruition. In relation to certain stories, e.g. the "barren wife" stories, they serve even further purposes; but we shall deal with these later (see pp. 139-141).

STORY PATTERNS AND PATTERNS OF STORIES

There is nothing particularly significant about a story pattern in itself. Stories are told and tend to be told in a certain way depending for the most part on their content or the purpose of the storyteller, either of which may account for the regular sequence of similar story elements which constitute a story pattern.

Patterns of stories, however, whether the pattern be formed by a group of similar stories told in succession or by a group of similar stories repeated not successively but at regular intervals, can be significant, for the simple reason that as a general rule such a pattern is not the result of chance but of intent, and the pattern reveals the intent.

---

[51] One may cite as examples Luke's Journey to Jerusalem narrative arrangement, Matthew's division of Our Lord's discourses into five major sermons, and John's arrangement according to feasts and according to pairings of miracles with related discourses.

The observant reader of the Yahwist's saga will readily recognize the recurrence of stories having the same basic pattern or regular sequence of similar story elements. This is obvious in the structure of many of the obstacle stories. It is obvious also in the sequence of sin, punishment, forgiveness found in the stories of Gn 2-11. The reader, however, will also notice that in addition to following the same basic pattern for each of these stories in Gn 2-11, the author groups the stories in a series in such a way that he succeeds in forming a pattern or regular sequence of stories having the same story pattern. Thus, in the stories of Gn 2-11 each story not only has the same basic pattern of story elements—sin, punishment, forgiveness—but the sequence of these stories is so regular that taken together the group of stories (Adam and Eve story, Cain and Abel story, flood story, and probably also the Tower of Babel story) form a pattern.

The presumption underlying such a pattern is that it is not accidental but intentional. As a consequence, a study of patterns of stories, presuming the pattern of Gn 2-11 is not isolated, should lead, as in the case of the foreshadowing texts, divine soliloquies, divine dialogues, theological comments, and genealogies, to another window on the author's mind and to another key to his theological intent.

Besides grouping successively stories of the same pattern, as in Gn 2-11, it is noteworthy that certain other stories having the same pattern occur, not successively, but at regular intervals. This is the case, for example, with the barren-wife stories. In each case the story pattern is the same—the wife is barren but eventually, usually in answer to prayer, God grants her children. This is true of Sarah,[52] of Rebecca,[53] of Rachel,[54] and in a somewhat different way—the barrenness is as it were an "enforced" barrenness—of Tamar.[55]

If this story pattern occurred only once or twice, its occurrence might indicate nothing more than that the Yahwist had stories of the same pattern about two different wives; perhaps because these

---

[52] Gn 16:1-2 and 21:1-2.
[53] Gn 25:21.
[54] Gn 29:31 and 30:22.
[55] Gn 38:6ff.

wives had been indeed barren in precisely the way described. It is
another thing, however, when the same story pattern is repeated
three or four times and each time concerns one of the matriarchs
of Israel!

Other patterns of stories not unlike the barren-wife pattern are
the "promise" stories, the "two-brother" stories, the sanctuary eti-
ologies, and the "anti-Canaanite" stories. In the account of the life
of each of the patriarchs there occurs almost without exception at
least one of each of these story patterns.

There are promise stories involving Abraham,[56] Isaac,[57] Jacob.[58]

There are two-brother stories involving Ishmael and Isaac,[59]
Esau and Jacob,[60] and in a different way Joseph and his brothers
(Gn 37).

In each patriarch's life there is at least one sanctuary legend,
e.g. Abraham in relation to Shechem (Gn 12:6-7) and Mamre
(Gn 18:1-15); Isaac in relation in Beersheba (Gn 21:33); Jacob
in relation to Bethel (Gn 28:1-22) and Penuel (Gn 32:22-31).

The anti-Canaanite stories begin in Gn 9:18-27 with the curse
of Canaan and continue in varying patterns in the lives of Abraham (Gn 18-19); Isaac—he is not to marry a Canaanite wife—(Gn
24:1-3); and Jacob—his difficulties with Esau, the eponymous
father of the Edomites, probably fit into this pattern (Gn 27 and
32).

The significance of each of these patterns of stories is not always
easy to determine. The mere fact, however, that there is a pattern
with its consequent repetition would seem to indicate at the very
least that the Yahwist is aiming for that emphasis which repetition
normally contributes. This would seem to be the main point of the
promise stories. Such repetition leaves no doubt about the importance of the promises to the patriarchs in the mind of the Yahwist.

In the barren-wife stories it is not unlikely that the Yahwist is
indulging in an anti-fertility cult polemic at least by insinuation,

---

[56] Gn 13:15-16; 12:2, 7; 15:18; 18:18; 22:15-18; 24:7.

[57] Gn 26:2-5, 24.

[58] Gn 27:29; 28:10-15.

[59] Gn 16 and 21.

[60] Gn 27:41-45; 32:4-13.

the innuendo being that the true Israelite seeks children from Yahweh and not from the gods of the fertility cult.[61]

The anti-Canaanite stories appear to be part of a continuous polemic against the fertility cult. The two-brother stories are not easily explained unless their meaning is exhausted by the "election" theme explanation.[62]

DEMYTHOLOGIZING AND RETHEOLOGIZING

It is only if one defines a myth in the older but still popular sense as a fictitious story about the gods and their activities terrestrial and extraterrestrial that one can properly speak of the Yahwist's methodology in Gn 2-11 as demythologizing. What he has done for the most part is take pagan myths and mythological motifs and remove from them anything that might smack of polytheism and polytheistic theology.[63]

If myth is understood in the sense given it by recent authors such as F. Cassirer, J. L. McKenzie,[64] and M. Burrows[65] as an at-

---

[61] The barren-wife motif is theologically summarized in the words of Jacob to Rachel: "Am I in God's place? It is he who has refused you motherhood" (Gn 30:2). The text is from the Elohist, but it adequately expresses what presumably were the similar sentiments of the Yahwist.

[62] Another pattern of stories that may be significant in the Yahwist's saga is the pattern that shows a remnant saved from destruction to be the seed-bearers and hope for the fulfillment of the promises. Thus Noah and his sons escaping the flood are a remnant. Lot and his family escaping from Sodom are a remnant. In Gn 32:9 it is said that Jacob returning to Canaan divided his possessions in such a way that if Esau attacked the group left might be a "remnant" which escaped. Similarly when the Yahwist puts his theological comment on the lips of Joseph in Gn 45:7 he has Joseph explain that Yahweh had protected him "in order to preserve a remnant on earth, and to keep you alive as a great remnant which escaped."

[63] Cf. W. F. Albright, New Horizons in Biblical Research, pp. 32ff.

[64] McKenzie is certainly right when he says: "What distinguishes these passages of the OT from ancient myths is not the patterns of thought and language, which seem in every respect to be the same, but the Hebrew idea of God as known through His revelation of Himself. This knowledge they themselves attributed to a personal encounter with God, and in this respect the unknown reality is not entirely unknown. When we compare the thought processes of the OT with the processes of Semitic myth, we observe that the OT rejects all elements which are out of character with the God whom they knew. But what they knew of God could be expressed only through symbolic form and concrete cosmic event, and

tempt to present in symbolic story-form some transcendental reality or truth intuitively grasped, then one cannot speak of demythologizing at all, since the Yahwist does not properly remove the symbolic story-form element but simply depaganizes the myth or mythological motif and, after depaganizing it, retheologizes it *as a myth* for his own theological purposes.[66]

The Yahwist's "depaganizing-retheologizing" technique can be appreciated by comparing his account of the flood with the Mesopotamian account in the Gilgamesh epic.[67] Depaganization is accomplished in short order by replacing the many gods of the myth with the one God, Yahweh; and by making the *raison d'être* of the flood, not the pique of the gods disturbed in their rest by the clamor of mankind, but the righteous anger of Yahweh at the widespread corruption of men.[68]

Already well on its way to retheologization by the removal of polytheistic elements and their replacement by Yahwistic elements, the myth is further retheologized by the Yahwist's theological comment in Gn 6:5-6 and by his divine soliloquies in Gn 6:7 and Gn 8:21-22. The comment and the soliloquies give the bor-

---

the relations of God with the world and with man were perceived and expressed through the same patterns and processes which elsewhere we call mythical. This is the quality of OT thought and language, by whatever term it may be designated" (*Dictionary of the Bible*, p. 599).

[65] Burrows defines myth as "a symbolic, approximate expression of truth which the human mind cannot perceive sharply and completely but can only glimpse vaguely, and therefore cannot adequately or accurately express. . . . Myth implies not falsehood but truth; not primitive, naive misunderstanding but an insight more profound than scientific description and logical analysis can ever achieve" (*An Outline of Biblical Theology*, pp. 115-116).

[66] R. Balducelli, in a review (*CBQ* 29, 1967, p. 627), speaks of mythological thinking and expression as ". . . a mythic mode of cognitional effort . . . which is the kind of effort that attempts to answer ultimate questions arising from existence as experienced, by correlating domestic and familiar reality to cosmic and primordial events which it creates by imagining them with the mechanics of subjective projection." R. Otto, *The Idea of the Holy*, p. 19, speaks of "numen and numinous" as formulations of man's *a priori* experience of the divine. It may well be asked if myth is not an expression of this experience.

[67] *ANET*, pp. 93-95; N. K. Sandars, *The Epic of Gilgamesh*; A. Heidel, *The Gilgamesh Epic and Old Testament Parallels*.

[68] Cf. B. W. Anderson, *Understanding the Old Testament*, pp. 164-165: "Even the slightest change in an old story, one as minor as the addition of 'Yahweh' was enough to bring about a complete change in meaning."

rowed mythological motif a theological bent consonant in every way with the message of Gn 3 and 4.[69]

The myth with which the flood story is introduced—the marriage of the sons of God with the daughters of men—is more difficult to explain. It would not appear, on the surface at least, that the Yahwist has demythologized or depaganized it even to the extent of removing the polytheistic elements. As it stands it is an etiological myth which explains how the giants mentioned in Gn 6:4 came into existence.

Von Rad explains the "sons of God" as angels and can claim some justification for this interpretation in the fact that the expression is used in a number of places in this sense (cf. Ps 29:1; 89:7; 82:6; 1 Kgs 22:19-22; Job 1:6). In these examples it is clear that Israel has anthropomorphized God as a king surrounded by his court and counselors. The pagan myth-makers had done the same long before. In the myths it is the high god surrounded by lesser gods. Israel's conceptualization of God as king necessarily reduced these lesser gods to non-gods or ministering angels.

The Yahwist, however, does not appear to reduce these sons of God to non-gods. He appears to have left the myth unchanged and even seems to have taken it seriously. But some allowance must be made for humor and irony. The Yahwist's audience would certainly recognize in the story an allusion to the ludicrous belief of the Canaanite religion that by means of sacred prostitution—sexual intercourse with male and female prostitutes at the Canaanite shrines—it was possible to enter into special relationship with the god or goddess represented by the sacred prostitute (see p. 63). The Yahwist's capacity for ribald polemic is more than evident in his story of the origin of the Moabites and the Ammonites in Gn 19:30-38. And his penchant for irony and humor com-

---

[69] In relation to history, there is no reason to believe the Yahwist was unduly concerned with history in expropriating the flood myth. His use of the story is purely functional. It shows God's hatred of sin. The same can be said for his expropriation and exploitation of the "sons of God and daughters of men" myth in Gn 6:1-4 and his paradise myth in Gn 2-3. There is every reason to believe that in all of these the Yahwist is using symbolic presentations, easily understood by his audience, to communicate his intuitive theological insights. One should not confuse the reality of the truth perceived with its symbolic presentation (cf. J. L. McKenzie, *Myths and Realities*, pp. 146-181).

bined is part and parcel of the famous "bargaining" dialogue between Yahweh and Abraham in Gn 18:22-32.

The Tower of Babel story (Gn 11:1-9) is another example of a depaganized, retheologized myth. The myth, however, has been much more radically altered than the flood myth or the sons of God and daughters of men myth.

Originally a Babylonian myth celebrating the building of a Ziggurat in Babylon for the god, Marduk, the Yahwist has retold it to make it a satire on man's hubris—the story of how man's pride can lead him to the heights of stupidity! The following version of the story is taken from Tablet VI of Enuma Elis (*ANET*, p. 68):

> The Anunnaki opened their mouths and said to Marduk, their lord:
> "Now, O lord, thou who has caused our deliverance,
> What shall be our homage to thee?
> Let us build a shrine whose name shall be called
> 'Lo, a chamber for our nightly rest'; let us repose in it."
> When Marduk heard this, brightly glowed his features, like the day:
> "Like that of lofty Babylon, whose building you have requested,
> Let its brickwork be fashioned. You shall name it: The Sanctuary."
> The Anunnaki applied the implement; for one whole year they molded bricks.
> When the second year arrived, they raised high the head of Esagila equaling Apsu.
> Having built a stage-tower as high as Apsu,
> They set up in it an abode for Marduk, Enlil, and Ea.
> In their presence he adorned it in grandeur.
> To the base of Esharra its horns look down.
> After they had achieved the building of Esagila,
> The Anunnaki themselves erected their shrines.

The Yahwist's tower is in Shinar, an ancient name for Babylon. It is built of bricks "with its top reaching heaven" and is named Babel. Coincidence could hardly account for such similarities. The differences, however, are significant. The Yahwist demythologizes the myth by making Yahweh the protagonist and by putting in Yahweh's mouth the poignantly satirical soliloquy in Gn 11:6-7:

> 'So they are all a single people with a single language!' said Yahweh. 'This is but the start of their undertakings! There will be nothing too hard for them to do. Come, let us go down and confuse their language on the spot so that they can no longer understand one another.'

If it is asked why the Yahwist used myths and mythological motifs as vehicles for his theological *modus operandi* in Gn 2-11, the answer is hardly profound. It was, as far as we know, the only way he could communicate these particular truths to that particular audience. It was the literary vehicle his audience was accustomed to at that time and for many centuries afterwards. It was, one could say, the only way he could communicate with his audience and "speak their language." Going from the known to the unknown has always been a basic principle of good teachers. The myths were known. They were fertile ground for a good teacher. As Avery Dulles says: "The primitive pagan myths, which gave concrete expression to man's longing for divine deliverance from the hostile powers, are gradually answered by divine revelation. As the answer is heard and assimilated, the myths are progressively purified, broken, and sublimated."[70]

For those of us who have seen the end of an age in which the Church came perilously close—in the popular estimation if never in fact—to saying that one could not properly understand theology except through the concepts and language of scholastic philosophy and theology, the use of such a vehicle should be more reassuring than disturbing.[71] Man seeks the truth. What avenue the truth takes—logical discourse, art, or myth—is a matter of secondary importance.[72]

SUGGESTED READINGS

R. A. F. MacKenzie, "The Divine Soliloquies in Genesis", *CBQ* 17 (1955), 157-166.

————. *Faith and History in the Old Testament*, 54-81.

---

[70] "Symbol, Myth, and the Biblical Revelation," *TS* (March, 1966), quoted from *New Theology No. 4*, eds. M. E. Marty and D. G. Peerman (New York: Macmillan, 1967), p. 58.

[71] M. McLuhan and G. B. Leonard rightly understand myths in their observation that "New Materials may be learned just as were the great myths of past cultures— as fully integrated systems that resonate on several levels and share the qualities of poetry and song" ("The Future of Education," *Look*, Feb. 21, 1967, pp. 24-25).

[72] In discussing both the origin and the interpretation of myth it is good to remember the observation of Claudel Strauss: "What primitive man sought above all else was not truth but coherence; not scientific distinctions between true and false, but a vision of the world that would satisfy his soul."

G. Duckworth, *Foreshadowing and Suspense in the Epics of Homer, Apollonius, and Vergil.*

A. Bentzen, *Introduction to the Old Testament* I, 141-144; 203-205; II, 57-59.

C. H. Lohr, "Oral Techniques in the Gospel of Matthew", *CBQ* 23 (1961), 403-435.

R. A. Bowman, "Genealogy" in *Interpreter's Dictionary of the Bible* II, 362-365.

B. Lonergan, *Insights*, 530-594.

B. S. Childs, *Myth and Reality in the Old Testament.*

J. L. McKenzie, *Myths and Realities.*

E. Cassirer, *The Philosophy of Symbolic Forms:* Vol. II *Mythical Thought.*

L. Hartman, "Myth" in *EDB*, 1584-1588.

J. Barr, "The Meaning of 'Mythology' in Relation to the Old Testament," *VT* 9 (1959), 1-10.

N. M. Sarna, *Understanding Genesis.*

A. Heidel, *The Gilgamesh Epic and Old Testament Parallels.*

D. W. Thomas, *Documents from Old Testament Times.*

B. W. Anderson, *Creation versus Chaos.*

Chapter VI

THE YAHWIST'S
THEOLOGY

INTERPRETING THE YAHWIST

The interpretation of the Yahwist's theology requires reconstructing from his saga the basic pattern of theological insights which existed in his mind.

More appositely, interpretation of the Yahwist's theology presents the problem—which is the problem of every modern interpreter of ancient texts—of trying to extricate the specific intention of a particular text or group of texts from the world view of the author in which it is embedded and make it intelligible for the reader of today.

It is, of course, taken for granted, based upon belief in the inspired character of the Divine Word, that this pattern of theological insights, which existed in the mind of the Yahwist and finds its expression in the intention behind the content of his saga, corresponds in its essentials to that ultimate pattern of ideas, organically and hierarchically structured, which existed in and was communicated by the mind of God.[1]

The existence of this pattern, however, as well as its hierarchical structure is not a matter of faith but must be demonstrated and educidated by the interpreter if he wishes to be serious in his

---

[1] Many of the Yahwist's insights, especially his psychological insights, would appear to be things known largely by instinct and intuition. Besides inspiration and beyond inspiration he himself could probably appeal only to those elements of conviction—*raisons du coeur*, as Pascal called them—which depend on the experience of life and reality and not on mere abstract reasoning.

147

claim to be a genuine interpreter of the biblical theologian's mind and work.

It is here that the interpreter faces his major difficulties. He must not only discover the principal theological insights of the theologian and the hierarchical order of these insights in the theologian's mind; he must, as well, successfully communicate them to a new audience with a different background, different needs, different challenges, and a greatly expanded world view. B. Lonergan poses the problem as follows:

> The problem of interpretation can best be introduced by distinguishing between expression, simple interpretation, and reflective interpretation.
>
> As has been seen, an expression is a verbal flow governed by a practical insight (F) that depends upon a principal insight (A) to be communicated, upon a grasp (B) of the anticipated audience's habitual intellectual development (C), and upon a grasp (D) of the deficiencies in insight (E) that have to be overcome if the insight (A) is to be communicated.
>
> By an interpretation will be meant a second expression addressed to a different audience. Hence, since it is an expression, it will be guided by a practical insight (F') that depends upon a principal insight (A') to be communicated, upon a grasp (B') of the anticipated audience's habitual intellectual development (C'), and upon a grasp (D') of the deficiencies in insight (E') that have to be overcome if the principal insight (A') is to be communicated.
>
> In the simple interpretation the principal insight (A') to be communicated *purports to coincide* with the principal insight (A) of the original expression. Hence, differences between the practical insights (F) and (F') depend directly upon differences between the habitual insights (B) and (B'), (D) and (D'), and remotely upon differences between the habitual developments (C) and (C'), and the deficiencies (E) and (E').[2]

A study of the Yahwist's audience and the Yahwist's sources has been prefaced to a study of the Yahwist's theology in the hope that it would provide a grasp (B) of his audience's habitual intellectual development (C) and a grasp (D) of the deficiencies in insight (E) of that audience that the Yahwist had to overcome in order to communicate his principal insights (A).

---

[2] *Insight: A Study of Human Understanding*, pp. 562ff.

A study of the Yahwist's opus and the Yahwist's methodology has been prefaced to a study of his theology in the hope that it would assist the reader, in each case, to grasp the principal insight (A) which is expressed by the Yahwist in a verbal flow or expression that is governed by a practical insight (F) which is communicated, upon a grasp (B) of his audience's habitual intellectual development (C) and a grasp (D) of the deficiencies in insight (E) of his audience that he had to overcome in order to communicate his principal insights (A).

In addition to discovering and interpreting the theological insights of the Yahwist's mind, the interpreter faces the ungrateful and self-defeating task of dissecting and fragmentizing a narrative of great artistic genius. As G. von Rad says, the Yahwist's narrative genius

> . . . is anything but the bluntness and naiveté of an archaic narrator. It is rather the candor and lack of hesitation which is only the mark of a lofty and mature way of thinking. This glasslike, transparent, and fragile way of thinking in the Yahwistic narrative makes of every exposition, which inevitably coarsens the original text, a difficult and almost insoluble task.[3]

In addition to these difficulties the interpreter must analyze carefully the insights he discovers. He must ask himself which insights communicated by the author are *explicitly and designedly* inculcated; which are nothing more than conventionalized convictions of faith shared by all and passed on by the author as a matter of course; which constitute an isolation and development of religious convictions hitherto latent or bound up with other religious convictions; and, finally, which are totally new insights, either directly revealed to the theologian or deduced by him for the first time under the influence of inspiration.[4] Lastly, he will have to

---

[3] *Genesis*, p. 24f.

[4] The Yahwist's faith, which in its subjective and objective totality must be considered the proximate source of his theological teaching, undoubtedly contained much that he could explicitly express and much that was only implicit to him and which as a consequence he perhaps could have expressed if he had tried or if a challenge had presented itself in such a way as to pose a question of faith. On the other hand, there must have been a number of questions to which he did not advert at all, or if he did advert to them, felt himself incapable of providing solutions.

ask himself which insights the theologian himself possessed but either did not directly teach or did not with full confidence embrace. One may cite as an example of this the Yahwist's teaching on marriage in Gn 2-3 and ask, how many of his insights here are expressed only in reaction to the Baal fertility cult degradation of women, and how many he himself embraced and taught with full conviction. In like manner and in the same chapters one might ask if the Yahwist's insight into the nature of sin went so far as an understanding of "original" sin.[5]

In the brief exposition of the Yahwist's theology presented below, no attempt will be made to determine the exact order of the Yahwist's insights. If this were attempted, it is the writer's opinion that the order of insights would begin with Yahweh, the Lord of History, and move down through the Kingdom of God, the salvific Love of God, and so on.

The presentation followed seeks rather a pedagogical arrangement of the Yahwist's principal insights without arranging them in exact order and without attempting to either discover or interpret the more numerous but secondary insights present in his saga.

The saga was not written to be a studied exposition of the Yahwist's theology but to respond to the needs of a specific audience. It is more, therefore, of the nature of a "tract for the times" than a theological opus. As a consequence, one should not expect the Yahwist to present the exact structure of his theological insights, but to structure his insights in a manner that will correspond to the needs of his audience.[6]

Nor will this study attempt to assess the "total impact" of the saga—that elusive something that is more than the sum of the parts, which is the interior vision of the author more or less ade-

One may cite evolution as a question to which he did not advert at all and the mystery of man's liberty and God's supreme power and knowledge as a question to which his attention may have been drawn but which he found, as so many theologians after him, insoluble.

[5] See "New Thinking on Original Sin" in *Herder Correspondence*, Vol. 4, No. 5 (1967), pp. 135-141; Z. Alczeghy and M. Flick, "An Evolutionary View of Original Sin," *TD* 15 (1967), pp. 197-202.

[6] See P. Schoonenberg, "The Dutch Catechism Defended," *Herder Correspondence*, March, 1967, pp. 94-95; *ibid*, May 1967, pp. 156-160.

quately communicated by his artistic presentation as a whole, and which can be realized but not expressed by the lettered and unlettered alike, because it stirs in them an elemental response like a sunset or a storm or a musical masterpiece. In the presentation of the Yahwist's theology, those insights will be emphasized which the Yahwist intentionally and designedly inculcated; and it will be the burden of the presentation to demonstrate that intent and design. To the degree that the insights here hopefully presented are genuine, the perceptive reader will be able, with the help of his own insights, to perhaps experience that "total impact."

Whatever the hierarchy of insights that governed the Yahwist's thinking and writing, one must be content to begin with those directive ideas which it is the burden of the saga as a whole to impress upon the minds of the tenth century Israelites for whom it was written.[7] These directive ideas or theological insights would appear to be as follows:

1. God has freely and deliberately chosen Israel from among all the nations of mankind.

2. He has made this choice of Israel out of love for Israel and for mankind.

3. In making this choice He has manifested Himself as the Lord of History who has a benevolent design or plan. The fulfillment of this plan is directed to the welfare and happiness of all mankind and not just Israel.

4. The complicating factor in the fulfillment of this plan is man's God-given freedom which permits him to obstruct the design and plan of God. The redeeming factor in the tragedy of man's abuse of freedom is the steadfast love of God which leads Him to forgive his sinful creatures and permit them to begin again.

5. So that the new beginnings may terminate happily God has entered into a covenant relationship with Israel and the Davidic dynasty whereby they will be instructed in his love and in his designs for mankind.

---

[7] One must remember that this hierarchy might have been more clearly and cogently expressed if the Yahwist had been writing for a more sophisticated audience and at a time when theology and theologizing were not in their infancy.

6. So instructed and guided Israel has a mission to mankind.

Since these directive ideas are expressed to a specific audience, they are necessarily conditioned by the intellectual, political, and religious situation of that audience. It is this situation that explains the author's use of myths, legends, patriarchal and national traditions, allusions to fertility cult Baalism, and the saga form of expression. The audience as always conditions not only the content but the literary container of the content.

ELECTION

The Yahwist's insight that God has singled out Israel as a nation from all the other nations making up the family of mankind would appear to be based, as are the majority of his insights, upon the faith-conviction of his people, who had been led to this conviction by the interventions of God in their history as far back as the time of the Patriarchs. He inculcates this directive idea of election theologically by means of his elimination-of-peoples-process, his emphasis on the call of certain great men in Israel's history, his foreshadowing texts, and his obstacle stories.

By his elimination-of-peoples-process (see pp. 131-136), which is accomplished by a clever arrangement of Israel's genealogies, the Yahwist shows that of all the nations descended from Eve, "the mother of all the living" (Gn 3:20), God's choice falls upon one nation. Of Eve's children Abel is eliminated by Cain (Gn 4:8-16). Cain's descendants are listed (Gn 4:17-24) and then disappear from the development of the saga.[8] The saga carries on with Seth (Gn 4:25ff) and his descendants down to Noah and his sons, Shem, Ham, and Japheth. Japheth and Ham (Gn 10:2-20) are eliminated and the story continues with the descendants of Shem (Gn 11:10-26), from whom eventually is born Abraham. With Abraham's birth the Yahwist finishes his primeval history, but not before he has established links between Abraham and Adam via Seth, Noah, and Shem.

In the patriarchal history Ishmael and his descendants are eliminated from the saga after Gn 25:18 and Esau's descendants after

---

[8] See pp. 132-133 for the ambiguity in the Yahwist's genealogy of Cain.

Gn 36:43. The line of election is shown to run from Abraham to Isaac to Jacob, from whom are born the twelve sons who become the forefathers of the twelve tribes of Israel, the chosen nation. In Gn 38:27-30 the Yahwist goes one step further in his use of genealogies to show election by focusing upon the descendants of Judah, from whom some seventy years before the time of the Yahwist there is born David (cf. also Gn 49:8-10 as confirmation for the Yahwist's intent in Gn 38:27-30).[9]

Within the chosen line of descendants certain men are singled out, favored in a special way, and given specific functions to perform in relation to the chosen nation. These men are: Abraham, the father of the Chosen People; Joseph, the protector of the Chosen People; Moses, the creator of the Chosen Nation; Joshua, the conqueror of the Promised Land; and, less clearly, David the founder of an empire and the augury of Israel's mission to mankind. What is notable about these men is their charismatic function. Their vocation is to serve the designs of God in bringing about the formation of the Chosen People.[10]

The Yahwist's use of foreshadowing texts to inculcate the election of Israel and the line of David is clear in the series of foreshadowing texts that points to a great nation that will come from the seed of Abraham[11] and a king who will come from the tribe of Judah.[12] The series foreshadowing the Exodus[13] and the series foreshadowing Israel's conquest of Edom[14] serve further to single out Israel from all the nations and to show God's special election of this nation in contradistinction to all others.

The Yahwist's obstacle stories emphasize the election of Israel by throwing into even greater prominence the infallible nature of the promises upon which the election of Israel was based. The promise to Abraham in Gn 12:2 "I will make you a great na-

---

[9] The easiest way to see the pedagogical purpose of the genealogies as elimination and selection is to trace them backwards instead of forwards. The only one that goes all the way back to Adam is Israel's.

[10] See H. H. Rowley, *The Biblical Doctrine of Election*, pp. 95ff.

[11] Gn 12:1-3; 26:3-4; 28:13-15.

[12] Gn 49:8-12; Nm 24:7, 17-19.

[13] Gn 15:13-16; 45:7; 48:21; Ex 3:8.

[14] Gn 25:23; 27:29,40; Nm 24:17-19.

tion . . ."[15] focuses the attention of the reader from here on upon the fulfillment of the promise through the rise of a nation that can trace its roots and its very existence back to this promise.

In the ensuing narrative the obstacle stories, by threatening the fulfillment of the promise, serve by that very fact to keep it uppermost in the mind of the audience. The obstacle stories continually remind the audience that God has overcome all obstacles to the fulfillment of his promise. The fact that God overcomes the weak faith of Abraham (Gn 12:10-20), the sterility and old age of Sarah (Gn 16:1; 18:9-15), the perils to Jacob in Mesopotamia (Gn 28-32) and to the twelve tribes in Egypt (Ex 1-14) and in Transjordan (Nm 10-24) throws into even greater prominence not only the fact of Israel's election but the determination of God to fulfill his promise of election, by bringing into existence the nation Israel despite the most insurmountable of human obstacles.

In the Yahwist's teaching on election, it is worthy of note that election is not a matter of "many are called but few are chosen." Israel alone is called and Israel alone is chosen. The nations, however, who are not called and not chosen are not thereby rejected. They are simply not chosen in the way and for the purpose for which Israel was chosen.

The elimination-of-peoples-process, for example, does not eliminate the nations from God's love and concern. It serves simply to single out Israel from among the nations and inculcate the truth that in God's designs Israel has a special place. Israel, in other words, is positively elected. The other nations are simply not elected; but neither are they rejected. They come from the same mother as Israel (Eve); they are related to the ancestors of Israel (the relationship of Ham and Japheth to Shem, of Ishmael to Isaac, of Esau to Jacob); and eventually, according to God's loving design and plan, they will share in the blessing bestowed upon Israel (Gn 12:2-3). God's love and concern for those not elected, except in and through Israel, is carefully inculcated by the Yahwist in a number of texts and stories.[16] Thus God explains how

---

[15] Cf. also the repetition of the promise in 12:7; 13:14-17; 15:4-5; 18:17-19; 26:3-4; 28:13-15; 32:12.

[16] Gn 4:15-16; 8:21-22; 9:22; 16:7-14; 18:23-33; 27:1ff.

and why Israel is elected. He does not "reveal" or "unveil" the story of his love for every other people.

There are authors who believe the doctrine of election was first developed in the book of Deuteronomy (circa 700 B.C.). The Yahwist, however, was no stranger to the doctrine nor were Israel's earliest psalm writers. R. de Vaux is surely right when he says: "Certainly the book of Deuteronomy is responsible for the final theological elaboration of this doctrine, but it is not quite true to say it created it. In different ways the doctrine had already been prepared."[17] The Yahwist's covenant theology (see pp. 181-188) would certainly presume a firm conviction of Israel's election.

SUGGESTED READINGS

H. H. Rowley, *The Biblical Doctrine of Election.*

G. E. Wright, *The Old Testament Against Its Environment*, 46-54.

G. E. Mendenhall, "Election" in *Interpreter's Dictionary of the Bible* II.

R. de Vaux, "Israel—People of God," *The Critic* xxiv (1965).

E. Jacob, *Theology of the Old Testament*, 201-208.

L. Koehler, *Old Testament Theology*, 81-82.

GOD'S LOVE

In the words of Jeremiah God says to Israel: "I have loved you with an everlasting love, so I am constant in my affection for you" (Jer 31:3). The Yahwist is equally convinced of God's love, not only for Israel but for all mankind; but he is not so demonstrative in his language. He believes that actions speak louder than words. Consequently he portrays for his audience not a God who says "I have loved you with an everlasting love," but a God who from the beginning of time manifests his love for mankind and for Israel by his active interventions in history.

He shows God pouring out his gifts upon Adam—placing him in a garden of delights; giving him Eve as a helpmate and filling him with such joy that he cries out: "This at last is bone from my

---

[17] "Israel—People of God" (*The Critic* xxiv, 1965, p. 58). Cf. also G. E. Mendenhall, under "Election," in *I.D.B.*, II (1962), p. 79; and E. W. Nicholson, *Deuteronomy and Tradition*, pp. 97ff.

bones, and flesh from my flesh . . ." (Gn 2:15, 23); forgiving him when he falls; making garments of skin for him and his wife when he sends them out of the garden (Gn 3:21ff).

Cain the murderer is given a sign that will protect him "to prevent whoever might come across him from striking him down" (Gn 4:15). Such a theological comment, so brief yet so poignant, suffuses even the story of the first murderer in the warmth of divine love and forgiveness.

At the end of his flood account the Yahwist composes a divine soliloquy and has God say to himself: "Never again will I curse the earth because of man, because his heart contrives evil from his infancy. Never again will I strike down every living thing as I have done. As long as earth lasts, sowing and reaping, cold and heat, summer and winter, day and night shall cease no more" (Gn 8:21-22).

The whole point of the progress-of-evil theme in Gn 2-11—from the sin of Adam to the sin of Cain to the sin of the sons of God with the daughters of men that brings on the flood and finally the revolt of mankind as a group in the Tower of Babel story—is the love of a God who sees that his creatures will ruin themselves if he does not lead them gently and with compassion back to himself.

It is no accident, therefore, that after the dispersion of the peoples in Gn 11, following the Tower of Babel revolt story, the Yahwist records immediately the call of Abraham and the divine promise to him that "all the tribes of the earth shall bless themselves by you" (Gn 12:1-3). As G. von Rad says in his epilogue to the Yahwistic primeval history:

> We stand here, therefore, at the point where primeval history and sacred history dovetail, and thus at one of the most important places in the entire Old Testament. . . . The question about God's salvation for all nations remains open and unanswerable in *primeval* history. But our narrator *does* give an answer, namely, at the point where sacred history begins. Here in the promise that is given concerning Abraham something is again said about God's saving will and indeed about a salvation extending far beyond the limits of the covenant people to 'all the families of the earth.'[18]

---

[18] *Genesis,* pp. 149-150.

In the patriarchal history promises and blessings abound. But what is more important, the God who walked in the garden with Adam (Gn 3:8) and made garments for Adam and his wife before sending them out of the garden (Gn 4:21) speaks familiarly with Abraham, enters into a covenant with him (Gn 15), is filled with compassion for Ishmael and Hagar (Gn 16:7-14), visits Abraham at his camping place by the terebinths of Mamre (Gn 18:1ff), and will not destroy the wicked inhabitants of the plain cities if Abraham can find among them even ten good men (Gn 18:23-33).

In the Joseph story the point made is that God so loves the forefathers of Israel that even when they sin against their brother Joseph, he turns their sin to good by raising up Joseph as their protector in Egypt. The Joseph, who says to his brothers after he has convinced them of his forgiveness and love: "God sent me before you to make sure that your race would have survivors in the land and to save your lives, many lives at that" (Gn 45:7), is made by this theological comment of the Yahwist what the father is in the New Testament parable of the Prodigal Son—a picture of the God whose love and forgiveness no outrage can destroy.

The sin-deliverance stories that occur so frequently throughout the Yahwist's saga are to be interpreted in this way. The inference to be drawn from these stories is not just that Israel or mankind is forever rebelling against God, but that God so loves Israel and mankind that he is forever constrained to forgive and start over again with his rebellious sons.

Since, as E. Jacob rightly asserts, "The idea of education as the Israelite conceived it is inseparable from punishment and he who abstains from punishment would be a bad pedagogue,"[19] it is clear that for an Israelite the Yahwist's recounting of punishment for sin would not be interpreted as a sign of rejection but as a sign of educative love (cf. Prv 22:15).[20]

Finally, one must not forget the Yahwist's emphasis upon Israel's election. Since election presupposes love, the Yahwist's continued emphasis on Israel's election should be viewed as a testimony to his belief in God's love for Israel.

---

[19] *Theology of the Old Testament*, p. 111.

[20] See H. H. Rowley, *The Biblical Doctrine of Election*, p. 53f.

THE LORD OF HISTORY

The God who promises and elects (Gn 12:1-3), exercises providential care for his elect (Gn 37-50), intervenes with power (Ex 1-14), covenants with his elect (Ex 19-24), and punishes-educates (Gn 2-11; Ex and Nm passim), is a God with a long-range plan and the power and will to implement that plan. He is in short the Lord of History. As L. Koehler says: ". . . everything that remains to be said about the revelation of God in the Old Testament, however rich in content and significance it may be, is but a corollary of the statement, 'God is the Lord.' This statement is the backbone of Old Testament Theology."[21]

There is no human hero in the Yahwist's saga—not Abraham or Jacob or Joseph or Moses. There is no human hero because the protagonist of the saga is the Lord God. For the Yahwist it is the same Lord of History who lovingly places the man in the garden, regretfully opens the floodgates of heaven, decisively calls Abraham out of Mesopotamia, dexterously positions Joseph in Egypt, powerfully intervenes at the Red Sea, solemnly covenants at Sinai, and paternally educates in the desert. What G. von Rad says about the episodes dealing with Moses is true of the saga as a whole:

> Great as was the veneration of the writers for this man to whom God had been pleased to reveal Himself, in all these stories it is not Moses himself, Moses the man, but God who is the central figure. God's words and God's deeds, these are the things that the writers intend to set forth. We shall find that this principle applies to all the early narratives of Israel; they are stories of God's great acts of salvation, of His enduring patience, and also of His judgments and His vengeance; in no single case is a man—be he the very greatest among the sons of men—the central figure. The aim of all these stories is to render honor to God, to glorify His deeds, His patience, and the faithfulness that He has been pleased to reveal.[22]

The centrality of the sovereignty of God—the Lord of History

---

[21] *Old Testament Theology*, p. 35. G. von Rad, *Old Testament Theology* II, pp. 425-426, discusses the impact of the Lord of History concept on Israel's historical writing.

[22] *Moses*, p. 8.

theme—in the Yahwist's saga is evident in many places.[23] It is basic to the connection between the Tower of Babel story in which "the Lord scattered them (the nations) over the whole face of the earth" and the call of Abraham (Gn 12:1-3) through whose descendants the nations will once more be gathered together to worship the Lord of History with one united voice.[24] It is at the heart of the Yahwist's portrayal of God influencing events in Egypt, in Mesopotamia, in Palestine, in Philistia, in Transjordan, and in the desert. The Joseph story, the Pharaoh versus Yahweh story, the Balaam story—all are grounded in the Yahwist's insight into the nature of God as Lord of History.

The foreshadowing texts as a group, but especially the programmatic texts in Gn 12:1-3 and 49:8-12; the divine soliloquies in the paradise story and the flood story (Gn 2:18; 3:22; 6:3, 7; and 8:21-22); the divine dialogues between God and the serpent, God and Adam, God and Eve, God and Cain, God and Abraham (Gn 3; 4; 18:23-33), and the theological comments in the Joseph story (especially Gn 45:5, 8) are all expressions in different ways of the Yahwist's conviction that Yahweh is truly the Lord of History.

If it is true that the Yahwist envisions a return of mankind in the future to that happy state of subjection to the Lord of History manifested by Adam (in whom all nations were contained) before the fall, it is nonetheless certain that the Yahwist's conception of history is not cyclical but linear.[25]

---

[23] Whatever the origin of the Yahwist's insight into the nature of God as the Lord of History (and it is probably the inspired deduction he came to from the promises made to the patriarchs, worked out in the exodus events, and fulfilled in part at least through the kingdom of David), he did not hesitate to make this insight the backbone of his saga. The observation of E. Jacob is relevant here: "Real History is born only when a religious or philosophical principle establishes some relationship between the course of events" (*Theology of the Old Testament*, p. 184).

[24] What the Yahwist realized only inchoatively has been expressed beautifully by Vatican II: "The eternal Father, by a free and hidden plan of his own wisdom and goodness created the whole world. His plan was to raise men to participation of the divine life . . . he planned to assemble in the holy Church all those who would believe in Christ" (*Dogmatic Constitution on the Church*, par. 2).

[25] To the degree that the Yahwist can be said to look for a return to the beginning, his theology is at least latently eschatological. If the introductory words of Gn 49, which speak of "what lies before . . . in time to come," are the words of the Yahwist, as are the words of Gn 49:8-12, there is all the more reason for seeing latent eschatology in the Yahwist's conception of history. See D. S. Russell, *The Method and Message of Jewish Apocalyptic*, pp. 213-217.

The wheel of history—if the Yahwist's foreshadowing in Gn 3:15 is to be believed—will eventually return man to the happy state he enjoyed before the fall, but men will turn the wheel themselves, freely and with the help of God's love and the enlightenment of his revelation. The wheel will turn, but not in the air and not deterministically. It will roll ahead through time impelled by men patiently educated by God to respond to his love and so fulfill his plan.

Thus Adam is free. Cain is free. Joseph's sinful brothers are free. The Israelites in the desert are free. Man sins freely throughout the saga, but he also responds freely, and it is ultimately through this response of love and fidelity that the Yahwist sees the fulfillment of God's plan. One might almost say that the Yahwist's presentation of Abraham's education in faith was intended by him as paradigmatic for his audience.

That God has a plan of salvation, the Yahwist shows by means of his foreshadowing texts and divine soliloquies; by means of his elimination-of-peoples-process; by means of promises made and promises fulfilled—even long centuries after the making of the promises; by linking the Primeval History with the Patriarchal History and the Patriarchal History with the National History; by laying a solid bond of continuity between the vocation of the Patriarchs, the vocation and mission of Moses, and the vocation and mission of the Davidic dynasty.

That this plan envisions all mankind and not only the chosen nation is made clear in the call of Abraham (Gn 12:2-3) in whom "all the tribes of the earth" are to be blessed. It is also indicated in the intercession of Abraham for the inhabitants of the plain cities (Gn 18:23-33) and in the ministry of Joseph in Egypt.[26] It is especially clear in the Primeval History as a whole and in the promise made to Eve (the mother of all the living) that her descendants will crush the head of the serpent, who through his victory over Adam (the father of all mankind) has temporarily conquered.

---

[26] Joseph is a source of "blessing" to Egypt and to that degree may have been intended by the Yahwist as an example of how the nations are blessed through the seed of Abraham as indicated in the programmatic foreshadowing text of Gn 12:1-3.

The Yahwist is convinced that the God of Israel is unique and not the least of the characteristics that made Him unique—utterly different from the gods of the nations and "wholly other"—was his supreme power not only over the world but over history. As J. L. McKenzie puts it:

> The historical thrust of the Israelite faith is one of the great sources of its dynamism; it is also one of the features which distinguishes it most sharply from the religions of Canaan. The will of Yahweh realizes itself in history and not in the mythological event. Yahweh is not involved in nature, but exercises supreme cosmic power; thus Yahweh is not involved in history, but exercises supreme historical power corresponding to his power in nature. Indeed the two are not really considered in the Israelite faith as two domains of power, but as a single domain. And as there is no parallel to the supreme cosmic dominion of Yahweh in other religions, so there is no parallel to his supreme historical dominion. With Israel there appears for the first time the idea of history as a unified process directed by a supreme intelligence and will towards a purpose. Israel therefore engaged in history with the assurance which comes from a sense of destiny.[27]

SUGGESTED READINGS

X. Léon-Dufour, *Vocabulaire de Théologie Biblique:* articles on "Dessein de Dieu," "Promesses," "Volonté de Dieu."

W. Eichrodt, *Theology of the Old Testament* I, 228ff; 381ff; 472-480.

E. Jacob, *Theology of the Old Testament,* 183-232. ✓

L. Koehler, *Old Testament Theology,* 30-35; 75-84; 92-98.

Th. Vriezen, *An Outline of Old Testament Theology,* 227ff.

G. Knight, *A Christian Theology of the Old Testament,* 218-224.

H. W. Robinson, *Inspiration and Revelation in the Old Testament,* 106-159.

A. Toynbee, *A Study of History* (abridged edition of vol. I-VI), 247-254.

R. G. Collingwood, *The Idea of History,* 67f; 181; 238; 264.

G. von Rad, *Old Testament Theology* I, 48-56; 308-318. ⌐

---

[27] *The World of the Judges,* p. 108.

J. H. Wright, "The Eternal Plan of Divine Providence," *TS*, March
'66, 27-57.
R. Latourelle, "Revelation, History, and the Incarnation" *TD*, 13,
29-34.

SIN—PUNISHMENT—FORGIVENESS

At the very beginning of his saga the Yahwist theologizes on the
most elemental of man's problems—the problem of evil and suffering in a world created by a good and loving God. The problem is
perennial. The author of Job will attack it in the 6th century. The
author of Wisdom in the first century. After the coming of Christ
the early Church Fathers will deal with the question in relation to
Gnosticism and St. Augustine in relation to Manicheism. To this
day no thoroughly satisfactory solution has been proposed.

In dealing with the Yahwist's theology of sin and suffering, it
should be remembered that the theology in Gn 2-11 is retrospec-
tive theology—a picture of what must have been in the beginning
based upon what the Yahwist deduced from the state of man in
his own time and from his own analysis of Israel's history with
God as far back as the time of the Patriarchs.

It should be remembered that what the Yahwist says about sin
and suffering and evil—inasmuch as he deals with these as elemental problems transcending time—must be distinguished from
his presentation. What he says—his solution such as it is—remains
perennial teaching. The way he says it—his presentation of the
problem—is conditioned by his audience and their particular
needs in the 10th century B.C. The interpreter must distinguish
between the Yahwist's teaching and his presentation, the way he
distinguishes between the teaching of Job and its presentation to
a 6th century audience, or the teaching of St. Augustine and its
presentation to a 5th century A.D. audience.

Finally, considering the developed theology of sin already evident in the 10th century Succession History (2 Sm 9-20; 1 Kgs
1-2), the interpreter should ask himself what is already common
and accepted doctrine on sin (cf. for example the teaching on sin
in 2 Sm 12) and what is new in Gn 2-11.

At all times, of course, the interpreter should remember that the

Yahwist's theology of sin is not only doctrinal but polemical. His presentation is geared to combat sin as he found it in its most detestable form in his own time in Israel's turning to the Baal fertility cult.

To begin with, it may be presumed that in view of his positive insights on Israel's election, on the love of God for Israel, and on Israel's place in the Lord of History's plan for mankind, the Yahwist was realist enough to face the fact that God's plan for his chosen people was not proceeding without obstruction. Tradition made it clear to him that even in the halcyon days of the Exodus and the stirring events of Sinai Israel had not responded with enthusiasm to God's love and to God's elective purpose. The murmuring in the desert between Egypt and Sinai (Ex 16), the apostasy at Sinai (Ex 32-34), the complaints and rebellions in the course of the march from Sinai to the plains of Moab (Nm 10-25), and the repeated apostasies in the period of the Judges all posed the problem—what is wrong with Israel . . . what is wrong with man . . . why does Israel continually turn away from the good God who has loved her, elected her, and destined her for great things in his redemptive plan?

It may be presumed likewise that the situation in the Yahwist's own time afforded him no great comfort. The Succession History showed sin rampant even in the life of David and his sons. Canaanite religion was strong in the land and Israelites in appreciable numbers were seeking the good things of life from the fertility gods. Solomon himself was influenced by his pagan wives and had already introduced the worship of the Baal gods into the holy city of Jerusalem (1 Kgs 11:1ff). There was prosperity in Israel but there was also suffering.

It was indeed easy to say that God is good, that God has elected Israel, that God loves Israel. But how explain physical suffering? How explain hard work come to nothing against the uncertainties of blight and drought? How explain the suffering that for many seemed as close to man as his clothing in so many areas of his life and for so long?

The Yahwist does not sound the problem to the depths. He gives the basic answer that nondualistic theologians have given down the centuries. God is indeed good and evil does not come

from Him. Man is free (he takes this elemental truth for granted)
and in the exercise of his freedom has elected evil. Suffering,
therefore, is the consequence of man's willful turning away from
God. The practical, though not the theoretical, solution is for man
to turn back to God, trust Him, do His will and leave to Him the
the fulfillment of His plan for His people.

A theoretical solution of the problem does not seem to have
been one of the clear insights of the Yahwist. He has almost all the
elements for the later teaching of St. Paul on original sin (cf. Rom
5:1ff), but he nowhere explicitly draws the same conclusion as
St. Paul.[28]

The Yahwist's contribution to the solution of the problem of
evil, it must be remembered, is conditioned in its presentation
both by the audience for whom it was destined and by the traditions whose literary forms he was bound to respect if he wished
to present his solution. To have any impact on his audience, his
presentation had to be pertinent to their needs and expressed in
a literary form they would understand. This meant dealing with
Israel's traditions theologically.

Israel's traditions had already conditioned her to think of God
as one who out of love had chosen her and delivered her from the
bondage of Egypt, who when she sinned punished but always delivered her and started over again with new overtures of love and
forgiveness.

In addition to her patriarchal and exodus traditions Israel was
acquainted with many of the age-old myths that were part of her
ancient Mesopotamian background and part of her more recent
acquaintance with the fertility cult rituals and literature of the
Canaanites. All of these were grist for the Yahwist's literary mill.
His problem, however, was how to use these sources, how arrange
them, how depaganize and transform them—where there was
question of sources which had originally been the vehicle for un-
orthodox religious teaching. Most of these problems are dealt with
in the major commentaries. We shall attempt to deal with the implications of Gn 2-11 as a whole and with the story pattern and
pattern of stories used by the Yahwist in this section of his saga.

---

[28] A. Dubarle, *The Biblical Doctrine of Original Sin*, pp. 1, 9-87; 171ff; and
"Original Sin and Modern Science," *The Pope Speaks*, XI 3, pp. 229-235.

The pattern of each of the stories in Gn 2-11 is practically identical—sin, punishment, forgiveness—with two notable and significant exceptions, the first at the beginning in Gn 2 and the second at the end in Gn 11. In Gn 2-3 the story pattern has one additional element—the description of man's original happy state before the fall. In Gn 11 the Tower of Babel story lacks the last element—forgiveness.

The similarity of the story elements in the pattern is clear. In each story there is a sin element. Adam and Eve disobey. Cain murders. The sons of God and the daughters of men fornicate. Canaan sins in some way against his father, Noah. The nations at the Tower of Babel assert themselves against God.

In each story there is a punishment element. Adam and Eve lose paradise. Cain is condemned to be a wanderer. The flood follows the sins of the sons of God and the daughters of men. Canaan is cursed for the sin of his father Ham. All mankind is scattered like Cain after the revolt at the Tower of Babel.

In each story there is a forgiveness element. Adam and Eve are forgiven and given a mark of God's concern in his making of clothes for them. Cain is forgiven and given a mark to protect him. After the flood God says: "Never again will I strike down every living thing as I have done. As long as earth lasts, sowing and reaping, cold and heat, summer and winter, day and night shall cease no more" (Gn 8:21-22). Mankind is given a new lease on life. Nothing is said about the forgiveness of Canaan, the son of Noah, but for a good pedagogical reason as we shall show. Neither is there any immediate evidence of forgiveness after the sin at the Tower of Babel.

THE LORD OF LIFE AND FERTILITY

In addition to the sin-punishment-forgiveness pattern of each story, another factor, which is not so much an element as it is an atmosphere, must be considered. It is the atmosphere or the motif of "fertility" that runs through almost all the stories. Only in the Tower of Babel story will the reader find lacking some connection between man's sins and the fertility motif. This factor, while readily clear and even obvious to the Yahwist's audience, is not so obvious to moderns. If the reader will read Gn 2-11 with two questions constantly uppermost in his mind—namely, who gives fertility and who is responsible for its loss?—he will come to some perhaps surprising answers.

The saga opens with the infertile earth dry and barren because "Yahweh God had not sent rain on the earth" (Gn 2:5). Man himself is intimately associated with this infertile earth. He is formed from it by the Divine Potter and becomes a living being when God breathes into his nostrils "the breath of life." His name "Adam"—man—is a play upon the Hebrew word for earth—"Adamah," as one might speak of a man as an "earthling," from the "earth."

God then plants a "garden" supplied with a superabundance of water—"A river flowed from Eden to water the garden"—and fertility—"Yahweh God caused to spring up from the soil every kind of tree, enticing to look at and good to eat" (Gn 2:8-10). Man is taken from the infertile earth and placed in the fertile garden provided by God.

In the story of the fall the fertility motif enters again in different forms. The tempter, symbolized by the serpent, is almost certainly to be identified as the fertility cult religion of Canaan.[29] For the Yahwist, as L. Hartman says, ". . . all the abominable rites which were practiced among the pagans and among his own people in as far as they were unfaithful to the worship of the Lord, in order to placate the nature gods and thereby ensure fertility in man and beast, in field and plant, were sinful magic, the symbol and personification of which was the serpent. Only the Lord can give the true fruit of the tree of life."[30]

When Adam and Eve sin, they are removed from the fertile garden to the infertile earth outside, following a divine judgment which decrees as the punishment for sin "pains in childbearing"

---

[29] See the comment of J. L. McKenzie (*DB*, p. 791): "Some modern interpreters have suggested that the seduction of man and woman by the serpent is a mythological representation of the seduction of Israel by the deities of fertility, which to the writer of the story is the fundamental sin of Israel."

[30] "Sin in Paradise" *CBQ* 20 (1958), 26-40; also J. L. McKenzie, *Myths and Realities*, pp. 166-175; also H. Renckens, *Israel's Concept of the Beginning*, pp. 268-271.

for the woman and a recalcitrant earth for the man who is henceforth condemned to wrest a living from the soil in the sweat of his
brow (Gn 3:16-19).

In the Cain-Abel story the fertility motif recurs. After the murder of Abel, God says: ". . . Listen to the sound of your brother's
blood, crying out to me from the ground ("adamah"). Now be
accursed and driven from the ground that has opened its mouth
to receive your brother's blood at your hands" (Gn 4:10-11). In
the Baal texts from Ras Shamra, it is significant that Baal is punished for the crime of fratricide and as a result there is a period
of barrenness. As J. Gray says: "The connection between fratricide
and sterility is, of course, familiar to anthropologists and is expressed in the Old Testament in God's curse on Cain. . . ."[31]

In relation to a possible anti-Canaanite element in the Cain-
Abel story, it is perhaps of some significance that Cain, the murderer, is an agriculturist like the Canaanites; while Abel, like the
Israelites, is a shepherd. The reactionary movement of the Recha-
bites (cf. Jer 35), inasmuch as it was a strictly Yahwistic extremist
sect that insisted on a seminomadic mode of life as against a settled, agrarian mode of life, may well provide the background for
the specific characterization of Cain and Abel.[32]

The story of the sons of God fornicating with the daughters of
men would appear to have no immediate contact with the fertility
cult. But it is possible, in a culture which knew only too well the
practice of sacred prostitution, that the author is here alluding to
that depraved ritual custom of the Canaanites. The Confraternity
Bible note on Dt 23:18f is enlightening in this regard: "The pagans believed that they could enter into special relationships with
their gods and goddesses by having sexual relations with the
pagan priests and priestesses who prostituted themselves for this
purpose. . . ."

In the fertility cult ritual it is significant that sacred prostitution
climaxes the rites which hail the return of the rains and fertility.
In the punishment which follows the fornication of the sons of
God with the daughters of men the rains come with a vengeance.

---

[31] *The Legacy of Canaan*, pp. 67, 83, 88.

[32] R. de Vaux, *Ancient Israel*, pp. 14f.

The flood covers the earth, and everything upon its fertile surface is swept away by the cleansing waters (Gn 7:20-23).[33]

In the Noah story there is only a tenuous connection between the earth and the Ham-Canaan sin. For his sin, which follows upon Noah's unwitting drunkenness, Canaan, like the serpent in 3:14 and Cain in 4:11, is cursed. Unlike the other sin-punishment stories nothing is said about the forgiveness of Canaan and the reason would appear to be that Canaan, like the serpent in Gn 3:14, is cursed not so much for himself as that he is the embodiment in the nation that comes from him of the fertility cult religion of the Canaanites and as such is not only at enmity with the descendants of the woman but with God Himself.

One may wonder if there is not here some allusion to the vices of drunkenness and sexual perversion prevalent among the agricultural Canaanites but virtually unknown among the semi-nomadic Israelites, at least in the early period of their history. The institution of the Nazarite vow which entailed among other things abstention from all products of the vine would appear to have come into existence in protest against the wine-bibbing of the Canaanites.[34]

Only the final episode in Gn 2-11, the Tower of Babel story, would seem to have no connection with the fertility motif. Mankind settles in the land of Shinar and attempts to build a life and make a name for itself apart from and independent of God (11:4). The author implies this sin is *hubris*, the presumption of man to run the world by himself, independent of the Lord of History. The tower is an invasion of heaven! For this sin mankind is scattered by the Lord over the face of the earth (11:9).

It is difficult to assess the total impact of Gn 2-11 on a 10th century Israelite audience. The nature of the material, however, and the religious needs of the audience make a number of doctrinal points reasonably certain.

To begin with, the use of a series of stories, each of which contains the same story elements and each of which reflects in some

---

[33] R. de Vaux, *op. cit.*, pp. 117f. J. Gray associates this Genesis story with an episode in the Ras Shamra mythology involving the God El's begetting of the divine twins *Shr and Slm*.

[34] R. de Vaux, *op. cit.*, p. 466; and G. von Rad, *Theology of the O.T.*, p. 62.

way the fertility motif, would certainly point to design on the part of the author and to his intention of inculcating certain teachings. While the succession of stories with a fertility motif background might be explained by the undoubted prevalence of the fertility cult throughout the whole of the Middle East for so many centuries, the consistent association of the stories with the sin and punishment of man would seem to indicate a polemic against Canaanite religion. In passing, it should be noted that the author is not against sex or sexuality; quite the opposite. He is against the abuse of these God-given faculties and their near deification by the Canaanites. If Israel's religious enemies had been Puritans or Jansenists, the Yahwist would probably have given us a series of stories which exalted in all their positive goodness the gifts of sex and sexuality. The author of the Canticle of Canticles will do this at a later and more opportune time.

The stories as a group emphasize, it would seem, the truth that Yahweh and not Baal is the true Lord of life and fertility! Thus, in Gn 2:4b-14 Yahweh not only creates heaven and earth but prepares for man a superfertile, superlatively watered garden. In Gn 3 man loses the fertile garden precisely because he apostatized from the true God of fertility to follow the false gods of fertility symbolized by the serpent.

Tending to confirm this interpretation are the following: the series of stories which deal with sin and punishment; the divine dialogues in 3:16-19; 4:6-15; the curse on Canaan in 9:25-27; the frequent stories with an anti-Canaanite bias in the rest of the saga; and especially the barren-wife stories. More positively one can cite the fertility blessings on Jacob in Gn 27:27-28; on Judah in 49:10-12; on Joseph in 49:22-25; the description of the Promised Land God is about to give them as a land "flowing with milk and honey" (Nm 14:7); and lastly the blessings of fertility given to Jacob (Gn 30:33-43) and especially to Joseph in Egypt, where the blessing of Joseph redounds as a blessing on the Egyptians (Gn 41).

The Yahwist, in short, is contrasting Yahwism with Baalism.[35]

---

[35] Opposition to elements of Canaanite religion in the saga reveals a good deal about the theologian's conception of Yahweh and Yahwism. Use of the principle of polarity for educing doctrine—i.e. distinguishing doctrines through polarity of

He is teaching his 10th century audience that Yahweh and not Baal is the source of good, the giver of life and fertility to man and field and flock. Distress in childbearing, an infertile and recalcitrant soil—these come from Yahweh, indeed, but as a punishment for apostasy to the false fertility gods. Suffering is not a matter of chance but comes as the just and educative punishment of a loving God who has been offended by his creatures. Sin, freely willed by man in his turning away from God, is the fundamental cause of suffering. Whatever the sin of the first man and woman (and the Yahwist makes no pretence of saying exactly what it was beyond indicating it was a sin of *hubris*), he presents that sin as he knew sin in his own time—as a turning away from Yahweh to follow the false religion of the fertility gods.[36]

Sin is a personal offense against God. Consequently sinners are accountable to God for their sins. The point is not so much taught as taken for granted, and perhaps because this refined notion of sin was already common teaching by the time of the Yahwist. It would seem quite clear in 2 Sm 12 where David realizes his sins of murder and adultery are sins against God. Moreover, in the Joseph story (Gn 37-50), which was probably written in the time of David, the author has Joseph, tempted to commit adultery by his employer's wife, express this truth as a truth taken for granted: "How could I do anything so wicked, and sin against God?" (Gn 39:9).

In addition to inculcating who the true Lord of fertility is, Gn 2-11 serves another function. The series of similar stories as a series shows that man left to himself is prone to greater and greater sins. The sinfulness and weakness of man is inculcated by the

---

doctrines even where the theologian wrongly adduces one pole, provided he thinks it is the opposite of what he holds—must nonetheless be used with great caution. The positive pole and everything that distinguishes it, not just the negative pole, must be emphasized.

[36] The Yahwist's insights on the forces of evil, whether they are in man or outside of man, are not clear. In Gn 4:7 he pictures sin as it were waiting for man to rush upon him and overpower him. In conjunction with the serpent-tempter picture in Gn 3, it would appear that he sees sin-evil as a principle outside man. E. Jacob's statement, however, ". . . the identification of the serpent with Satan . . . only draws the final consequences of what the story-teller in Gn had already glimpsed . . ." (*Theology of the Old Testament*, p. 282), would appear to attribute to the Yahwist a conclusion or at least a half-formed insight which the Yahwist himself might very well never recognize.

progress of sin from the disobedience of Adam to the fratricide of Cain, the insensate vengeance of Lamech, the general corruption of mankind before the flood, the drunkenness of Noah and the perversion of Canaan after the flood, and finally the ultimate revolt of all mankind at the Tower of Babel. The theological comment in 6:3 and the divine soliloquies in 6:5-7 and 8:21-22 express in direct discourse what is taught by the series of stories as a group.

The continual turning away from God to self against the best interests of self and the continual return of God to forgive and begin again indicate that the Yahwist, speaking for God, is attempting to convince his audience of a truth enunciated later by Our Lord: "Without me you can do nothing." The discourses attributed to God by the Yahwist would seem to confirm this analysis.[37] The saga as a whole and Gn 2-11 in particular call upon the Israelites to shun the fertility cult religion and return to the good God who has elected them out of love and destined them for a prominent part in the fulfillment of his salvific plan for all mankind. Later on the author of Deuteronomy will say the same thing, though in a different way:

> You must fear Yahweh your God, you must serve him, by his name you must swear. Do not follow other gods, gods of the peoples round you, for Yahweh your God who dwells among you is a jealous God; his anger could blaze out against you and wipe you from the face of the earth (Dt 6:13-15).

It is in relation to these last points perhaps that the Yahwist's omission of the forgiveness element in the Tower of Babel story can best be understood. Once he has roundly inculcated the proneness of man to sin and the inability of man to save himself from the onslaughts of sin, the Yahwist can hope that his audience will appreciate to the full the significance of God's intervention in human history by the calling of Abraham out of Mesopotamia, his promise to make a great nation out of him, to bless him, make his name great, and in him bless all the nations of the earth (Gn 12:1-3).

---

[37] Cf. Gn 3:14-19; 4:9-15; 6:5-8; 8:21; 11:6-7.

The forgiveness element in the Tower of Babel story is not really omitted at all. It is found in the story that follows. The nations scattered all over the earth in the Tower of Babel story (Gn 11:9), because they attempted to "make a name" for themselves independent of God (11:4), will be gathered together again in him in whom "all the tribes of the earth" are to be blessed. What the nations had sought, "to make a name for themselves," is promised to Abraham and his seed: "I will . . . make your name so famous that it will be used as a blessing" (Gn 12:2).[38]

IMMORTALITY

If, as has been suggested, the element of forgiveness, missing in the Tower of Babel story, is really implicit in the whole account that follows, beginning with the call of Abraham and the promises made to him which would eventually involve all the nations, then the link created here by the Yahwist between the primeval history and the patriarchal history suggests the possibility of other links.

Some of these have already been suggested, namely, the links between the anti-Canaanite stories of the primeval history and the anti-Canaanite stories in the patriarchal and national histories, the links between the teaching that Yahweh is the true Lord of fertility in the primeval history and the barren-wife stories in the patriarchal history, and finally the links between the foreshadowing texts in Gn 3:15 and 9:25-27 in the primeval history with the foreshadowing texts dealing with the rise of Israel and her kings in the patriarchal history.

These links suggest the possibility of a more important, though far more elusive, link between the additional story element in Gn 2-3—the description of man's happy state before the fall—and the whole of the patriarchal and national history that follows.

The link is not easily demonstrated and particularly because it involves the much disputed text of Gn 3:15. As is well known, when the Yahwist placed in the mouth of God the words of prom-

---

[38] The catchword "great" recurs in the Isaac cycle in Gn 26:13 and in relation to Gn 12:2, the promise of blessing, as can be seen from the words of Abimelech in Gn 26:28-29.

ise contained in the foreshadowing of Gn 3:15—a promise that involved the conquest of the serpent who had turned the first man and woman against God—he laid the foundation—quite innocently —for an exegetical marathon that continues to this day.

Exegetes for centuries have pursued unsuccessfully the meaning of this text, which was certainly clear to the Yahwist and probably equally clear to his unlettered audience in the 10th century B.C. The explanation given below (cf. pp. 196-203ff) sees this text as a foreshadowing text and interprets its ambiguities in the light of the later, clearer foreshadowing texts in the same series. It is here suggested that this interpretation may help to explain the purpose of the additional story element in the sin-punishment-forgiveness story of Gn 2-3—the description of the happy state of man before the fall—and perhaps show its link with the patriarchal and national history that follows in the second and third parts of the saga.

Presuming always that the Yahwist was attempting to teach his 10th century audience certain theological truths and presuming as well that he did not underestimate the ability of his audience to grasp what he was teaching, we must ask what connection the Yahwist's audience would see between the description of man's happy state before the fall and the two promises which form the axes of the whole saga, namely, the promise to Adam and Eve that their descendants would conquer the serpent and the promise to Abraham in Gn 12:1-3 with its sequel in the history that follows.

Several factors must be considered. First, it is quite possible that the Yahwist had only one purpose in mind in opening his saga with a picture of Yahweh as creator and giver of fertility. By so doing he demonstrated from the beginning the basic truth that Yahweh and not Baal was the true Lord of fertility.

But other factors must be weighed. God not only gives fertility; he makes a promise, implicit at least, that man will be immortal. For the ancients this meant being "like gods" (note how the serpent plays upon this idea in 3:5); and while it was generally held that man could not become immortal like the gods because the gods had decreed death for mankind, it was not considered absolutely impossible. The dialogue between Aqhat and the warrior-

goddess Anath in the Tale of Aqhat reflects the Ugaritic attitude
toward immortality:

> Then quoth the Maiden Anath:
> "Ask for life, O Aqhat the Youth.
> Ask for life and I'll give it thee
> For deathlessness, and I'll bestow't on thee.
> I'll make thee count years with Baal,
> With the sons of El shalt thou count months.
> And Baal when he gives life gives a feast,
> Gives a feast to the life-given and bids him drink;
> Sings and chants over him,
> Sweetly serenades him:
> So give I life to Aqhat the Youth."
> But Aqhat the Youth answers:
> "Fib not to me, O Maiden;
> For to a Youth thy fibbing is loathsome.
> Further life—how can mortal attain it?
> How can mortal attain life enduring?
> Glaze will be poured on my head,
> Plaster upon my pate;
> And I'll die as everyone dies,
> I too shall assuredly die. . . ."[39]

The Epic of Gilgamesh related the unsuccessful quest of Gilgamesh for immortality; but it also acknowledged that at least one
man and one woman by the direct will of the gods had been
granted immortality. This is accomplished, in the Akkadian version of the myth, by the will of the god, Enlil, who says to Utnapishtim and his wife after the flood that they will be "like unto us
gods":

> Thereupon Enlil went aboard the ship.
> Holding me by the hand, he took me aboard.
> He took my wife aboard and made her kneel by my side.
> Standing between us, he touched our foreheads to bless us:
> 'Hitherto Utnapishtim has been but human.
> Henceforth Utnapishtim and his wife shall be like unto us gods.
> Utnapishtim shall reside far away, at the mouth of the rivers!'
> Thus they took me and made me reside far away,
> At the mouth of the rivers.

---

[39] ANET, p. 151.

But now, who will for thy sake call the gods to Assembly
That the life which thou seekest thou mayest find?[40]

In the earlier Sumerian version of the myth, King Ziusudra is deified by being given "life like a god" and "breath eternal" and is then sent to live in Dilmun "the place where the sun rises." The text clearly deals with the theme of immortality:

Ziusudra, the king,
Prostrated himself before Anu and Enlil.
Anu and Enlil cherished Ziusudra,
Life like that of a god they give him,
Breath eternal like that of a god they bring down for him.
Then, Ziusudra the king,
The preserver of the name of vegetation and of the seed of mankind,
In the land of crossing, the land of Dilmun, the place where the sun
    rises, they caused to dwell.[41]

Still more important, in the Yahwist's saga as well as in the Epic of Gilgamesh, it is a serpent who prevents man from enjoying the immortality promised by God and symbolized by the tree of life. Gilgamesh's quest for immortality brought him to the tree of life. It is the sequel, however, that is important:

Gilgamesh says to him, to Urshanabi, the boatman:
"Urshanabi, this plant is a plant apart,
Whereby a man may regain his life's breath.
I will take it to ramparted Uruk,
Will cause (. . . .) to eat the plant . . . !
Its name shall be 'Man Becomes Young in Old Age.'
I myself shall eat it
And thus return to the state of my youth."
After twenty leagues they broke off a morsel,
After thirty further leagues they prepared for the night.
Gilgamesh saw a well whose water was cool.
He went down into it to bathe in the water.
A serpent snuffed the fragrance of the plant;
It came up from the water and carried off the plant.
Going back it shed its slough.[42]

---

[40] ANET, p. 95.
[41] ANET, p. 44.
[42] ANET, p. 96.

Finally, and most significant of all, it would appear that while the Yahwist depaganizes and retheologizes the Mesopotamian flood story, he also deliberately changes its conclusion. Noah and his wife, the counterparts of Ziusudra and Utnapishtim and his wife, *do not* receive the gift of immortality from God!

What are we to deduce from the Yahwist's reuse and reorganization of these Mesopotamian myths? The least we can deduce is that neither he nor his audience was unmindful or ignorant of man's desire to live forever. The mythical treatments of man's search for immortality were in written form at least 500 to 1000 years before the time of the Yahwist. The theme was not new. We may also deduce that the differences in the stories, especially in what relates to immortality, may well have much to tell us about the Yahwist's theology.[43]

In the myths, the gods have no intention of sharing their immortality with men. Only two—*by way of exception*—are granted the gift of immortality. In the Yahwist's saga immortality is promised to man from the beginning. It is the *ordinary lot of man*, provided he obeys God! Man does not, like Gilgamesh, have to search in vain for the tree of life. It is given to him from the beginning. It stands secure in his grasp in the midst of the garden.

In the Gilgamesh epic, Gilgamesh, who represents every man striving for immortality, has the tree of life in his hands but loses it because a serpent chances by and steals it while he rests. In the Yahwist's saga it is through the intervention of the serpent, representing the fertility cult religion of Canaan, that man loses the gift of immortality. But—where Gilgamesh weeps for the immortality which he has apparently irrevocably lost because of the serpent—the Yahwist presents God promising man that he will someday conquer his adversary the serpent. Gilgamesh is left without hope. Adam has a promise!

Here we come to the nub of the problem. Would the 10th century Yahwist, who was certainly acquainted with the Mesopota-

---

[43] The Yahwist, however much he has to say about sin, is unquestionably an optimist, whose theology stands out in stark contrast to the pessimism of the pagans (Cf. R. MacKenzie, *Faith and History in the Old Testament*, pp. 11-25). He insists on the goodness of Yahweh, on Yahweh's determination to save, on the goodness of man, of marriage, of creation. In any age his message would be cheerful. In the 10th century B.C. it was positively evangelical.

mian myths mentioned above, have intended his audience to understand that the conquest of the serpent meant the eventual regaining of the immortality enjoyed by the first man and woman before the fall? It is by no means improbable.

It has been generally held that certain knowledge of the future life with God was not common knowledge among the Jews until the second century B.C. The prophets certainly do not take it for granted. Nor do the authors of Job, Ecclesiastes, and Sirach. This would appear to make most improbable any knowledge of the doctrine in the time of the Yahwist who lived so long before any of these authors. But the state of the question must be understood. The Yahwist does not teach immortality with God after death as the common lot of men in the same way as Daniel 12, Wisdom 1-5, 2 Maccabees 5-6, or the New Testament. All he does is insinuate that in God's good time the gift of immortality, generally considered to have been denied to men by the decree of the gods, will be given to the seed of the woman (mankind in general) as it was to the few by the Mesopotamian gods after the flood. What the Yahwist presents is more a hope than a doctrinal teaching on immortality. And it is a hope that is not unknown to Israel's psalmists even before the exile, however little the actual teaching on immortality is developed. In relation to the psalms it is interesting to note the statement of M. Dahood:

> Perhaps the most significant contribution to biblical theology that flows from the translations based on the new philological principles concerns the subject of resurrection and immortality. If the translations and exegesis propounded for such passages as Pss i 3-6, v 9, xi 7, xvi 10-11, xvii 15, xxi 7, xxvii 13, xxxvi 9-10, xxxvii 37-38, xli 13, lvi 14, lxxiii 23-24, bear up under criticism, then the treatment of these topics in standard biblical theologies will need drastic revision. . . . the opinion of Sigmund Mowinckel that "neither Israel nor early Judaism knew of a faith in any resurrection nor is such a faith represented in the psalms" will not survive serious scrutiny.[44]

We have said the Yahwist insinuates that in God's good time the gift of immortality will be given to the seed of the woman so

---

[44] *Psalms*, Anchor Bible, vol I, p. xxxvi.

recently deprived of it through the intervention of the serpent.
The statement is based upon a link between Gn 3:15 and the narrative which precedes it and a further link between Gn 3:15 and
Gn 12:1-3. Such links are difficult to prove. They can be suggested,
however, and either accepted or rejected according to how well
they fit the immediate context and the ideological background of
the author and his audience.

A link between Gn 3:15 and the preceding narrative is inherently probable on both counts. Both the Yahwist and his audience
were acquainted with the myths which dealt with the search for
immortality; otherwise the use of the myths by the Yahwist is inexplicable. According to the context, the serpent and the man and
the theme of immortality are certainly the concern of the author
before the fall. The conquest of the man by the serpent causes
man to lose his gift of immortality. Should not then the eventual
conquest of the serpent by the seed of the woman, foretold and
promised in Gn 3:15, effect the restoration of that which the serpent had caused man to lose? The deduction would not seem too
difficult for the Yahwist's audience. And the idea itself is certainly
not too abstruse for so perceptive a theologian as the Yahwist.

The further link between Gn 3:15 and Gn 12:1-3 and its sequel
in Israel's history leans heavily upon the link between the end of
the primeval history and the beginning of the patriarchal history.
If, as G. von Rad says, the election and blessing of Abraham is
"the point where primeval history and sacred history dovetail,"[45]
then it is certain that the Yahwist intended to link his theological
construction in Gn 2-11 with his more historical narrative which
follows. It would follow too, as a consequence, that the reader may
expect to see more than one link between the primeval history and
the later parts of the saga. The most obvious links, of course, are
the genealogies, the promises, and the anti-Canaanite stories.

That the promise of Gn 3:15, already linked with the loss of
immortality in the previous pericope, is also linked with the
promise to Abraham in Gn 12:1-3 is suggested on at least two
counts. First, it is indisputable that both Gn 3:15 and Gn 12:1-3
look to the future. And since both come from the same author and

---

[45] *Genesis,* p. 149.

are in all probability foreshadowing texts, there is no good reason why they should not look to the same future.

Secondly, it is a stylistic characteristic of the Yahwist to make a promise and then introduce numerous obstacles to its fulfillment. This is quite evident with regard to the promise made in Gn 12:1-3. The same characteristic, however, is evident in the Yahwist's treatment of the promise in Gn 3:15. Far from seeing immediate fulfillment in a rapid conquest of the serpent, the prophecy seems lost to sight in the chapters that follow. The serpent's success with Adam is repeated with Cain, with all mankind before the flood and with all mankind after the flood. All seems hopeless until the call of Abraham. It does not as a consequence seem unlikely that the Yahwist meant it this way—that the first step in the fulfillment of Gn 3:15 should be the call of Abraham in Gn 12:1-3.

Much more could be said for the theological insights of the Yahwist in the theological construct of Gn 2-12 and the reader is urged to consult the commentaries, especially Chaine and Von Rad. There remains the matter of evaluation. First, the difficult matter of evaluating the actual insights of the Yahwist in Gn 2-12 as distinct from the theological insights already part and parcel of Israelite religious teaching in the 10th century. Second, the more difficult task of evaluating the degree of personal conviction with which the Yahwist accepted his own insights. And third, the most difficult of all, the task of evaluating the degree of acceptance the Yahwist demanded from his readers in presenting to them his insights.

One may ask, to be more concrete, whether in the matter of marriage, as presented in Gn 2, the Yahwist truly attained those insights—monogamy and indissolubility—which we today take for granted as the basic properties of marriage. If he did indeed perceive the sense and significance of monogamous, indissoluble marriage, did he, living in a thoroughly unsympathetic, polygamous Israelite environment, feel thoroughly secure and convinced in the truth of his insight?[46]

Even granting the fact of the insight (which is not easily

---

[46] Much to the point here is the dictum of Oliver Wendell Holmes: "All values are anticipations of the future."

granted) and the Yahwist's conviction that his insights represented the truth of the matter, we may very well ask with what
binding force did the Yahwist present his teaching to his contemporaries? It is perhaps significant that he nowhere concludes one
of his didactic stories with a command such as that of Our Lord
at the end of the parable of the Good Samaritan: "Go thou and do
likewise!" It is certain that he nowhere demands the putting away
of extra wives and concubines. And there is no reason to believe
he would have been considered anything but an idiot if he had
conducted a monogamy crusade in 10th century Israel. Most dis-
concerting of all, his teaching, if such it was on the unity and indissolubility of marriage, remains a dead letter until the time of
Christ. The same, of course, could be said for his insights on
immortality.

How then are we to evaluate the Yahwist's insights? As genuine
insights, indeed; but born out of time, ahead of time, in some
cases. As such, they are presented rather than taught. This is true
of much in the Yahwist's saga. He drafts no credo. But he presents
to his readers in a positive, almost impressionistic way, that interior vision of a complex but organically structured world view
given to him by the Spirit.

SUGGESTED READINGS

H. Renckens, *Israel's Concept of the Beginning*, 159ff.
W. Eichrodt, *Theology of the Old Testament* II, 81-118.
J. Guillet, *Themes of the Bible*, 104-109.
A. Dubarle, *The Biblical Doctrine and Original Sin*, 9-87.
L. Koehler, *Old Testament Theology*, 166-180.
J. L. McKenzie, *Myths and Realities*, 85-200.
B. Childs, *Myth and Reality in the Old Testament*.
J. Barr, "The Meaning of 'Mythology' in relation to the OT," *VT* 9
    (1959).
✓ A. Suelzer, *The Pentateuch*, 22-40. ✓
E. Jacob, *Theology of the Old Testament*, 281-297.
P. Grelot, *Man and Wife in Scripture*, 14-56.
B. Lonergan, *Insight*, 530-549.
Vatican II, *Pastoral Constitution on the Church in the Modern
    World*, nn. 13-18.

H. W. Wolff, "The Kerygma of the Yahwist," *Interpretation* 20 (1966), 129-158.

COVENANT THEOLOGY

The Sinai covenant may rightly be termed the climax of the Yahwist's saga—whatever one thinks about the anticlimactic events which follow in the narrative of Nm 10-24. On the basis of structure alone, the saga culminates on Sinai. The primeval history leads up to Abraham and the patriarchs; the patriarchal history leads up to Israel in Egypt; and Israel in Egypt leads up to the national history in Exodus-Numbers which receives its *raison d'être* from the covenant.

The Yahwist's abiding interest in genealogies, promises, and the themes of divine election and the Lord of History make little sense except in view of the covenant. Through the covenant, the promises, election, genealogies, and the guidance and protection of the Lord of History come to a focus, when Israel becomes the Kingdom of God on earth. Toward this event, therefore, all Israel's prior history converges; and even the great intervention of God in the Exodus experience is only the last step toward the summit of Sinai. Sinai is to the Old Testament what Calvary is to the New.

In his descriptions of the Sinai covenant[47] and the Abrahamitic covenant,[48] the Yahwist would appear to be dependent upon tradition. In his description of the Adamitic covenant, if one admits covenant characteristics in the construction of the Adam story in Gn 2-3, the Yahwist would appear to be dependent only upon his own insight and literary genius.[49]

Whatever view is taken of the covenant in the Yahwist's saga, certain questions inevitably arise. In view of what has been said about the Hittite suzerainty treaties in recent years, one may ask whether the Yahwist received from tradition a covenant form based upon the suzerainty treaties or upon some other form.

In view of the Yahwist's occasional anachronisms in his patri-

---

[47] Ex 19:10-15; 24:12-15; 34:1ff according to Noth's analysis of the text.

[48] Gn 15:1-4, 6-12, 17-21 according to Speiser's analysis of the text.

[49] A. Schökel, "Sapiential and Covenant Themes in Gn 2-3" in *TD* 13, 1965, pp. 3-9.

archal history, one may further ask whether he received from tradition or freely created the form in which the covenant with Abraham is described.

Finally, in view of the Yahwist's obvious reconstructions in the
primeval history, one may first suspect and then forthrightly ask
whether the Yahwist did not construct the account of the fall in
Gn 2-3 in such a way that it would anticipate the sequence of
events that preceded and followed the Sinai experience.

If, as seems probable, the Yahwist did not receive from tradition
a covenant form description based upon the suzerainty treaties,
the further questions arise: first, in what form did Moses himself
present to the Israelites the making of the Sinai covenant? and
second, did Moses present the covenant in two forms, the first of
which was based upon the form of the suzerainty treaties and
which came down as the traditional form in the northern kingdom
as testified to by the book of Deuteronomy; the second of which—
sacrificial form, meal etc—came down in the southern kingdom as
testified to in the Yahwist's saga?[50]

In dealing with the covenant form in Ex 19-24, it will be good
to recall that a covenant form deals with the externalization of an
agreement between two parties acknowledging the existence of
certain rights or obligations. The way in which the agreement is
externalized, i.e. the form of the covenant, can vary greatly. Our
first question deals with the form of the covenant in Ex 19-24, not
the covenant itself.

D. McCarthy rightly says: "Investigation of the events and the
documents of Sinai (Ex 19-24) seems to show little or nothing of
the literary form of the covenant. There is simply no place in
which the curses and blessings appear."[51] Without these one cannot speak of a suzerainty pact literary form.

In Ex 24, no matter how one analyzes the text (vv 1-2, 9-12

---

[50] These questions have been dealt with at some length by Murray Newman in
his book, *The People of the Covenant.* For a rebuttal of von Rad's opinion, that the
Yahwist was the first to combine the Exodus and Sinai traditions, see A. Weiser,
The Old Testament: Its Formation and Development, pp. 83-99; also H. H. Huff-
mon's, "The Exodus, Sinai and the Credo" in *CBQ* 27 (1965), pp. 101-113; and
B. Anderson, *Understanding the Old Testament,* p. 63.

[51] "Covenant in the Old Testament: The Present State of Enquiry," *CBQ* 27
(1965), p. 230.

J author and vv 3-8 E author according to *BJ* and many others; or vv 1-11 E author and 12-15 J author according to Noth) one arrives at a covenant form based either upon a blood sacrifice (24:5-8) or upon a meal sacrifice (24:11). Neither here nor in Ex 34, which is almost universally attributed to the J author, is there any indication of "blessings and curses" which are an essential element of the suzerainty treaty form.

One may observe in favor of the suzerainty parallel that the final compilers of the Pentateuch let Israel's history in Ex 1-18 serve as an historical prologue and that the decalogue in Ex 20 or the cultic decalogue in Ex 34 served as the customary treaty form of stipulations. One still searches in vain, however, for any clear evidence of the treaty element of blessings and curses. If these existed in the traditions and were incorporated in the sagas of the Yahwist and Elohist, then for some unknown reason they were eliminated by the final compiler. But since they are so manifest in Deuteronomy, which was well known to the final compiler during the exile, their omission can only be explained by the obvious inference that they did not exist in the Yahwistic and Elohistic traditions at least in the form in which those traditions came down to the compiler. A possible but farfetched explanation might be that the compilers let the numerous curses and blessings in Dt 28 serve as the final element of the suzerainty form. Leaving aside such stretching of the evidence, one may conclude with McCarthy:

> The evidence is overwhelming that there is a very strong cultic element in the most antique presentation of Israel's special relationship, its covenant relationship, with Yahweh. Covenant meal, sacrifice, and especially the overpowering experience of the theophany presented in the cult were certainly elements connected with and integral to the covenant. The God who appears on Sinai, a God appearing in cultic circumstances, as all agree, is such that his mere appearance founds the relationship between him and the people and supplies a sufficient ground for the demands he put upon them.[52]

More to the point, however, one may ask if the Yahwist, who

---

[52] D. McCarthy, *op. cit.*, p. 231.

throughout his saga repeatedly mentions in one form or another "curses and blessings"[53] does not avoid the covenant form found in the Hittite suzerainty treaties, precisely because he does not concede that Israel can be cursed (cf. Nm 22-24), however convinced he is of Israel's sinfulness. We deal here obviously with an extremely difficult insight, which is debatable on many counts.

Speaking of Gn 15, one may observe that on first view the account of the covenant given here does not appear early. The foreshadowing text in vv 13-16 is obviously late. The same may be said for the theological tone of the statement in v 6: "Abram put his faith in Yahweh, who counted this as making him justified."[54] Also to be considered are the words of God to Abraham in Gn 15:7: "I am Yahweh . . . who brought you out of Ur of the Chaldaeans," words which re-echo suspiciously the preamble of the Sinai covenant in Ex 20:2: "I am Yahweh your God who brought you out of the land of Egypt, out of the house of slavery."

On the other hand, the incident in Gn 15:2-4, according to which Abraham's slave will be his heir if a son is not born to him, has the ring of high antiquity. As Albright has recently suggested, the incident is best explained on the basis of documents of 15th century Nuzi which testify to an Amorite custom according to which a man could borrow money without alienating his ancestral property by adopting the money lender as son. If he then died without issue, the money lender (or whomever he had adopted to take care of him in his old age) became his heir. The custom has no parallel in later law and is entirely peculiar to the patriarchal period.[55]

The same can be said for the narrative in 15:9-12, 17-18. Speiser shows that the fiery oven and the flaming torch are found in Akkadian texts pertaining to magic, where they are listed in incantations against witches. Their antiquity may be vouched for.[56] "Small wonder, therefore," Speiser observes, "that the description touches on magic and carries with it a feeling of awe and mystery

---

[53] Gn 3:14-19; 9:25-27; 12:1-3; Nm 22-24.

[54] G. von Rad, *The Problem of the Hexateuch and Other Essays*, pp. 125-130.

[55] W. F. Albright, *From Abraham to Ezra*, p. 8.

[56] E. Speiser, *Genesis*, p. 113.

which, thanks to the genius of the narrator, can still grip the reader after all the intervening centuries."[57]

The question of covenant form becomes even more difficult when one considers the Yahwist's account in Gn 2-3. Recent authors speak of Gn 2-3 as reconstructed history—the story namely of "what must have been" (cf. von Rad, Dubarle, Vawter, Renckens, McKenzie). If Gn 2-3 is reconstructed history, one may ask three questions about the material in this reconstruction: 1. What is the origin of the myths upon which the Adam and Eve story is based? 2. What is the origin of the doctrine taught in the story? 3. What is the origin of the form or format according to which the material is presented?

The first and second questions have been adequately discussed in recent years. McKenzie has argued a good case for the Mesopotamian origin of the material upon which Gn 2-3 is based,[58] and Hartman a good case for the Yahwist's knowledge of God, Israel, and Israel's sin in his own time as the source from which he drew the doctrine taught in Gn 2-3.[59]

The third question requires a lengthier answer. Since the Yahwist based his theological conclusions in Gn 2-3 on the history of Israel's relations with God as known from the patriarchal and national history, one may suspect that he reconstructed not only much of his doctrine from Israel's history but also the pattern or form of his narrative as well.

To begin with, the pattern of Gn 2-3 is not unfamiliar. It has four parts: God's goodness, man's revolt, divine punishment, divine forgiveness. The same pattern recurs in the following stories of the primeval history and in the national history as well, especially in Ex 14-16; 32-34; and Nm 10-21 passim. The Yahwist, it appears, has reconstructed the paradise story and the fall of man according to the classical pattern of Salvation History.

In addition to the Salvation History pattern for the story as a whole, the Yahwist would appear to have introduced into the first part of his story another pattern almost as familiar. To ap-

---

[57] *ibid.*, p. 115.

[58] J. L. McKenzie, *Myths and Realities*, pp. 152ff; 176ff.

[59] L. Hartman, "Sin in Paradise," *CBQ*, 20 (1958), pp. 26-40.

preciate this pattern, the reader must look at it with the eyes of an Israelite. What familiar motifs, he must ask, would an Israelite sense in the sequence of events preceding the sin of Adam? First, there is the careful account of what God has done for the man— the benefits he has conferred upon him in creating him, preparing a garden for him, and then taking him from the infertile earth outside and putting him in the garden. There is then the imposition of a single stipulation or command. Finally, there is the promise of blessing (immortality) and the threat of a curse (loss of immortality). Following this first scene comes the story of the fall, which comes about as a result of man's refusal to observe the stipulation, and, consequent upon the fall, the realization of the threat of a curse.

In this first scene, the account of God's goodness to man has the familiar ring of an historical prologue. Taking the man from outside the garden and placing him in a terrain fertile and abundantly watered is a description of the exodus in miniature (through which God 'took' Israel out of Egypt) and also, in miniature, a description of the taking possession of the promised land (a land which, in the words of the scouts sent out by Moses, flows "with milk and honey"). Following this prologue is the single stipulation: ". . . . of the tree of the knowledge of good and evil you are not to eat" and the threat of a curse instead of a blessing in the words "for on the day you eat of it you shall most surely die" (Gn 2:17).

It is to be noted that the Garden is given to Adam not just as a place in which to dwell, but "to cultivate and take care of it." These terms, as A. Schökel points out, are "technical terms used frequently for the service of God and observance of the commandments. They express responsibility, the burden of man faced with the divine initiative. The vocabulary of this verse is thus of great theological weight. God's gifts and his demand reflect the minor or covenant pattern."[60] The description, one might say, has so many overtones of covenant theology that it is not difficult to believe the Yahwist had the covenant pattern in mind and used it for his reconstruction.

---

[60] "Sapiential and Covenant Themes in Gn 2-3," *TD* 13 (1965), p. 7.

Three conclusions emerge from our study of the Yahwist's covenant theology. First, the Yahwist is covenant minded. We find some form of covenant in every section of his saga—a covenant based on the suzerainty treaty form evoked by allusions and overtones in Gn 2-3; a covenant based upon an ancient Mesopotamian form in Gn 15; and a more familiar type of covenant based upon sacrifice and a meal in Ex 24.

Secondly, it cannot be proved from the immediate text of Ex 19-24 that the Yahwist knew any tradition of a covenant based upon the suzerainty treaty form. The broad context of his saga, however, indicates his knowledge of a tradition according to which Israel's relationship with God was expressed by a form based upon the suzerainty treaties. This would appear evident in the veiled allusions to a covenant in Gn 2 and especially in the repetition at regular intervals and at salient points in the saga to the "blessing-curse" motif.[61] Joshua 24 may be cited as evidence of the general antiquity of the form in Israelite tradition.

Thirdly, and most important, the pastoral purpose of the saga as a whole is to inculcate a genuine covenant relationship to God— a relationship which involves an attitude of trust in one who has shown such concern for Israel's good (especially Gn 2-3) and a response of love to be manifested by obedience to the will of him who had chosen her as his own (especially in Gn 22, in the Joseph story, and in the omnipresent pattern of sin, punishment, reconciliation). The Yahwist seems to say to Israel what Our Lord later said to his apostles: "If you love me, keep my commandments." Or, in the words of the preacher in Deuteronomy:

See, today I set before you life and prosperity, death and disaster. If you obey the commandments of Yahweh your God . . . you will live and increase, and Yahweh your God will bless you. . . . But if your heart strays, if you refuse to listen, if you let yourself be drawn into worshipping other gods and serving them, I tell you today, you will most certainly perish. . . . I set before you life or death, blessing or curse. Choose life, then, so that you and your descendants may live, in the love of Yahweh your God, obeying his voice, clinging to him; for in this your life consists . . . (30:15-20).

---

[61] Gn 3; 4; 9:25-27; 12:1-3; 49:1ff; Nm 22-24.

We may conclude by observing that the Yahwist's insistence on covenant theology is directly related to the central theme of his saga—the kingdom of God, founded by God, in Israel, at Sinai, as the vehicle or institution through which the divine plan for the salvation of mankind would eventually be worked out.

That God alone is the true King of Israel and that it is Israel's privilege and duty to do God's will "on earth as it is in heaven" is central to the Yahwist's theology but, in his time and in Israel's history, another factor—a human kingship—was at work. As a theologian the Yahwist was faced with the problem of assessing the place of this new factor not only in Israel's history but in Israel's theology.

SUGGESTED READINGS

W. Eichrodt, *Theology of the Old Testament*, 36ff and passim.

E. Jacob, *Theology of the Old Testament*, 209-217.

D. McCarthy, *Treaty and Covenant*, 152-177.

G. E. Mendenhall, "Covenant Forms in Israelite Times" *BA* (1954), 50-75.

M. Noth, *Exodus*, 151-201; 258-267.

M. Kline, *Treaty of the Great King*.

J. Bright, *A History of Israel*, 203-208.

H. Cazelles, "Connexions et structure de Gen. XV" *RB* 69 (1962) 231-249.

H. B. Huffmon, "The Exodus, Sinai and the Credo" *CBQ* 27 (1965), 101-113.

A. Schökel, "Sapiential and Covenant Themes in Gn 2-3" *TD* 13 (1965), 3-9.

W. Eichrodt, "Covenant and Law" *Interpretation* July 1966, 305-326.

G. von Rad, *Genesis*, 154-156.

————. *The Problem of the Hexateuch and Other Essays*.

M. Newman, *The People of the Covenant*.

A. Weiser, *The Psalms*, 35-51.

R. Clements, *Abraham and David*, 15-22.

W. Beyerlin, *Origins and History of the Oldest Sinaitic Traditions*.

THE MONARCHY

The kingdom of God, in which God is the king and Israel is the kingdom, is central to the Yahwist's saga. Nevertheless another king, the Davidic king, has a part to play in the kingdom.

Allusions to the Davidic dynasty at key points in the saga suggest this. The Yahwist includes a story about Judah, the forefather of David, which concludes with part of the genealogy of David (Gn 38:27-29). He gives the hero's part to Judah in the Joseph story (Gn 37-50). And he goes out of his way to foreshadow the hegemony of Judah in Gn 49:8-12 and the rise of David in Nm 24:17-19.[62]

The apparent emphasis on the choice of the second-born over the firstborn throughout the Yahwist's saga would be an additional indication of the Yahwist's interest in the monarchy if it could be proved that this emphasis was meant as an apologia for David or Solomon.[63] In relation to such an apologia it should be noted that one purpose of the Rise of David History was to establish the legitimacy of David's dynasty. The same can be said for the purpose of the Succession History in relation to Solomon. Also to be noted is the emphasis on a "chosen seed" in Gn 3:15; 12:1-3; 49:8-12; and 2 Sm 7. It is true that these points would not be obvious to modern readers, but to the Yahwist's audience the overtones even of particular words would have been more than audible.[64]

The dynasty of David, therefore, has a role to play in the Yahwist's saga. How much of a role, however, it is not easy to say. Nor is it a simple matter to determine what part the Yahwist expected the dynasty to play in the mission and history of Israel. He was in favor of the dynasty undoubtedly. But whether he saw it as a passing phenomenon or as an institution ordained by

---

[62] There is, of course, no question about it if the Yahwist's saga, as some authors like to think, terminated in 1 or 2 Samuel.

[63] Cf. J. L. McKenzie, "The Theologies of the Old Testament" in *Leblond Lectures*, p. 2f.

[64] The idea has been well expressed by Oliver Wendell Holmes: "A word is not a crystal, transparent and unchanged; it is the skin of a living thought and may vary greatly in color and content according to the circumstances and the time in which it is used."

God to fulfill a definite and important function in the divine plan for the salvation of the world, is difficult to say.

Even if it be admitted that the Yahwist posited an absolute place for the dynasty in the divine plan, it must still be asked how he conceived the function of the kings in the salvific mission of the kingdom of God. It may also be asked to what extent the Yahwist trusted the kings to fulfill this function. One cannot forget his experience of Saul and David, not to mention Solomon.[65] W. Eichrodt puts it this way:

> The monarchy enabled religion to shape the life of the nation and to give visible form to its relation to the one divine Lord. But it likewise brought with it the danger of creating a national particularism which by giving a false primacy to outward forms would obscure the role of service for which the nation existed and thus cripple the universalist forces of religion.[66]

If we are to understand the place of the monarchy in the Yahwist's theology, we must not only ask of the saga the right questions, we must in addition keep in mind two salutary cautions. First, we must restrict ourselves to the theological sources in possession of the Yahwist in the 10th century B.C. We cannot, in other words, presume the theological development which the dynastic oracle of Nathan in 2 Sm 7 underwent in the centuries following David. In the time of the Yahwist, the revelation of a promised perpetuity for the Davidic dynasty was a new datum of belief. It had not been subjected to the glacier-weight and glacier-shaping process of history. The Yahwist had not yet experienced second thoughts about the dynasty like Isaiah nor disillusionment like Jeremiah. The distilled essence of the revelation took form long after his time.

Second, the interpreter must remember that the Yahwist was severely restricted by the very nature of his saga and his saga

---

[65] G. von Rad is very conscious of the tension the Yahwist must have experienced. He says: ". . . the institution of the monarchy was a new comer at this time in Israel. Indeed, it was born out of season. Consequently, it was inevitable that its relationship with the central tradition of faith was strained at the very outset. And right down to the end, the monarchy never succeeded in extricating itself from this strain" (*Theology of the Old Testament*, p. 40).

[66] *Old Testament Theology* I, p. 455.

materials in any attempts to give an adequate theology of the monarchy. His saga dealt with periods of Israel's history long antedating (at least 250 years) the monarchy and the Davidic dynasty. As a consequence, anything he wanted to say about either of these would have to be either literally dragged in and patched on to the saga, as for example the foreshadowing texts were; or it would have to be said by indirection, by contrast, by suggestion, by implication. Since his saga terminated well before the origin of the monarchy and the promise to the dynasty, he would have no other means unless he had used blatantly obvious foreshadowing speeches—a procedure used extensively by the later "D" author, as for example in Dt 17:14-20, but nowhere utilized by the Yahwist, who is content to use shorter and simpler foreshadowing techniques.[67]

With regard to asking the right questions one may begin by asking: if it be granted that the Yahwist attributed to the monarchy and the Davidic dynasty a function in God's salvific plan, did he intend as well to explain, either positively or negatively, the nature of this function. It cannot be denied that the Yahwist may have been stumped by the question, or, if not stumped by the question, may have found it impossible to express his answer by means of the saga. As H. S. Hughes observes:

> The Historian will not call the shots. Yet like other types of scientists he will delimit what is possible, what is probable, and what is almost certain. Most of the time he will do it by indirection, by simply organizing his statement of past events so that they move toward other events that lie in the future. This we call retrospective prediction. For the subsequent series of events does not really lie in the future—the *historian's* future—but merely in the future of the participants in the initial series. Such predictions are by definition accurate: here we recall the historian's privileged position of knowing the outcome. But what happens when the chain of retrospection comes to an end? What is the historian to do when he reaches his own present—when he loses his special knowledge and becomes a blind participant like anyone else, peering into the future as best he may? Does he give up the predictive character of his thought?

---

[67] Vergil brought Rome into the *Aeneid*. Since the setting of the Aeneid is well before 753 B.C., he did it in the only way possible—by the foreshadowing technique.

Does he radically recast the structure of his narrative sentences so as to shut off their built-in motion toward the future? I do not think he does so, and I do not think he ought to do so. He can and does continue just as before. He continues to project his line of analysis into a future that is now actually, rather than merely by literary convention, unknown to him. . . ."[68]

We can begin with the theological basis upon which the Yahwist would have depended for anything he would teach concerning the Davidic dynasty. This is agreed, almost universally, to have been the Nathan Oracle in 2 Sm 7.

The Oracle testified to the theological fact that God had promised perpetuity to the dynasty of David. The acceptance of the Oracle and the credence given to it are testified to by numerous inspired authors down the centuries of Israel's tradition.[69]

That the theological fact was credited even earlier would seem a valid deduction from 2 Sm 23:1-7[70] and from the two documents dealing with David and his dynasty found in 1 Sm 16-31 and 2 Sm 9-20; 1 Kgs 1-2. The dynastic oracle of Nathan would appear to play a very large part in the motivation and theology of both these 10th century documents.

It is reasonable to hold, therefore, that the Yahwist's theological patrimony contained not only the revelations made in patriarchal and Mosaic times but the new revelation made to Israel by Nathan in his oracle dealing with the future of the David dynasty.

We have already seen how the Yahwist organized and integrated into his saga the patriarchal and mosaic revelation. It remains to be seen whether he did the same for the revelation made to David.

Since the Yahwist utilized the devices of promises, genealogies, and foreshadowing texts to organize and integrate his theological presentation in the saga, it is to these devices we should look for his possible integration of the Nathan Oracle with the revelation made to Israel in patriarchal and Mosaic times.

---

[68] *History as Art and as Science*, pp. 87-88.

[69] Pss 89, 132, 2, 72, 110; Is 7-11; Mi 5:1-5; Am 9:11-15; Ho 2:19-24; 1 Chr 17:7-14.

[70] H. W. Hertzberg, *1 & 2 Samuel*, pp. 399ff.

The Yahwist initiates his presentation of the Lord of History's salvific plan with the promise to the woman in Gn 3:15—a promise that is at the same time definite as a promise but vague as to content. He next uses the promise device in the programmatic promise made to Abraham in Gn 12:1-3. He concludes with the promise made to Judah in Gn 49:8-12 and Nm 24:17-19.

What is to be noted is that the Yahwist no place explicitly tells of the fulfillment of these promises. The most he does is to indicate the beginning of the fulfillment of Gn 12:1-3, and by insinuation the earlier promise in Gn 3:15, in the words of Yahweh to Moses in Ex 3:6-10, especially the words: "I am the God of your father, the God of Abraham, the God of Isaac and the God of Jacob. . . . I have seen the miserable state of my people in Egypt. . . . I mean to deliver them out of the hands of the Egyptians and bring them up out of that land to a land rich and broad, a land where milk and honey flow, the home of the Canaanites, the Hittites, the Amorites, the Perizzites, the Hivites and the Jebusites."

One may with some reason believe that the Yahwist and his audience saw an even fuller measure of fulfillment of the "land-promise" in the "great nation" established by David's 10th century conquests. To be noted in relation to the land promise is the fact that, in the promise texts dealing with the land to be given to the great nation which will proceed from the seed of Abraham, the nations and peoples mentioned are generally those who in the early 10th century became subject to Israel through the conquests of David, namely, the Canaanites, Hittites, Amorites, Perizzites, Hivites and Jebusites.[71] The Jebusites are particularly significant since they were the inhabitants of Jerusalem, which fell to Israel only in the time of David. If this inference is valid, one may speak of integration of the promise made to David in 2 Sm 7 with the earlier promises made to Judah, to Abraham, and perhaps even to the woman of Gn 3:15.

In relation to the Yahwist's genealogical device, it has already been seen that he used this device as an elimination-of-peoples-process which terminated in the election of Israel alone among

[71] Cf. G. von Rad, *The Problem of the Hexateuch*, pp. 72-74.

all the nations of the earth (see pp. 131-136). By this device the Yahwist moves unerringly from Adam to Seth to Noah to Sem to Abraham to Isaac to Jacob (Israel). The question may be asked whether the Yahwist discarded his genealogical device with the arrival on the scene of the twelve tribes of Israel. Three pericopes from his saga indicate he did not, and, two of these indicate he continued to use the device but this time to single out the family of David.

l,   The first of these is the story of Judah and Tamar in Gn 38, a story which terminates with the descendants of Judah by Tamar. From Tamar are born Perez and Zerah (Gn 38:27-29). Other sources testify that David was descended from the line of Perez.[72] What is significant about the pericope is its formal similarity with the other genealogical narratives, and in particular with the account of the births of Esau and Jacob in Gn 25:20-26. In each case the mother is barren (though for different reasons); twins are born, but the second is preferred to the first. Thus in Gn 38 when the time of Tamar's delivery comes, Zerah puts forth his hand but then withdraws to allow Perez to enter the world first (vv 28-29). The pattern established earlier in the accounts of the births of Ishmael and Isaac, Esau and Jacob, whereby God's choice of the second rather than the firstborn is made manifest, is thus repeated—this time in a line that points directly to David.

2   The second example of the Yahwist's use of the genealogical device following the arrival of the twelve tribes of Israel on the scene is found in Gn 48:8-20. It follows the same general pattern of the second son preferred to the first (vv 12-14), but this time terminates in Ephraim and Manasseh, the sons of Joseph, and is, therefore, inconclusive in any argumentation in favor of the Davidic dynasty.

3   The third example follows the pattern only in a wide sense, but it does follow the pattern. In Gn 49:1ff, an eleventh century poetic work which has been redacted by the Yahwist and into which he has interpolated some or all of what is contained in vv 8-12, the first three sons of Jacob are, as it were, eliminated and the blessing promise of the patriarch falls upon the fourth-born Judah to whom is promised royal power.

[72] Cf. Ruth 4:18ff; Nm 26:21; 1 Chr 2:3ff.

It should be noted that the arrangement of the genealogies, if not throughout, at least in Gn 29:31—30:24 and in Gn 49, gives every indication of being the work of the Yahwist himself rather than an arrangement he had received from tradition.

One gathers this from the marked difference between the Yahwist's arrangement (Reuben, Simeon, Levi, Judah, etc., as in Gn 49) and the arrangements in Dt 33 (Reuben, Judah, Levi, Benjamin, etc.); in Nm 26 (Reuben, Simeon, Gad, Judah, Issachar, etc.); and perhaps also Jgs 5, where the canticle of Deborah (which is, however, incomplete with regard to the roster of tribes and, therefore, not trustworthy as a source for comparisons) cites the tribes in the following order: Ephraim, Benjamin, Machir, Zebulun, Issachar, Reuben, Gilead, Dan, Asher, Zebulun, Naphtali.

The Yahwist's incorporation of stories about Reuben (Gn 35:22), Simeon and Levi (Gn 34:29) lays the ground for the rejection of these tribes and would seem preparatory to his arrangement in Gn 49.

The inference drawn from these texts is surely not foolproof. But one may at least suspect from the pattern of Gn 38:27-29 and Gn 49:8-12 that the Yahwist has used his genealogical device not only to single out Israel from the nations but to single out Judah and David from the tribes and clans of Israel. Since the Yahwist in Gn 11-12 links the scattering of the nations with the call of Abraham and the nation that was to come from him, one may with reason conjecture that the mission of the chosen nation and the mission of the chosen dynasty in some way coincide. One might even wonder if the Yahwist did not in this way intend to subtly instruct the king of his day on the principal duty of a Davidic king.

The third device used by the Yahwist to integrate and organize his theological presentation is the foreshadowing technique (see pp. 123-127). Of the several series of foreshadowing texts, the Edom series (Gn 25:23; 27:29, 40; Nm 24:17) is significant for two reasons. First, it leads directly to the time of David and Solomon and highlights the idea of conquest and domination, a theme adumbrated in Gn 3:15 and emphasized in a more general way in Gn 49:8-12 and Nm 24:17-19. Second, the Edom series indicates that the rise of David entered the mind of the Yahwist in the composition of his saga at least as early as the patriarchal history.

Whether the rise of David entered the Yahwist's mind even earlier in the composition of his saga and whether he integrated his theology of the Davidic dynasty with his primeval history depends upon how one interprets the series of foreshadowing texts which begins with Gn 3:15 and runs through Gn 9:26-27; 12:1-3 (cf. also 26:3-4; 27:29; 28:14-15); 49:8-12 and Nm 24:17-19. If it can be proved that these texts constitute a genuine series, then one may legitimately conclude that the Yahwist has indeed integrated the revelation made to David not only with the theology of the patriarchal and national periods of Israel's history but with his reconstruction of the primeval history and the salvific plan outlined in Gn 2-12.

Gn 3:15 has long resisted any kind of satisfying interpretation. If it can be shown to be the first in a series of foreshadowing texts which concludes with Gn 49:8-12 and Nm 24:17-19, then, on the basis of the last characteristic of foreshadowing texts, namely, that foreshadowing usually proceeds from obscure to clear and from the general to the specific, its obscure terms can be interpreted in the light of these clearer, later texts in the series (see p. 123).

Since the Gn 49 text which speaks of "The sceptre shall not pass from Judah," and the Nm 24 text, which speaks of an Israelite king who will conquer Edom, are generally interpreted as referring to the rise of the Davidic dynasty and Israel's conquest of Canaan, there is a distinct possibility that the obscure foreshadowing in Gn 3:15 is to be interpreted as referring to the conquest of Canaan by Israel under the Davidic dynasty or, to be more in line with the theological thought of the Yahwist, the conquest of the forces of anti-God—represented by the false religion of Canaan in the time of the Yahwist—by the hand of Israel and her divinely established Davidic dynasty.

In brief we may say that the meaning of the terms in Gn 3:15, though purposely vague at the beginning of the saga so as not to destroy the element of suspense, is nevertheless clear to the 10th century audience of the Yahwist. For that audience, the serpent would be a symbol representing the false religion of the Canaanites.[73] The seed of the serpent would represent the devotees of the fertility cults. The seed of the woman would represent the people of God in general and the Davidic dynasty in particular since it is through these that God intends to destroy false religion and bring to fulfillment his plan for the salvation of the world.

Without elaborating on the interpretation of the individual terms of Gn 3:15, it will be sufficient to demonstrate that Gn 3:15 is truly a foreshadowing text in the series that ends with Gn 49 and Nm 24. If this can be proved, its interpretation can be based with some probability on these later more explicit foreshadowing texts in the same series. To demonstrate that Gn 3:15 is truly a foreshadowing text, it will be necessary to show that it has all or most of the characteristics found in those other texts which are more obviously and certainly foreshadowing texts, namely, the Exodus and Edom texts.

The first of these characteristics—the recurrence of the foreshadowing texts after the manner of a refrain—depends on demonstrating that Gn 3:15 is truly a foreshadowing text. We shall not begin by begging the question.

The second characteristic—the placing of foreshadowing texts in the mouth of God or some important individual—is true of Gn 3:15. The whole foreshadowing text, which runs from 3:14 to 3:19 is placed by the Yahwist in the mouth of God.

The third characteristic of foreshadowing texts is verified in Gn 3:15 inasmuch as its basic ideas—curse of the serpent, enmities between descendants of the serpent and descendants of the woman, and even some of its key words (curse and seed or their equivalents)—recur in later foreshadowing texts in the same series.[74]

Thus in Gn 9:25-27, the key word "curse" recurs and significantly in direct relation to Canaan, the seed of the serpent. In Noah's words to his son, Ham, it is Canaan, like the serpent in Gn 3:14, who is cursed: "Accursed be Canaan. He shall be his broth-

---

[73] A number of fine articles have been published on the symbolism in the paradise story. Among the best: L. Hartman, "Sin in Paradise," *CBQ* 20 (1958); C. Stuhlmueller, "The Mother of Emmanuel," *Marian Studies* 12 (1961), pp. 165-204; S. Rowe, "An Exegetical Approach to Gn 3:15," *Marian Studies* 12 (1961), pp. 49-79; B. Rigaux, "La Femme et son lignage dans Genèse III, 14-15," *RB* 61 (1954), pp. 329-345 (Engl. trans. in *Theology Digest* 6, 1958).

[74] Cf. Léon-Dufour, *Vocabulaire de Théologie Biblique*, p. 571, "Malédiction."

ers' meanest slave." Also significant in Gn 9:26 is the subjection of Canaan to Shem, from whom proceed Abraham, Isaac, Jacob, Judah, and eventually David. The text, like Gn 3:15, speaks of a subjection of the seed of the serpent: "Blessed by Yahweh, God of Shem, let Canaan be his slave!"

The narrative of Genesis continues in the patriarchal history with *blessings* on the righteous line of Shem and *curses* on the evil line of Canaan.[75] As a consequence it is not insignificant that in the following foreshadowing text in the series, namely Gn 12:1-3, God says to Abraham: "I will bless those who bless you: I will curse those who slight you." Nor is it insignificant in Nm 22-24 that the point of the Balaam story is precisely that Balaam cannot *curse* Israel, but must on the contrary *bless* her.[76]

The other key word in Gn 3:14ff is the word "seed." From Gn 4 down to Gn 49:8-12, the storyteller concentrates on those descendants of the woman who will be the *blessed* and chosen seed: namely, the line of descendants that runs through Seth, Noah, Shem, Abraham, Isaac, Jacob, Judah to David. In the foreshadowing text in Gn 12:2 the blessing of Abraham consists in making a great nation from the *seed* of the renowned patriarch. In Gn 49:8-12 the blessing of Judah consists in the promise of a king who will spring from the seed of Judah, who himself has descended from the seed of Jacob, Isaac, and Abraham.

The fourth characteristic—the tendency of foreshadowing texts to give the general outline or direction that the story will take—is likewise verified in Gn 3:15. When the storyteller speaks of the "seed of the woman," his audience naturally asks who is this seed? In the rest of Genesis the Yahwist goes about identifying the seed of the woman. Step by step he eliminates the different nations born from the first woman. Of all the descendants of Eve, only the line that begins with Seth and runs through Noah, Shem, Abraham, Isaac and Jacob to terminate in Judah and his royal offspring

---

[75] H. W. Wolff, "The Kerygma of the Yahwist," *Interpretation* 20 (1966), pp. 139-155 finds the basic kerygma of the Yahwist precisely in the blessing motif, first enunciated in Gn 12:3b and thereafter repeated regularly both in relation to Abraham's descendants and in relation to the nations for whom Abraham's descendants are a source of divine blessing.

[76] On Balaam's curse, cf. C. Westermann, *Basic Forms of Prophetic Speech*, p. 194.

is followed from beginning to end. Thus, the whole elimination-of-peoples-process used by the storyteller is foreshadowed in the opposition between the seed of the woman and the seed of the serpent.

When the storyteller speaks about "enmities" between the seed of the woman and the seed of the serpent, his audience quite naturally asks who is the seed of the serpent and why the enmities? To answer this question the storyteller throughout Genesis and Numbers continually reminds his audience of the iniquities of the Canaanites and of the duty of the chosen seed of the woman to avoid and oppose the Canaanites.

Thus, the first murderer is Cain. Like the Canaanites who were predominantly an agricultural people, Cain is a tiller of the soil. Like the serpent cursed by God in 3:14, Cain too is cursed (4:11). Cain's victim, on the other hand, is Abel, a herdsman like the Israelites. Noah plants a vineyard and, like the Canaanites, one of whose many vices was drunkenness, gets drunk. When he is drunk and naked in his tent, only Ham looks upon his father in his drunken nakedness. For this Canaanitish lack of decency, Ham's son, Canaan, not Ham himself, is cursed—and significantly in terms that re-echo the curse of the serpent in Gn 3:14 and the curse of Cain in Gn 4:11.

In the patriarchal history Abraham cannot find ten good men in Sodom and Gomorrah. For their crimes, which the author indicates are the unnatural sexual vices the Canaanites had made a part of their fertility rites, the five plain cities are wiped off the map (Gn 19). The Yahwist, moreover, goes on to complacently recount the incestuous origin of the Moabites and Ammonites (Gn 19:30-38) and selects a number of stories from the patriarchal traditions to show the patriarchal repugnance for the intermarriage of the chosen seed with the depraved Canaanite women (Gn 24:3; 27:46; 28:1).

Finally, when the storyteller predicts that the seed of the woman will crush the head of the serpent, the audience again quite naturally asks who is this seed of the woman who will conquer the seed of the serpent?[77]

---

[77] The meaning of the verb *suph* in Gn 3:15 is disputed. Later texts in the same series substantiate the opinion of those who see in the head-heel contrast a fore-

The storyteller answers this question by eliminating from the seed of the first woman all except that elect line of blessed descendants which begins with Seth, runs through Noah, Shem, and Abraham and terminates with the royal, conquering seed of Judah in Gn 49:8-12 and Nm 24:17. The audience, if it is following the foreshadowing and the story that flows from it, must conclude that it is the seed of Judah, the dynasty of David, which will, according to God's will and plan, conquer the seed of the serpent and recover for mankind that blessed communion with God which was man's glory before the fall.

A reading of the following texts, the majority foreshadowing texts with a few additional texts taken from Yahwistic soliloquies and dialogues, will indicate the tight thread of continuity in the saga and the value of the foreshadowing technique in effecting unity in the overall story. Key words or their equivalents are italicized.

> Because you have done this, be *accursed* beyond all cattle . . . I will make you *enemies* of each other: . . . *your offspring and her offspring*. It will *crush* your head and you will strike its heel (Gn 3:14f).

> Now be *accursed* (Cain) and driven from the ground that has opened its mouth to receive your brother's blood at your hands (Gn 4:11).

> Yahweh smelt the appeasing fragrance and said to himself, 'Never again will I *curse* the earth because of man . . .' (Gn 8:21).

> *Accursed* be *Canaan*. He shall be his brothers' meanest *slave*. . . . *Blessed* be Yahweh, God of *Shem*, let *Canaan* be his *slave!* May God extend Japheth, may he live in the tents of Shem, and may *Canaan* be his *slave!* (Gn 9:25-27).

> . . . I will make you (*seed*) a great nation; I will *bless* you and make your name so famous . . . I will *bless* those who bless you; I will

shadowing of the woman's seed conquering the seed of the serpent (see Rowe, *op. cit.*, 65-66). The verb *suph* is found only in two other places: Job 9:17; Ps 139:11. One may note in passing the similarity of the basic notion in Gn 3:15 with the common symbolic description of conquest by the foot upon the head as in Ps 110:1; Jos 10:24-25. If this interpretation is correct then Gn 3:15 would be only an obscure expression of what is clearly said in Ps 110:1: ". . . I will make your enemies a footstool for you."

curse those who slight you . . . (Gn 12:2ff and cf. repetition of blessing on Isaac and Jacob in 26:3-4; 27:29; 28:14-15, and the curse-
blessing motif in the Balaam story).

Judah, your brothers shall praise you: you grip your *enemies by the
neck* . . . *like a lion he crouches and lies down, or a lioness: who
dare rouse him?* The *sceptre* shall not pass from Judah . . . (Gn
49:8ff).

How fair are your tents, O Jacob! . . . His *king* is greater than Agag,
his *majesty* is exalted. . . . *He has crouched,* he has lain down, *like
a lion, like a lioness; who dare rouse him?* Blessed be those who
bless you, and accursed be those who *curse* you! (Nm 24:5ff and
cf. Gn 12:3; Gn 49:8ff).

I see him—but not in the present . . . : a *star* from Jacob takes the
leadership, a *sceptre* arises from Israel (cf. Gn 49:10). It crushes
the brows of Moab . . . Edom (cf. Edom foreshadowing texts) becomes a conquered land; a conquered land is Seir. Israel exerts his
strength, Jacob *dominates his enemies* . . . (Nm 24:17-19; and cf.
Gn 3:15; also Nm 23:25-26 and Gn 12:3 in relation to the curse-
blessing motif).

Some confirmation of this hypothesis may be found in the con-
vergence of ideas first enunciated in Gn 3:15, namely, the idea of
"conquest" and the idea of a determined "seed" of the "mother of
all the living" which will crush the head of the serpent.

The identification of the "seed" is followed out in the elimination-of-peoples-process by means of the Yahwist's genealogical
device and certainly terminates in the nation Israel. It is not unlikely, as suggested earlier, that the Yahwist goes one step further
in his use of the genealogical device by using it to point to David
in the Judah-Tamar genealogy (Gn 38:27-29) and in the blessing-
promise made to Judah (Gn 49:8-12). If this deduction is valid,
the Yahwist has gone one step further in his identification of the
seed of the woman by identifying it with the Davidic dynasty.

The other idea first enunciated in Gn 3:15, the idea of "conquest," is pursued in a twofold manner. First, the author shows by
his foreshadowing texts that certain nations will be subject to the
nation, Israel. This is particularly true of Canaan (Gn 9:25-27)
and Edom (Gn 25:23; 27:29, 40). But later on the Yahwist clearly
foreshadows the conquest of Edom by David, not only in Gn

27:40, but also in Nm 24:17-19, where Edom is expressly named as one of the nations which will be crushed by the "star" that rises from Israel.

It may be objected that the "conquest" implied in Gn 3:15 is a spiritual conquest (the reversal of the spiritual fall of man brought about by the serpent) as suggested earlier (see p. 178) and the conquest of Canaan and Edom is physical. But one must remember that throughout the saga the attitude of the Yahwist toward the Canaanites is ambivalent. In the foreshadowing texts he appears to be speaking only about the physical conquest of Canaan. Other texts which witness to his polemic against Canaan's fertility cult indicate that "conquest" to the Yahwist meant not only victories in the wars against the Canaanites in the time of David but victory in *the* war against the false religion of the Canaanites.

If it be granted that the Yahwist did indeed integrate the Nathan oracle with the revelation made to Israel in Patriarchal and Mosaic times and attributed to the Davidic dynasty a function in God's salvific plan, there still remains the vexing question of what this function entailed and how the Yahwist expressed and inculcated it.

Admittedly, it is difficult to determine the Yahwist's mind on the function of the monarchy and the Davidic dynasty in Israel and in the kingdom of God on earth. It is, to begin with, not even certain that he intended to express himself on the subject. As mentioned earlier, whatever the Yahwist had to say on the subject would have had to be expressed by indirection for the most part.

We may begin then by pointing to the Yahwist's ambivalent expressions dealing with the idea of "conquest." Since the Yahwist has made reasonably clear his attitude toward the Canaanite fertility cult religion as the real enemy of God, man, and the kingdom of God, might not his audience (and the king) see the function of the dynasty in the carrying out of the plan of salvation to consist primarily in the waging of this spiritual warfare against the forces of anti-God?

Also to be considered is the Yahwist's anti-Canaanite animus which runs throughout his primeval history and patriarchal history and is put into programmatic form in Ex 23:23-26 and 34:11-17. M. Noth considers the material a Deuteronomic interpolation (compare Dt 7:1-6) and he is probably correct.[78] On the other hand, the Deuteronomic tradition is later and there is no good reason why in its earliest form such a text would not have come from the Yahwist. The theological content, if not the phraseology, is typically Yahwistic. It is not difficult to imagine the Yahwist proposing the following program not only to the Israelites but to their kings as well:

> Mark, then, what I command you today. I mean to drive out the Amorites before you, the Canaanites, the Hittites, the Perizzites, the Hivites, the Jebusites. Take care you make no pact with the inhabitants of the land you are about to enter, or this will prove a pitfall at your very feet. You are to tear down their altars, smash their standing-stones, cut down their sacred poles. You shall bow down to no other god, for Yahweh's name is the Jealous One; he is a jealous God. Make no pact with the inhabitants of the land or, when they prostitute themselves to their own gods and sacrifice to them, they may invite you and you may consent to eat from their victim; or else you may choose wives for your sons from among their daughters and these, prostituting themselves to their own gods, may induce your sons to do the same (Ex 34:11-16).

Again, some significance may be attached to the imbalance in the amount of space allotted by the Yahwist to the national history (approximately 500 verses) in comparison to the amount of space allotted to the patriarchal history (approximately 800 verses).[79] Might this not be an indirect way of pointing to the function of the Davidic dynasty by insinuating that the true heroes of Yahwism are men like Abraham who "put his faith in Yahweh, who counted this as making him justified" (Gn 15:6) and who allowed himself to be guided by God to the fulfillment of his plan for the salvation of mankind?

One might further ask if the Yahwist did not designedly emphasize the faith of the patriarchs as a lesson for the kings, whose principal function would be to testify to Israel's faith in the divine promises and the divine plan for Israel. Indeed, one is tempted

---

[78] *Exodus*, p. 262.

[79] See p. 34. See also H. W. Wolff, "The Kerygma of the Yahwist," *Interpretation* 20 (1966), p. 147. The patriarchal tradition, therefore, appears to have been enlarged because in it the meaning of Gn 12:3b is carried out basically.

to believe that when the Yahwist composed the divine soliloquy of Gn 18:17-19, he was interpreting God's will not only for Abraham and his descendants in general but for the kings especially:

> Shall I conceal from Abraham what I am going to do, seeing that Abraham will become a great nation with all the nations of the earth blessing themselves by him? For I have singled him out to command his sons and his household after him to maintain the way of Yahweh by just and upright living. In this way Yahweh will carry out for Abraham what he has promised him.

Lastly, one may wonder if the Yahwist's portrayal of Moses and the patriarchs in "charismatic" rather than "royal" colors is not meant to remind the kings that God alone is true king of Israel and that men, however great their power, are nothing more than his charismatic instruments. The burden of the Rise of David History, which was to show that David was indeed the charismatic elect of Yahweh, would here be reflected in the Yahwist's theology.[80]

SUGGESTED READINGS

B. Anderson, *Understanding the Old Testament*, 160-187.
H. W. Hertzberg, *1 & 2 Samuel*, 130-134.
J. Gray, *1 & 2 Kings*, 20-27.
E. Jacob, *Theology of the Old Testament*, 234-239.
G. von Rad, *Old Testament Theology*, 36-68.
J. L. McKenzie, *Myths and Realities*, 203-250.
―――. "Theologies of the Old Testament" in *Leblond Lectures*, 1-8.
J. Bright, *A History of Israel*, 164-208.
S. Mowinckel, *He That Cometh*, 21ff.
W. Eichrodt, *Theology of the Old Testament*, 47ff; 436-458.
R. de Vaux, *Ancient Israel*, 91-114.
P. J. Calderone, *Dynastic Oracle and Suzerainty Treaty*.
W. Brueggermann, "David and His Theologian," *CBQ* 30 (1968), 156-181.

---

[80] On the Yahwist's possible concept of the king in Israel's future, cf. M. Buber, *The Prophetic Faith*, pp. 151-154.

UNIVERSALISM

The unsympathetic reader may well find scandalous the Yahwist's confident avowal of his nation's election by God. The idea of a "chosen people" warms no one's heart, for it implies, and rightfully, that no other nation has been chosen in the same way as Israel. Even though this does not imply the rejection of the "unchosen" (see p. 154), the scandal remains. And its full import can only be appreciated when the reader has fully convinced himself that the Yahwist is truly a universalist. A relative universalism, if we may use the term, would considerably reduce the scandal. If the Yahwist, in other words, was only thinking of the middle eastern nations he was acquainted with, one might, with an understanding toleration of national pride, excuse him. He would not be the first to be carried away by an excess of enthusiasm for an empire builder like David, nor the last to think that history had reached its zenith in his nation and in his nation's influence upon the world.[81]

It is a different matter entirely if the Yahwist was a true universalist. If he was indeed thinking of all mankind from the beginning down to his own time and into the future, then his idea of election must be either the arrogance of a rampant nationalist, the effrontery of a small intellect, or the magnificent deduction of a truly great inspired theologian.

On the one hand, one cannot discount megalomania without discounting the lessons of history and, on the other, one cannot ignore reality without asking how an insignificant individual in a third-rate "empire" of the Middle East, living at least two centuries before the realization of the Assyrian Empire, four centuries before the advent of the Neo-Babylonian empire of Nebuchadnezzar, and six centuries before the empire of Alexander, could have

---

[81] That David's empire-building was the catalyst for the Yahwist's theologizing in a universalist vein has not without good reason been suggested by Otto Eissfeldt: "The creation of a large and powerful united Israelite empire as it was achieved by David must have produced an atmosphere of national exaltation, which was very congenial to the composition of historical works. . . . Thus it is a natural assumption, and one that has often been made, that it was David's deeds or the recollection of them which first led a particular individual to set out a presentation of Israel's history linking it with the history of humanity" (*The Old Testament: an Introduction*, p. 140).

the effrontery to claim that God had chosen his nation—and his nation alone—to be the vehicle for the salvation-happiness of all mankind.[82]

It is necessary, therefore, to be reasonably clear about the nature of the Yahwist's universalism. Was it absolute or relative? If absolute, what led the Yahwist to such a conception? Was it his own proper deduction from Israel's deposit of revelation, or had some earlier theologian received it by revelation or deduced it prior to him?

It is customary to base the Yahwist's absolute universalism on such texts as Gn 12:3; 22:18; 26:4 and 28:14. All of these, however, are simply repetitions of God's promise in Gn 12:3, which is the primary text: "all the tribes of the earth shall bless themselves by you." As J. Chaine, G. von Rad, and E. Speiser have pointed out, the Hebrew verb form for "bless" can be translated "shall bless themselves." The consequent translation is obviously susceptible of the meaning that Israel will be so bountifully blessed that when nations seek for a blessing or invoke a blessing on others they will say: "May we (or you) be blessed as was the seed of Abraham." In such a translation absolute universalism is reasonably doubtful.[83]

What is doubtful, however, in the immediate text can be clarified by the broader context of the saga and especially by the evident intent of the primeval history. The Yahwist makes it more than clear in Gn 2-11 that his interests are both religious and universal. He is talking about all men, about mankind as a whole. The

---

[82] The great development in universalist thinking in the prophets Isaiah and Micah inclines some authors to date the origin of true religious universalism to the reign of King Hezekiah (715-689). See Y. Kaufman, *The Religion of Israel*, pp. 386-395; H. Renckens, *Israel's Concept of the Beginning*, pp. 135-155.

[83] Speiser's note on Gn 12:3 runs as follows: "The Heb. form is often translated 'shall be blessed,' inasmuch as it is Niphal, which is generally, though not always, passive. There are however, parallel passages with the Hithpael (see xxii 18, xxvi 4), a form that can be reflexive or reciprocal, but not passive. What the clause means, therefore, is that the nations of the world will point to Abraham as their ideal, either in blessing themselves (Dr.), or one another (Ehrl.). The passive, on the other hand, would imply that the privileges to be enjoyed by Abraham and his descendants shall be extended to other nations. The distinction may be slight on the surface, yet it is of great consequence theologically. Nor may one disregard the evidence from linguistic usage" (*Genesis*, p. 86). J. Chaine agrees with this translation (*Le Livre de la Genèse*, p. 181) as does G. von Rad (*Genesis*, pp. 155f), though without denying to the text a true universalist import.

universality of his outlook is made clear in a number of ways. To begin with, the woman is said to be ". . . the mother of all those who live" (Gn 3:20). After the flood the Yahwist says of Noah and his sons: "These three were Noah's sons, and from these the whole earth was peopled" (Gn 9:19). Finally, in the Tower of Babel story, the immediate link with the Abraham story and the Abraham promise in 12:1-3, the Yahwist's language is again manifestly universalist: "Throughout the earth men spoke the same language, with the same vocabulary. . . . It was named Babel therefore, because there Yahweh confused the language of the whole earth. It was from there that Yahweh scattered them over the whole face of the earth" (Gn 11:1, 9).

It may be objected that these universalist elements were part and parcel of the Mesopotamian myths used by the Yahwist and represent, as a consequence, nothing more than the timeless and limitless view of the ancient mythmakers.

The objection would be well taken if the Yahwist had done nothing more than let the myths speak for themselves. However, he has not done this. He has gone out of his way to emphasize the universalist element. This is evident, though perhaps not persuasively so, in the theological comment already quoted in Gn 3:20: "The man named his wife 'Eve' because she was the mother of all those who live." It would seem more than clear in the other theological comments of the Yahwist and particularly in his divine soliloquies, e.g.:

Yahweh said, 'My spirit must not forever be disgraced in man, for he is but flesh; his life shall last no more than a hundred and twenty years' (Gn 6:3).

Yahweh saw that the wickedness of man was great on the earth, and that the thoughts in his heart fashioned nothing but wickedness all day long. Yahweh regretted having made man on the earth, and his heart grieved. 'I will rid the earth's face of man, my own creation,' Yahweh said 'and of animals also, reptiles too, and the birds of heaven; for I regret having made them' (Gn 6:5-8).

Yahweh smelt the appeasing fragrance and said to himself, 'Never again will I curse the earth because of man, because his heart contrives evil from his infancy. Never again will I strike down every living thing as I have done. As long as earth lasts, sowing and reaping, cold and heat, summer and winter, day and night shall cease no more' (Gn 8:21-22).

'So they are all a single people with a single language!' said Yahweh. 'This is but the start of their undertakings! There will be nothing too hard for them to do. Come, let us go down and confuse their language on the spot so that they can no longer understand one another' (Gn 11:6-7).

The universalist element in these theological formulations of the Yahwist is so striking that it is difficult to explain except as the product of a truly enlightened theological mind. It must be recognized, too, that however one translates Gn 12:3 and its companion texts (18:17-19; 22:18; 26:4 and 28:14) the ideological background against which they are to be understood is the universalism of Gn 2-11.[84]

The same can be said for such other texts of dubious universalist import as Gn 18:25 and 49:10. In the light of the primeval history and its link with the promise to Abraham in Gn 12:1-3, these texts can no longer be interpreted as simply applicable to the surrounding nations in the time of Abraham and David. The Yahwist's horizons are unlimited. W. Zimmerli has expressed it well:

> Beyond the promise of the land and increasing posterity, there is promised, in the coming history of Israel, a fulfillment of blessing thoroughly capable of constituting a universal counter-history to the world-wide history of curse related in Gn 3-11 (J). The old patriarchal history, which looked forward to fulfillment in the Conquest, is thereby placed in the tension of a much farther-looking expectation of fulfillment. For Abraham's posterity finally to become a people and to possess the land of Canaan—this alone would not mean the full realization of the promise. The program of the Yahwist is here greater than the fulfillment about which he himself will later tell. Beyond his account of fulfillment, promise yet unredeemed will remain open.[85]

Added support for the Yahwist's absolute universalism is supplied by his genealogies. They manifestly include all the descend-

---

[84] See G. von Rad, *Genesis*, pp. 155f. Also M. Noth: "The Yahwistic narrative conceives the history of Israel as part of a universal divine purpose for the blessing of humanity" (*The History of Israel*, p. 138).

[85] W. Zimmerli, "Promise and Fulfillment," in *Essays on Old Testament Hermeneutics*, p. 93.

ants of the mother of all the living and so insistent are they in identifying the nations of mankind that any reference to the nations in the Yahwist's saga must be understood against the background of the genealogies. By themselves, the genealogies testify to the universalism of the Yahwist.

Finally, it is not without reason that in view of such a universalist outlook, the Yahwist's most universalist statement of all—the promise to the woman in Gn 3:15 that her seed (mankind) would conquer the serpent—has been looked upon down the centuries as a proto-evangelium announcing the ultimate salvation of all mankind. The election of Israel as a consequence must be seen against this most universal of all promises. And it is against this background that much of the radical scandal of election in the Yahwist's saga is significantly mitigated. For Israel, as the "D" author will insist and as the prophets will confirm, is not alone in God's plan. God's plan is for all mankind. Israel is the first of many.[86]

The full implications of election in relation to all mankind are brought out for the first time in the Epistles of St. Paul, particularly in Romans and Ephesians. An earlier theology of election against a universalist background was developed by Deutero-Isaiah during Israel's Babylonian exile. Its dependence upon the theology of first Isaiah, Micah, and the Yahwist would seem obvious.

Whether the Yahwist was the earliest theologian in Israel to look beyond the promises to the nation to promises that involved the totality of mankind is difficult to determine. It would seem from the fact that the universalist elements in the saga—the primeval history as a whole and the foreshadowing texts which elaborate the revelation made to the Patriarchs—come from the pen of the Yahwist that the universalist element in itself was not necessarily original to the patriarchal revelation and tradition but was retrojected by the Yahwist either from later revelation or as a result of his own inspired theologizing.[87]

---

[86] See H. H. Rowley, *The Biblical Doctrine of Election*, pp. 63-68.

[87] G. von Rad, *Genesis*, p. 23, says: "The promise in Gn 12:1ff contains three promises of blessing: (1) Abraham will be blessed and become a great nation, (2) Yahweh will give the land to Abraham's seed (v 7), (3) in Abraham all nations of

Whether the Yahwist was the first to see the universal implications of the revelation made to the patriarchs and the revelation made to Moses at the time of the exodus and the Sinai pact is difficult to say. Universalism could have been present, however implicitly, at least as early as the patriarchs and certainly by the time of the Mosaic revelations. In order to date with any certitude the origin of universalist thought in Israel one would have to establish and evaluate earlier sources untouched by the Yahwist. These earlier sources exist, namely, the patriarchal traditions in general, the canticles of Miriam (Ex 15) and Deborah (Jgs 5), the covenant renewal text of Joshua 24, and perhaps the cultic credos of Dt 6:20-25 and 26:5-9. Unambiguous universalism, however, cannot be found in any of these. Until a better case for universalism can be made in these earlier sources, the palm must go to the Yahwist.

How the Yahwist arrived at such a stupendous insight as the universality of God's plan for mankind can be neither deduced a priori nor demonstrated a posteriori. The workings of a theologian's mind are antecedent to his theology, and the assistance of inspiration, for all that it gives a guarantee to the truth of his conclusions, does not in any way clarify the means by which he arrived at them.

The Yahwist nowhere tells us he received this insight as a direct revelation. One might conclude, therefore, barring an earlier direct revelation to either the patriarchs or Moses, that the Yahwist deduced his universalism from those elements of revelation which were already part of Israel's deposit of faith and from which, given the occasion, a theologian could theologize to such further conclusions as those under consideration.

These elements would be, unless we are much mistaken, the nature of God as God of love and Lord of History, the salvation history interventions of God in Israel's history from the time of the patriarchs down through the period of the exodus and up to the time of the promise to the Davidic dynasty, and the already

---

the earth will be blessed (v 3). The first two promises were already known to the Yahwist from the tradition of the patriarchal sagas, the third, however, obviously arose from none of the older traditions but directly from the authority of his prophetic inspiration . . ." See also, H. W. Wolff, "The Kerygma of the Yahwist," *Interpretation* 20 (1966), pp. 137-147.

mentioned scandal implicit in the election of one nation by a God of love who is creator of all men and Lord of all history.

Living in the great days of Solomon and faced with the puzzle of Israel's destiny, the Yahwist may well have meditated upon his nation's religious heritage and deduced with the assistance of inspiration that Israel's destiny lay not in power politics but in bringing to all nations what God had already so graciously given to her.[88]

SUGGESTED READINGS

Y. Kaufman, *The Religion of Israel*, 386-395.
E. Lewy, *The Growth of the Pentateuch*, 201ff.
G. von Rad, *Genesis*, 148ff.
W. Harrelson, "Blessing" in *The Interpreter's Dictionary of the Bible* I, 446ff.
J. Chaine, *Le Livre de la Genèse*, 181ff.

---

[88] See G. von Rad, *The Problem of the Hexateuch*, p. 66, "(The Yahwist) proclaims, in a manner which is neither rationally justifiable nor yet capable of detailed explanation, that the ultimate purpose of the redemption which God will bring about in Israel is that of bridging the gulf between God and the entire human race."

BIBLIOGRAPHY

The literature on biblical theology is immense and the titles selected here represent for the most part works found valuable by the author. For a more comprehensive bibliography the reader is urged to consult R. C. Dentan's *Preface to Old Testament Theology*, pp. 127-144. Titles available in paperback are indicated by PB. Works referred to in the footnotes and in the suggested readings appended to each chapter are here given in alphabetical order and with full bibliographical particulars.

Ackroyd, P. R., "Recent Biblical Theologies: VII. G.A.F. Knight's 'A Christian Theology of the Old Testament,'" *Expository Times* 73 (1962).

Actemeier, P. J. and E., *The Old Testament Roots of our Faith* (Nashville: Abingdon, 1962).

Albright, W. F., *New Horizons in Biblical Research* (London: Oxford University Press, 1966).

————. *The Biblical Period from Abraham to Ezra* (Pittsburgh: Biblical Colloquium, 1950). PB: Harper, 1963.

————. *From the Stone Age to Christianity* (Baltimore: Johns Hopkins, 1940). PB: Anchor, 1957.

————. *Yahweh and the Gods of Canaan* (Garden City: Doubleday, 1968).

Allmen, J. J. von (ed.), *A Companion to the Bible* (London: 1958).

Alt, A., *Essays on Old Testament History and Religion* (Garden City: Doubleday, 1968).

Anderson, B. W. (ed.), *The Old Testament and Christian Faith* (New York: Harper & Row, 1963).

————. *Understanding the Old Testament* (Englewood Cliffs: Prentice-Hall, 1957, rev. ed. 1966).

————. *Creation versus Chaos* (New York: Association Press, 1967).

Anderson, G. W., "Recent Biblical Theologies: V. Th. C. Vriezen's 'Outline of Old Testament Theology,'" *Expository Times* 73 (1962).

Baab, O. J., *The Theology of the Old Testament* (Nashville: Abingdon Press, 1949).

✓ Barr, J., "The Meaning of 'Mythology' in Relation to the Old Testament," *VT* 9 (1959).

———. *The Semantics of Biblical Language* (London: Oxford University Press, 1961).

———. *Old and New in Interpretation* (New York: Harper & Row, 1966).

———. "Recent Biblical Theologies: VI. Gerhard von Rad's 'Theologie des Alten Testaments,'" *Expository Times* 73 (1962).

Barthelemy, D., *God and His Image* (New York: Sheed and Ward, 1966).

Benoit, P., *Aspects of Biblical Inspiration* (Chicago: The Priory Press, 1965).

Bentzen, A., *Introduction to the Old Testament*, I-II, 2nd ed. (Copenhagen: G.E.C. Gad, 1952).

Beyerlin, W., *Origins and History of the Oldest Sinaitic Traditions* (Oxford: Basil Blackwell, 1965).

Blenkinsopp, J., "Biblical and Dogmatic Theology: the Present Situation," *CBQ* 26 (1964).

Bowman, R. A., "Genealogy," *Interpreter's Dictionary of the Bible* (Nashville: Abingdon).

Bright, J., *Early Israel in Recent History Writing* (London: SCM Press, 1956).

———. "Recent Biblical Theologies: VIII. Edmond Jacob's 'Theology of the Old Testament,'" *Expository Times* 73 (1962).

———. *A History of Israel* (Philadelphia: Westminster, 1959).

———. *The Authority of the Old Testament* (Nashville: Abingdon, 1967).

Buber, M., *The Prophetic Faith* (New York: Macmillan, 1949). PB: Harper & Row, 1960.

———. *Moses* (London: East & West Library, 1946).

Buttrick, G. A. et al. (eds.) *The Interpreter's Dictionary of the Bible* (IDB). 4 vols (Nashville: Abingdon, 1962).

Calderone, P. J., *Dynastic Oracle and Suzerainty Treaty* (Studies published by the Faculty of Loyola House of Studies, Ateneo de Manila University, 1966).

Cassirer, E., *The Philosophy of Symbolic Forms:* Mythical Thought (New Haven: Yale University Press, 1955).

Cassuto, U., *La Questione della Genesi* (Florence: 1934).

Cazelles, H., "Pentateuque," in *Dictionnaire de la Bible Supplément*.

———. "Connexions et structure de Gen. XV" *RB* 69 (1962).

Childs, B., *Myth and Reality in the Old Testament* (London: SCM Press, 1960).

Clements, R. E., *Prophecy and Covenant* (Naperville: Allenson, 1965).

————. *Abraham and David* (Naperville: Allenson, 1967).

Collingwood, R. G., *The Idea of History* (New York: Oxford University Press, 1956).

Crowe, F., "On the Method of Theology," *TS* 23 (1962).

Cullmann, O., *Salvation in History* (New York: Harper & Row, 1967).

/Cwickowski, F. J., "Biblical Theology as Historical Theology," *CBQ* 24 (1962).

Dahood, M., *Psalms*, Anchor Bible (New York: Doubleday, 1967).

Danielou, J., *In the Beginning . . . Genesis I-III* (Baltimore: Helicon, 1965).

DeVaux, R., *Ancient Israel: Its Life and Institutions* (New York: McGraw-Hill, 1965).

Dillon, D. A., "Biblical and Systematic Theology: The Basic Issues," *Proceedings: CTSA* 21 (1966).

Dion, H. M., "The Patriarchal Traditions and the Literary Form of the Oracle of Salvation," *CBQ* 29 (1967).

Driver, S., *An Introduction to the Literature of the Old Testament* (Cleveland: The World Publishing Co., 1956). PB: 1956.

Dubarle, A. M., *The Biblical Doctrine of Original Sin* (New York: Herder & Herder, 1964).

————. "History and Myth in Genesis," *Theology Digest* 6 (1958).

Duckworth, G. E., *Foreshadowing and Suspense in the Epics of Homer, Apollonius, and Vergil* (Princeton: Princeton University Press, 1933).

Dufour, X. L., et al. (eds.), *Vocabulaire de Théologie Biblique* (Paris: Les Éditions du Cerf, 1962).

Eichrodt, W., *Theology of the Old Testament*, 2 vols. (Philadelphia: Westminster, 1961).

Eissfeldt, O., *Introduction to the Old Testament* (New York: Harper & Row, 1965).

Eliade, M., *Cosmos and History: The Myth of the Eternal Return* (New York: Harper Torchbook, PB: 1954).

————. *The Sacred and the Profane: The Nature of Religion* (New York: Harper Torchbook, PB: 1961).

Ellis, P. F., *The Men and the Message of the Old Testament* (Collegeville, Minn.: Liturgical Press, 1963).

Finnegan, J., *Light from the Ancient Past* (Princeton: Princeton University Press, 1959).

Fitzmyer, J. A., *Pauline Theology—A Brief Sketch* (Englewood Cliffs: Prentice-Hall, 1967).

Frankfurt, H., and H. A., *The Intellectual Adventure of Ancient Man* (Chicago: University of Chicago Press, 1946. PB: Penguin, 1949).

Gelin, A., *Sin in the Bible* (New York: Desclée, 1965).

Gleason, R. W., *Yahweh: The God of the Old Testament* (Englewood Cliffs: Prentice-Hall, 1964).

Goff, B. S., "The Lost Yahwistic Account of the Conquest of Canaan," *JBL* 53 (1934).

Gordon, C., "The Story of Jacob and Laban in the Light of the Nuzi Tablets," *BASOR* 66 (1937).

Gottwald, N. K., "Recent Biblical Theologies: IX. Walther Eichrodt's 'Theology of the Old Testament,'" *Expository Times* 74 (1963).

Gray, J., *The Legacy of Canaan*, 2nd ed. (Leiden: Brill, 1965).

———. *I & II Kings* (Philadelphia: Westminster, 1963).

Grelot, P., *Man and Wife in Scripture* (New York: Herder & Herder, 1964).

Guillet, J., *Themes of the Bible* (Notre Dame: Fides, 1960).

Gunkel, H., *The Legends of Genesis* (New York: Schocken Books, 1964).

Hahn, H. F., *The Old Testament in Modern Research* (Philadelphia: Fortress Press, 1966).

Harrelson, W., *Interpreting the Old Testament* (New York: Holt, Rinehart and Winston, 1964).

———. "Blessing," *Interpreter's Dictionary of the Bible* (Nashville: Abingdon).

Hartman, L., *Encyclopedic Dictionary of the Bible* (New York: McGraw-Hill, 1963).

Hebert, A. G., *The Old Testament from Within* (London: Oxford, 1962).

Heidel, A., *The Gilgamesh Epic and Old Testament Parallels* (Chicago: University of Chicago Press, 1946).

Henry, A. M. (ed.) *Introduction to Theology,* Theology Library, Vol. I (Chicago: Fides Publishers Association, 1958).

Hertzberg, H. W., *I & II Samuel* (London: SCM Press, 1964).

Holt, J. M., *The Patriarchs of Israel* (Nashville: Vanderbilt University Press, 1964).

Huffmon, H. B., "The Exodus, Sinai and the Credo," *CBQ* 27 (1965).

Hughes, H. S., *History as Art and Science* (New York: Harper & Row, 1964).

Hunt, I., *The World of the Patriarchs* (Englewood Cliffs: Prentice-Hall, 1967).

Imschoot, van P., *The Theology of the Old Testament* (New York: Desclée, 1965).

Jacob, E., *Theology of the Old Testament* (New York: Harper & Row, 1958).

Kapelrud, A., *The Ras Shamra Discoveries and the Old Testament* (Oklahoma: University of Oklahoma Press, 1963).

Kaufman, Y., *The Religion of Israel* (Chicago: University of Chicago Press, 1960).

Kirk, G. S., "The Homeric Poems as History," *Cambridge Ancient History*, rev. ed., fasc. 22.

Knight, G. A. F., *A Christian Theology of the Old Testament* (London: SCM Press, 1965).

Köhler, L., *Old Testament Theology* (Philadelphia: Westminster, 1957).

Kramer, S. N., *History Begins at Sumer* (Garden City: Doubleday, 1959).

Kraus, H. J., *Worship in Israel* (Richmond: John Knox Press, 1966).

Latourelle, R., *Theology of Revelation* (New York: Alba House, 1967).

Lewy, E., *The Growth of the Pentateuch* (New York: Bookman Associates, 1955).

Lohfink, N., "Inerrancy in Scripture," *Theology Digest* 13 (1965).

————. "Genesis 2-3 as Historical Etiology," *Theology Digest* 13 (1965).

Lohr, C. H., "Oral Techniques in the Gospel of Matthew," *CBQ* 23 (1961).

Lonergan, B., *Insight: A Study of Human Understanding* (New York: Longmans, 1957).

Lund, W. W., *Chiasmus in the New Testament: A Study in Formgeschichte* (Chapel Hill: University of North Carolina Press, 1942).

MacKenzie, R. A. F., "The Divine Soliloquies in Genesis," *CBQ* 17 (1955).

————.*Faith and History in the Old Testament* (New York: Macmillan, 1963).

Maertens, T., *A Feast in Honor of Yahweh* (Notre Dame: Fides, 1965).

Maly, E., *The World of David and Solomon* (Englewood Cliffs: Prentice-Hall, 1967).

Marty, M., "The Bible and Tradition," *The Critic* (Aug.-Sept. 1965).

McCarthy, D., *Treaty and Covenant, a Study in Form in the Ancient Oriental Documents and in the Old Testament* (Rome: Pontifical Biblical Institute, 1963).

————. "Covenant in the Old Testament: The Present State of Inquiry," *CBQ* 27 (1965).

McCarthy, D. J. and Callen, W. B. (eds.), *Modern Biblical Studies* (Milwaukee: Bruce, 1967).

McKenzie, J. L., *The Two-Edged Sword* (Milwaukee: Bruce, 1956).

————. "The Task of Biblical Theology," *The Voice of St. Mary's Seminary* 36 (1959).

————. *Myths and Realities* (Milwaukee: Bruce, 1964).

————. *The World of the Judges* (Englewood Cliffs: Prentice-Hall, 1967).

————. "Problems of Hermeneutics in Roman Catholic Exegesis," *JBL* 77 (1958).

Mendenhall, G., *Law and Covenant in Israel and the Ancient Near East* (Pittsburgh: Biblical Colloquium, 1955).

————. "The Hebrew Conquest of Palestine," *BA* 25 (1962).

Moltmann, J., *The Theology of Hope* (New York: Harper & Row, 1967).

Most, W. G., "Theology of Redemption in a Covenant Framework," *CBQ* 29 (1967).

Mowinckel, S., *The Old Testament as Word of God* (Nashville: Abingdon Press, 1959).

————. *He That Cometh* (Nashville: Abingdon Press, 1956).

Muilenburg, J., "Preface to Hermeneutics," *JBL* 77 (1958).

Murphy, J., "The Relationship between the Testaments," *CBQ* 26 (1964).

Newman, M. L., *The People of the Covenant: A Study of Israel from Moses to the Monarchy* (Nashville: Abingdon Press, 1962).

Nicholson, E. W., *Deuteronomy and Tradition* (Philadelphia: Fortress Press, 1967).

Nielsen, E., *Oral Tradition* (London: SCM Press, 1954).

North, C. N., *The Old Testament Interpretation of History* (London: 1946).

————. "The Place of Oral Tradition in the Growth of the Old Testament," *Expository Times*, LXI (1949-50).

Noth, M., *Exodus* (Philadelphia: Westminster, 1962).

———. *The Laws in the Pentateuch and Other Studies* (Philadelphia: Fortress Press, 1967).

Novak, M., "The Philosophy Implicit in Biblical Studies," *CBQ* 22 (1960).

O'Callaghan, R., *Aram Naharaium: A Contribution to the History of Upper Mesopotamia in the Second Millennium B.C.* (Rome: Pontifical Biblical Institute, 1948).

O'Collins, G. G., "Spes Quaerens Intellectum," *Interpretation* 22 (Jan. 1968).

Otto, R., *The Idea of the Holy* (New York: Oxford University Press, 1958).

Piper, O., "Biblical Theology and Systematic Theology," *JBR* 25 (1957).

Plastaras, J., *The God of Exodus* (Milwaukee: Bruce, 1966).

Porteous, N. W., "The Theology of the Old Testament," *Peake's Commentary on the Bible* (London: Nelson, 1962).

Pritchard, J. B. (ed.), *Ancient Near Eastern Texts Relating to the Old Testament*, 2nd ed. (Princeton: Princeton University Press, 1955).

Rad, G. von, *Moses* (London: Lutterworth, 1960).

———. *Genesis* (Philadelphia: Westminster, 1961).

———. *Old Testament Theology*, I: *The Theology of Israel's Historical Traditions* (New York: Harper & Row, 1962); II: *The Theology of Israel's Prophetic Traditions* (1965).

———. *The Problem of the Hexateuch and Other Essays* (New York: McGraw-Hill, 1966).

———. *Deuteronomy* (Philadelphia: Westminster, 1966).

———. "History and the Patriarchs," *Expository Times* 72 (1961).

Renckens, H., *Israel's Concept of the Beginning* (New York: Herder & Herder, 1964).

Rigaux, B., "The Woman and Her Seed in Genesis 3:14-15," *Theology Digest* 6 (1958).

Robinson, H. W., *The Religious Ideas of the Old Testament*. Rev. ed. by L. H. Brockington (Naperville: Allenson, 1956).

———. *Inspiration and Revelation in the Old Testament* (New York: Oxford University Press, 1946). PB: Oxford, 1962.

Robinson, J. M. "Scripture and Theological Method," *CBQ* 27 (1965).

Robinson, J. M. & Cobb, J. B. (eds.), *The New Hermeneutic* (New York: Harper & Row, 1964).

Rowley, H. H., *The Biblical Doctrine of Election* (London: Lutter-worth, 1950).

————. *The Faith of Israel: Aspects of Old Testament Thought* (London: SCM Press, 1956). PB: SCM Press.

————. *From Joseph to Joshua* (London: Oxford University Press, 1950).

Salm, L. (ed.), *Studies in Salvation History* (Englewood Cliff: Prentice-Hall, 1964).

Sandars, N. K., *The Epic of Gilgamesh* (Baltimore: Penguin, 1960).

Sarna, N. M., *Understanding Genesis* (New York: McGraw-Hill, 1966).

Schillebeeckx, E., *Revelation and Theology* (New York: Sheed & Ward, 1967).

Schökel, L. A., *The Inspired Word* (New York: Herder & Herder, 1965).

————. "Argument d'Écriture et théologie biblique dans l'enseignement théologique," *NRT* 81 (1959).

————. "Sapiential and Covenant Themes in Gn 2-3," *TD* 13 (1965).

Schoonenberg, P., *Man and Sin* (Notre Dame: University of Notre Dame Press, 1965).

Snaith, N., *Distinctive Ideas of the Old Testament* (London: Epworth, 1947). PB: Schocken, 1965.

Speiser, E. A., *Genesis*, Anchor Bible (Garden City: Doubleday, 1964).

Spicq, C., "The Work of Biblical Theology," *Theology Digest* 7 (1959).

Stamm, J. J. and Andrew, M. E., *The Ten Commandments in Recent Research* (Naperville: Allenson, 1967).

Stendahl, K., "Biblical Theology," *Interpreter's Dictionary of the Bible* (Nashville: Abingdon, 1962).

Strobel, "Myth in the Old Testament," *Theology Digest* 14 (1966).

Suelzer, A., *The Pentateuch* (New York: Herder & Herder, 1964).

Thomas, D. W., *Documents from Old Testament Times* (New York: Harper & Row, 1958). PB: Harper Torchbook, 1961.

Vandenhaar, G. A., "The Status of Scholastic Philosophy in Theology Today," *Proceedings: CTSA* 21 (1966).

Vawter, B., *A Path Through Genesis* (New York: Sheed & Ward, 1956).

————. "The Fuller Sense: Some Considerations," *CBQ* 26 (1964).

Vorgrimler, H., (ed.), *Dogmatic vs Biblical Theology* (Baltimore: Helicon, 1964).

Vos, G., *Biblical Theology* (Grand Rapids: Eerdmans, 1948).

Vriezen, Th. C., *An Outline of Old Testament Theology* (Oxford: Blackwell, 1958).

Watson, P. S., "The Nature and Function of Biblical Theology," *Expository Times* 73 (1962).

Weiser, A., *The Old Testament: Its Formation and Development* (New York: Association Press, 1961).

———. *The Psalms* (Philadelphia: Westminster, 1962).

Westermann, C., (ed.), *Essays on Old Testament Hermeneutics* (Richmond: John Knox, 1963).

———. "God and His People," *Theology Digest* 14 (1966).

Wolff, H. W., "The Kerygma of the Yahwist," *Interpretation* 20 (1966).

Wright, G. E., *The Old Testament Against its Environment* (London: SCM Press, 1950).

———. *God Who Acts* (London: SCM Press, 1952).

Wright, J. H., "The Eternal Plan of Divine Providence, *TS* 13 (1966).

Appendix

THE YAHWIST SAGA

GENESIS

Paradise

2 At the time when Yahweh God made earth and heaven •there was as yet no 5
wild bush on the earth nor had any wild plant yet sprung up, for Yahweh God
had not sent rain on the earth, nor was there any man to till the soil. •However, 6
a flood was rising from the earth and watering all the surface of the soil. •Yahweh 7
God fashioned man of dust from the soil. Then he breathed into his nostrils a
breath of life, and thus man became a living being.

Yahweh God planted a garden in Eden which is in the east, and there he put 8
the man he had fashioned. •Yahweh God caused to spring up from the soil every 9
kind of tree, enticing to look at and good to eat, with the tree of life and the tree
of the knowledge of good and evil in the middle of the garden. •A river flowed 10
from Eden to water the garden, and from there it divided to make four streams.
The first is named the Pishon, and this encircles the whole land of Havilah where 11
there is gold. •The gold of this land is pure; bdellium and onyx stone are found 12
there. •The second river is named the Gihon, and this encircles the whole land 13
of Cush. •The third river is named the Tigris, and this flows to the east of Ashur. 14
The fourth river is the Euphrates. •Yahweh God took the man and settled him 15
in the garden of Eden to cultivate and take care of it. •Then Yahweh God gave 16
the man this admonition, 'You may eat indeed of all the trees in the garden.
Nevertheless of the tree of the knowledge of good and evil you are not to eat, 17
for on the day you eat of it you shall most surely die.'

Yahweh God said, 'It is not good that the man should be alone. I will make 18
him a helpmate.' •So from the soil Yahweh God fashioned all the wild beasts 19
and all the birds of heaven. These he brought to the man to see what he would
call them; each one was to bear the name the man would give it. •The man gave 20
names to all the cattle, all the birds of heaven and all the wild beasts. But no
helpmate suitable for man was found for him. •So Yahweh God made the man 21
fall into a deep sleep. And while he slept, he took one of his ribs and enclosed
it in flesh. •Yahweh God built the rib he had taken from the man into a woman, 22
and brought her to the man. •The man exclaimed: 23

'This at last is bone from my bones,
and flesh from my flesh!
This is to be called woman,
for this was taken from man.'

This is why a man leaves his father and mother and joins himself to his wife, 24
and they become one body.

Now both of them were naked, the man and his wife, but they felt no 25
shame in front of each other.

The Fall

3 The serpent was the most subtle of all the wild beasts that Yahweh God 1
had made. It asked the woman, 'Did God really say you were not to eat from
any of the trees in the garden?' •The woman answered the serpent, 'We may eat 2

the fruit of the trees in the garden. ·But of the fruit of the tree in the middle of 3
the garden God said, "You must not eat it, nor touch it, under pain of death". '
Then the serpent said to the woman, 'No! You will not die! ·God knows in fact 5
that on the day you eat it your eyes will be opened and you will be like gods,
knowing good and evil.' ·The woman saw that the tree was good to eat and 6
pleasing to the eye, and that it was desirable for the knowledge that it could give.
So she took some of its fruit and ate it. She gave some also to her husband who
was with her, and he ate it. ·Then the eyes of both of them were opened and they 7
realised that they were naked. So they sewed fig-leaves together to make themselves loin-cloths.

The man and his wife heard the sound of Yahweh God walking in the 8
garden in the cool of the day, and they hid from Yahweh God among the trees
of the garden. ·But Yahweh God called to the man. 'Where are you?' he asked. 9
'I heard the sound of you in the garden;' he replied 'I was afraid because I was 10
naked, so I hid.' ·'Who told you that you were naked?' he asked 'Have you been 11
eating of the tree I forbade you to eat?' ·The man replied, 'It was the woman you 12
put with me; she gave me the fruit, and I ate it'. ·Then Yahweh God asked the 13
woman, 'What is this you have done?' The woman replied, 'The serpent tempted
me and I ate.'

Then Yahweh God said to the serpent, 'Because you have done this,   14
   'Be accursed beyond all cattle,
   all wild beasts.
   You shall crawl on your belly and eat dust
   every day of your life.
   I will make you enemies of each other: 15
   you and the woman,
   your offspring and her offspring.
   It will crush your head
   and you will strike its heel.'
To the woman he said: 16
   'I will multiply your pains in childbearing,
   you shall give birth to your children in pain.
   Your yearning shall be for your husband,
   yet he will lord it over you.'
To the man he said, 'Because you listened to the voice of your wife and ate 17
from the tree of which I had forbidden you to eat,
   'Accursed be the soil because of you.
   With suffering shall you get your food from it
   every day of your life.
   It shall yield you brambles and thistles,   18
   and you shall eat wild plants.
   With sweat on your brow   19
   shall you eat your bread,
   until you return to the soil,
   as you were taken from it.
   For dust you are
   and to dust you shall return.'
The man named his wife 'Eve' because she was the mother of all those who 20
live. ·Yahweh God made clothes out of skins for the man and his wife, and 21
they put them on. ·Then Yahweh God said, 'See, the man has become like 22

one of us, with his knowledge of good and evil. He must not be allowed to
stretch his hand out next and pick from the tree of life also, and eat some
and live for ever.' ·So Yahweh God expelled him from the garden of Eden, 23
to till the soil from which he had been taken. ·He banished the man, and in 24
front of the garden of Eden he posted the cherubs, and the flame of a flashing
sword, to guard the way to the tree of life.

Cain and Abel

4 The man had intercourse with his wife Eve, and she conceived and gave birth 1
to Cain. 'I have acquired a man with the help of Yahweh' she said. ·She gave 2
birth to a second child, Abel, the brother of Cain. Now Abel became a shepherd
and kept flocks, while Cain tilled the soil. ·Time passed and Cain brought some 3
of the produce of the soil as an offering for Yahweh, ·while Abel for his part 4
brought the first-born of his flock and some of their fat as well. Yahweh looked
with favour on Abel and his offering. ·But he did not look with favour on Cain 5
and his offering, and Cain was very angry and downcast. ·Yahweh asked 6
Cain, 'Why are you angry and downcast? ·If you are well disposed, ought you 7
not to lift up your head? But if you are ill disposed, is not sin at the door like
a crouching beast hungering for you, which you must master?' ·Cain said to 8
his brother Abel, 'Let us go out'; and while they were in the open country,
Cain set on his brother Abel and killed him.

Yahweh asked Cain, 'Where is your brother Abel?' 'I do not know' he 9
replied. 'Am I my brother's guardian?' ·'What have you done?' Yahweh 10
asked. 'Listen to the sound of your brother's blood, crying out to me from the
ground. ·Now be accursed and driven from the ground that has opened its 11
mouth to receive your brother's blood at your hands. ·When you till the ground 12
it shall no longer yield you any of its produce. You shall be a fugitive and a
wanderer over the earth.' ·Then Cain said to Yahweh, 'My punishment is 13
greater than I can bear. ·See! Today you drive me from this ground. I must 14
hide from you, and be a fugitive and a wanderer over the earth. Why, whoever
comes across me will kill me!' ·'Very well, then,' Yahweh replied 'if anyone 15
kills Cain, sevenfold vengeance shall be taken for him.' So Yahweh put a mark
on Cain, to prevent whoever might come across him from striking him down.
Cain left the presence of Yahweh and settled in the land of Nod, east of Eden. 16

The descendants of Cain

Cain had intercourse with his wife, and she conceived and gave birth to Enoch. 17
He became builder of a town, and he gave the town the name of his son
Enoch. ·Enoch had a son, Irad, and Irad became the father of Mehujael; 18
Mehujael became the father of Methushael, and Methushael became the father
of Lamech. ·Lamech married two women: the name of the first was Adah 19
and the name of the second was Zillah. ·Adah gave birth to Jabal: he was the 20
ancestor of the tent-dwellers and owners of livestock. ·His brother's name was 21
Jubal: he was the ancestor of all who play the lyre and the flute. ·As for Zillah, 22
she gave birth to Tubal-cain: he was the ancestor of all metalworkers, in
bronze or iron. Tubal-cain's sister was Naamah.

Lamech said to his wives: 23

'Adah and Zillah, hear my voice,
Lamech's wives, listen to what I say:
I killed a man for wounding me,

a boy for striking me.
Sevenfold vengeance is taken for Cain,　　　　　　24
but seventy-sevenfold for Lamech.'

Seth and his descendants

Adam had intercourse with his wife, and she gave birth to a son whom she 25
named Seth, 'because God has granted me other offspring' she said 'in place
of Abel, since Cain has killed him'. •A son was also born to Seth, and he named 26
him Enosh. This man was the first to invoke the name of Yahweh. 5
He gave him the name Noah because, he said, 'Here is one who will give us, 29
in the midst of our toil and the labouring of our hands, a consolation derived
from the ground that Yahweh cursed'. . . .

Sons of God and daughters of men

6 When men had begun to be plentiful on the earth, and daughters had been 1
born to them, •the sons of God, looking at the daughters of men, saw they 2
were pleasing, so they married as many as they chose. •Yahweh said, 'My spirit 3
must not for ever be disgraced in man, for he is but flesh; his life shall last no
more than a hundred and twenty years'. •The Nephilim were on the earth at 4
that time (and even afterwards) when the sons of God resorted to the daughters
of man, and had children by them. These are the heroes of days gone by, the
famous men.

The corruption of mankind

Yahweh saw that the wickedness of man was great on the earth, and that 5
the thoughts in his heart fashioned nothing but wickedness all day long. •Yahweh 6
regretted having made man on the earth, and his heart grieved. •'I will rid 7
the earth's face of man, my own creation,' Yahweh said 'and of animals also,
reptiles too, and the birds of heaven; for I regret having made them.' •But 8
Noah had found favour with Yahweh.
. . . . . .

Preparation for the flood

7 Yahweh said to Noah, 'Go aboard the ark, you and all your household, 1
for you alone among this generation do I see as good man in my judgement.
Of all the clean animals you must take seven of each kind, both male and 2
female; of the unclean animals you must take two, a male and its female •(and 3
of the birds of heaven also, seven of each kind, both male and female), to
propagate their kind over the whole earth. •For in seven days' time I mean to 4
make it rain on the earth for forty days and nights, and I will rid the earth of
every living thing that I made.' •Noah did all that Yahweh ordered. . . . 5
Noah with his sons, his wife, and his sons' wives boarded the ark to escape 7
the waters of the flood. •(Of the clean animals and the animals that are not 8
clean, of the birds and all that crawls on the ground, •two of each kind boarded 9
the ark with Noah, a male and a female, according to the order God gave Noah.)
Seven days later the waters of the flood appeared on the earth. . . . •It rained 12
on the earth for forty days and forty nights. . . . And Yahweh closed the door
behind Noah.

The flood

... The waters swelled, lifting the ark 17
until it was raised above the earth. ... •Everything with the breath of life in 22
its nostrils died, everything on dry land. •Yahweh destroyed every living thing 23
on the face of the earth, man and animals, reptiles, and the birds of heaven. He
rid the earth of them, so that only Noah was left, and those with him in the ark.

The flood subsides

8

. . . . . .

Rain ceased to fall from heaven; •the waters gradually ebbed from the 3
earth.

. . . . . .

At the end of forty days Noah opened the porthole he had made in the ark 6
and he sent out the raven. ... •Then he sent out the dove, to see whether 8
the waters were receding from the surface of the earth. •The dove, finding 9
nowhere to perch, returned to him in the ark, for there was water over the whole
surface of the earth; putting out his hand he took hold of it and brought it back
into the ark with him. •After waiting seven more days, again he sent out the 10
dove from the ark. •In the evening, the dove came back to him and there it was 11
with a new olive-branch in its beak. So Noah realised that the waters were
receding from the earth. •After waiting seven more days he sent out the dove, 12
and now it returned to him no more. ... •Noah lifted back the hatch of the ark 13
and looked out. The surface of the ground was dry!

. . . .

Noah built an altar for Yahweh, and choosing from all the clean animals 20
and all the clean birds he offered burnt offerings on the altar. •Yahweh smelt 21
the appeasing fragrance and said to himself, 'Never again will I curse the earth
because of man, because his heart contrives evil from his infancy. Never again
will I strike down every living thing as I have done.

> 'As long as earth lasts,   22
> sowing and reaping,
> cold and heat,
> summer and winter,
> day and night
> shall cease no more.'

9

. . . . . .

Noah and his sons

The sons of Noah who went out from the ark were Shem, Ham and 18
Japheth; Ham is the ancestor of the Canaanites. •These three were Noah's 19
sons, and from these the whole earth was peopled.
Noah, a tiller of the soil, was the first to plant the vine. •He drank some 21
of the wine, and while he was drunk he uncovered himself inside his tent.
Ham, Canaan's ancestor, saw his father's nakedness, and told his two brothers 22
outside. •Shem and Japheth took a cloak and they both put it over their 23

shoulders, and walking backwards, covered their father's nakedness; they kept their faces turned away, and did not see their father's nakedness. ·When Noah 24 awoke from his stupor he learned what his youngest son had done to him. And he said: 25

'Accursed be Canaan.
He shall be his brothers'
meanest slave.'

He added: 26

'Blessed be Yahweh, God of Shem,
let Canaan be his slave!
May God extend Japheth, 27
may he live in the tents of Shem,
and may Canaan be his slave!'

· · · · · ·

Genealogies

10

· · · · · ·

Cush became the father of Nimrod who was the first potentate on earth. 8 He was a mighty hunter in the eyes of Yahweh, hence the saying, 'Like Nimrod, 9 a mighty hunter in the eyes of Yahweh'. ·First to be included in his empire 10 were Babel, Erech and Accad, all of them in the land of Shinar. ·From this 11 country came Ashur, the builder of Nineveh, Rehoboth-ir, Calah, ·and Resen 12 between Nineveh and Calah (this is the great city).

Misraim became the father of the people of Lud, of Anam, Lehab, Naphtuh, 13 Pathros, Cusluh and Caphtor, from which the Philistines came. 14

Canaan became the father of Sidon, his first-born, then Heth, ·and the 16 Jebusites, the Amorites, Girgashites, ·Hivites, Arkites, Sinites, ·Arvadites, 18 Zemarites, Hamathites; later the Canaanite tribes scattered. ·The Canaanite 19 frontier stretched from Sidon in the direction of Gerar and as far as Gaza, then in the direction of Sodom, Gomorrah, Admah and Zeboim, and as far as Lesha. . . . ·Shem also was the father of children, the ancestor of all the sons 21 of Eber and the elder brother of Japheth.

· · · · · ·

Arpachshad became the father of Shelah, and Shelah became the father 24 of Eber. ·To Eber were born two sons: the first was called Peleg, because it was 25 in his time that the earth was divided, and his brother was called Joktan. ·Joktan 26 became the father of Almodad, Sheleph, Hazarmaveth, Jerah, ·Hadoram, 27 Uzal, Diklah, ·Obal, Abima-el, Sheba, ·Ophir, Havilah, Jobab; all these are 29 sons of Joktan. ·They occupied a stretch of country from Mesha in the direction 30 of Sephar, the eastern mountain range.

· · · · · ·

The tower of Babel

11 Throughout the earth men spoke the same language, with the same vocab- 1 ulary. ·Now as they moved eastwards they found a plain in the land of 2 Shinar where they settled. ·They said to one another, 'Come, let us make 3 bricks and bake them in the fire'.—For stone they used bricks, and for mortar they used bitumen.—·'Come,' they said 'let us build ourselves a town and a 4

tower with its top reaching heaven. Let us make a name for ourselves, so that
we may not be scattered about the whole earth.'

Now Yahweh came down to see the town and the tower that the sons of 5
man had built. •'So they are all a single people with a single language!' said 6
Yahweh. 'This is but the start of their undertakings! There will be nothing
too hard for them to do. •Come, let us go down and confuse their langage 7
on the spot so that they can no longer understand one another.' •Yahweh 8
scattered them thence over the whole face of the earth, and they stopped
building the town. •It was named Babel therefore, because there Yahweh 9
confused the language of the whole earth. It was from there that Yahweh
scattered them over the whole face of the earth.

· · · · · ·

The descendants of Terah

. . . Haran died in the presence of his father Terah in his native 28
land, Ur of the Chaldaeans. •Abram and Nahor both married: Abram's wife 29
was called Sarai, Nahor's wife was called Milcah, the daughter of Haran, father
of Milcah and Iscah. •Sarai was barren, having no child. 30

· · · · · ·

THE STORY OF ABRAHAM

The call of Abraham

12 Yahweh said to Abram, 'Leave your country, your family and your father's 1
house, for the land I will show you. •I will make you a great nation; 2
I will bless you and make your name so famous that it will be used as
a blessing.

'I will bless those who bless you: 3
I will curse those who slight you.
All the tribes of the earth
shall bless themselves by you.'

So Abram went as Yahweh told him, and Lot went with him. . . . . *They set
off for the land of Canaan, and arrived there.*

Abram passed through the land as far as Shechem's holy place, the Oak 6
of Moreh. At that time the Canaanites were in the land. •Yahweh appeared 7
to Abram and said, 'It is to your descendants that I will give this land'. So
Abram built there an altar for Yahweh who had appeared to him. •From there 8
he moved on to the mountainous district east of Bethel, where he pitched his
tent, with Bethel to the west and Ai to the east. There he built an altar to
Yahweh and invoked the name of Yahweh. •Then Abram made his way stage 9
by stage to the Negeb.

Abraham in Egypt

When famine came to the land Abram went down into Egypt to stay there 10
for the time, since the land was hard pressed by the famine. •On the threshold 11
of Egypt he said to his wife Sarai, 'Listen! I know you are a beautiful woman.
When the Egyptians see you they will say, "That is his wife", and they will 12
kill me but spare you. •Tell them you are my sister, so that they may treat me 13
well because of you and spare my life out of regard for you.' •When Abram 14
arrived in Egypt the Egyptians did indeed see that the woman was very beautiful.

When Pharaoh's officials saw her they sang her praises to Pharaoh and the 15
woman was taken into Pharaoh's palace. ·He treated Abram well because of 16
her, and he received flocks, oxen, donkeys, men and women slaves, she-donkeys
and camels. ·But Yahweh inflicted severe plagues on Pharaoh and his household 17
because of Abram's wife Sarai. ·So Pharaoh summoned Abram and said, 'What 18
is this you have done to me? Why did you not tell me she was your wife? ·Why 19
did you say, "She is my sister", so that I took her for my wife? Now, here is
your wife. Take her and go!' ·Pharaoh committed him to men who escorted 20
him back to the frontier with his wife and all he possessed.

Abraham and Lot separate

13 From Egypt Abram returned to the Negeb with his wife and all he 1
possessed, and Lot with him. ·Abram was a very rich man, with livestock, 2
silver and gold. ·By stages he went from the Negeb to Bethel, where he had first 3
pitched his tent, between Bethel and Ai, ·at the place where he had formerly 4
erected the altar. Here Abram invoked the name of Yahweh.

Lot, who was travelling with Abram, had flocks and cattle of his own, and 5
tents too. . . . ·Dispute broke out between the herdsmen of Abram's livestock 7
and those of Lot's. (The Canaanites and the Perizzites were then living in the
land.) ·Accordingly Abram said to Lot, 'Let there be no dispute between me 8
and you nor between my herdsmen and yours, for we are brothers. ·Is not the 9
whole land open before you? Part company with me: if you take the left, I will
go right; if you take the right, I will go left.'

Looking round, Lot saw all the Jordan plain, irrigated everywhere—this 10
was before Yahweh destroyed Sodom and Gomorrah—like the garden of
Yahweh or the land of Egypt, as far as Zoar. ·So Lot chose all the Jordan 11
plain for himself and moved off eastwards. . . . pitching his tents on the out-
skirts of Sodom. ·Now the people of Sodom were vicious men, great sinners 13
against Yahweh.

Yahweh said to Abram after Lot had parted company with him, 'Look 14
all round from where you are towards the north and the south, towards
the east and the west. ·All the land within sight I will give to you and your 15
descendants for ever. ·I will make your descendants like the dust on the ground: 16
when men succeed in counting the specks of dust on the ground, then they will
be able to count your descendants! ·Come, travel through the length and 17
breadth of the land, for I mean to give it to you.'

So Abram went with his tents to settle at the Oak of Mamre, at Hebron, 18
and there he built an altar to Yahweh.

The campaign of the four great kings

14 It was in the time of Amraphel king of Shinar, Arioch king of Ellasar, 1
Chedor-laomer king of Elam, and Tidal king of the Goiim. ·These made 2
war on Bera king of Sodom, Birsha king of Gomorrah, Shinab king of Admah,
Shemeber king of Zeboiim, and the king of Bela (that is, Zoar).

These latter all banded together in the Valley of Siddim (that is, the Salt 3
Sea). For twelve years they had been under the yoke of Chedor-laomer, 4
but in the thirteenth year they revolted. ·In the fourteenth year Chedor-laomer 5
arrived and the kings who were on his side. They defeated the Rephaim at
Asteroth-karnaim, the Zuzim at Ham, the Emim in the plain of Kiriathaim,
the Horites in the mountainous district of Seir as far as El-paran, which is on 6

the edge of the wilderness. ·Wheeling round, they came to the Spring of 7
Judgement (that is, Kadesh); they conquered all the territory of the Amalekites
and also the Amorites who lived in Hazazon-tamar. ·Then the kings of Sodom, 8
Gomorrah, Admah, Zeboiim and Bela (that is, Zoar) marched out and took
up battle positions against them in the Valley of Siddim, ·against Chedor-laomer 9
king of Elam, Tidal king of the Goiim, Amraphel king of Shinar and Arioch
king of Ellasar: four kings against five! ·Now there were many bitumen wells 10
in the Valley of Siddim, and in their flight the kings of Sodom and Gomorrah
fell into them, while the rest took refuge in the mountains. ·The conquerors 11
seized all the possessions of Sodom and Gomorrah, and all their provisions,
and made off. ·They also took Lot (the nephew of Abram) and his possessions 12
and made off; he was living at Sodom.

A survivor came to tell Abram the Hebrew, who was living at the Oak of the 13
Amorite Mamre, the brother of Eshcol and Aner; these were allies of Abram.
When Abram heard that his kinsman had been taken captive, he mustered 14
his supporters, the members of his household from birth, numbering three
hundred and eighteen, and led them in pursuit as far as Dan. ·He and his servants 15
fell on them by night and defeated them, pursuing them as far as Hobah, north
of Damascus. ·He recaptured all the goods, along with his kinsman Lot and 16
his possessions, together with the women and people.

Melchizedek

When Abram came back after the defeat of Chedor-laomer and the kings 17
who had been on his side, the king of Sodom came to meet him in the Valley
of Shaveh (that is, the Valley of the King). ·Melchizedek king of Salem 18
brought bread and wine; he was a priest of God Most High. ·He pronounced 19
this blessing:
> 'Blessed be Abram by God Most High, creator of heaven and earth, 20
> and blessed be God Most High for handing over your enemies to you'.

And Abram gave him a tithe of everything.

The king of Sodom said to Abram, 'Give me the people and take the 21
possessions for yourself'. ·But Abram replied to the king of Sodom, 'I raise my 22
hand in the presence of Yahweh, God Most High, creator of heaven and earth:
not one thread, not one sandal strap, nothing will I take of what is yours; you 23
shall not say, "I enriched Abram". ·For myself, nothing. There is only what 24
my men have eaten, and the share belonging to the men who came with me,
Eshkol, Aner and Mamre; let them take their share.'

The divine promises and Covenant

15 It happened some time later that the word of Yahweh was spoken to 1
Abram in a vision, 'Have no fear, Abram, I am your shield; your reward
will be very great'.

'My Lord Yahweh,' Abram replied 'what do you intend to give me? I go 2
childless . . .' ·Then Abram said, 'See, you have given me no descendants; 3
some man of my household will be my heir'. ·And then this word of Yahweh 4
was spoken to him, 'He shall not be your heir; your heir shall be of your own
flesh and blood'. . . . ·Abram put his faith in Yahweh, who counted this as 6
making him justified.

'I am Yahweh' he said to him 'who brought you out of Ur of the Chaldaeans 7
to make you heir to this land.' ·'My Lord Yahweh,' Abram replied 'how am I 8

to know that I shall inherit it?' •He said to him, 'Get me a three-year-old heifer, 9
a three-year-old goat, a three-year-old ram, a turtledove and a young pigeon'.
He brought him all these, cut them in half and put half on one side and half 10
facing it on the other; but the birds he did not cut in half. •Birds of prey came 11
down on the carcases but Abram drove them off.

Now as the sun was setting Abram fell into a deep sleep, and terror seized 12
him. •*Then Yahweh said to Abram, 'Know this for certain, that your descendants* 13
will be exiles in a land not their own, where they will be slaves and oppressed
for four hundred years. •But I will pass judgement also on the nation that 14
enslaves them and after that they will leave, with many possessions. •For your 15
part, you shall go to your fathers in peace; you shall be buried at a ripe old
age. •In the fourth generation they will come back here, for the wickedness 16
of the Amorites is not yet ended.'

When the sun had set and darkness had fallen, there appeared a smoking 17
furnace and a firebrand that went between the halves. •That day Yahweh 18
made a Covenant with Abram in these terms:

> 'To your descendants I give this land,
>   from the wadi of Egypt to the Great River,

the river Euphrates, •the Kenites, the Kenizzites, the Kadmonites, •the Hittites, 20
the Perizzites, the Rephaim, •the Amorites, the Canaanites, the Girgashites, and 21
the Jebusites'.

The birth of Ishmael

16 Abram's wife Sarai had borne him no child, but she had an Egyptian 1
maidservant named Hagar. •So Sarai said to Abram, 'Listen, now! Since 2
Yahweh has kept me from having children, go to my slave-girl. Perhaps
I shall get children through her.' Abram agreed to what Sarai had said. . . . •Sarai 3
took Hagar her Egyptian slave-girl and gave her to Abram as his wife. •He went 4
to Hagar and she conceived. And once she knew she had conceived, her mistress
counted for nothing in her eyes. •Then Sarai said to Abram 'May this insult to 5
me come home to you! It was I who put my slave-girl into your arms but now
she knows that she has conceived, I count for nothing in her eyes. Let Yahweh
judge between me and you.' •'Very well,' Abram said to Sarai 'your slave-girl is 6
at your disposal. Treat her as you think fit.' Sarai accordingly treated her so
badly that she ran away from her.

The angel of Yahweh met her near a spring in the wilderness, the spring 7
that is on the road to Shur. •He said, 'Hagar, slave-girl of Sarai, where have 8
you come from, and where are you going?' 'I am running away from my mistress
Sarai' she replied. •The angel of Yahweh said to her, 'Go back to your mistress 9
and submit to her'. •The angel of Yahweh said to her, 'I will make your 10
descendants too numerous to be counted'. •Then the angel of Yahweh said 11
to her:

> 'Now you have conceived, and you will bear a son,
>   and you shall name him Ishmael,
>   for Yahweh has heard your cries of distress.
> A wild-ass of a man he will be,   12
>   against every man, and every man against him,
>   setting himself to defy all his brothers.'

Hager gave a name to Yahweh who had spoken to her: 'You are El Roi', 13

for, she said, 'Surely this is a place where I, in my turn, have seen the one who
sees me?' ·This is why this well is called the well of Lahai Roi; it is between 14
Kadesh and Bered. ·Hagar bore Abram a son, and Abram gave to the son that 15
Hagar bore the name Ishmael. . . .

The apparition at Mamre

18 Yahweh appeared to him [Abraham] at the Oak of Mamre while he was 1
sitting by the entrance of the tent during the hottest part of the day.
He looked up, and there he saw three men standing near him. As soon as he saw 2
them he ran from the entrance of the tent to meet them, and bowed to the
ground. ·'My lord,' he said 'I beg you, if I find favour with you, kindly do not 3
pass your servant by. ·A little water shall be brought; you shall wash your feet 4
and lie down under the tree. ·Let me fetch a little bread and you shall refresh 5
yourselves before going further. That is why you have come in your servant's
direction.' They replied, 'Do as you say'.

Abraham hastened to the tent to find Sarah. 'Hurry,' he said 'knead three 6
bushels of flour and make loaves.' ·Then running to the cattle Abraham took 7
a fine and tender calf and gave it to the servant, who hurried to prepare it.
Then taking cream, milk and the calf he had prepared, he laid all before them, 8
and they ate while he remained standing near them under the tree.

'Where is your wife Sarah?' they asked him. 'She is in the tent' he replied. 9
Then his guest said, 'I shall visit you again next year without fail, and your 10
wife will then have a son'. Sarah was listening at the entrance of the tent behind
him. ·Now Abraham and Sarah were old, well on in years, and Sarah had ceased 11
to have her monthly periods. ·So Sarah laughed to herself, thinking, 'Now 12
that I am past the age of child-bearing, and my husband is an old man, is pleasure
to come my way again?' ·But Yahweh asked Abraham, 'Why did Sarah laugh 13
and say, "Am I really going to have a child now that I am old?" ·Is anything 14
too wonderful for Yahweh? At the same time next year I shall visit you again
and Sarah will have a son.' ·'I did not laugh' Sarah said, lying because she 15
was afraid. But he replied, 'Oh yes, you did laugh'.

Abraham intercedes

From there the men set out and arrived within sight of Sodom, with 16
Abraham accompanying them to show them the way. ·Now Yahweh had 17
wondered, 'Shall I conceal from Abraham what I am going to do, ·seeing that 18
Abraham will become a great nation with all the nations of the earth blessing
themselves by him? ·For I have singled him out to command his sons and his 19
household after him to maintain the way of Yahweh by just and upright living.
In this way Yahweh will carry out for Abraham what he has promised him.'
Then Yahweh said, 'How great an outcry there is against Sodom and Gomorrah! 20
How grievous is their sin! ·I propose to go down and see whether or not they 21
have done all that is alleged in the outcry against them that has come up to me.
I am determined to know.'

The men left there and went to Sodom while Abraham remained standing 22
before Yahweh. ·Approaching him he said, 'Are you really going to destroy 23
the just man with the sinner? ·Perhaps there are fifty just men in the town. 24
Will you really overwhelm them, will you not spare the place for the fifty just
men in it? ·Do not think of doing such a thing: to kill the just man with the 25
sinner, treating just and sinner alike! Do not think of it! Will the judge of

the whole earth not administer justice?' •Yahweh replied, 'If at Sodom I find 26
fifty just men in the town, I will spare the whole place because of them'.

Abraham replied, 'I am bold indeed to speak like this to my Lord, I who 27
am dust and ashes. •But perhaps the fifty just men lack five: will you destroy 28
the whole city for five?' 'No,' he replied 'I will not destroy it if I find forty-five
just men there.' •Again Abraham said to him, 'Perhaps there will only be forty 29
there'. 'I will not do it' he replied 'for the sake of the forty.'

Abraham said, 'I trust my Lord will not be angry, but give me leave to speak: 30
perhaps there will only be thirty there'. 'I will not do it' he replied 'if I find
thirty there.' •He said, 'I am bold indeed to speak like this, but perhaps there 31
will only be twenty there'. 'I will not destroy it' he replied 'for the sake of the
twenty.' •He said, 'I trust my Lord will not be angry if I speak once more: 32
perhaps there will only be ten'. 'I will not destroy it' he replied 'for the sake
of the ten.'

When he had finished talking to Abraham Yahweh went away, and Abraham 33
returned home.

The destruction of Sodom

19 When the two angels reached Sodom in the evening, Lot was sitting at 1
the gate. As soon as Lot saw them he rose to meet them and bowed to
the ground. •'I beg you, my lords,' he said 'please come down to your servant's 2
house to stay the night and wash your feet. Then in the morning you can
continue your journey.' 'No,' they replied 'we can spend the night in the open
street.' •But he pressed them so much that they went home with him and 3
entered his house. He prepared a meal for them, baking unleavened bread,
and they ate.

They had not gone to bed when the house was surrounded by the men of 4
the town, the men of Sodom both young and old, all the people without
exception. •Calling to Lot they said, 'Where are the men who came to you 5
tonight? Send them out to us so that we may abuse them.'

Lot came out to them at the door, and having closed the door behind him 6
said, 'I beg you, my brothers, do no such wicked thing. •Listen, I have two 8
daughters who are virgins. I am ready to send them out to you, to treat as it
pleases you. But as for the men, do nothing to them, for they have come under
the shadow of my roof.' •But they replied, 'Out of the way! Here is one who 9
came as a foreigner, and would set himself up as a judge. Now we will treat
you worse than them.' Then they forced Lot back and moved forward to break
down the door. •But the men reached out, pulled Lot back into the house, 10
and shut the door. •And they struck the men who were at the door of the house 11
with blindness, from youngest to oldest, and they never found the doorway.

The men said to Lot, 'Have you anyone else here? Your sons, your daughters 12
and all your people in the town, take them out of the place. •We are about 13
to destroy this place, for there is a great outcry against them, and it has reached
Yahweh. And Yahweh has sent us to destroy them.' •Lot went to speak to 14
his future sons-in-law who were to marry his daughters. 'Come,' he said
'leave this place, for Yahweh is about to destroy the town.' But his sons-in-law
thought he was joking.

When dawn broke the angels urged Lot, 'Come, take your wife and these 15
two daughters of yours, or you will be overwhelmed in the punishment of the
town'. •And as he hesitated, the men took him by the hand, and his wife and 16

his two daughters, because of the pity Yahweh felt for him. They led him out and left him outside the town.

As they were leading him out he said, 'Run for your life. Neither look behind 17 you nor stop anywhere on the plain. Make for the hills if you would not be overwhelmed.' •'No, I beg you, my lord,' Lot said to them •'your servant has 19 won your favour and you have shown great kindness to me in saving my life. But I could not reach the hills before this calamity overtook me, and death with it. •The town over there is near enough to flee to, and is a little one. 20 Let me make for that—is it not little?—and my life will be saved.' •He 21 answered, 'I grant you this favour too, and will not destroy the town you speak of. •Hurry, escape to it, for I can do nothing until you reach it.' That 22 is why the town is named Zoar.

As the sun rose over the land and Lot entered Zoar, •Yahweh rained on 24 Sodom and Gomorrah brimstone and fire from Yahweh. •He overthrew these 25 towns and the whole plain, with all the inhabitants of the towns, and everything that grew there. •But the wife of Lot looked back, and was turned into a 26 pillar of salt.

Rising early in the morning Abraham went to the place where he had stood 27 before Yahweh, •and looking towards Sodom and Gomorrah, and across all 28 the plain, he saw the smoke rising from the land, like smoke from a furnace.

Thus it was that when God destroyed the towns of the plain, he kept 29 Abraham in mind and rescued Lot out of disaster when he overwhelmed the towns where Lot lived.

The origin of the Moabites and the Ammonites

After leaving Zoar Lot settled in the hill country with his two daughters, 30 for he dared not stay at Zoar. He made his home in a cave, himself and his two daughters.

The elder said to the younger, 'Our father is an old man, and there is not 31 a man in the land to marry us in the way they do the world over. •Come let 32 us ply our father with wine and sleep with him. In this way we shall have children by our father.' •That night they made their father drunk, and the 33 elder slept with her father though he was unaware of her coming to bed or of her leaving. •The next day the elder said to the younger, 'Last night I slept 34 with my father. Let us make him drunk again tonight, and you go and sleep with him. In this way we shall have children by our father.' •They made their 35 father drunk that night too, and the younger went and slept with him, but he was unaware of her coming to bed or of her leaving. •Both Lot's daughters 36 thus became pregnant by their father. •The elder gave birth to a son whom 37 she named Moab; and he is the ancestor of the Moabites of our own times. The younger also gave birth to a son whom she named Ben-ammi; and he is 38 the ancestor of the Bene-ammon of our own times.
. . . . . .

The birth of Isaac

21 Yahweh dealt kindly with Sarah as he had said, and did what he had 1 promised her. •So Sarah conceived and bore a son to Abraham in his 2 old age. . . .

. . . Abraham planted a tamarisk at Beersheba and there he invoked Yahweh, 33 the everlasting God. . . .

The sacrifice of Isaac

22 It happened some time later that God put Abraham to the test. 'Abraham, 1 Abraham' he called. 'Here I am' he replied. ·'Take your son,' God said 2 'your only child Isaac, whom you love, and go to the land of Moriah. There you shall offer him as a burnt offering, on a mountain I will point out to you.'

Rising early next morning Abraham saddled his ass and took with him two 3 of his servants and his son Isaac. He chopped wood for the burnt offering and started on his journey to the place God had pointed out to him. ·On the third 4 day Abraham looked up and saw the place in the distance. ·Then Abraham said 5 to his servants, 'Stay here with the donkey. The boy and I will go over there; we will worship and come back to you.'

Abraham took the wood for the burnt offering, loaded it on Isaac, and 6 carried in his own hands the fire and the knife. Then the two of them set out together. ·Isaac spoke to his father Abraham, 'Father' he said. 'Yes, my son' 7 he replied. 'Look,' he said 'here are the fire and the wood, but where is the lamb for the burnt offering?' ·Abraham answered, 'My son, God himself will provide 8 the lamb for the burnt offering'. Then the two of them went on together.

When they arrived at the place God had pointed out to him, Abraham built 9 an altar there, and arranged the wood. Then he bound his son Isaac and put him on the altar on top of the wood. ·Abraham stretched out his hand and seized 10 the knife to kill his son.

But the angel of Yahweh called to him from heaven. 'Abraham, Abraham' 11 he said. 'I am here' he replied. ·'Do not raise your hand against the boy' the 12 angel said. 'Do not harm him, for now I know you fear God. You have not refused me your son, your only son.' ·Then looking up, Abraham saw a ram 13 caught by its horns in a bush. Abraham took the ram and offered it as a burnt offering in place of his son. ·Abraham called this place 'Yahweh pro- 14 vides', and hence the saying today: On the mountain Yahweh provides.

The angel of Yahweh called Abraham a second time from heaven. ·'I swear 16 by my own self—it is Yahweh who speaks—because you have done this, because you have not refused me your son, your only son, ·I will shower blessings on you, 17 I will make your descendants as many as the stars of heaven and the grains of sand on the seashore. Your descendants shall gain possession of the gates of their enemies. ·All the nations of the earth shall bless themselves by your descendants, 18 as a reward for your obedience.'

Abraham went back to his servants, and together they set out for Beersheba, 19 and he settled in Beersheba.

The descendants of Nahor

It happened some time later that Abraham received word that Milcah, too, 20 had now borne sons to his brother Nahor: ·Uz his first-born, Buz his brother, 21 Kemuel Aram's father, ·Chesed, Hazo, Pildash, Jidlaph, Bethuel ·(and Bethuel 23 was the father of Rebekah). These are the eight children Milcah gave Nahor, Abraham's brother. ·He had a concubine named Reumah, and she too had 24 children: Tebah, Gaham, Tahash and Maacah.

The tomb of the patriarchs

23 . . . She [Sarah] died at Kiriath-arba, or Hebron, in the land of Canaan, 2 and Abraham went in to mourn and grieve for her.

Then leaving his dead, Abraham spoke to the sons of Heth: •'I am a stranger 4
and a settler among you' he said. 'Let me own a burial-plot among you, so that
I may take my dead wife and bury her.' •The sons of Heth gave Abraham this 5
answer, 'Listen, my lord, you are God's prince amongst us; bury your dead in 6
the best of our tombs; not one of us would refuse you his tomb and keep
you from burying your dead'.

Abraham rose and bowed to the ground before the people of the land, the 7
sons of Heth, •and spoke to them. 'If' he said 'you are willing for me to take 8
my dead wife and bury her, then listen to me. Intercede for me with Ephron,
Zohar's son, to give me the cave he owns at Machpelah, which is on the edge of 9
his land. Let him make it over to me in your presence at its full price, for me
to own as a burial-plot.' •Now Ephron was sitting among the sons of Heth, and 10
Ephron the Hittite answered Abraham in the hearing of the sons of Heth and
of all the citizens of the town. •'My lord, listen to me' he said. 'I give you the 11
land and I give you the cave on it; I make this gift in the sight of the sons of my
people. Bury your dead.'

Abraham bowed before the people of the land •and he spoke to Ephron 13
in the hearing of the people of the land, 'Oh, if it be you. . . But listen to me.
I will pay the price of the land; accept it from me and I will bury my dead there.'
Ephron answered Abraham, •'My lord, listen to me. A property worth four 15
hundred shekels of silver, what is a little thing like that between me and you?
Bury your dead.' •Abraham agreed to Ephron's terms, and Abraham weighed 16
out for Ephron the silver he had stipulated in the hearing of the sons of Heth,
namely four hundred shekels of silver, according to the current commercial rate.

Thus Ephron's field at Machpelah opposite Mamre, the field and the cave 17
that was on it, and all the trees that were on it, the whole of its extent in every
direction, passed •into Abraham's possession in the sight of the sons of Heth 18
and of all the citizens of the town. •After this Abraham buried his wife Sarah 19
in the cave of the field of Machpelah opposite Mamre, in the country of
Canaan. •And so the field and the cave that was on it passed from the sons of 20
Heth into Abraham's possession to be owned as a burial-plot.

The marriage of Isaac

24 By now Abraham was an old man well on in years, and Yahweh had blessed 1
him in every way. •Abraham said to the eldest servant of his house- 2
hold, the steward of all his property, 'Place your hand under my thigh, •I would 3
have you swear by Yahweh, God of heaven and God of earth, that you will not
choose a wife for my son from the daughters of the Canaanites among whom
I live. •Instead, go to my own land and my own kinsfolk to choose a wife for my 4
son Isaac.' •The servant asked him, 'What if the woman does not want to come 5
with me to this country? Must I take your son back to the country from which
you came?' •Abraham answered, 'On no account take my son back there. 6
Yahweh, God of heaven and God of earth, took me from my father's home, and 7
from the land of my kinsfolk, and he swore to me that he would give this country
to my descendants. He will now send his angel ahead of you, so that you may
choose a wife for my son there. •And if the woman does not want to come 8
with you, you will be free from this oath of mine. Only do not take my son back
there.' •And the servant placed his hand under the thigh of his master Abraham, 9
and swore to him that he would do it.

The servant took ten of his master's camels and something of the best of all 10 his master owned, and set out for Aram Naharaiim and the town of Nahor. In the evening, at the time when women go down to draw water, he made the 11 camels kneel outside the town near the well. •And he said, 'Yahweh, God of my 12 master Abraham, be with me today, and show your kindness to my master Abraham. •Here I stand by the spring as the young women from the town come out 13 to draw water. •To one of the girls I will say: Please tilt your pitcher and let me 14 drink. If she answers, "Drink, and I will water your camels too", may she be the one you have chosen for your servant Isaac; by this I shall know you have shown your kindness to my master.'

He had not finished speaking when Rebekah came out. She was the daughter 15 of Bethuel, son of Milcah, wife of Abraham's brother Nahor. She had a pitcher on her shoulder. •The girl was very beautiful, and a virgin; no man had touched 16 her. She went down to the spring, filled her pitcher and came up again. •Running 17 to meet her, the servant said, 'Please give me a little water to drink from your pitcher'. •She replied, 'Drink, my lord', and she quickly lowered her pitcher on 18 her arm and gave him a drink. •When she had finished letting him drink, she said, 19 'I will draw water for your camels, too, until they have had enough'. •She 20 quickly emptied her pitcher into the trough, and ran to the well again to draw water, and drew water for all the camels •while the man watched in silence, 21 wondering whether Yahweh had made his journey successful or not.

When the camels had finished drinking, the man took a gold ring weighing 22 half a shekel, and put it through her nostrils, and put on her arms two bracelets weighing ten gold shekels, •and he said, 'Whose daughter are you? Please tell me. 23 Is there room at your father's house for us to spend the night?' •She answered, 24 'I am the daughter of Bethuel, the son whom Milcah bore to Nahor'. •And she 25 went on, 'We have plenty of straw and fodder, and room to lodge'. •Then the 26 man bowed down and worshipped Yahweh •saying, 'Blessed be Yahweh, God 27 of my master Abraham, for he has not stopped showing kindness and goodness to my master. Yahweh has guided my steps to the house of my master's brother.'

The girl ran to her mother's house to tell what had happened. •Now Rebekah 28 had a brother called Laban, and Laban ran out to the man at the spring. •As soon 30 as he had seen the ring and the bracelets his sister was wearing, and had heard his sister Rebekah saying, 'This is what the man said to me', he went to the man and found him still standing by his camels at the spring. •He said to him, 'Come 31 in, blessed of Yahweh, why stay out here when I have cleared the house and made room for the camels?' •The man went to the house, and Laban unloaded the 32 camels. He provided straw and fodder for the camels and water for him and his companions to wash their feet.

They offered him food, but he said, 'I will eat nothing before I have said 33 what I have to say'. Laban said, 'Speak'. •He said, 'I am the servant of Abraham. 34 Yahweh has overwhelmed my master with blessings, and Abraham is now very 35 rich. He has given him flocks and herds, silver and gold, men slaves and women slaves, camels and donkeys. •Sarah, my master's wife, bore him a son in his old 36 age, and he has made over all his property to him. •My master made me take 37 this oath, "You are not to choose a wife for my son from the daughters of the Canaanites in whose country I live. •Curse you if you do not go to my father's 38 home and to my kinsfolk to choose a wife for my son." •I said to my master: 39 Suppose the woman will not agree to come with me? •and his reply was, "Yahweh, in whose presence I have walked, will send his angel to make your journey 40 successful; you shall choose a wife for my son from my kinsfolk and from my

father's house. •So doing, you will be free from my curse: you will have gone to 41
my family, and if they refuse you, you will be free from my curse." •Arriving 42
today at the spring I said: Yahweh, God of my master Abraham, show me, I
pray, if you intend to make my journey successful. •Here I stand, by the 43
spring: when a girl comes out to draw water and I say to her: Please let me drink
a little water from your pitcher, •and she replies, "Drink by all means, and I will 44
draw water for your camels too", may she be the wife Yahweh has chosen for my
master's son: •I was still turning this over in my mind when Rebekah came out, 45
her pitcher on her shoulder. She came down to the spring and drew water. I said
to her: Please give me a drink. •Quickly she lowered her pitcher saying, "Drink, 46
and I will water your camels too". •I asked her: Whose daughter are you? 47
She replied, "I am the daughter of Bethuel, whom Milcah bore to Nahor". Then
I put this ring through her nostrils and these bracelets on her arms. •I bowed 48
down and worshipped Yahweh, and I blessed Yahweh, God of my master
Abraham, who had so graciously led me to choose the daughter of my master's
brother for his son. •Now tell me whether you are prepared to show kindness 49
and goodness to my master; if not, say so, and I shall know what to do.'

Laban and Bethuel replied, 'This is from Yahweh; it is not in our power to 50
say yes or no to you. •Rebekah is there before you. Take her and go; and let her 51
become the wife of your master's son, as Yahweh has decreed.' •On hearing this 52
Abraham's servant prostrated himself on the ground before Yahweh. •He brought 53
out silver and gold ornaments and clothes which he gave to Rebekah; he also
gave rich presents to her brother and to her mother.

They ate and drank, he and his companions, and they spent the night there. 54
Next morning when they were up, he said, 'Let me go back to my master'. •Re- 55
bekah's brother and mother replied, 'Let the girl stay with us a few days, perhaps
ten; after that she may go'. •But he replied. 'Do not delay me; it is Yahweh who 56
has made my journey successful; let me leave to go back to my master'. •They 57
replied, 'Let us call the girl and find out what she has to say'. •They called 58
Rebekah and asked her, 'Do you want to leave with this man?' 'I do' she replied.
Accordingly they let their sister Rebekah go, with her nurse, and Abraham's 59
servant and his men. •They blessed Rebekah in these words: 60

'Sister of ours, increase
to thousands and tens of thousands!
May your descendants gain possession
of the gates of their enemies!'

Rebekah and her servants stood up, mounted the camels, and followed the man. 61
The servant took Rebekah and departed.

Isaac, who lived in the Negeb, had meanwhile come into the wilderness of 62
the well of Lahai Roi. •Now Isaac went walking in the fields as evening fell, and 63
looking up saw camels approaching. •And Rebekah looked up and saw Isaac. She 64
jumped down from her camel, •and asked the servant, 'Who is that man walking 65
through the fields to meet us?' The servant replied, 'That is my master'; then she
took her veil and hid her face. •The servant told Isaac the whole story, 66
and Isaac led Rebekah into his tent and made her his wife; and he loved her. 67
And so Isaac was consoled for the loss of his mother.

The descendants of Keturah

25 Abraham married another wife whose name was Keturah; •and she bore 2
him Zimram, Jokshan, Medan, Midian, Ishbak and Shuah.—•Jokshan 3

was the father of Sheba and Dedan, and the sons of Dedan were the Asshurites, the Letushim and the Leummin.—·The sons of Midian are Ephah, Epher, 4 Hanoch, Abida and Eldaah. All these are sons of Keturah.

Abraham gave all his possessions to Isaac. ·To the sons of his concubines 6 Abraham gave presents, and during his lifetime he sent them away from his son Isaac eastward, to the east country. . . . ·And Isaac lived near the well of Lahai 11 Roi.

. . . . . .

THE STORY OF ISAAC AND JACOB

The birth of Esau and Jacob

. . . Isaac prayed to Yahweh on behalf of his wife, for she was 21 barren. Yahweh heard his prayer, and his wife Rebekah conceived. ·But the 22 children struggled with one another inside her, and she said, 'If this is the way of it, why go on living?' So she went to consult Yahweh, ·and he said to her: 23

'There are two nations in your womb,
your issue will be two rival peoples.
One nation shall have the mastery of the other,
and the elder shall serve the younger.'

When the time came for her confinement, there were indeed twins in her 24 womb. ·The first to be born was red, and as though he were completely wrapped 25 in a hairy cloak; so they named him Esau. ·Then his brother was born, with his 26 hand grasping Esau's heel; so they named him Jacob. . . .

·When the boys grew up Esau became a skilled hunter, a man of the 27 open country. Jacob on the other hand was a quiet man, staying at home among the tents. ·Isaac preferred Esau, for he had a taste for wild game; but Rebekah 28 preferred Jacob.

Esau gives up his birthright

Once, Jacob had made a soup, and Esau returned from the countryside ex- 29 hausted. ·Esau said to Jacob, 'Let me eat the red soup, that red soup there; I 30 am exhausted'—hence the name given to him, Edom. ·Jacob said, 'First sell me 31 your birthright, then'. ·Esau said, 'Here I am, at death's door; what use will my 32 birthright be to me?' ·Then Jacob said, 'First give me your oath'; he gave him his 33 oath and sold his birthright to Jacob. ·Then Jacob gave him bread and lentil soup, 34 and after eating and drinking he got up and went. That was all Esau cared for his birthright.

Isaac at Gerar

26 There was a famine in the land—a second one after the famine which took 1 place in the time of Abraham—and Isaac went to Abimelech, the Philistine king at Gerar. ·Yahweh appeared to him and said, 'Do not go down into Egypt; 2 stay in the land I shall tell you of. ·Remain for the present here in this land, and I 3 will be with you and bless you. For it is to you and your descendants that I will give all these lands, and I will fulfil the oath I swore to your father Abraham. ·I 4 will make your descendants as many as the stars of heaven, and I will give them all these lands; and all the nations in the world shall bless themselves by your descendants ·in return for Abraham's obedience; for he kept my charge, my 5 commandments, my statutes and my laws.' ·So Isaac stayed at Gerar. 6

When the people of the place asked him about his wife he replied, 'She is my 7
sister', for he was afraid to say, 'She is my wife', in case they killed him
on Rebekah's account, for she was beautiful. •When he had been there some time, 8
Abimelech the Philistine king happened to look out of the window and saw Isaac
fondling his wife Rebekah. •Abimelech summoned Isaac and said to him, 'Surely 9
she must be your wife! How could you say she was your sister?' Isaac answered
him, 'Because I thought I might be killed on her account'. •Abimelech said, 10
'What is this you have done to us? One of my subjects might easily have slept
with your wife, and then you would have made us incur guilt.' •Then Abimelech 11
issued this order to all the people: 'Whoever touches this man or his wife shall be
put to death'.

Isaac sowed his crops in that land, and that year he reaped a hundredfold. 12
Yahweh blessed him •and the man became rich; he prospered more and more 13
until he was very rich indeed. •He had flocks and herds and many servants. The 14
Philistines began to envy him.

The wells between Gerar and Beersheba

The Philistines had sealed all the wells dug by his father's servants, filling them 15
with earth. These had existed from the time of his father Abraham. •Abimelech 16
said to Isaac, 'Leave us, for you have become much more powerful than we are'.
So Isaac left; he pitched camp in the Valley of Gerar and there he stayed. •Isaac 18
dug again the wells made by the servants of his father Abraham and sealed by
the Philistines after Abraham's death, and he gave them the same names as his
father had given them.

Isaac's servants dug in the valley and found a well of spring-water. •But the 20
shepherds of Gerar quarrelled with Isaac's shepherds, saying, 'That water is
ours!' So Isaac named the well Esek, because they had quarrelled with him. •They 21
dug another well, and there was a quarrel about that one too; so he named it
Sitnah. Then he left there, and dug another well, and since there was no quarrel 22
about this one, he named it Rehoboth, saying, 'Now Yahweh has made room for
us, so that we may thrive in the land.'

From here he went up to Beersheba. •Yahweh appeared to him that night and 24
said:

> 'I am the God of your father Abraham.
> Do not be afraid, for I am with you.
> I will bless you and make your descendants many in number
> on account of my servant Abraham.'

There he built an altar and invoked the name of Yahweh. There he pitched his 25
tent, and there Isaac's servants sank a well.

The alliance with Abimelech

Abimelech came from Gerar to see him, with his adviser Ahuzzath and the 26
commander of his army, Phicol. •Isaac said to them, 'Why do you come to me 27
since you hate me, and have made me leave you?' •'It became clear to us that 28
Yahweh was with you:' they replied 'and so we said, "Let there be a sworn treaty
between ourselves and you, and let us make a covenant with you". •Swear not to 29
do us any harm, since we never molested you but were unfailingly kind to you
and let you go away in peace. Now you have Yahweh's blessing.' •He then made 30
them a feast and they ate and drank.

Rising early in the morning, they exchanged oaths. Then Isaac bade them 31

farewell and they went from him in peace. ·Now it was on the same day that 32
Isaac's servants brought him news of the well they had dug. 'We have found
water!' they said to him. ·So he called the well Sheba, and hence the town is 33
named Beersheba to this day.

. . . . . .

Jacob obtains Isaac's blessing by cunning

27 Isaac had grown old, and his eyes were so weak that he could no longer see. 1
He summoned his elder son Esau, 'My son!' he said to him, and the latter
answered, 'I am here'. ·Then he said, 'See, I am old and do not know when I may 2
die. ·Now take your weapons, your quiver and bow; go out into the country and 3
hunt me some game. ·Make me the kind of savoury I like and bring it to me, 4
so that I may eat, and give you my blessing before I die.'

Rebekah happened to be listening while Isaac was talking to his son Esau. So 5
when Esau went into the country to hunt game for his father, ·Rebekah 6
said to her son Jacob, 'I have just heard your father saying to your brother
Esau, ·"Bring me some game and make a savoury for me. Then I shall eat, 7
and bless you in the presence of Yahweh before I die." ·Now my son, listen to 8
me and do as I tell you. ·Go to the flock, and bring me back two good kids, so 9
that I can make the kind of savoury your father likes. ·Then you can take it to 10
your father for him to eat so that he may bless you before he dies.'

Jacob said to his mother Rebekah, 'Look, my brother Esau is hairy, while I am 11
smooth-skinned. ·If my father happens to touch me, he will see I am cheating 12
him, and I shall bring down a curse on myself instead of a blessing.' ·But his 13
mother answered him, 'On me be the curse, my son! Just listen to me; go and
fetch me the kids.' ·So he went to fetch them, and he brought them to his mother, 14
and she made the kind of savoury his father liked. ·Rebekah took her elder son 15
Esau's best clothes, which she had in the house, and dressed her younger son
Jacob in them, ·covering his arms and the smooth part of his neck with the skins 16
of the kids. ·Then she handed the savoury and the bread she had made to her 17
son Jacob.

He presented himself before his father and said, 'Father'. 'I am here;' was the 18
reply 'who are you, my son?' ·Jacob said to his father, 'I am Esau your first-born; 19
I have done as you told me. Please get up and take your place and eat the game I
have brought and then give me your blessing.' ·Isaac said to his son, 'How quickly 20
you found it, my son!' 'It was Yahweh your God' he answered 'who put it in my
path.' ·Issac said to Jacob, 'Come here, then, and let me touch you, my son, to 21
know if you are my son Esau or not'. ·Jacob came close to his father Issac, who 22
touched him and said, 'The voice is Jacob's voice but the arms are the arms of
Esau!' ·He did not recognise him, for his arms were hairy like his brother Esau's, 23
and so he blessed him. ·He said, 'Are you really my son Esau?' And he replied, 24
'I am'. ·Isaac said, 'Bring it here that I may eat the game my son has brought, 25
and so may give you my blessing'. He brought it to him and he ate; he offered
him wine, and he drank. ·His father Isaac said to him, 'Come closer, and kiss me, 26
my son'. ·He went closer and kissed his father, who smelled the smell of his 27
clothes. He blessed him saying:

'Yes, the smell of my son
is like the smell of a fertile field blessed by Yahweh.
May God give you   28
dew from heaven,

> and the richness of the earth,
> abundance of grain and wine!
> May nations serve you   29
> and peoples bow down before you!
> Be master of your brothers;
> may the sons of your mother bow down before you!
> Cursed be he who curses you;
> blessed be he who blesses you!'

As soon as Isaac had finished blessing Jacob, and just when Jacob was leaving 30 the presence of his father Isaac, his brother Esau returned from hunting: ·He too 31 made a savoury and brought it to his father. He said to him, 'Father, get up and eat the game your son has brought and then give me your blessing!' ·His father 32 Isaac asked him, 'Who are you?' 'I am your firstborn son, Esau' he replied. ·At 33 this Isaac was seized with a great trembling and said, 'Who was it, then, that went hunting and brought me game? Unsuspecting I ate before you came; I blessed him, and blessed he will remain!' ·When Esau heard his father's words, he cried 34 out loudly and bitterly to his father, 'Father, bless me too!' ·But he replied, 'Your 35 brother came by fraud and took your blessing'. ·Esau said, 'Is it because his name 36 is Jacob, that he has now supplanted me twice? First he took my birthright, and look, now he has taken my blessing!' 'But' he added 'have you not kept a blessing for me?' ·Isaac answered Esau, 'See, I have made him your master; I have given 37 him all his brothers as servants, I have provided him with grain and wine. What can I do for you, my son?' ·Esau said to his father, 'Was that your only blessing, 38 father? Father, give me a blessing too.' Isaac remained silent, and Esau burst into tears. ·Then his father Isaac gave him this answer: 39

> 'Far from the richness of the earth
> shall be your dwelling-place,
> far from the dew that falls from heaven.
> You shall live by your sword,   40
> and you shall serve your brother.
> But when you win your freedom,
> you shall shake his yoke from your neck.'

Esau hated Jacob because of the blessing his father had given him, and thought 41 thus to himself, 'The time to mourn for my father will soon be here. Then I will kill my brother Jacob.' ·When the words of Esau, her elder son, were repeated to 42 Rebekah, she sent for her younger son Jacob and said to him, 'Look, your brother Esau means to take revenge and kill you. ·Now, my son, listen to me; go away 43 and take refuge with my brother Laban in Haran. ·Stay with him a while, until 44 your brother's fury cools, ·until your brother's anger against you cools and he 45 forgets what you have done to him. Then I will send someone to bring you back. Why should I lose you both on the same day?'

28

· · · · · · ·

Jacob's dream

Jacob left Beersheba and set out for Haran. ·When he had reached a certain 11 place he passed the night there, since the sun had set. . . . ·And Yahweh was 13 there, standing over him, saying, 'I am Yahweh, the God of Abraham your father, and the God of Isaac. I will give to you and your descendants the land

on which you are lying. •Your descendants shall be like the specks of dust on the 14
ground; you shall spread to the west and the east, to the north and the south,
and all the tribes of the earth shall bless themselves by you and your descendants.
Be sure that I am with you; I will keep you safe wherever you go, and bring you 15
back to this land, for I will not desert you before I have done all that I have
promised you.' •Then Jacob awoke from his sleep and said, 'Truly, Yahweh is in 16
this place and I never knew it!' . . . •He named the place Bethel, but before that 19
the town was called Luz.

. . . . . .

Jacob arrives at Laban's home

29 Moving on, Jacob went to the land of the sons of the East. •He looked and 2
there in the fields was a well with three flocks of sheep lying beside it, for
this well was used for watering the flocks. Now the stone on the mouth of the
well was a large one; •so they used to gather all the flocks there, and then roll the 3
stone off the mouth of the well, to water the sheep; then they put the stone back
in its place over the mouth of the well. •Jacob said to the shepherds, 'Brothers, 4
where are you from?' They replied, 'We are from Haran'. •Then he asked them, 5
'Do you know Laban, the son of Nahor?' 'We know him' they replied. •Then he 6
asked them, 'Does all go well with him?' 'Yes,' they replied 'and here comes his
daughter Rachel with the sheep.' •Then he said, 'See, it is still broad daylight; it is 7
not yet time to bring the animals in. Water the sheep and go and take them back
to pasture.' •But they answered, 'We cannot do that until all the flocks are gath- 8
ered and they roll the stone off the mouth of the well; then we shall water the
sheep'.

He was still talking to them, when Rachel came with the sheep belonging to 9
her father, for she was a shepherdess. •As soon as Jacob saw Rachel, the daughter 10
of his uncle Laban, and the sheep of his uncle Laban, he came up and, rolling the
stone off the mouth of the well, he watered the sheep of his uncle Laban. •Jacob 11
kissed Rachel and burst into tears. •He told Rachel he was her father's kinsman 12
and Rebekah's son, and she ran to tell her father. •As soon as he heard her speak 13
of his sister's son Jacob, Laban ran to meet him; and embracing him he kissed
him warmly, and brought him to his house. Jacob told Laban every thing that
had happened, •and Laban said to him, 'Truly you are my bone and flesh!' 14
. . .

Jacob's two marriages

Laban said to Jacob, 'Because you are my kinsman, are you to work for me 15
without payment? Tell me what wages you want.' •Now Laban had two daugh- 16
ters, the elder named Leah, and the younger Rachel. •There was no sparkle in 17
Leah's eyes, but Rachel was shapely and beautiful, •and Jacob had fallen in 18
love with Rachel. So his answer was, 'I will work for you seven years to win
your younger daughter Rachel'. •Laban replied, 'It is better for me to give her to 19
you than to a stranger; stay with me'.

To win Rachel, therefore, Jacob worked seven years, and they seemed to him 20
like a few days because he loved her so much. •Then Jacob said to Laban, 'Give 21
me my wife, for my time is finished, and I should like to go to her'. •Laban gath- 22
ered all the people of the place together, and gave a banquet. •But when night 23
came he took his daughter Leah and brought her to Jacob, and he slept with her.
(Laban gave his slave-girl Zilpah to be his daughter Leah's slave.) •When morn- 25

ing came, there was Leah. So Jacob said to Laban, 'What is this you have done
to me? Did I not work for you to win Rachel? Why then have you tricked
me?' ·Laban answered, 'It is not the custom in our country to give the younger 26
before the elder. ·Finish this marriage week and I will give you the other one too 27
in return for your working with me another seven years'. ·Jacob did this, and 28
when the week was over, Laban gave him his daughter Rachel as his wife.
(Laban gave his daughter Rachel his slave-girl Bilhah to be her slave.) ·So Jacob 30
slept with Rachael also, and he loved Rachel more than Leah. He worked with
Laban another seven years.

The sons of Jacob

Yahweh saw that Leah was neglected, so he opened her womb, while Rachel 31
remained barren. ·Leah conceived and gave birth to a son whom she named 32
Reuben, 'Because' she said 'Yahweh has seen my misery; now my husband will
love me'. ·Again she conceived and gave birth to a son, saying, 'Yahweh has 33
heard that I was neglected, so he has given me this one too'; and she named him
Simeon. ·Again she conceived and gave birth to a son, saying, 'This time my hus- 34
band will be united to me, for I have now borne three sons to him'; accordingly,
she named him Levi. ·Again she conceived and gave birth to a son, saying, 'This 35
time I will give glory to Yahweh'; accordingly she named him Judah. Then she
had no more children.

30 *Rachel, seeing that she herself gave Jacob no children, became jealous of* 1
her sister. And she said to Jacob, 'Give me children, or I shall die!' ·This 2
made Jacob angry with Rachel, and he retorted, 'Am I in God's place? It is he
who has refused you motherhood.' ·So she said, 'Here is my slave-girl, Bilhah. 3
Sleep with her so that she may give birth on my knees; through her, then, I too
shall have children!' ·So she gave him her slave-girl Bilhah as a wife. Jacob slept 4
with her, ·and Bilhah conceived and gave birth to a son by Jacob. ·*Then Rachel* 6
said, 'God has done me justice; yes, he has heard my prayer and given me a son'.
Accordingly she named him Dan. ·Again Rachel's slave-girl Billhah conceived 7
and gave birth to a second son by Jacob. ·Then Rachel said, 'I have fought God's 8
fight with my sister, and I have won'; so she named him Naphtali.

Now Leah, seeing that she had no more children, took her slave-girl Zilpah 9
and gave her to Jacob as a wife. ·So Leah's slave-girl Zilpah gave birth to a son 10
by Jacob. ·Then Leah exclaimed, 'What good fortune!' So she named him Gad. 11
Leah's slave-girl Zilpah gave birth to a second son by Jacob. ·Then Leah said, 13
'What happiness! Women will call me happy!' So she named him Asher.

Going out when they were harvesting the corn, Reuben found some man- 14
drakes and brought them to his mother Leah. Rachel said to Leah, 'Please give
me some of your son's mandrakes'. ·But Leah replied, 'Is it not enough to have 15
taken my husband that you should want to take my son's mandrakes too?' So
Rachel said, 'Very well, he shall sleep with you tonight in return for your son's
mandrakes'. ·When Jacob came back from the fields that night, Leah went out to 16
meet him, saying, 'You must come to me, for I have hired you at the price of my
son's mandrakes'. So he slept with her that night. ·*God heard Leah, and she* 17
conceived and gave birth to a fifth son by Jacob. ·*Then Leah said, 'God has paid* 18
me my wages for giving my slave-girl to my husband'. So she named him Issachar. ·*Again Leah conceived and gave birth to a sixth son by Jacob,* ·*saying,* 20
'God has given me a fine gift; now my husband will honour me, for I have borne

six children to him'. So she named him Zebulun. •Later she gave birth to a   21
daughter and named her Dinah.

Then God remembered Rachel; he heard her and opened her womb. •She   23
conceived and gave birth to a son, saying, 'God has taken away my shame'. •So   24
she named him Joseph, saying, 'May Yahweh give me another son!'

How Jacob becomes rich

When Rachel had given birth to Joseph, Jacob said to Laban, 'Release me, and   25
then I can go home to my own country. •Give me my wives for whom I have   26
worked for you, and my children, so that I can go. You know very well the work
I have done for you.' •Laban said to him, 'If I have won your friendship. . . I   27
learned from the omens that Yahweh had blessed me on your account. •So name   28
your wages,' he added 'and I will pay you.' •He answered him, 'You know very   29
well how hard I have worked for you, and how your stock has fared in my
charge. •The little you had before I came has increased enormously, and Yahweh   30
has blessed you wherever I have been. But when am I to provide for my own
House?' Laban said, 'How much am I to pay you?' And Jacob replied, 'You will   31
not have to pay me anything: if you do for me as I propose, I will be your shepherd once more and look after your flock.

'Today I will go through all your flock. Take out of it every black animal   32
among the sheep, and every speckled or spotted one among the goats. Such shall
be my wages, •and my honesty will answer for me later: when you come to check   33
my wages, every goat I have that is not speckled or spotted, and every sheep that
is not black shall rank as stolen property in my possession.' •Laban replied,   34
'Good! Let it be as you say.' •That same day he took out the striped and speckled   35
he-goats and all the spotted and speckled she-goats, every one that had white on
it, and all the black sheep. He handed them over to his sons, •and put three days'   36
journey between himself and Jacob. Jacob took care of the rest of Laban's flock.

Jacob gathered branches in sap, from poplar, almond and plane trees, and   37
peeled them in white strips, laying bare the white on the branches. •He put the   38
branches he had peeled in front of the animals, in the troughs in the channels
where the animals came to drink; and the animals mated when they came to
drink. •They mated therefore in front of the branches and so produced striped,   39
spotted and speckled young. •As for the sheep, Jacob put them apart, and he   40
turned the animals towards whatever was striped or black in Laban's flock. Thus
he built up droves of his own which he did not put with Laban's flock. •Moreover,   41
whenever the sturdy animals mated, Jacob put the branches where the animals
could see them, in the troughs, so that they would mate in front of the branches.
But when the animals were feeble, he did not put them there; thus Laban got the   42
feeble, and Jacob the sturdy, •and he grew extremely rich, and became the owner   43
of large flocks, with men and women slaves, camels and donkeys.

Jacob's flight

31 Jacob learned that the sons of Laban were saying, 'Jacob has taken every-   1
thing that belonged to our father; it is at our father's expense that he
has acquired all this wealth'. •Jacob saw from Laban's face that things were   2
not as they had been. •Yahweh said to Jacob, 'Go back to the land of your   3
forefathers and to your kindred; and I will be with you'. •So Jacob had Rachel   4
and Leah called to the fields where his flocks were, •and he said to them, 'I can   5
see from your father's face that I am out of favour with him now; but the

God of my father has been with me. ·You yourselves know that I have worked 6
for your father with all my strength. ·Your father has tricked me, ten times 7
changing my wages, yet God has not allowed him to harm me. ·Whenever he 8
said, "The spotted ones shall be your wages," all the animals produced spotted
young; whenever he said, "The striped ones shall be your wages", all the animals produced striped young. ·Thus God has taken your father's livestock and 9
given it to me. ·It happened at the time when the animals were on heat, that in a 10
dream I looked up and saw that the males covering the females of the flock were
striped or spotted or piebald. ·In the dream the angel of God called to me, 11
"Jacob!" And I answered: I am here. ·He said, "Look up and see: all the males 12
covering the females of the flock are striped or spotted or piebald, for I have
seen all that Laban has done to you. ·I am the God of Bethel where you poured 13
oil on a monument, and where you made a vow to me. Now get ready to leave
this country and return to the land of your birth".'

In answer Rachel and Leah said to him, 'Have we any share left in the inher- 14
itance of our father's House? ·Does he not treat us as foreigners, for he has sold 15
us and gone on to use up all our money? ·Surely all the riches God has taken 16
from our father belong to us and to our children. So do all that God has told
you.'

Jacob made ready and put his children and his wives on camels, ·and he drove 18
all his livestock before him—with all he had acquired, the livestock belonging
to him which he had acquired in Paddan-aram—to go to his father Isaac in the
land of Canaan. ·When Laban had gone to shear his flock, Rachel stole the 19
household idols belonging to her father. ·Jacob outwitted Laban the Aramaean by 20
giving him no inkling of his flight. ·He fled with all he had and went away, cross- 21
ing the River and making for Mount Gilead.

Laban pursues Jacob

Three days later Laban was told that Jacob had fled. ·Taking his brothers 23
with him he pursued him for seven days and overtook him at Mount Gilead.
God came by night in a dream to Laban the Aramaean and said to him, 'On no 24
account say anything whatever to Jacob'. ·Laban caught up with Jacob, who had 25
pitched his tent in the hills; and Laban pitched camp on Mount Gilead.

Laban said to Jacob, 'What have you done, tricking me and driving my daugh- 26
ters off like prisoners of war? ·Why did you flee in secret, stealing away without 27
letting me know so that I could send you on your way rejoicing, with songs and
the music of tambourines and lyres? ·You did not even let me kiss my sons and 28
daughters. You have behaved like a fool. ·It is in my power to do you harm, but 29
the God of your father said to me last night, "On no account say anything whatever to Jacob". ·Now it may be you really went because you had such a longing 30
for your father's House, but why did you steal my gods?'

Jacob answered Laban, 'I was afraid, thinking you were going to snatch your 31
daughters from me. ·But whoever is found in possession of your gods shall not 32
remain alive. In the presence of our brothers, examine for yourself what I have,
and take what is yours.' Now Jacob did not know that Rachel had stolen them.
Laban went into Jacob's tent, and then into Leah's tent and the tent of the two 33
slave-girls, but he found nothing. He came out of Leah's tent and went into
Rachel's. ·Now Rachel had taken the household idols and put them in the camel's 34
litter, and was sitting on them. Laban went through everything in the tent but
found nothing. ·Then Rachel said to her father, 'Do not look angry, my lord, 35

because I cannot rise in your presence, for I am as women are from time to time'. Laban searched but did not find the idols.

Then Jacob lost his temper and took Laban to task. And Jacob said to Laban, 36 'What is my offence, what is my crime, that you have set on me? •You have gone 37 through all my belongings; have you found anything belonging to your House? Produce it here in the presence of my brothers and yours, and let them decide between the two of us. •In all the twenty years I have been with you, your ewes 38 and your she-goats have never miscarried, and I have eaten none of the rams from your flock. •As for those mauled by wild beasts, I have never brought them 39 back to you, but have borne the loss myself; you claimed them from me, whether I was robbed by day or robbed by night. •In the daytime the heat has consumed 40 me, and at night the cold has gnawed at me, and sleep has fled from my eyes. These twenty years I have been in your house; fourteen years I have worked for 41 you for your two daughters, and six years for your flock; and ten times you have changed my wages. •If the God of my father, the God of Abraham, the Kinsman 42 of Isaac, had not been with me, you would have sent me away empty-handed. But God has seen my weariness and the work done by my hands, and last night he delivered judgement.'

A treaty between Jacob and Laban

Laban gave Jacob this answer, 'These daughters are my daughters and these 43 sons are my sons; these sheep are my sheep, and all that you see belongs to me. But what can I do today about my daughters, and about the sons they have borne? •Come now, let us make a covenant, you and I. . ., and let it serve as a 44 witness between us.'

Then Jacob took a stone and set it up as a monument. •Jacob said to his 46 kinsmen, 'Collect some stones', and gathering some stones they made a cairn. They had a meal there, on the cairn, and •Laban called it Jegar-sahadutha while 47 Jacob called it Galeed. •Laban said, 'May this cairn be a witness between us 48 today'. That is why he named it Galeed, •and also Mizpah, because he said, 'Let 49 Yahweh act as watchman between us when we are no longer in sight of each other. •If you ill-treat my daughters or marry other women in addition to 50 my daughters, even though no one be with us, remember: God is witness between us.' •Then Laban said to Jacob, 'Here is this cairn I have thrown up 51 between us, and here is the monument. •This cairn is a witness, and the 52 monument bears witness: I must not pass this cairn to attack you, and you must not pass this cairn and this monument to attack me. •May the God of 53 Abraham and the god of Nahor judge between us.' Then Jacob swore by the Kinsman of his father Isaac. •He offered a sacrifice on the mountain and invited 54 his brothers to the meal. They ate the meal, and passed the night on the mountain.

32

· · · · · ·

Jacob prepares for his meeting with Esau

Jacob sent messengers ahead of him to his brother Esau in the land of Seir, 3 the countryside of Edom, •with these instructions, 'Say this to my lord Esau, 4 "Here is the message of your servant Jacob: I have been staying with Laban till

now, and have acquired oxen, beasts of burden and flocks, and men and women 5
slaves. I send news of this to my lord in the hope of winning your approval".'
The messengers returned to Jacob and told him, 'We went to your brother Esau, 6
and he is already on his way to meet you; there are four hundred men with him'.
Jacob was greatly afraid and distressed. He divided the people with him, and 7
the flocks and cattle, into two companies, •saying, 'If Esau comes to one of the 8
companies and attacks it, the other company will be left to escape'. •Jacob said, 9
'O God of my father Abraham, and God of my father Isaac, Yahweh who said
to me, "Go back to your country and family, and I will make you prosper", •I 10
am unworthy of all the kindness and goodness you have shown your servant. I
had only my staff when I crossed the Jordan here, and now I can form two companies. •I implore you, save me from my brother's clutches, for I am afraid of 11
him; he may come and attack us and the mothers and their children. •Yet it was 12
you who said, "I will make you prosper, and make your descendants like the
sand on the seashore, so many that it cannot be counted".' •Then Jacob passed 13
that night there.
From what he had with him he chose a gift for his brother Esau: •two hundred 14
she-goats and twenty he-goats, two hunderd ewes and twenty rams, •thirty camels 15
in milk with their calves, forty cows and ten bulls, twenty she-asses and ten donkeys. •He put them in the charge of his servants, in separate droves, and he told 16
his servants, 'Go ahead of me, leaving a space between each drove and the next'.
He gave the first this order: 'When my brother Esau meets you and asks, "To 17
whom do you belong? Where are you going? Whose are those animals that you
are driving?" •you will answer, "To your servant Jacob. They are a gift sent to 18
my lord Esau. Jacob himself is following".' •He gave the same order to the second 19
and the third, and to all who were following the droves, 'That is what you must
say to Esau when you find him. •You must say, "Yes, your servant Jacob himself 20
is following".' For he argued, 'I shall conciliate him by sending a gift in advance;
so when I come face to face with him he may perhaps receive me favourably'.
The gift went ahead of him, but he himself spent that night in the camp.

Jacob wrestles with God

That same night he rose, and taking his two wives and his two slave-girls and 22
his eleven children he crossed the ford of the Jabbok. •He took them and sent 23
them across the stream and sent all his possessions over too. •And Jacob was 24
left alone.
And there was one that wrestled with him until daybreak •who, seeing that he 25
could not master him, struck him in the socket of his hip, and Jacob's hip was
dislocated as he wrestled with him. •He said, 'Let me go, for day is breaking'. 26
But Jacob answered, 'I will not let you go unless you bless me'. •He then asked, 27
'What is your name?' 'Jacob', he replied. •He said, 'Your name shall no longer 28
be Jacob, but Israel, because you have been strong against God, you shall
prevail against men'. •Jacob then made this request, 'I beg you, tell me your 29
name', but he replied, 'Why do you ask my name?' And he blessed him there.
Jacob named the place Peniel, 'Because I have seen God face to face,' he said 30
'and I have survived'. •The sun rose as he left Peniel, limping because of his 31
hip. •That is the reason why to this day the Israelites do not eat the sciatic nerve 32
which is in the socket of the hip; because he had struck Jacob in the socket of
the hip on the sciatic nerve.

The meeting with Esau

33 Looking up Jacob saw Esau arriving with four hundred men. Accordingly 1
he divided the children between Leah, Rachel and the two slave-girls. •He 2
put the slave-girls and their children in front, with Leah and her children following, and Rachel and Joseph behind. •He himself went ahead of them and bowed 3
to the ground seven times before going up to his brother. •But Esau ran to meet 4
him, took him in his arms and held him close and wept. •Then looking up he 5
saw the women and children. 'Who are these with you?' he asked. Jacob answered, 'The children whom God has bestowed on your servant'. •The slave-girls 6
then came up with their children, and they all bowed low. •Leah also came up 7
along with her children, and they all bowed low. Finally Rachel and Joseph came
up and bowed low.

Esau asked, 'What was the meaning of all the company that I have met?' 8
'It is to win my lord's favour' he replied. •'Brother, I have plenty,' Esau answered 9
'keep what is yours.' •Jacob protested, 'Please, if I have found favour with you, 10
accept the gift I offer. To speak truly, I came into your presence as into the
presence of God, but you have received me kindly. •So accept the gift I have 11
brought for you; since God has been generous to me, I have all I need.' And he
urged him, and Esau accepted.

Jacob leaves Esau

Esau said, 'Let us break camp and move off; I will lead you'. •But Jacob 13
replied, 'My lord is aware that the children are weak, and that I must consider
the sheep and the cows that have calved. If they are driven too hard, even for
one day, the whole drove will die. •May it please my lord to go on ahead of his 14
servant. For my part, I will move at a slower pace, to suit the flock I am driving
and the children, until I join my lord in Seir.' •Then Esau said, 'But I must at 15
least leave you some of the people accompanying me'. 'Why?' Jacob asked 'All I
desire is to win your favour.' •So that day Esau resumed his journey to Seir. 16
But Jacob left for Succoth, where he built himself a house and made shelters 17
for his livestock; that is why the place was given the name of Succoth.

Jacob arrived safely at the town of Shechem in Canaanite territory, on his 18
return from Paddan-aram. . . .

The rape of Dinah

34 Dinah, who was Jacob's daughter by Leah, went out to visit the women of 1
that region. •Shechem, the son of Hamor the Hivite, who was ruler of that 2
region, saw her, carried her off and raped her, and so dishonoured her. •But he 3
was captivated by Dinah, the daughter of Jacob; he fell in love with the young
girl and comforted her. •Accordingly Shechem said to his father Hamor, 'Get me 4
this young girl, I want to marry her'. •Meanwhile, Jacob had heard how his 5
daughter Dinah had been dishonoured, but since his sons were out in the countryside with his livestock, Jacob said nothing until they came back.

A matrimonial alliance with the Shechemites

Hamor the father of Shechem went out to talk to Jacob. •When Jacob's son 7
returned from the countryside and heard the news, these men were outraged and
infuriated that Shechem had insulted Israel by raping Jacob's daughter—an
offence that could not be overlooked. •Hamor said to them, 'The heart of my son 8
Shechem is set on your daughter; I beg you, let him marry her. •Ally yourselves 9

with us by marriage; give us your daughters and take our daughters for yourselves. •Stay with us and the land shall be open to you to live in or move through 10
or own.' •Shechem said to the father and brothers of the young girl, 'If only I can 11
win your favour, I will give you whatever you ask. •Demand from me a huge 12
bridal price and gifts; I will give you as much as you ask. Only let me marry the
young girl.'

Then came the answer Jacob's sons gave to Shechem and his father Hamor, 13
a crafty answer because he had dishonoured their sister Dinah. •'We cannot do 14
such a thing' they said to them. 'To give our sister to an uncircumcised man
would be a disgrace for us. •We can agree only on one condition: that you be- 15
come like us by circumcising all your males. •Then we will give you our daugh- 16
ters, taking yours for ourselves; and we will stay with you to make one nation.
But if you do not listen to us on this matter of circumcision we shall take our 17
daughter and go.' •Hamor and Shechem, Hamor's son, were pleased with what 18
they heard. •The young man did not hesitate about doing this, for he was deeply 19
in love with Jacob's daughter. Moreover he was the most important person in his
father's household.

Hamor and his son Shechem went to the gate of their town and spoke to their 20
fellow townsmen saying, •'These men are friendly; let them stay with us in 21
the land, and move about as freely as they like. Let us marry their daughters and
give our daughters to them. •But these men will agree to stay with us and become 22
a single nation only on this condition: all males must be circumcised as they are.
Will not their livestock, their goods and all their cattle belong to us, if only we 23
agree to let them stay with us?' •All the citizens of the town agreed to the pro- 24
posal made by Hamor and his son Shechem, and so all the males were circumcised.

The treacherous revenge of Simeon and Levi

Now on the third day, when they were still in pain, Jacob's two sons Simeon 25
and Levi, brothers of Dinah, took their swords and marched into the town
unsuspected; they killed all the males. •They put Hamor and his son Shechem to 26
the sword, took Dinah from Shechem's house and came away. •Jacob's sons 27
attacked the wounded and pillaged the town because their sister had been dishonoured. •They took away their flocks, cattle, donkeys and whatever there 28
was in the town and in the countryside. •They carried off all their riches, all 29
their little children and their wives, and looted everything to be found in their
houses.

Jacob said to Simeon and Levi, 'You have done me harm, putting me in 30
bad odour with the people of this land, the Canaanites and the Perizzites. I have
few men, whereas they will unite against me to defeat me and destroy me and my
family.' •They retorted, 'Is our sister to be treated like a whore?' 31

35
. . . . . .

Reuben's incest

Israel left and pitched his tent beyond Migdal-eder. •While Israel was living 22
in that district, Reuben went and slept with Bilhah his father's concubine, and
Israel learned of it.

. . . . . .

37

THE STORY OF JOSEPH

Joseph and his brothers

. . . . .

Joseph was seventeen years old. As he was still young, he was shepherding the 2
flock with his brothers, with the sons of Bilhah and Zilpah his father's wives.
Joseph informed their father of the evil spoken about them.

Israel loved Joseph more than all his other sons, for he was the son of his old 3
age, and he had a coat with long sleeves made for him. ·But his brothers, seeing 4
how his father loved him more than all his other sons, came to hate him so much
that they could not say a civil word to him.

Now Joseph had a dream, and he repeated it to his brothers. ·'Listen' he 5
said 'to this dream I have had. ·We were binding sheaves in the countryside; and 6
my sheaf, it seemed, rose up and stood upright; then I saw your sheaves gather 7
round and bow to my sheaf.' ·'So you want to be king over us,' his brothers 8
retorted 'or to lord it over us?' And they hated him still more, on account of his
dreams and of what he said. ·He had another dream which he told to his broth- 9
ers. 'Look, I have had another dream' he said. 'I thought I saw the sun, the moon
and eleven stars, bowing to me.' ·He told his father and brothers, and his father 10
scolded him. 'A fine dream to have!' he said to him. 'Are all of us then, myself,
your mother and your brothers, to come and bow to the ground before you?'
His brothers were jealous of him, but his father kept the thing in mind.   11

Joseph sold by his brothers

His brothers went to pasture their father's flock at Shechem. ·Then Israel 13
said to Joseph, 'Are not your brothers with the flock at Shechem? Come, I am
going to send you to them.' 'I am ready' he replied. ·He said to him, 'Go and 14
see how your brothers and the flock are doing, and bring me word'. He sent him
from the valley of Hebron, and Joseph arrived at Shechem.

A man found him wandering in the countryside and the man asked him, 'What 15
are you looking for?' ·'I am looking for my brothers' he replied. 'Please tell me 16
where they are pasturing their flock.' ·The man answered, 'They have moved on 17
from here; indeed I heard them say, "Let us go to Dothan" '. So Joseph went
after his brothers and found them at Dothan.

They saw him in the distance, and before he reached them they made a plot 18
among themselves to put him to death. ·'Here comes the man of dreams' they 19
said to one another. ·'Come on, let us kill him and throw him into some well; 20
we can say that a wild beast devoured him. Then we shall see what becomes of
his dreams' . . . . ·Then they sat down to eat.   25

Looking up they saw a group of Ishmaelites who were coming from Gilead,
their camels laden with gum, tragacanth, balsam and resin, which they were taking down into Egypt. ·Then Judah said to his brothers, 'What do we gain by kill- 26
ing our brother and covering up his blood? ·Come, let us sell him to the Ishmael- 27
ites, but let us not do any harm to him. After all, he is our brother, and our own
flesh.' His brothers agreed. . . . ·They sold Joseph to the Ishmaelites for twenty 28
silver pieces, and these men took Joseph to Egypt. . . .

The story of Judah and Tamar

38 It happened at that time that Judah left his brothers, to go down and stay 1
with an Adullamite called Hirah. ·There Judah saw the daughter of a 2
Canaanite called Shua. He made her his wife and slept with her. ·She conceived 3
and gave birth to a son whom she named Er. ·She conceived again and gave birth 4
to a son whom she named Onan. ·Yet again she gave birth to a son whom she 5
named Shelah. She was at Chezib when she gave birth to him.

Judah took a wife for his first-born Er, and her name was Tamar. ·But Er, 7
Judah's first-born, offended Yahweh greatly, so Yahweh brought about his
death. ·Then Judah said to Onan, 'Take your brother's wife, and do your duty 8
as her brother-in-law, to produce a child for your brother'. ·But Onan, knowing 9
the child would not be his, spilt his seed on the ground every time he slept with
his brother's wife, to avoid providing a child for his brother. ·What he did was 10
offensive to Yahweh, so he brought about his death also. ·Then Judah said to 11
his daughter-in-law Tamar, 'Return home as a widow to your father, and wait
for my son Shelah to grow up', for he was thinking, 'He must not die like his
brothers'. So Tamar went back home to her father.

A long time passed, and then Shua's daughter, the wife of Judah, died. After 12
Judah had been comforted he went up to Timnah to the men who sheared his
sheep, himself and Hirah, his Adullamite friend. ·This was reported to Tamar, 13
'Listen, your father-in-law is going up to Timnah for the shearing of his sheep'.
She therefore changed her widow's clothes, wrapped a veil around her, and sat 14
down, heavily swathed, where the road to Enaim branches off the road to Timnah. Shelah had now grown up, as she saw, and yet she had not been given to
him as his wife.

Judah, seeing her, took her for a prostitute, since her face was veiled. ·Going 16
up to her on the road, he said, 'Come, let me sleep with you'. He did not know
that she was his daughter-in-law. 'What will you give me to sleep with me?' she
asked. ·'I will send you a kid from the flock' he answered. 'Agreed, if you give 17
me a pledge until you send it' she answered. ·'What pledge shall I give you?' he 18
asked. 'Your seal, your cord and the stick you are holding' she answered. He
gave them to her and slept with her, and she conceived by him. ·Then she rose 19
and left him, and taking off her veil she put on her widow's weeds.

Judah sent the kid by his Adullamite friend to recover the pledge from the 20
woman. But he did not find her. ·He inquired from the men of the place, 'Where 21
is the prostitute who was by the roadside at Enaim?' 'There has been no prostitute there', they answered. ·So returning to Judah he said, 'I did not find her. 22
What is more, the men of the place told me there had been no prostitute there.'
'Let her keep what she has' Judah replied 'or we shall become a laughing-stock. 23
At least I sent her this kid, even though you did not find her.'

About three months later it was reported to Judah, 'Your daughter-in-law has 24
played the harlot; furthermore, she is pregnant, as a result of her misconduct'.
'Take her outside and burn her' said Judah. ·But as she was being led off she sent 25
this message to her father-in-law, 'It was the man to whom these things belong
who made me pregnant. Look at them' she said 'and see whose seal and cord
and stick these are.' ·Judah examined them and then said, 'She is in the right, 26
rather than I. This comes of my not giving her to my son Shelah to be his wife.'
He had no further intercourse with her.

When the time for her confinement came she was found to have twins in her 27

womb. •During the delivery one of them put out a hand, and the midwife caught 28
it and tied a scarlet thread to it, saying, 'This is the first to arrive'. •But he drew 29
his hand back, and it was his brother who came out first. Then she said, 'What
a breach you have opened for yourself!' So he was named Perez. •Then his 30
brother came out with the scarlet thread on his hand, so he was named Zerah.

Joseph's early days in Egypt

39 Now Joseph had been taken down into Egypt. Potiphar the Egyptian, one 1
of Pharaoh's officials and commander of the guard, bought him from the
Ishmaelites who had brought him down there. •Yahweh was with Joseph, and 2
everything went well with him. He lodged in the house of his Egyptian master,
and when his master saw how Yahweh was with him and how Yahweh made 3
everything succeed that he turned his hand to, •he was pleased with Joseph and 4
made him his personal attendant; and his master put him in charge of his
household, entrusting everything to him. •And from the time he put him in 5
charge of his household and all his posessions, Yahweh blessed the Egyptian's
household out of consideration for Joseph; Yahweh's blessing extended to all his
possessions, both household and estate. •So he left Joseph to handle all his pos- 6
sessions, and with him at hand, concerned himself with nothing beyond the food
he ate.

The attempt to seduce Joseph

Now Joseph was well built and handsome, •and it happened some time later 7
that his master's wife looked desirously at him and said, 'Sleep with me'. •But he 8
refused, and answered his master's wife, 'Because of me, my master does not
concern himself with what happens in the house; he has handed over all his
possessions to me. •He is no more master in this house than I am. He has with- 9
held nothing from me except yourself, because you are his wife. How could I
do anything so wicked, and sin against God?' •Although she spoke to Joseph day 10
after day he would not agree to sleep with her and surrender to her.

But one day Joseph in the course of his duties came to the house, and there 11
was not a servant there indoors. •The woman caught hold of him by his tunic 12
and said, 'Sleep with me'. But he left the tunic in her hand and ran out of the
house. •Seeing he had left the tunic in her hand and left the house, •she called 14
her servants and said to them, 'Look at this! He has brought us a Hebrew to insult us. He came to me to sleep with me, but I screamed, •and when he heard me 15
scream and shout he left his tunic beside me and ran out of the house.'

She put the tunic down by her side until the master came home. •Then she 17
told him the same tale, 'The Hebrew slave you bought us came to insult me.
But when I screamed and called out he left his garment by my side and made 18
his escape.' •When the master heard his wife say, 'This is how your slave treated 19
me', he was furious. •Joseph's master had him arrested and committed to the 20
gaol where the king's prisoners were kept.

Joseph in gaol

And there in gaol he stayed. •But Yahweh was with Joseph. He was kind to 21
him and made him popular with the chief gaoler. •The chief gaoler put Joseph 22
in charge of all the prisoners in the gaol, making him responsible for everything
done there. •The chief gaoler did not need to interfere with Joseph's administra- 23

tion, for Yahweh was with him, and Yahweh made everything he undertook successful.

. . . . . .

Pharaoh's dreams

41 *Two years later it happened that Pharaoh had a dream: he was standing* 1
by the Nile, •and there, coming up from the Nile, were seven cows, sleek 2
and fat, and they began to feed among the rushes. •And seven other cows, ugly 3
and lean, came up from the Nile after them; and these went over and stood
beside the other cows on the bank of the Nile. •The ugly and lean cows ate the 4
seven sleek and fat cows. Then Pharaoh awoke.
    He fell asleep and dreamed a second time: there, growing on one stalk, were 5
seven ears of corn full and ripe. •And sprouting up after them came seven ears of 6
corn, meagre and scorched by the east wind. •The scanty ears of corn swallowed 7
the seven full and ripe ears of corn. Then Pharaoh awoke; it was a dream.

. . . . . .

    Then Pharaoh had Joseph summoned, and they hurried him from prison. He 14
shaved and changed his clothes, and came into Pharaoh's presence. •Pharaoh 15
said to Joseph, 'I have had a dream which no one can interpret. But I have heard
it said of you that when you hear a dream you can interpret it.' •Joseph answered 16
Pharaoh, 'I do not count. It is God who will give Pharaoh a favourable answer.'

. . . . . .

    Joseph told Pharaoh, 'Pharaoh's dreams are one and the same: God has re- 25
vealed to Pharaoh what he is going to do. •The seven fine cows are seven years 26
and the seven ripe ears of corn are seven years; it is one and the same dream.
The seven gaunt and lean cows coming up after them are seven years, as are the 27
seven shrivelled ears of corn scorched by the east wind: there will be seven years
of famine. •It is as I have told Pharaoh: God has revealed to Pharaoh what he is 28
going to do. •Seven years are coming, bringing great plenty to the whole land 29
of Egypt, •but seven years of famine will follow them, when all the plenty in 30
the land of Egypt will be forgotten, and famine will exhaust the land. •The 31
famine that is to follow will be so very severe that no one will remember what
plenty the country enjoyed. •The reason why the dream came to Pharaoh twice 32
is because the event is already determined by God, and God is impatient to bring
it about.

. . . . . .

Joseph's promotion

    Pharaoh and all his ministers approved of what he had said. •Then Pharaoh 38
asked his ministers, 'Can we find any other man like this, possessing the spirit of
God?' •So Pharaoh said to Joseph, 'Seeing that God has given you knowledge 39
of all this, there can be no one as intelligent and wise as you. •You shall be my 40
chancellor, and all my people shall respect your orders; only this throne shall set
me above you.' •Pharaoh said to Joseph, 'I hereby make you governor of the 41
whole land of Egypt'. •Pharaoh took the ring from his hand and put it on Jo- 42
seph's. He clothed him in fine linen and put a gold chain round his neck. •He 43
made him ride in the best chariot he had after his own, and they cried before
him 'Abrek'. This is the way he was made governor of the whole land of Egypt.

. . . . . .

Then the seven years of plenty that there had been in the land of Egypt came 53
to an end. ·The seven years of famine began to come as Joseph had said. There 54
was famine in every country, but there was bread to be had throughout the land
of Egypt. ·When the whole country began to feel the famine, the people cried 55
out to Pharaoh for bread. But Pharaoh told all the Egyptians, 'Go to Joseph and
do what he tells you'.—·There was famine all over the world.—Then Joseph 56
opened all the granaries and sold grain to the Egyptians. The famine grew worse
in the land of Egypt. ·People came to Egypt from all over the world to buy grain 57
from Joseph, for the famine had grown severe throughout the world.

The first meeting between Joseph and his brothers

42 *Jacob, seeing that there was grain for sale in Egypt, said to his sons, 'Why* 1
do you stand looking at one another?' ·'I hear' he said 'that there is grain 2
for sale in Egypt. Go down and buy grain for us there, that we may survive and
not die.' ·So ten of Joseph's brothers went down to buy grain in Egypt. ·But 4
Jacob did not send Joseph's brother Benjamin with his brothers. 'Nothing must
happen to him' he said.

Israel's sons with others making the same journey went to buy grain, for there 5
was famine in the land of Canaan. ·It was Joseph, as the man in authority over 6
the country, who sold the grain to all comers. So Joseph's brothers went and
bowed down before him, their faces touching the ground. . . .

So Joseph recognised his brothers, but they did not recognise him. ·Joseph, 9
remembering the dreams he had had about them, said to them, 'You are spies.
You have come to discover the country's weak points.' ·'No, my lord,' they told 10
him 'your servants have come to buy food. ·We are all sons of the same man. 11
We are honest men, your servants are not spies.' ·'Not so!' he replied 'It is the 12
country's weak points you have come to discover.' ·'Your servants are twelve 13
brothers,' they said 'sons of the same man, from the land of Canaan. The young-
est, we should explain, is at present with our father, and the other one is no
more.' Joseph answered them, 'It is as I said, you are spies. . . . ·Then he kept 17
them all in custody for three days.

On the third day Joseph said to them, 'Do this and you shall keep your lives, 18
for I am a man who fears God. ·If you are honest men let one of your brothers 19
be kept in the place of your detention; as for you, go and take grain to relieve
the famine of your families. ·You shall bring me your youngest brother; this way 20
your words will be proved true, and you will not have to die!' This they did.
. . . Of their number he took Simeon and had him bound while they looked on. 24

Jacob's sons return to Canaan

Joseph gave the order to fill their panniers with corn, to put back each man's 25
money in his sack, and to give them provisions for the journey. This was done
for them. ·They loaded the grain on their donkeys and went away. ·But when 27
they camped for the night one of them opened his corn-sack to give fodder to his
donkey and saw his money in the mouth of his sack. ·He said to his brothers, 28
'My money has been put back; here it is in my corn-sack'. Their hearts sank, and
they looked at one another in panic, saying, 'What is this that God has done to
us?'
· · · · · ·

Jacob's sons leave again with Benjamin

43 But the country was hard-pressed by famine, ·and when they had finished 2 eating the grain they had brought from Egypt their father said to them, 'Go back and buy us a little food'. ·'But the man expressly warned us' Judah told 3 him. 'He said, "You will not be admitted to my presence unless your brother is with you". ·If you are ready to send our brother with us, we are willing to go 4 down and buy food for you. ·But if you are not ready to send him we will not go 5 down, for the man told us, "You will not be admitted to my presence unless your brother is with you".' ·Then Israel said, 'Why did you bring this misery on me 6 by telling the man you had another brother?' ·They replied, 'He kept questioning 7 us about ourselves and our kinsfolk, "Is your father still alive?" and, "Have you a brother?" That is why we told him. How could we know he was going to say, "Bring your brother down here"?' ·Judah said to his father Israel, 'Send the boy 8 with me. Let us start off and go, so that we may save our lives and not die, we, you, and our dependants. ·I will go surety for him, and you can hold me respon- 9 sible for him. If I do not bring him back to you and set him before you, let me bear the blame all my life. ·Indeed, if we had not wasted so much time we 10 should have been back again by now!'

Then their father Israel said to them, 'If it must be so, then do this: take some 11 of the land's finest products in your panniers, and carry them down to the man as a gift, a little balsam, a little honey, gum, tragacanth, resin, pistachio nuts and almonds. ·Take double the amount of money with you and return the money put 12 back in the mouths of your sacks; it may have been a mistake. ·Take your 13 brother, and go back to the man. ·May El Shaddai move the man to be kind to 14 you, and allow you to bring back your other brother and Benjamin. As for me, if I must be bereaved, bereaved I must be.'

The meeting with Joseph

The men took this gift; they took double the amount of money with them, 15 and Benjamin. They started off and went down to Egypt. They presented themselves to Joseph. ·When Joseph saw Benjamin with them he said to his cham- 16 berlain, 'Take these men to the house. Slaughter a beast and prepare it, for these men are to eat with me at midday.' ·The man did as Joseph had ordered, and 17 took the men to Joseph's house.

The men were afraid at being taken to Joseph's house, thinking, 'We are being 18 taken there because of the money replaced in our corn-sacks the first time. They will set on us; they will fall on us and make slaves of us, and take our donkeys too.' ·So they went up to Joseph's chamberlain and spoke to him at the entrance 19 to the house. ·'By your leave, sir,' they said 'we came down once before to buy 20 food, ·and when we reached camp and opened our corn-sacks, there was each 21 man's money in the mouth of his sack, to its full amount. But we have brought it back with us, ·and we have brought more money with us to buy food. We do 22 not know who put our money in our corn-sacks.' ·'Peace to you,' he replied 23 'do not be afraid. Your God and your father's God has put a treasure in your corn-sacks. Your money reached me safely.' And he brought Simeon out to them.

The man took the men into Joseph's house. He offered them water to wash 24 their feet, and gave their donkeys fodder. ·They arranged their gift while they 25 waited for Joseph to come at midday, for they had heard they were to dine there.

When Joseph arrived at the house they offered him the gift they had with 26
them, and bowed before him to the ground. ·But he greeted them kindly, asking, 27
'Is your father well, the old man you told me of? Is he still alive?' ·'Your servant 28
our father is well,' they replied 'he is still alive', and they bowed low in homage.
Looking up he saw his brother Benjamin, his mother's son. 'Is this your young- 29
est brother,' he asked 'of whom you told me?' Then he said to him, 'God be
good to you, my son'. ·Joseph hurried out, for his heart was moved at the sight 30
of his brother and he was near to weeping. He went into his room and there he
wept. ·After bathing his face he returned and, controlling himself, gave the 31
order: 'Serve the meal'. ·He was served separately; so were they, and so were the 32
Egyptians who ate in his household, for Egyptians cannot take food with Hebrews; they have a horror of it. ·They were placed opposite him each according 33
to his rank, from the eldest to the youngest, and the men looked at one another in
amazement. ·He had portions carried to them from his own dish, the portion for 34
Benjamin being five times larger than any of the others. They drank with him
and were happy.

Joseph's cup in Benjamin's sack

44 Joseph gave this order to his chamberlain: 'Fill these men's sacks with as 1
much food as they can carry, and put each man's money in the mouth of
his sack. ·And put my cup, the silver one, in the mouth of the youngest one's 2
sack as well as the money for his grain.' He carried out the instructions Joseph
had given.

When morning came and it was light, the men were sent off with their don- 3
keys. ·They had scarcely left the city, and had not gone far before Joseph said 4
to his chamberlain, 'Away now and follow those men. When you catch up with
them say to them, "Why did you reward good with evil? ·Is this not the one my 5
lord uses for drinking and also for reading omens? What you have done is
wrong." '

So when he caught up with them he repeated these words. ·They asked him, 7
'What does my lord mean? Your servants would never think of doing such a
thing. ·Look, the money we found in the mouths of our corn-sacks we brought 8
back to you from the land of Canaan. Are we likely to have stolen silver or gold
from your master's house? ·Whichever of your servants is found to have it shall 9
die, and we ourselves shall be slaves of my lord.' ·'Very well, then,' he replied 'it 10
shall be as you say. The one on whom it is found shall become my slave, but the
rest of you can go free.' ·Each of them quickly lifted his corn-sack to the 11
ground, and each opened his own. ·He searched them, beginning with the eldest 12
and ending with the youngest, and found the cup in Benjamin's sack. ·Then they 13
tore their clothes, and when each man had reloaded his ass they returned to the
city.

When Judah and his brothers arrived at Joseph's house he was still there, so 14
they fell on the ground in front of him. ·'What is this deed you have done?' Jo- 15
seph asked them. 'Did you not know that a man such as I am is a reader of
omens?' ·'What can we answer my lord?' Judah replied 'What can we say? How 16
can we clear ourselves? God himself has uncovered your servants' guilt. Here
we are then, my lord's slaves, we no less than the one in whose possession the
cup was found.' ·'I could not think of doing such a thing' he replied. 'The man 17
in whose possession the cup was found shall be my slave, but you can go back
safe and sound to your father.'

Judah intervenes

Then Judah went up to him and said, 'May it please my lord, let your servant 18
have a word privately with my lord. Do not be angry with your servant, for you
are like Pharaoh himself. •My lord questioned his servants, "Have you father or 19
brother?" •And we said to my lord, "We have an old father, and a younger 20
brother born of his old age. His brother is dead, so he is the only one left of his
mother, and his father loves him." •Then you said to your servants, "Bring him 21
down to me that my eyes may look on him". •We replied to my lord, "The boy 22
cannot leave his father. If he leaves him, his father will die." •But you said to 23
your servants, "If your youngest brother does not come down with you, you will
not be admitted to my presence again". •When we went back to your servant my 24
father, we repeated to him what my lord had said. •So when our father said, 25
"Go back and buy us a little food", •we said, "We cannot go down. If our 26
youngest brother is with us, we will go down, for we cannot be admitted to the
man's presence unless our youngest brother is with us." •So your servant our 27
father said to us, "You know that my wife bore me two children. •When one left 28
me, I said that he must have been torn to pieces. And I have not seen him to this
day. •If you take this one from me too and any harm comes to him, you will 29
send me down to Sheol with my white head bowed in misery." •If I go to your 30
servant my father now, and we have not the boy with us, he will die as soon as
he sees the boy is not with us, for his heart is bound up with him. Then your 31
servants will have sent your servant our father down to Sheol with his white
head bowed in grief. •Now your servant went surety to my father for the boy. I 32
said: If I do not bring him back to you, let me bear the blame before my father
all my life. •Let your servant stay, then, as my lord's slave in place of the boy, 33
I implore you, and let the boy go back with his brothers. •How indeed could I 34
go back to my father and not have the boy with me? I could not bear to see the
misery that would overwhelm my father.'

Joseph makes himself known

45 Then Joseph could not control his feelings in front of all his retainers, and 1
he exclaimed, 'Let everyone leave me'. No one therefore was present with
him while Joseph made himself known to his brothers, •but he wept so loudly 2
that all the Egyptians heard, and the news reached Pharaoh's palace.

Joseph said to his brothers, 'I am Joseph. Is my father really still alive?' His 3
brothers could not answer him, they were so dismayed at the sight of him. Then
Joseph said to his brothers, 'Come closer to me'. When they had come closer 4
to him he said, 'I am your brother Joseph whom you sold into Egypt. •But now, 5
do not grieve, do not reproach yourselves for having sold me here, since God
sent me before you to preserve your lives. •For this is the second year there has 6
been famine in the country, and there are still five years to come of no ploughing or reaping. •God sent me before you to make sure that your race would have 7
survivors in the land and to save your lives, many lives at that. •So it was not 8
you who sent me here but God, and he has made me father to Pharaoh, lord of
all his household and administrator of the whole land of Egypt.

'Return quickly to your father and tell him, "Your son Joseph says this: God 9
has made me lord of all Egypt. Come down to me at once. •You shall live in 10
the country of Goshen where you will be near me, you, your children and your
grandchildren, your flocks, your cattle and all your possessions. •I will provide 11

for you there, for there are still five years of famine, and I do not want you to
be in need, you and your household and all you have." •You can see with your 12
own eyes, and my brother Benjamin can see too that it is my own mouth speaking to you. •Give my father a full report of all the honour I enjoy in Egypt, and 13
of all you have seen. Then hurry and bring my father down here.'

Then throwing his arms around the neck of his brother Benjamin he wept; 14
and Benjamin wept on his shoulder. •He kissed all his brothers, weeping over 15
them. After which his brothers talked with him.

Pharaoh's invitation

News reached Pharaoh's palace that Joseph's brothers had come, and Pha- 16
raoh was pleased to hear it, as were his servants. •Pharaoh told Joseph, 'Say to 17
your brothers, "Do this: load your beasts and go off to the land of Canaan.
Fetch your father and families, and come back to me. I will give you the best 18
the land of Egypt offers, and you shall feed on the fat of the land." •And you, 19
for your part, give them this command: "Do this: take waggons from the land
of Egypt, for your little ones and your wives. Get your father and come. •Never 20
mind about your property, for the best that the land of Egypt offers is yours." '

The return to Canaan

Israel's sons did as they were told. Joseph gave them waggons as Pharaoh 21
had ordered, and he gave them provisions for the journey. •To each and every 22
one he gave a festal garment, and to Benjamin three hundred shekels of silver
and five festal garments. •And he sent his father ten donkeys laden with the 23
best that Egypt offered, and ten she-donkeys laden with grain, bread and food
for his father's journey. •Then he sent his brothers on their way. His final words 24
to them were, 'Do not be upset on the journey'.

And so they left Egypt. When they reached the land of Canaan and their 25
father Jacob, •they gave him this report, 'Joseph is still alive. Indeed it is he who 26
is administrator of the whole land of Egypt.' But he was as one stunned for he
did not believe them. •However, when they told him all Joseph had said to 27
them, and when he saw the waggons that Joseph had sent to fetch him, the
spirit of their father Jacob revived, •and Israel said, 'That is enough! My son 28
Joseph is still alive. I must go and see him before I die.'

Jacob leaves for Egypt

46 Israel left with his possessions, and reached Beersheba. Then he offered 1
sacrifices to the God of his father Isaac. . . .

Israel sent Judah ahead to Joseph, so that the latter might present himself 28
to him in Goshen. When they arrived in the land of Goshen, •Joseph had his 29
chariot made ready and went up to meet his father Israel in Goshen. As soon as
he appeared he threw his arms round his neck and for a long time wept on his
shoulder. •Israel said to Joseph, 'Now I can die, now that I have seen you again, 30
and seen you still alive'.

Then Joseph said to his brothers and his father's family, 'I will go up and 31
break the news to Pharaoh. I will tell him, "My brothers and my father's family
who were in the land of Canaan have come to me. •The men are shepherds and 32
look after livestock, and they have brought their flocks and cattle and all their
possessions." •Thus, when Pharaoh summons you and asks, "What is your occu- 33
pation?", •you are to say, "Ever since our boyhood your servants have looked 34

after livestock, we and our fathers before us". And so you will be able to stay in the land of Goshen.' For the Egyptians have a horror of all shepherds.

Pharaoh grants an audience

47 So Joseph went and told Pharaoh, 'My father and brothers, along with 1 their flocks and cattle and all their possessions, have come from the land of Canaan and are now in the land of Goshen'. ·He had taken five of his brothers, 2 and he now presented them to Pharaoh. ·Pharaoh asked his brothers, 'What 3 is your occupation?' and they gave Pharaoh the answer, 'Your servants are shepherds, like our fathers before us'. ·They went on to tell Pharaoh, 'We have 4 come to stay for the present in this land, for there is no pasture for your servants' flocks, the land of Canaan is hard-pressed by famine. Now give your servants leave to stay in the land of Goshen.' ·Then Pharaoh said to Joseph, ·'They 6 may stay in the land of Goshen, and if you know of any capable men among them, put them in charge of my own livestock'.

· · · · · ·

Joseph's agrarian policy

There was no bread in the whole land, for the famine had grown so severe 13 that the land of Egypt and the land of Canaan were weakened with hunger. Joseph accumulated all the money there was to be found in the land of Egypt 14 and in the land of Canaan, in return for the grain which men were buying, and he brought the money to Pharaoh's palace.

When all the money in the land of Egypt and in the land of Canaan had run 15 out, the Egyptians all came to Joseph: 'Give us bread' they said. 'Have we to perish before your eyes? For our money has come to an end.' ·Joseph answered, 16 'Hand over your livestock; I am willing to give you bread in exchange for your livestock, if your money has come to an end'. ·So they brought their livestock 17 to Joseph, and Joseph gave them bread, in exchange for horses and livestock, whether sheep or cattle, and for donkeys. Thus he fed them that year with bread, in exchange for all their livestock.

When that year was over, they came to him the next year, and said to him, 18 'We cannot hide it from my lord: the truth is, our money has run out and the livestock is in my lord's possession. There is nothing left for my lord except our bodies and our land. ·Have we to perish before your eyes, we and our land? 19 Buy us and our land in exchange for bread; we with our land will be Pharaoh's serfs. But give us something to sow, that we may keep our lives and not die and the land may not become desolate.'

Thus Joseph acquired all the land in Egypt for Pharaoh, since one by one the 20 Egyptians sold their estates, so hard-pressed were they by the famine, and the whole country passed into Pharaoh's possession. ·As for the people, he reduced 21 them to serfdom from one end of Egypt to the other. ·The only land he did 22 not acquire belonged to the priests, for the priests received an allowance from Pharaoh and lived on the allowance that Pharaoh gave them. Therefore they did not have to sell their land.

Then Joseph said to the people, 'This is how we stand: I have bought you 23 out, with your land, on Pharaoh's behalf. Here is seed for you so that you can sow the land. ·But when harvest comes you must give a fifth to Pharaoh. The 24 other four-fifths you can have for sowing your fields, to provide food for yourselves and your households, and food for your dependants.' ·'You have saved our 25

lives' they replied. 'If we may enjoy my lord's favour, we will be Pharaoh's serfs.'
So Joseph made a statute, still in force today, concerning the soil of Egypt: a fifth 26
goes to Pharaoh. The land of the priests alone did not go to Pharaoh.

Jacob's last wishes

The Israelites stayed in the land of Egypt, in the country of Goshen. . . . 27
When Israel's time to die drew near he called his son Joseph and said to him, 29
'If I enjoy your favour, place your hand under my thigh and promise to be kind
and good to me, do not bury me in Egypt. ·When I sleep with my fathers, carry 30
me out of Egypt and bury me in their tomb.' 'I will do as you say' he replied.
'Swear to me' he insisted. So he swore to him, and Israel sank back on the pillow. 31

Jacob adopts Joseph's two sons and blesses them

48

. . . . . .

When Israel saw Joseph's two sons, he asked, 'Who are these?' ·'They are my 9
sons, whom God has given me here' Joseph told his father. 'Then bring them
to me,' he said 'that I may bless them.' ·Israel's sight was failing because of his 10
great age, and so he could not see. Joseph therefore made them come closer to
him and he kissed and embraced them. ·Then Israel said to Joseph, 'I did not 11
think that I should see you again, but God has let me see your family as well'.
Joseph took them from his lap and bowed to the ground.　　　　　　　　　12
Joseph took hold of the two of them, Ephraim with his right hand so that he 13
should be on Israel's left, and Manasseh with his left hand, so that he should be
on Israel's right, and brought them close to him. ·But Israel held out his right 14
hand and laid it on the head of Ephraim, the younger, and his left on the head
of Manasseh, crossing his hands—Manasseh was, in fact, the elder. ·Then he 15
blessed Joseph saying:
'May God in whose presence my fathers Abraham and Isaac walked,
　may God who has been my shepherd from my birth until this day,
　may the angel who has been my saviour from all harm, bless these boys,　　16
　may my name live on in them, and the names of my fathers Abraham
　　　and Isaac.
　May they grow and increase on the earth.'
Joseph saw that his father was laying his right hand on the head of Ephraim, 17
and this upset him. He took his father's hand and tried to shift it from the head
of Ephraim to the head of Manasseh. ·Joseph protested to his father, 'Not like 18
that, father! This one is the elder; put your right hand on his head.' ·But his 19
father refused. 'I know, my son, I know' he said. 'He too shall become a people;
he too shall be great. Yet his younger brother shall be greater than he, and his
descendants shall become a multitude of nations.'
So he blessed them that day saying:　　　　　　　　　　　　　　　　　20
　　　　　　'May you be a blessing in Israel; may they say,
　　　　　　"God make you like Ephraim and Manasseh!" '
In this way he put Ephraim before Manasseh.
Then Israel said to Joseph, 'Now I am about to die. But God will be with you 21
and take you back to the country of your fathers. ·As for me, I give you a She- 22
chem more than your brothers, the one I took from the Amorites with my sword
and my bow.'

Jacob's blessings

49

. . . . . .

'Gather round, sons of Jacob, and listen;   2
listen to Israel your father.
Reuben, you are my first-born,   3
my vigour, and the first-fruit of my manhood,
foremost in pride, foremost in strength,
uncontrolled as a flood: you shall not be foremost,   4
for you mounted your father's bed,
and so defiled my couch, to my hurt.
'Simeon and Levi are brothers,   5
they carried out their malicious plans.
Let my soul not enter into their counsel   6
nor my heart join in their company,
for in their rage they have killed men,
in their fury they hamstrung bulls.
Accursed be their rage for its ruthlessness,   7
their wrath for its ferocity.
I will divide them among Jacob,
I will scatter them among Israel.
'Judah, your brothers shall praise you: 8
you grip your enemies by the neck,
your father's sons shall do you homage,
Judah is a lion cub,   9
you climb back, my son, from your kill;
like a lion he crouches and lies down,
or a lioness: who dare rouse him?
'The sceptre shall not pass from Judah,   10
nor the mace from between his feet,
until he come to whom it belongs,
to whom the peoples shall render obedience.
He ties up his young ass to the vine,   11
to its stock the foal of his she-ass.
He washes his coat in wine,
his cloak in the blood of the grape;
his eyes are cloudy with wine,   12
his teeth are white with milk.
'Zebulun lives by the shore of the sea,   13
he is a sailor on board the ships,
he has Sidon close by him.
'Issachar is a strong ass,   14
lying down in the midst of the sheepfolds.
He saw how good it was to take his ease,   15
how pleasant was the country,
so he bowed his shoulders for the load,
he became a slave to forced labour.
'Dan is judge of his people   16

like each one of the tribes of Israel.
May Dan be a serpent on the road,   17
a viper on the path,
who bites the horse on the hock
and its rider falls backward.
'I trust in your salvation, Yahweh.   18
'Gad, robbers rob him,   19
and he, he robs and pursues them.
'Asher, his bread is rich,   20
he provides food fit for a king.
'Naphtali is a swift hind,   21
dropping beautiful fawns.
'Joseph is a fruitful creeper near the spring,   22
whose tendrils climb over the wall.
Bowmen provoked him,
they drew and assailed him.   23
But their bow was broken by a mighty one,   24
the sinews of their arms were parted
by the hands of the Mighty One of Jacob,
by the name of the Stone of Israel,
by the God of your father who assists you,   25
by El Shaddai who blesses you:
with blessings of heaven above,
blessings of the deep lying below,
blessings of breasts and womb,
blessings of grain and flowers,   26
blessings of ancient mountains;
bounty of the everlasting hills;
may they descend on Joseph's head,
on the brow of the dedicated one among his brothers.
'Benjamin is a ravening wolf,   27
in the morning he devours his prey,
in the evening he is still dividing the spoil.'

. . . . . .

Jacob's funeral

50 At this Joseph threw himself on his father, covering his face with tears and 1
kissing him. •Then Joseph ordered the doctors in his service to embalm his 2
father. The doctors embalmed Israel, •and it took them forty days, for embalming 3
takes forty days to complete.

The Egyptians mourned him for seventy days. •When the period of mourning 4
for him was over, Joseph said to Pharaoh's household, 'If I may presume to enjoy
your favour, please see that this message reaches Pharaoh's ears, •"My father 5
made me swear an oath: I am about to die, he said, I have a tomb which I dug
for myself in the land of Canaan, and there you must bury me. So now I seek
leave to go up and bury my father, and then I shall come back".' •Pharaoh re- 6
plied, 'Go up and bury your father, in accordance with the oath he made you
swear'.

Joseph went up to bury his father, all Pharaoh's servants and the palace digni- 7
taries going up with him, joined by all the dignitaries of the land of Egypt, •as 8

well as all Joseph's family and his brothers, along with his father's family. They left no one in the land of Goshen but their dependants, with their flocks and their cattle. ·Chariots also and horsemen went up with them; it was a very large retinue. 9

On arriving at Goren-ha-atad, which is across the Jordan, they performed 10 there a long and solemn lamentation, and Joseph observed three days' mourning for his father. ·When the Canaanites, the inhabitants of the land, witnessed the 11 mourning at Goren-ha-atad they exclaimed, 'This is a solemn act of mourning for the Egyptians'. For this reason they call this place Abel-mizraim—it is across the Jordan. . . . ·Then Joseph returned to Egypt, he and his brothers, along with 14 all those who had come up with him for his father's burial.

EXODUS

1

. . . . . .

The Hebrews oppressed

Then there came to power in Egypt a new king who knew nothing of Joseph. 8
'Look,' he said to his subjects 'these people, the sons of Israel, have become so 9
numerous and strong that they are a threat to us. ·We must be prudent and 10
take steps against their increasing any further, or if war should break out, they
might add to the number of our enemies. They might take arms against us and
so escape out of the country.' ·Accordingly they put slave-drivers over the 11
Israelites to wear them down under heavy loads. In this way they built the
store-cities of Pithom and Rameses for Pharaoh. ·But the more they were 12
crushed, the more they increased and spread, and men came to dread the sons 14
of Israel. . . .

Pharaoh then gave his subjects this command· 'Throw all the boys born to 22
the Hebrews into the river, but let all the girls live'.

The birth of Moses

2

There was a man of the tribe of Levi who had taken a woman of Levi as his 1
wife. ·She conceived and gave birth to a son and, seeing what a fine child he 2
was, she kept him hidden for three months. ·When she could hide him no longer, 3
she got a papyrus basket for him; coating it with bitumen and pitch, she put the
child inside and laid it among the reeds at the river's edge. ·His sister stood 4
some distance away to see what would happen to him.

Now Pharaoh's daughter went down to bathe in the river, and the girls 5
attending her were walking along by the riverside. Among the reeds she noticed
the basket, and she sent her maid to fetch it. ·She opened it and looked, and 6
saw a baby boy, crying; and she was sorry for him. 'This is a child of one of the
Hebrews' she said. ·Then the child's sister said to the Pharaoh's daughter, 7
'Shall I go and find you a nurse among the Hebrew women to suckle the child
for you?' ·'Yes, go' Pharaoh's daughter said to her; and the girl went off to find 8
the baby's own mother. ·To her the daughter of Pharaoh said, 'Take this child 9
away and suckle it for me. I will see you are paid.' So the woman took the child
and suckled it. ·When the child grew up, she brought him to Pharaoh's daughter 10
who treated him like a son; she named him Moses because, she said, 'I drew
him out of the water'.

Moses escapes to Midian

Moses, a man by now, set out at this time to visit his countrymen, and he saw 11
what a hard life they were having; and he saw an Egyptian strike a Hebrew, one
of his countrymen. ·Looking round he could see no one in sight, so he killed the 12

Egyptian and hid him in the sand. •On the following day he came back, and there 13
were two Hebrews, fighting. He said to the man who was in the wrong, 'What
do you mean by hitting your fellow countryman?' •'And who appointed you' 14
the man retorted. •'to be prince over us, and judge? Do you intend to kill me as
you killed the Egyptian?' Moses was frightened. 'Clearly that business has
come to light' he thought. •When Pharaoh heard of the matter he would have 15
killed Moses, but Moses fled from Pharaoh and made for the land of Midian.
And he sat down beside a well.

Now the priest of Midian had seven daughters. They came to draw water and 16
fill the troughs to water their father's sheep. •Shepherds came and drove them 17
away, but Moses came to their defence and watered their sheep for them. •When 18
they returned to their father Reuel, he said to them, 'You are back early today!'
'An Egyptian protected us from the shepherds;' they said 'yes, and he drew 19
water for us and watered the flock.' •'And where is he?' he asked his daughters. 20
'Why did you leave the man there? Ask him to eat with us.' •So Moses settled 21
with this man, who gave him his daughter Zipporah in marriage. •She gave birth 22
to a son, and he named him Gershom because, he said, 'I am a stranger in a
foreign land'.

. . . . . .

The burning bush

3 *Moses was looking after the flock of Jethro, his father-in-law. He led his flock* 1
to the far side of the wilderness and came to Horeb, the mountain of God.
There the angel of Yahweh appeared to him in the shape of a flame of fire, 2
coming from the middle of a bush. Moses looked; there was the bush blazing
but it was not being burnt up. •'I must go and look at this strange sight,' Moses 3
said 'and see why the bush is not burnt.' •Now Yahweh saw him go forward 4
to look . . . .

And Yahweh said, 'I have seen the miserable state of my people in Egypt. 7
I have heard their appeal to be free of their slave-drivers. Yes, I am well aware
of their sufferings. •I mean to deliver them out of the hands of the Egyptians and 8
bring them up out of that land to a land rich and broad, a land where milk and
honey flow, the home of the Canaanites, the Hittites, the Amorites, the Perizzites,
the Hivites and the Jebusites. . . .'

Moses instructed for his mission

'Go and gather the elders of Israel together and tell them, "Yahweh, the God 16
of your fathers, has appeared to me,—the God of Abraham, of Isaac, and of
Jacob; and he has said to me: I have visited you and seen all that the Egyptians
are doing to you. •And so I have resolved to bring you up out of Egypt where 17
you are oppressed, into the land of the Canaanites, the Hittites, the Amorites,
the Perizzites, the Hivites and the Jebusites, to a land where milk and honey
flow." •They will listen to your words, and with the elders of Israel you are to 18
go to the king of Egypt and say to him, "Yahweh, the God of the Hebrews, has
come to meet us. Give us leave, then, to make a three days' journey into the
wilderness to offer sacrifice to Yahweh our God." •For myself, knowing that 19
the king of Egypt will not let you go unless he is forced by a mighty hand, •I shall 20
show my power and strike Egypt with all the wonders I am going to work there.
After this he will let you go. . . .'

Moses granted miraculous powers

4 Then Moses answered, 'What if they will not believe me or listen to my words 1
and say to me, "Yahweh has not appeared to you"?' . . . •"So that they may 5
believe that Yahweh, the God of their fathers, the God of Abraham, the God of
Isaac, and the God of Jacob, has really appeared to you,' •[Again] Yahweh spoke 6
to Moses, 'Put your hand into your bosom.' He put his hand into his bosom and
when he drew it out, his hand was covered with leprosy, white as snow. •'Put 7
your hand back into your bosom.' He put his hand back into his bosom and when
he drew it out, there it was restored, just like the rest of his flesh. . . .

Aaron, the mouthpiece of Moses

Moses said to Yahweh, 'But, my Lord, never in my life have I been a man 10
of eloquence, either before or since you have spoken to your servant. I am a
slow speaker and not able to speak well.' •'Who gave man his mouth?' Yahweh 11
answered him. 'Who makes him dumb or deaf, gives him sight or leaves him
blind? Is it not I, Yahweh? •Now go, I shall help you to speak and tell you what 12
to say.'

'If it please you, my Lord,' Moses replied 'send anyone you will!' •At this, 14
the anger of Yahweh blazed out against Moses, and he said to him, 'There is your
brother Aaron the Levite, is there not? I know that he is a good speaker. Here
he comes to meet you. When he sees you, his heart will be full of joy. •You will 15
speak to him and tell him what message to give. I shall help you to speak, and
him too, and instruct you what to do. •He himself is to speak to the people 16
in your place; he will be your mouthpiece, and you will be as the god inspiring
him. . . .'

Moses returns to Egypt. He leaves Midian

Moses went away and returned to his father-in-law Jethro, and said to him, 18
'Give me leave to go back to my relatives in Egypt to see if they are still alive'.
And Jethro said to Moses, 'Go in peace'.

Yahweh said to Moses in Midian, 'Go, return to Egypt, for all those who 19
wanted to kill you are dead'. •So Moses took his wife and his son and, putting 20
them on a donkey, started back for the land of Egypt . . . .

The son of Moses circumcised

On the journey, when Moses had halted for the night, Yahweh came to meet 24
him and tried to kill him. •At once Zipporah, taking up a flint, cut off her son's 25
foreskin and with it she touched the genitals of Moses. 'Truly, you are a bridegroom of blood to me!' she said. •And Yahweh let him live. It was then that she 26
said, 'bridegroom of blood' on account of the circumcision.

Moses meets Aaron

Yahweh said to Aaron, 'Go into the wilderness to meet Moses'. And so he 27
went, and met him at the mountain of God; and he kissed him. •Moses then 28
told Aaron all that Yahweh had said when he set him his task and all the signs
he had ordered him to perform. •Moses and Aaron then went and gathered all 29
the elders of the sons of Israel together, •and Aaron told all that Yahweh had said 30
to Moses, and in the sight of the people he performed the signs. •The people were 31
convinced, and they rejoiced that Yahweh had visited the sons of Israel and
seen their misery, and they bowed down and worshipped.

The first audience with Pharaoh

5 After this, Moses and Aaron went to Pharaoh and said to him, 'This is what 1
Yahweh, the God of Israel, has said, "Let my people go, so that they may
keep a feast in the wilderness in honour of me." ' •'Who is Yahweh,' Pharaoh 2
replied 'that I should listen to him and let Israel go? I know nothing of Yahweh,
and I will not let Israel go.' •'The God of the Hebrews has come to meet us' they 3
replied. 'Give us leave to make a three days' journey into the wilderness to offer
sacrifice to Yahweh our God, or he will come down on us with a plague or with
the sword.' •The king of Egypt said to them, 'Moses and Aaron, what do you 4
mean by taking the people away from their work? Get back to your labouring.'
And Pharaoh said, 'Now that these common folk have grown to such numbers, 5
do you want to stop them labouring?'

Instructions to the slave-drivers

That same day, Pharaoh gave this command to the people's slave-drivers and 6
to the overseers. •'Up to the present, you have provided these people with straw 7
for brickmaking. Do so no longer; let them go and gather straw for themselves.
All the same, you are to get from them the same number of bricks as before, not 8
reducing it at all. They are lazy, and that is why their cry is, "Let us go and offer
sacrifice to our God". •Make these men work harder than ever, so that they do 9
not have time to stop and listen to glib speeches.'
The people's slave-drivers went out with the overseers to speak to the people. 10
'Pharaoh has given orders' they said: ' "I will not provide you with straw. •Go 11
out and collect straw for yourselves wherever you can find it. But your output
is not to be any less." ' •So the people scattered all over the land of Egypt to 12
gather stubble for making chopped straw. •The slave-drivers harassed them. 13
'Every day you must complete your daily quota,' they said 'just as you did when
straw was provided for you.' •And the foremen who had been appointed for the 14
sons of Israel by Pharaoh's slave-drivers were flogged, and they were asked,
'Why have you not produced your full amount of bricks as before, either yester-
day or today?'

The Hebrew foremen complain

The foremen for the sons of Israel went to Pharaoh and complained. 'Why 15
do you treat your servants so?' they said. •'No straw is provided for your servants 16
and still the cry is, "Make bricks!" And now your servants have been flogged! . . . '
'You are lazy, lazy' he answered 'that is why you say, "Let us go and offer 17
sacrifice to Yahweh". •Get back to your work at once. You shall not get any 18
straw, but you must deliver the number of bricks due from you.'

The dilemma of the foremen. Moses prays

The foremen for the sons of Israel saw themselves in a very difficult position 19
when told there was to be no reduction in the daily number of bricks. •As they 20
left Pharaoh's presence they met Moses and Aaron who were waiting for them.
'May Yahweh see your work and punish you as you deserve!' they said to them. 21
'You have made us hated by Pharaoh and his court; you have put a sword into
their hand to kill us.' •Once more Moses turned to Yahweh. 'Lord,' he said 22
to him 'why do you treat this people so harshly? Why did you send me here?
Ever since I came to Pharaoh and spoke to him in your name, he has ill-treated 23

this nation, and you have done nothing to deliver your people.' **6** Then Yahweh 1
said to Moses, 'You will see now how I shall punish Pharaoh. He will be forced
to let them go: yes, he will be forced to send them out of his land.'

· · · · · ·

7

· · · · · ·

The water turns to blood

Then Yahweh said to Moses, 'Pharaoh is adamant. He refuses to let the 14
people go. •In the morning go to him as he makes his way to the water and 15
wait for him by the bank of the river. . . . •Say to him, "Yahweh, the God of 16
the Hebrews, has sent me to say: Let my people go to offer me worship in the
wilderness. Now, so far you have not listened. •Here is Yahweh's message: That 17
I am Yahweh you shall learn by this: . . . I will strike the water of the river and
it shall be changed into blood. •The fish in the river will die, and the river will 18
smell so foul that the Egyptians will not want to drink the water of it." '
. . . *Moses . . . raised his staff and in the sight of Pharaoh and his court he* 20
struck the waters of the river, and all the water in the river changed to blood.
The fish in the river died, and the river smelt so foul that the Egyptians found 21
it impossible to drink its water. . . . •Pharaoh turned away and went back into 23
his palace, taking no notice even of this. •Meanwhile, all the Egyptians dug holes 24
along the banks of the river in search of drinking water; they found the water of
the river impossible to drink. •After Yahweh had struck the river, seven days 25
passed.

The frogs

Then Yahweh said to Moses, 'Go to Pharoah and say to him, "This is 26
Yahweh's message: Let my people go to offer me worship. •If you refuse to let 27
them go, know that I will plague the whole of your country with frogs. •The 28
river will swarm with them; they will make their way into your palace, into
your bedroom, on to your bed, into the houses of your courtiers and of your
subjects, into your ovens, into your kneading bowls. •The frogs will even climb 29
all over you, over your courtiers, and over all your subjects." '
8 Yahweh said to Moses, 'Say this to Aaron, "Stretch our your hand 1
. . . . . over the rivers, the canals, the marshland, and make frogs swarm
all over the land of Egypt" '. •So Aaron stretched out his hand over the waters of 2
Egypt, and the frogs came up and covered the land of Egypt. •But the magicians 3
did the same with their witchcraft, and made frogs swarm all over the land of
Egypt.
Pharaoh summoned Moses and Aaron, 'Entreat Yahweh' he said 'to rid 4
me and my subjects of the frogs, and I promise to let the people go and offer
sacrifice to Yahweh.' •Moses answered Pharaoh, 'Take this chance to get the 5
better of me! When I pray on your account and for your courtiers, and for
your subjects, what time am I to fix for the frogs to leave you and your subjects
and your houses, and stay in the river?' •'Tomorrow' Pharaoh said. 'It shall 6
be as you say' answered Moses. 'By this you shall learn that Yahweh our God
has no equal. •The frogs will go from you and your palaces, your courtiers 7
and your subjects; they will stay in the river.' •When Moses and Aaron had 8
gone from Pharaoh's presence, Moses pleaded with Yahweh about the frogs

with which he had afflicted Pharaoh. ·And Yahweh granted Moses' prayer: 9
in house and courtyard and field the frogs died. ·They piled them up in heaps 10
and the land reeked of them. ·But as soon as he saw that relief had been granted, 11
Pharaoh became adamant again and, as Yahweh had foretold, he refused to
listen to Moses and Aaron.

· · · · · ·

The gadflies

Then Yahweh said to Moses, 'Get up early in the morning and wait for Pha- 16
raoh as he makes his way to the water. Say to him, "This is Yahweh's message:
Let my people go to offer me worship. ·But if you do not let my people go, I shall 17
send gadflies on you, on your courtiers and your palaces. The houses of the
Egyptians will be infested with them, and even the very ground they stand on.
But I shall set apart the land of Goshen, where my people live, on that day; 18
there will be no gadflies there, and so you may know that I, Yahweh, am in
the midst of the land, ·I shall make a distinction between my people and yours. 19
This sign shall take place tomorow." ' ·Yahweh did this, and great swarms of 20
gadflies found their way into Pharaoh's palace, into the houses of his courtiers,
and into all the land of Egypt, and ruined the country.

Pharaoh summoned Moses and Aaron. 'Go' he said 'and offer sacrifice to 21
your God, but in this country!' ·'That would not be right' Moses answered. 22
'We sacrifice to Yahweh our God animals which Egyptians count it sacrilege to
slaughter. If we offer in front of the Egyptians sacrifices that outrage them, will
they not stone us? ·We must make a three days' journey into the wilderness to 23
offer sacrifice to Yahweh our God, as he has commanded us.' ·Pharaoh replied, 24
'I will let you go to offer sacrifice to Yahweh your God in the wilderness,
provided you do not go far. And intercede for me.' ·'The moment I leave you,' 25
said Moses 'I will pray to Yahweh. Tomorrow morning the gadflies will leave
Pharaoh and his courtiers and his subjects. Only, Pharaoh must not play false
again, and refuse to let the people go to offer sacrifice to Yahweh.' ·So Moses 26
went out of Pharaoh's presence and prayed to Yahweh. ·And Yahweh did as 27
Moses asked; the gadflies left Pharaoh and his courtiers and his subjects; not
one remained. ·But Pharaoh was adamant this time too and did not let the 28
people go.

Death of the Egyptians' livestock

9 Then Yahweh said to Moses, 'Go to Pharaoh and say to him, "This is the 1
message of Yahweh, the God of the Hebrews: Let my people go to offer
me worship. ·If you refuse to let them go and detain them any longer, ·you 3
will find that the hand of Yahweh will fall on your livestock in the fields, horse
and donkey and camel, herd and flock, with a deadly plague. ·Yahweh will 4
discriminate between the livestock of Israel and of Egypt: nothing shall die of
all that belongs to the sons of Israel. ·Yahweh has fixed the hour. Tomorrow, 5
he has said, Yahweh will carry out this threat in all the land." ' Next day Yahweh 6
kept his word; all the Egyptians' livestock died, but none owned by the sons
of Israel died. ·Pharaoh had inquiries made, but it was true: none was dead of 7
the livestock owned by the sons of Israel. But Pharaoh became adamant again
and did not let the people go.

· · · · · ·

The hail

Then Yahweh said to Moses, 'Get up early in the morning and present yourself 13
to Pharaoh. Say to him, "This is the mesage of Yahweh, the God of the
Hebrews: Let my people go to offer me worship. . . . •High-handed with my 17
people still, you will not let them go. •Tomorrow, therefore, at about this time, 18
I will let fall so great a storm of hail as was never known in Egypt from the
day of its foundation. . . . " '

. . . And Yahweh thundered and rained down hail. Lightning struck the earth. 23
Yahweh rained down hail on the land of Egypt, . . . a greater storm of hail than 24
had ever been known in Egypt since it first became a nation. . . . It struck all the
crops in the fields, and it shattered every tree in the fields. •Only in the land of 26
Goshen where the Hebrews lived, was there no hail.

Pharaoh sent for Moses and Aaron. ' . . . •Entreat Yahweh to stop the thunder 28
and the hail; I promise to let you go, and you shall stay here no longer.' •Moses 29
answered him, 'The moment I leave the city I will stretch out my hands to
Yahweh. The thunder will stop, and there will be no more hail, so that you may
know that the earth belongs to Yahweh. . . . '

Moses left Pharaoh and went out of the city. He stretched out his hands to 33
Yahweh and the thunder and the hail stopped and the rain no longer poured
down on the earth. •When Pharaoh saw that rain and hail and thunder had 34
stopped, he sinned yet again. •He became adamant, he and his courtiers. The 35
heart of Pharaoh was stubborn and, as Yahweh had foretold through Moses,
he did not let the sons of Israel go.

The Locusts

10

. . . So Moses and Aaron went to Pharaoh. They 3
said to him, 'This is the message of Yahweh, the God of the Hebrews, "How
much longer will you refuse to submit to me? Let my people go to offer me
worship. •If you refuse to let my people go, then tomorrow I will send locusts 4
over your country. •They shall cover the surface of the soil so thick that the soil 5
will not be seen. They shall devour the remainder that is left to you, all that has
survived from the hail; they shall devour all your trees growing in the fields;
they shall fill your palaces, the houses of your courtiers, the houses of all the
Egyptians. •Your forefathers and their ancestors will never have seen the like 6
since first they lived in the country." ' Then Moses turned away and left Pharaoh's
presence. •And Pharaoh's courtiers said to him, 'How much longer is this man 7
to be the cause of our trouble? Let the people go to offer worship to Yahweh
their God. Do you not understand that Egypt is now on the brink of ruin?'
. . . . . .

Then Yahweh said to Moses, "Stretch out your hand over the land of Egypt 12
to bring the locusts. . . .' And Yahweh brought up an east wind over the land and 13
it blew all that day and night. By morning, the east wind had brought the locusts.
. . . On the whole territory of Egypt they fell, in numbers so great that such 14
swarms had never been seen before, nor would be again. . . .

Pharaoh sent urgently for Moses and Aaron. . . . •'Forgive my sin, I implore 17
you, this once, and entreat Yahweh your God just to rid me of this deadly
plague.' •So Moses left Pharaoh's presence and interceded with Yahweh. •Then 19

Yahweh made the wind veer till it blew so strongly from the west that it caught
up the locusts and carried them off towards the Sea of Reeds. *There was not one
locust left in the whole land of Egypt.* •*But Yahweh made Pharaoh's heart stub-* 20
born, and he did not let the sons of Israel go.

The darkness

Then Yahweh said to Moses, 'Stretch out your hand towards heaven, and 21
let darkness, darkness so thick that it can be felt, cover the land of Egypt'.
So Moses stretched out his hand towards heaven, and for three days there 22
was deep darkness over the whole land of Egypt. •No one could see anyone 23
else or move about for three days, but where the sons of Israel lived there was
light for them.

Pharaoh summoned Moses. 'Go and offer worship to Yahweh,' he said 24
'but your flocks and herds must remain here. Your children may go with you
too.' •Moses replied, 'But you must let us have means of offering sacrifices 25
and holocausts to Yahweh our God. •Our livestock, too, must go with us; 26
not one head of cattle must be left behind: it must be from our livestock that
we provide for the worship of Yahweh our God; until we reach the place, we
do not know ourselves what worship we shall have to offer Yahweh.'

But Yahweh made Pharaoh's heart stubborn, and he refused to let them go. 27
Pharaoh said to Moses, 'Out of my sight! Take care! Never appear before me 28
again, for on the day you do, you die!' •Moses replied, 'You yourself have said it: 29
never again shall I appear before you.'

Moses proclaims the death of the first-born

11

. . . . . .

Moses said, 'This is Yahweh's message, "Towards midnight I shall pass 4
through Egypt. •All the first-born in the land of Egypt shall die: from the first- 5
born of Pharaoh, heir to his throne, to the first-born of the maidservant at the
mill, and all the first-born of the cattle. •And throughout the land of Egypt 6
there shall be such a wailing as never was heard before, nor will be again. •But 7
against the sons of Israel, against man or beast, never a dog shall bark, so that
you may know that Yahweh discriminates between Egypt and Israel. •Then all 8
these courtiers of yours will come down to me and bow low before me and say:
Go away, you and all the people who follow you! After this, I shall go." ' And,
hot with anger, Moses left Pharaoh's presence.

. . . . . .

12

. . . . . .

Injunctions relating to the Passover

Moses summoned all the elders of Israel and said to them, 'Go and choose 21
animals from the flock on behalf of your families, and kill the Passover victim.
Then take a spray of hyssop, dip it in the blood that is in the basin, and with 22
the blood from the basin touch the lintel and the two doorposts. Let none of
you venture out of the house till morning. •Then, when Yahweh goes through 23
Egypt to strike it, and sees the blood on the lintel and on the two doorposts,

he will pass over the door and not allow the destroyer to enter your homes
and strike. . . . '

Death of the first-born

And at midnight Yahweh struck down all the first-born in the land of Egypt: 29
the first-born of Pharaoh, heir to his throne, the first born of the prisoner in his
dungeon, and the first-born of all the cattle. •Pharaoh and all his courtiers and 30
all the Egyptians got up in the night, and there was a great cry in Egypt, for
there was not a house without its dead. •And it was night when Pharaoh 31
summoned Moses and Aaron. 'Get up,' he said 'you and the sons of Israel, and
get away from my people. . . . '

Israel's departure

The sons of Israel left Rameses for Succoth. . . . •People of various sorts 38
joined them in great numbers; there were flocks, too, and herds in immense
droves. •They baked cakes with the dough which they had brought from Egypt, 39
unleavened because the dough was not leavened; they had been driven out of
Egypt, with no time for dallying, and had not provided themselves with food
for the journey.

13

· · · · · ·

From Succoth they moved on, and encamped at Etham, on the edge of the 20
wilderness. •Yahweh went before them, by day in the form of a pillar of cloud to 21
show them the way, and by night in the form of a pillar of fire to give them light:
thus they could continue their march by day and by night. •The pillar of cloud 22
never failed to go before the people during the day, nor the pillar of fire during
the night.

14

· · · · · ·

The Egyptians pursue the Israelites

When Pharaoh, king of Egypt, was told that the people had made their 5
escape, he and his courtiers changed their minds about the people. 'What have
we done,' they said 'allowing Israel to leave our service?' •So Pharaoh had his 6
chariot harnessed and gathered his troops about him, •taking six hundred of the 7
best chariots and all the other chariots in Egypt, each manned by a picked team.
. . . And as Pharaoh approached, the sons of Israel looked round—and there 10
were the Egyptians in pursuit of them! The sons of Israel were terrified and cried
out to Yahweh. . . . •Moses answered the people, 'Have no fear! Stand firm, and 13
you will see what Yahweh will do to save you today: the Egyptians you see
today, you will never see again. •Yahweh will do the fighting for you: you have 14
only to keep still.'

The crossing

· · · · · ·

. . . The pillar of cloud changed station from the front to the rear of them, and 19
remained there. •It came between the camp of the Egyptians and the camp of 20
Israel. The cloud was dark, and the night passed without the armies drawing any

closer the whole night long. •Moses stretched out his hand over the sea. Yahweh 21
drove back the sea with a strong easterly wind all night, and he made dry land
of the sea. . . . •In the morning watch, Yahweh looked down on the army of the 24
Egyptians from the pillar of fire and of cloud, and threw the army into confusion.
He so clogged their chariot wheels that they could scarcely make headway. 'Let 25
us flee from the Israelites,' the Egyptians cried 'Yahweh is fighting for them
against the Egyptians!' . . . •Moses stretched out his hand over the sea and, as 27
day broke, the sea returned to its bed. The fleeing Egyptians marched right into
it, and Yahweh overthrew the Egyptians in the very middle of the sea. . . . •That 30
day, Yahweh rescued Israel from the Egyptians, and Israel saw the Egyptians
lying dead on the shore. •Israel witnessed the great act that Yahweh had per- 31
formed against the Egyptians, and the people venerated Yahweh; they put their
faith in Yahweh and in Moses, his servant.

Song of victory

15 It was then that Moses and the sons of Israel sang this song in honour of 1
Yahweh:

'Yahweh I sing: he has covered himself in glory,
horse and rider he has thrown into the sea.
Yah is my strength, my song,   2
he is my salvation.
This is my God, I praise him;
the God of my father, I extol him.
Yahweh is a warrior;   3
Yahweh is his name.
The chariots and the army of Pharaoh he has hurled into the sea;   4
the pick of his horsemen lie drowned in the Sea of Reeds.
The depths have closed over them;   5
they have sunk to the bottom like a stone.
Your right hand, Yahweh, shows majestic in power,   6
your right hand, Yahweh, shatters the enemy.
So great your splendour, you crush your foes;   7
you unleash your fury, and it devours them like stubble.
A blast from your nostrils and the waters piled high;   8
the waves stood upright like a dyke;
in the heart of the sea the deeps came together.
"I will give chase and overtake," the enemy said   9
"I shall share out the spoil, my soul will feast on it;
I shall draw my sword, my hand will destroy them."
One breath of yours you blew, and the sea closed over them;   10
they sank like lead in the terrible waters.
Who among the gods is your like, Yahweh?   11
Who is your like, majestic in holiness,
terrible in deeds of prowess, worker of wonders?
You stretched your right hand out, the earth swallowed them!   12
By your grace you led the people you redeemed,   13
by your strength you guided them to your holy house.
Hearing of this, the peoples tremble;   14
pangs seize on the inhabitants of Philistia.
Edom's chieftains are now dismayed,   15

the princes of Moab fall to trembling,
Canaan's inhabitants are all unmanned.
On them fall terror and dread;   16
through the power of your arm they are still as stone
as your people pass, Yahweh,
as the people pass whom you purchased.
You will bring them and plant them on the   17
mountain that is your own,
the place you have made your dwelling, Yahweh,
the sanctuary, Yahweh, prepared by your own hands.
Yahweh will be king for ever and ever.'   18
Pharaoh's cavalry, both his chariots and horsemen, had indeed entered the 19
sea, but Yahweh had made the waters of the sea flow back on them, yet the sons
of Israel had marched on dry ground right through the sea.

· · · · · ·

ISRAEL IN THE DESERT

Marah

Moses made Israel move from their camp at the Sea of Reeds, and they made 22
for the wilderness of Shur where they travelled for three days without finding
water. ·They reached Marah but the water there was so bitter they could not 23
drink it; this is why the place was named Marah. ·The people grumbled at 24
Moses. 'What are we to drink?' they said. ·So Moses appealed to Yahweh, and 25
Yahweh pointed out some wood to him; this Moses threw into the water, and
the water was sweetened.

· · · · · ·

The Manna

16

· · · · · ·

Then Yahweh said to Moses, 'Now I will rain down bread for you from the 4
heavens. Each day the people are to go out and gather the day's portion; I propose
to test them in this way to see whether they will follow my law or not. ·On the 5
sixth day, when they prepare what they have brought in, this will be twice as
much as the daily gathering' . . . .
. . . Then Yahweh said to Moses, 'How much longer will you refuse to keep 28
my commandments and my laws? ·Listen! Yahweh has laid down the sabbath for 29
you; for this he gives you two days' food on the sixth day; each of you is to stay
where he is; on the seventh day no one is to leave his home.' ·So on the seventh 30
day the people abstained from all work.
The House of Israel named it 'manna'. It was like coriander seed; it was white 31
and its taste was like that of wafers made with honey. . . . ·The sons of Israel ate 35
manna for forty years, up to the time they reached inhabited country: they ate
manna up to the time they reached the frontier of the land of Canaan. . . .

The water from the rock

17 The whole community of the sons of Israel moved from their camp in the 1
wilderness of Sin at Yahweh's command, to travel the further stages; and

they pitched camp at Rephidim where there was no water for the people to drink. •So they grumbled against Moses. 'Give us water to drink' they said. 2 Moses answered them. 'Why do you grumble against me? Why do you put Yahweh to the test?' •But tormented by thirst, the people complained against 3 Moses. 'Why did you bring us out of Egypt?' they said. 'Was it so that I should die of thirst, my children too, and my cattle?' •Moses appealed to Yahweh. 4 'How am I to deal with this people?' he said. 'A little more and they will stone me!' •Yahweh said to Moses, 'Take with you some of the elders of Israel and 5 move on to the forefront of the people; take in your hand the staff with which you struck the river, and go. •I shall be standing before you there on the rock, 6 at Horeb. You must strike the rock, and water will flow from it for the people to drink.' This is what Moses did, in the sight of the elders of Israel. •The place 7 was named Massah and Meribah because of the grumbling of the sons of Israel and because they put Yahweh to the test by saying, 'Is Yahweh with us, or not?'

A battle against the Amalekites

The Amalekites came and attacked Israel at Rephidim. •Moses said to Joshua, 9 'Pick out men for yourself, and tomorrow morning march out to engage Amalek. I, meanwhile, will stand on the hilltop, the staff of God in my hand.' •Joshua did 10 as Moses told him and marched out to engage Amalek, while Moses and Aaron and Hur went up to the top of the hill. •As long as Moses kept his arms raised, 11 Israel had the advantage; when he let his arms fall, the advantage went to Amalek. But Moses' arms grew heavy, so they took a stone and put it under him and 12 on this he sat, Aaron and Hur supporting his arms, one on one side, one on the other; and his arms remained firm till sunset. •With the edge of the sword Joshua 13 cut down Amalek and his people. •Then Yahweh said to Moses, 'Write this 14 action down in a book to keep the memory of it, and say in Joshua's hearing that I shall wipe out the memory of Amalek from under heaven.' •Moses then built an 15 altar and named it Yahweh-nissi •because he said, 'Lay hold of the banner of 16 Yahweh! Yahweh is at war with Amalek from age to age!'

· · · · · ·

THE COVENANT AT SINAI

The Israelites come to Sinai

19

. . . And when they reached the wilderness of Sinai, there in the wilderness 2 they pitched their camp; there facing the mountain Israel pitched camp.

· · · · · ·

Preparing for the covenant

Yahweh said to Moses, 'Go to the people and tell them to prepare themselves 10 today and tomorrow. Let them wash their clothing and •hold themselves in 11 readiness for the third day, because on the third day Yahweh will descend on the mountain of Sinai in the sight of all the people. . . . When the ram's horn 13 sounds a long blast, they are to go up the mountain.'

So Moses came down from the mountain to the people and bade them prepare 14 themselves; and they washed their clothing. •Then he said to the people, 'Be 15 ready for the third day; do not go near any woman.'

The theophany on Sinai

Now at daybreak on the third day there were peals of thunder on the 16
mountain and lightning flashes, a dense cloud, and a loud trumpet blast, and
inside the camp all the people trembled. •Then Moses led the people out of 17
the camp to meet God; and they stood at the bottom of the mountain. •The 18
mountain of Sinai was entirely wrapped in smoke, because Yahweh had descended on it in the form of fire. Like smoke from a furnace the smoke went up,
and the whole mountain shook violently. •Louder and louder grew the sound 19
of the trumpet. Moses spoke, and God answered him with peals of thunder.
Yahweh came down on the mountain of Sinai, on the mountain top. . . .   20

. . . . . .

24

. . . . . .

Moses on the mountain

Yahweh said to Moses, 'Come up to me on the mountain and stay there 12
while I give you the stone tablets —the law and the commandments— that
I have written for their instruction'. •Accordingly Moses rose, he and his servant 13
Joshua, and they went up the mountain of God. •To the elders he had said, 14
'Wait here for us until we come back to you. You have Aaron and Hur with
you; if anyone has a difference to settle, let him go to them.' •And Moses went 15
up the mountain.

. . . . . .

The golden calf

32 When the people saw that Moses was a long time before coming down the 1
mountain, they gathered round Aaron and said to him, 'Come, make us
a god to go at the head of us; this Moses, the man who brought us up from
Egypt, we do not know what has become of him'. •Aaron answered them, 'Take 2
the gold rings out of the ears of your wives and your sons and daughters, and
bring them to me'. •So they all took the gold rings from their ears and brought 3
them to Aaron. •He took them from their hands and, in a mould, melted the 4
metal down and cast an effigy of a calf. 'Here is your God, Israel,' they cried
'who brought you out of the land of Egypt!' •Observing this, Aaron built an 5
altar before the effigy. 'Tomorrow' he said 'will be a feast in honour of
Yahweh.'

And so, early the next day they offered holocausts and brought communion 6
sacrifices; then all the people sat down to eat and drink, and afterwards got
up to amuse themselves.

Moses forewarned by Yahweh

Then Yahweh spoke to Moses, '*Go down now, because your people whom* 7
you brought out of Egypt have apostatised. •They have been quick to leave the 8
way I marked out for them; they have made themselves a calf of molten metal
and have worshipped it and offered it sacrifice. "Here is your God, Israel,"
they have cried "who brought you up from the land of Egypt!" ' •Yahweh said 9
to Moses, 'I can see how headstrong these people are! •Leave me, now, my 10
wrath shall blaze out against them and devour them; of you, however, I will
make a great nation.'

The prayer of Moses

But Moses pleaded with Yahweh his God. 'Yahweh,' he said 'why should 11
your wrath blaze out against this people of yours whom you brought out of the
land of Egypt with arm outstretched and mighty hand? ·Why let the Egyptians 12
say, "Ah, it was in treachery that he brought them out, to do them to death in
the mountains and wipe them off the face of the earth"? Leave your burning
wrath; relent and do not bring this disaster on your people. ·Remember Abraham, 13
Isaac and Jacob, your servants to whom by your own self you swore and made
this promise: I will make your offspring as many as the stars of heaven, and all
this land which I promised I will give to your descendants, and it shall be their
heritage for ever.' ·So Yahweh relented and did not bring on his people the 14
disaster he had threatened.

Moses breaks the tablets of the Law

Moses made his way back down the mountain with the two tablets of the 15
Testimony in his hands, tablets inscribed on both sides, inscribed on the front
and on the back. ·These tablets were the work of God, and the writing on them 16
was God's writing engraved on the tablets.

Joshua heard the noise of the people shouting. 'There is the sound of battle 17
in the camp', he told Moses. ·Moses answered him: 18

'No song of victory is this sound,
no wailing for defeat this sound;
it is the sound of chanting that I hear'.

As he approached the camp and saw the calf and the groups dancing, Moses' 19
anger blazed. He threw down the tablets he was holding and broke them at the
foot of the mountain. ·He seized the calf they had made and burned it, grinding 20
it into powder which he scattered on the water; and he made the sons of Israel
drink it. ·To Aaron Moses said, 'What has this people done to you, for you 21
to bring such a great sin on them?' ·'Let not my lord's anger blaze like this' 22
Aaron answered. 'You know yourself how prone this people is to evil. ·They said 23
to me, "Make us a god to go at our head; this Moses, the man who brought us
up from Egypt, we do not know what has become of him". ·So I said to them, 24
"Who has gold?", and they took it off and brought it to me. I threw it into the
fire and out came this calf.'

The zeal of the Levites

When Moses saw the people so out of hand—for Aaron had allowed them to 25
lapse into idolatry with enemies all round them—·he stood at the gate of the 26
camp and shouted, 'Who is for Yahweh? To me!' And all the sons of Levi rallied
to him. ·And he said to them, 'This is the message of Yahweh, the God of Israel, 27
"Gird on your sword, every man of you, and quarter the camp from gate to gate,
killing one his brother, another his friend, another his neighbour" '. ·The sons 28
of Levi carried out the command of Moses, and of the people about three
thousand men perished that day. ·'Today' Moses said 'you have won your- 29
selves investiture as priests of Yahweh at the cost, one of his son, another of his
brother; and so he grants you a blessing today.'
· · · · · ·

The Israelites ordered to depart

33 Yahweh said to Moses, 'Leave this place, with the people you brought out 1 of the land of Egypt, and go to the land that I swore to Abraham, Isaac and Jacob I would give their descendants. . . . •I will drive out the Canaanites, 2 the Amorites, the Hittites, the Perizzites, the Hivites, the Jebusites. •Go on to the 3 land where milk and honey flow. I shall not go with you myself—you are a head-strong people—or I might exterminate you on the way.' •On hearing these stern 4 words the people went into mourning, and no one wore his ornaments.

• • • • • •

Moses prays

Moses said to Yahweh, 'See, you yourself say to me, "Make the people go 12 on", but you do not let me know who it is you will send with me. Yet you your-self have said, "I know you by name and you have won my favour". •If indeed 13 I have won your favour, please show me your ways, so that I can understand you and win your favour. Remember, too, that this nation is your own people.' Yahweh replied, 'I myself will go with you, and I will give you rest'. •Moses 15 said, 'If you are not going with us yourself, do not make us leave this place. By what means can it be known that I, I and my people, have won your favour, 16 if not by your going with us? By this we shall be marked out, I and my people, from all the peoples on the face of the earth.' •Yahweh said to Moses, 'Again 17 I will do what you have asked, because you have won my favour and because I know you by name'.

• • • • • •

The tablets of the Law

34 Yahweh said to Moses, 'Cut two tablets of stone like the first ones and 1 come up to me on the mountain, and I will inscribe on them the words that were on the first tablets, which you broke. •Be ready by morning, and come 2 up to the mountain of Sinai at dawn; await my orders there at the top of the mountain. •No one must come up with you, no one be seen anywhere on the 3 mountain; even the flocks and herds may not graze in front of this mountain.' And so Moses cut two tablets of stone like the first and, with the two tablets 4 of stone in his hands, he went up the mountain of Sinai in the early morning as Yahweh had commanded him. •And Yahweh descended in the form of a cloud, 5 and Moses stood with him there.

• • • • • •

The Convenant

Yahweh said, 'I am about to make a covenant with you. In the presence of 10 all your people I shall work such wonders as have never been worked in any land or in any nation. All the people round you will see what Yahweh can do, for what I shall do through you will be awe-inspiring. . . .

'You shall bow down to no other god, for Yahweh's name is the Jealous One; 14 he is a jealous God. •Make no pact with the inhabitants of the land or, when they 15 prostitute themselves to their own gods and sacrifice to them, they may invite you and you may consent to eat from their victim; •or else you may choose wives 16 for your sons from among their daughters and these, prostituting themselves to their own gods, may induce your sons to do the same.

'You shall make yourself no gods of molten metal.   17

'You shall celebrate the feast of Unleavened Bread: you shall eat unleavened 18
bread, as I have commanded you, at the appointed time in the month of Abib,
for in the month of Abib you came out of Egypt.

'All that first issues from the womb is mine: every male, every first-born of 19
flock or herd. •But the first-born donkey you must redeem with an animal from 20
your flocks. If you do not redeem it, you must break its neck. You must redeem
all the first-born of your sons. And no one is to come before me empty-handed.

'For six days you shall labour, but on the seventh day you shall rest, even at 21
ploughing time and harvest.

'You shall celebrate the feast of Weeks, of the first-fruits of the wheat harvest, 22
and the feast of Ingathering at the close of the year.

'Three times a year all your menfolk must present themselves before the Lord 23
Yahweh, the God of Israel.

'When I have dispossessed the nations for you and extended your frontiers, 24
no one will covet your land, if you present yourselves three times in the year
before Yahweh your God.

'You must not offer the blood of the victim sacrificed to me at the same time 25
as you offer unleavened bread, nor is the victim offered at the feast of Passover
to be put aside for the following day.

'You must bring the best of the first-fruits of your soil to the house of Yahweh 26
your God.

'You must not boil a kid in its mother's milk.'

Yahweh said to Moses, 'Put these words in writing, for they are the terms of 27
the covenant I am making with you and with Israel'.

He stayed there with Yahweh for forty days and forty nights, eating and 28
drinking nothing. He inscribed on the tablets the words of the Covenant—the
Ten Words.

. . . . . .

NUMBERS

10

. . . . .

Moses' proposal to Hobab

Moses said to Hobab son of Reuel the Midianite, his father-in-law, 'We are 29
setting out for the land of which Yahweh has said: I will give it to you. Come
with us, and we will treat you well, for Yahweh has promised happiness to
Israel.' •'I will not come with you,' he answered 'I will go to my own land and 30
my own kindred.' •'Do not leave us,' Moses replied 'for you know where we 31
can camp in the wilderness, and so you will be our eyes. •If you come with us, 32
you will share in the blessing of the happiness with which Yahweh blesses us.'

The departure

They set out from the mountain of Yahweh and journeyed for three days. 33
The ark of the covenant of Yahweh went at their head for this journey of three
days, searching out a camping place for them.
In the daytime, the Cloud of Yahweh was over them whenever they left camp. 34
And as the ark set out, Moses would say, 35
'Arise, Yahweh, may your enemies be scattered
and those who hate you run
for their lives before you!'
And as it came to rest, he would say, . 36
'Come back, Yahweh,
to the thronging hosts of Israel'.

THE HALTS IN THE WILDERNESS

Taberah

11
Now the people set up a lament which was offensive to Yahweh's ears, 1
and Yahweh heard it. His anger blazed, and the fire of Yahweh burned
among them: it destroyed one end of the camp. •The people appealed to Moses,
and he interceded with Yahweh and the fire died down. •So the place was called 3
Taberah, because the fire of Yahweh had burned among them.

Kibroth-hattaavah. The people complain

The rabble who had joined the people were overcome by greed, and the sons 4
of Israel themselves began to wail again, 'Who will give us meat to eat?'
they said. •'Think of the fish we used to eat free in Egypt, the cucumbers, 5
melons, leeks, onions and garlic! •Here we are wasting away, stripped of 6
everything; there is nothing but manna for us to look at!'
The manna was like coriander seed, and had the appearance of bdellium. 7
The people went round gathering it, and ground it in a mill or crushed it with 8
a pestle; it was then cooked in a pot and made into pancakes. It tasted like cake

285

made with oil. ·When the dew fell on the camp at night-time, the manna fell 9
with it.

The prayer of Moses

Moses heard the people wailing, every family at the door of its tent. The 10
anger of Yahweh flared out, and Moses greatly worried over this. ·And he 11
spoke to Yahweh:

'Why do you treat your servant so badly? Why have I not found favour
with you, so that you load on me the weight of all this nation? ·Was it I who 12
conceived all this people, was it I who gave them birth, that you should say
to me, "Carry them in your bosom, like a nurse with a baby at the breast, to
the land that I swore to give their fathers"? ·Where am I to find meat to give 13
to all this people, when they come worrying me so tearfully and say, "Give us
meat to eat"? ·I am not able to carry this nation by myself alone; the weight 14
is too much for me. ·If this is how you want to deal with me, I would rather you 15
killed me! If only I had found favour in your eyes, and not lived to see such
misery as this!'

Yahweh replies

Yahweh said to Moses, 'Gather seventy of the elders of Israel, men you 16
know to be the people's elders and scribes. Bring them to the Tent of Meeting,
and let them stand beside you there. ·I will come down to speak with you; 17
and I will take some of the spirit which is on you and put it on them. So they
will share with you the burden of this nation, and you will no longer have to
carry it by yourself.

'To the people, say this, "Purify yourselves for tomorrow and you will have 18
meat to eat, now that you have wailed in the hearing of Yahweh and said: Who
will give us meat to eat? How happy we were in Egypt! So be it! Yahweh will
give you meat to eat. ·You shall eat it not for one day only, or two, or five 19
or ten or twenty, ·but for a full month, until you are sick of it and cannot bear 20
the smell of it, because you have rejected Yahweh who is with you, and have
wailed before him saying: Why did we ever leave Egypt?" '

Moses said, 'The people round me number six hundred thousand foot 21
soldiers, and you say, "I shall give them meat to eat for a whole month"! ·If all 22
the flocks and herds were slaughtered, would that be enough for them? If all
the fish in the sea were gathered, would that be enough for them?' ·Yahweh 23
answered Moses, 'Is the arm of Yahweh so short? You shall see whether the
promise I have made to you comes true or not.'

The spirit given to the elders

Moses went out and told the people what Yahweh had said. Then he gathered 24
seventy elders of the people and brought them round the Tent. ·Yahweh came 25
down in the Cloud. He spoke with him, but took some of the spirit that was
on him and put it on the seventy elders. When the spirit came on them they
prophesied, but not again.

Two men had stayed back in the camp; one was called Eldad and the other 26
Medad. The spirit came down on them; though they had not gone to the Tent,
their names were enrolled among the rest. These began to prophesy in the camp.
The young man ran to tell this to Moses, 'Look,' he said 'Eldad and Medad 27
are prophesying in the camp'. ·Then said Joshua the son of Nun, who had 28

served Moses from his youth, 'My Lord Moses, stop them!' •Moses answered 29
him, 'Are you jealous on my account? If only the whole people of Yahweh
were prophets, and Yahweh gave his Spirit to them all!' •Then Moses went back 30
to the camp, the elders of Israel with him.

The quails

A wind came from Yahweh and it drove quails in from the sea and brought 31
them down on the camp. They lay for a distance of a day's march either side
of the camp, two cubits thick on the ground. •The people were up all that day 32
and night and all the next day collecting quails: the least gathered by anyone
was ten homers; then they spread them out round the camp. •The meat was still 33
between their teeth, not even chewed, when the anger of Yahweh blazed out
against the people. Yahweh struck them with a very great plague.

The name given to this place was Kibroth-hattaavah, because it was there 34
that they buried the people who had indulged their greed.

From Kibroth-hattaavah the people set out for Hazeroth, and at Hazeroth 35
they pitched camp.

Hazeroth. Complaints of Miriam and Aaron

12 Miriam, and Aaron too, spoke against Moses in connexion with the 1
Cushite woman he had taken. (For he had married a Cushite woman.)
They said, 'Has Yahweh spoken to Moses only? Has he not spoken to us too?' 2
Yahweh heard this. •Now Moses was the most humble of men, the humblest 3
man on earth.

God's answer

Suddenly, Yahweh said to Moses and Aaron and Miriam, 'Come, all three 4
of you, to the Tent of Meeting'. They went, all three of them, •and Yahweh 5
came down in a pillar of cloud and stood at the entrance of the Tent. He called
Aaron and Miriam and they both came forward. •Yahweh said, 'Listen now 6
to my words:

> If any man among you is a prophet
> I make myself known to him in a vision,
> I speak to him in a dream.
> Not so with my servant Moses: 7
> he is at home in my house;
> I speak with him face to face,   8
> plainly and not in riddles,
> and he sees the form of Yahweh.

How then have you dared to speak against my servant Moses?'

The anger of Yahweh blazed out against them. He departed, •and as soon 10
as the cloud withdrew from the Tent, there was Miriam a leper, white as snow!
Aaron turned to look at her; she had become a leper.

The prayer of Aaron and Moses

Aaron said to Moses: 11
'Help me, my lord! Do not punish us for a sin committed in folly of which
we are guilty. •I entreat you, do not let her be like a monster, coming from its 12
mother's womb with flesh half corrupted.'

Moses cried to Yahweh, 'O God,' he said 'please heal her, I beg you!'   13

Then Yahweh said to Moses, 'If her father had done no more than spit in her 14
face, would she not be a thing of shame for seven days? Let her be shut outside
the camp for seven days, and then let her be brought in again.'

Miriam was shut outside the camp for seven days. The people did not set 15
out until she returned. •Then the people left Hazeroth, and camp was pitched 16
in the wilderness of Paran.

The reconnaissance in Canaan

13

• • • • • •

Moses sent them to reconnoitre the land of Canaan, 'Go up into the Negeb; 17
then go up into the highlands. •See what sort of country it is, and what sort 18
of people the inhabitants are, whether they are strong or weak, few or many,
what sort of country they live in, whether it is good or poor; what sort of towns 19
they have, whether they are open or fortified; •what sort of land it is, fertile 20
or barren, wooded or open. Be bold, and bring back some of the produce of
the country.'

It was the season for early grapes. •They went up to reconnoitre the land, 21
from the wilderness of Zin to Rehob, the Pass of Hamath. •They went up 22
by way of the Negeb as far as Hebron, where the Anakim lived, Ahiman, Sheshai
and Talmai. (Hebron was founded seven years before Tanis in Egypt.) •They 23
came to the Valley of Eshcol; there they lopped off a vine branch with a cluster
of grapes, which two of them carried away on a pole, as well as pomegranates
and figs. •This place was called the Valley of Eshcol after the cluster which 24
the sons of Israel had cut there.

The envoys' report

. . . They sought out Moses, Aaron and the whole community of Israel, 26
in the wilderness of Paran, at Kadesh. They made their report to them, and to
the whole community, and showed them the produce of the country.

They told them this story, 'We went into the land to which you sent us. 27
It does indeed flow with milk and honey; this is its produce. •At the same time, 28
its inhabitants are a powerful people; the towns are fortified and very big; yes,
and we saw the descendants of Anak there. •The Amalekite holds the Negeb 29
area, the Hittite, Amorite and Jebusite the highlands, and the Canaanite the
sea coast and the banks of the Jordan.'

Caleb harangued the people gathered about Moses: 'We must march in,' 30
he said 'and conquer this land: we are well able to do it'. •But the men who 31
had gone up with him answered, 'We are not able to march against this people;
they are stronger than we are. . . . Every man we saw there was of enormous
size. •Yes, and we saw giants there (the sons of Anak, descendants of the 33
Giants). We felt like grasshoppers, and so we seemed to them.'

The rebellion of Israel

14 At this, the whole community raised their voices and cried aloud, and 1
the people wailed all that night. . . . •And they said to one another, 'Let us 4
appoint a leader and go back to Egypt'.

• • • • • •

The anger of Yahweh. Moses makes an appeal

. . . And Yahweh said to Moses: 11
'How long will this people insult me? How long will they refuse to believe
in me despite the signs I have worked among them? •I will strike them with 12
pestilence and disown them. And of you I shall make a new nation, greater and
mightier than they are.'
Moses answered Yahweh:
'But the Egyptians already know that you, by your own power, have brought
this people out from their midst. •They have said as much to the inhabitants 14
of this country. They already know that you, Yahweh, are in the midst of this
people, and that you show yourself to them face to face; that it is you, Yahweh,
whose cloud stands over them, that you go before them in a pillar of cloud
by day and a pillar of fire by night. •If you destroy this people now as if it were 15
one man, then the nations who have heard about you will say, •"Yahweh was 16
not able to bring this people into the land he swore to give them, and so he
has slaughtered them in the wilderness". •No, my Lord! It is now you must 17
display your power, according to those words you spoke, •"Yahweh is slow to 18
anger and rich in graciousness, forgiving faults and transgression, and yet letting
nothing go unchecked, punishing the father's fault in the sons to the third and
fourth generation". •In the abundance, then, of your graciousness, forgive the 19
sin of this people, as you have done from Egypt until now.'

Pardon and punishment

Yahweh said, 'I forgive them as you ask. •But—as I live, and as the glory 21
of Yahweh fills all the earth—•of all the men who have seen my glory and the 22
signs that I worked in Egypt and in the wilderness, who have put me to the test
ten times already and not obeyed my voice, •not one shall see the land 23
I swore to give their fathers. Not one of those who slight me shall see it.
But my servant Caleb is of another spirit. Because he has obeyed me perfectly, 24
I will bring him into the land he has entered, and his race shall possess it. (The
Amalekite and the Canaanite dwell in the plain.) •Tomorrow you will turn 25
about and go back into the wilderness, in the direction of the Sea of Suph.'
. . . . . .

An abortive attempt by the Israelites

Moses reported these words to all the sons of Israel, and the people set up 39
a great outcry. •Then they rose early and set out for the heights of the highlands 40
saying, 'Look, we are setting out for this place, since Yahweh has told us that
we have sinned'. •Moses replied, 'Why disobey the command of Yahweh? Noth- 41
ing will come of it. •Do not go up, for Yahweh is not among you; do not get 42
yourselves beaten by your enemies. •Yes, there facing you are the Amalekite and 43
the Canaanite, and you will fall to their swords because you have turned away
from Yahweh, and Yahweh is not with you.' •Yet they set out presumptuously 44
towards the heights of the highlands. Neither the ark of the covenant of Yahweh
nor Moses left the camp. •The Amalekite and the Canaanite who lived in that 45
hill country came down and defeated them, and harried them all the way to
Hormah.
. . . . . .

The rebellion of Dathan and Abiram

16 . . . Dathan and Abiram sons of Eliab, and On son of Peleth (Eliab and 1
Peleth were sons of Reuben) ·rebelled against Moses. . . .

Moses summoned Dathan and Abiram, the sons of Eliab. They replied, 12
'We will not come. ·Was it not enough to take us from a land where milk and 13
honey flow to die in this wilderness, without seeking to lord it over us now?
There is no land flowing with milk and honey that you have brought us to, 14
nor have you given us fields and vineyards for our inheritance. Do you expect
this people to be blind? We will not come.' ·Moses flew into a rage and said to 15
Yahweh, 'Pay no heed to their offering. I have not taken so much as a donkey
from them, nor have I harmed any of them.'

The punishment

. . . . . .

Moses stood up and went to Dathan and Abiram; the elders of Israel followed 25
him. ·He said to the community, 'Stand away, I beg you, from the tents of these 26
perverse men, and touch nothing that belongs to them, for fear that with all
their sins you too will be swept away'. . . .

Dathan and Abiram had come out and were standing at their tent doors
with their wives and their sons and their young children. ·Moses said, 'By this 28
you will know that Yahweh himself has sent me to perform all these tasks and
that this is not my doing. ·If these people die a natural death such as men 29
commonly die, then Yahweh has not sent me. ·But if Yahweh does something 30
utterly new, if the earth should open its mouth and swallow them, themselves
and all that belongs to them, so that they go down alive to Sheol, then you will
know that these men have rejected Yahweh.'

The moment he finished saying all these words, the ground split open under 31
their feet, ·the earth opened its mouth and swallowed them, their families too. 32
. . . ·They went down alive to Sheol, they and all their possessions. The earth 33
closed over them and they disappeared from the midst of the assembly. ·At their 34
cries all the Israelites around them ran away. For they said, 'The earth must
not swallow us!'

. . . . . .

FROM KADESH TO MOAB

20 . . . The people settled at Kadesh. It was there that Miriam died and was 1
buried.

. . . . . .

Edom refuses right of way

Moses sent messengers from Kadesh, 'To the king of Edom: A message 14
from your brother Israel. You know well enough the extremity to which we have
been reduced. ·Our ancestors went down into Egypt, and there we stayed for a 15
long time. But the Egyptians treated us badly, as they did our ancestors. ·We 16
cried to Yahweh. He listened to us and sent an angel to bring us out of Egypt.
Now we are here at Kadesh, a town on the borders of your territory. ·We ask 17
permission to pass through your land. We will not cross any fields or vineyards;
we will not drink any water from the wells; we will keep to the king's highway
without turning to right or left until we are clear of your frontiers.' ·Edom 18

answered, 'You shall not pass through my country; if you do, I will come out to attack you'. •The answer of the sons of Israel was, 'We will keep to the high 19 road; if we use any of your water for myself and my cattle, I will pay for it. I am asking only to pass through on foot.' •Edom replied, 'You shall not pass', 20 and Edom marched out to meet them with many men and in great force. •At 21 Edom's refusal to allow Israel a passage through his territory, Israel turned away. · · · · · ·

The capture of Hormah

21 The king of Arad, a Canaanite living in the Negeb, learned that Israel was 1 coming by way of Atharim. He attacked Israel and took some prisoners. Israel then made this vow to Yahweh, 'If you deliver this people into my power, 2 I will lay their towns under ban'. •Yahweh heard the voice of Israel and delivered 3 the Canaanites into their power. And they laid them under ban, both them and their towns. This place was given the name Hormah.

The bronze serpent

. . . On the way the people lost patience. •They spoke against God and against 5 Moses, 'Why did you bring us out of Egypt to die in this wilderness? For there is neither bread nor water here; we are sick of this unsatisfying food.'

At this God sent fiery serpents among the people; their bite brought death 6 to many in Israel. •The people came and said to Moses, 'We have sinned by 7 speaking against Yahweh and against you. Intercede for us with Yahweh to save us from these serpents.' Moses interceded for the people, •and Yahweh answered 8 him, 'Make a fiery serpent and put it on a standard. If anyone is bitten and looks at it, he shall live.' •So Moses fashioned a bronze serpent which he put on 9 a standard, and if anyone was bitten by a serpent, he looked at the bronze serpent and lived.

By stages to Transjordania

. . . They set out from there and camped in the wadi Zered. •They set out from 13 there and camped beyond the Arnon. . .

This wadi in the desert begins in the land of the Amorites. For the Arnon is the frontier of Moab, between the Moabites and the Amorites. •Hence it is 14 written in the Book of the Wars of Yahweh:

> . . . Waheb by Suphah and the wadi Arnon 15
> and the slope of the ravine
> that runs down to the site of Ar
> and leans over the frontier of Moab. . .

and from there they went on to Beer. . . 16

It was of the well here that Yahweh had said to Moses, 'Call the people together and I will give them water'. •Then it was that Israel sang this song: 17

> 'For the well.
> Sing out for the well
> that was sunk by the princes 18
> and dug by the leaders of the people
> with the sceptre, with their staves.'

. . . . . and from Beer to Mattanah, •and from Mattanah to Nahaliel, and from 19 Nahaliel to Bamoth, •and from Bamoth to the valley that gives on to the country 20 of Moab, towards the heights of Pisgah which marks the edge of the desert and looks down on it.

The conquest of Transjordania

Israel sent messengers to say to Sihon, king of the Amorites, ·'I wish to pass 22 through your land. We will not stray into fields or vineyards; we will not drink any water from the wells; we will keep to the king's highway until we are clear of your frontiers.'

But Sihon would not give Israel leave to pass through his land. He gathered 23 all his people, marched into the desert to meet Israel, and reached Jahaz, where he gave battle to Israel. ·Israel struck him down with the edge of the sword and 24 conquered his country from the Arnon to the Jabbok, as far as the sons of Ammon, for Jazer was the Ammonite frontier.

Israel took all these towns, and occupied all the Amorite towns, Heshbon 25 and all the towns under its jurisdiction, ·Heshbon being the capital of Sihon, 26 king of the Amorites. It was the same Sihon who had waged war on the first king of Moab and captured all his territory as far as the Arnon. ·Hence the poets 27 sing:

Courage, Heshbon!
Well built and well founded,
city of Sihon!
For a fire came out of Heshbon,   28
a flame from the city of Sihon,
it devoured Ar of Moab,
it engulfed the heights of the Arnon.
Woe to you, Moab!   29
You are lost, people of Chemosh!
He has turned his sons into fugitives,
his daughters into captives
for Sihon, king of the Amorites.
Heshbon has destroyed   30
the little children as far as Dibon,
the women as far as Nophah,
the men as far as Medeba.

Israel settled in the land of the Amorites. ·Moses sent men to reconnoitre 32 Jazer, and Israel took it and all the towns in its jurisdiction and evicted the Amorites who dwelt there.

Then they turned and marched in the direction of Bashan. Og king of Bashan 33 marched out to meet them with all his people to give battle at Edrei. ·Yahweh 34 said to Moses, 'Do not be afraid of him, for I have given him into your power, him and all his people and his country. Deal with him as you dealt with Sihon, king of the Amorites, who lived in Heshbon.' ·So they defeated him, his sons and 35 all his people; not one of them escaped. And they took possession of his country.

22 Then the sons of Israel set out and pitched their camp in the plains of 1 Moab, beyond the Jordan opposite Jericho.

The king of Moab appeals to Balaam

. . . . . .

Now Balak son of Zippor was king of Moab at the time. ·He sent messengers 5 to summon Balaam son of Beor, at Pethor on the river, in the land of the sons of Amaw, saying, 'Look how this people coming from Egypt has overrun the whole countryside; they have settled at my door. •Come, please, and curse this 6 people for me, for they are stronger than I am. We may then be able to defeat them and drive them out of the country. For this I know: the man you bless is blessed, the man you curse is accursed.'

The elders of Moab and the elders of Midian set out, taking the fee for the 7 divination with them. They found Balaam and gave him Balak's message. •He 8 said to them, 'Stay the night here, and I will answer as Yahweh directs me.' So the chiefs of Moab stayed with Balaam. . . . •In the morning Balaam rose and 13 said to the chiefs sent by Balak, 'Go back to your country, for Yahweh will not let me go with you'. •So the chiefs of Moab rose and returned to Balak and said, 14 'Balaam would not come with us'.

And again Balak sent chiefs, more numerous and more renowned than the 15 first. •They came to Balaam and said, 'A message from Balak son of Zippor, 16 "Do not refuse, I beg you, to come to me. •I will load you with honours and do 17 whatever you say. Come, I beg you, and curse this people for me." ' •Balaam 18 answered the envoys of Balak, 'Even if Balak gave me his house full of silver and gold, I could not go against the order of Yahweh my God in anything, great or small. •Now please stay the night here yourselves, and I will learn what else 19 Yahweh has to tell me.' •*God came to Balaam during the night and said to him,* 20 '*Have not these men come to summon you? Get up, go with them. But you must do nothing except what I tell you.*' •In the morning Balaam rose and 21 saddled his she-donkey and set out with the chiefs of Moab.

Balaam's donkey

His going kindled the wrath of Yahweh, and the angel of Yahweh took his 22 stand on the road to bar his way. He was riding his donkey and his two servants were with him. •Now the donkey saw the angel of Yahweh standing on the road, 23 a drawn sword in his hand, and she turned off the road and made off across country. But Balaam beat her to turn her back on to the road.

The angel of Yahweh then took his stand on a narrow path among the 24 vineyards, with a wall to the right and a wall to the left. •The donkey saw the 25 angel of Yahweh and brushed against the wall, grazing Balaam's foot. Balaam beat her again.

The angel of Yahweh moved and took up his stand in a place so narrow that 26 there was no room to pass, right or left. •When the donkey saw the angel of 27 Yahweh, she lay down under Balaam. Balaam flew into a rage and beat her with his stick.

Then Yahweh opened the mouth of the donkey, who said to Balaam, 'What 28 have I done to you? Why beat me three times like this?' •Balaam answered the 29 donkey, 'Because you are playing the fool with me! If I had had a sword in my hand I would have killed you by now.' •The donkey said to Balaam, 'Am I not 30 your donkey, and have I not been your mount from your youth? In all this time, have I ever failed to serve you?' He answered, 'No'.

Then Yahweh opened the eyes of Balaam. He saw the angel of Yahweh 31 standing on the road, a drawn sword in his hand; and he bowed down and fell prostrate on his face. •And the angel of Yahweh said to him, 'Why did you beat 32 your donkey three times like that? I myself had come to bar your way; while I am here your road is blocked. •The donkey saw me and turned aside from me three 33 times. You are lucky she did turn aside, or I should have killed you by now,

though I would have spared her.' ·Balaam answered the angel of Yahweh, 34
'I have sinned. I did not know you were standing in my path. However, if you
are angry with me, I will go back.' ·The angel of Yahweh answered Balaam, 35
'Go with these men, but only say what I tell you to say.' So Balaam went with
the chiefs sent by Balak.

Balaam and Balak

Balak learned that Balaam was coming and went out to meet him, in the 36
direction of Ar of Moab, at the Arnon frontier on the country's furthest bound-
ary. ·Balak said to Balaam, 'Did I not send messengers to summon you? Why did 37
you not come to me? Did you think, perhaps, I could confer no honours on you?'
Balaam answered Balak, 'Here I am at your side. May I make myself clear 38
to you now? The word that God puts into my mouth, this I shall speak.'

24 ... Raising his eyes Balaam saw Israel, encamped by tribes; the spirit of 2
God came on him and he declaimed his poem. He said:
>   'The oracle of Balaam son of Beor,
>   the oracle of the man with far-seeing eyes,
>   the oracle of one who hears the word of God.   4
>   He sees what Shaddai makes him see,
>   receives the divine answer, and his eyes are opened.
>   How fair are your tents, O Jacob!   5
>   How fair your dwellings, Israel!
>   Like valleys that stretch afar,   6
>   like gardens by the banks of a river,
>   like aloes planted by Yahweh,
>   like cedars beside the waters!
>   A hero arises from their stock,   7
>   he reigns over countless peoples.
>   His king is greater than Agag,
>   his majesty is exalted.
>   God brings him out of Egypt,   8
>   he is like the wild ox's horns to him.
>   He feeds on the carcase of his enemies,
>   and breaks their bones in pieces.
>   He has crouched, he has lain down,   9
>   like a lion, like a lioness;
>   who dare rouse him?
>   Blessed be those who bless you,
>   and accursed be those who curse you!'

Balak flew into a rage with Balaam. He beat his hands together and said to 10
Balaam, 'I brought you to curse my enemies, and you bless them three times over!
Be off with you, and go home. I promised to load you with honours. Yahweh 11
himself has deprived you of them.' ·Balaam answered Balak, 'Did I not tell the 12
messengers you sent me: ·Even if Balak gave me his house full of gold and 13
silver I could not go against the order of Yahweh and do anything of my own
accord, good or evil; what Yahweh says is what I will say. ·Now that I am going 14
back to my own folk, let me warn you what this people will do to your people,
in time to come.' ·Then he declaimed his poem. He said: 15
>   'The oracle of Balaam son of Beor,
>   the oracle of the man with far-seeing eyes,

the oracle of one who hears the word of God,   16
of one who knows the knowledge of the Most High.
He sees what Shaddai makes him see,
receives the divine answer, and his eyes are opened.
I see him—but not in the present,   17
I behold him—but not close at hand:
a star from Jacob takes the leadership,
a sceptre arises from Israel.
It crushes the brows of Moab
the skulls of all the sons of Sheth.
Edom becomes a conquered land;   18
a conquered land is Seir.
Israel exerts his strength,   19
Jacob dominates his enemies
and destroys the fugitives from Ar.'
Balaam looked on Amalek and declaimed his poem. He said: 20
   'Amalek, first among the nations!
   But his posterity shall perish for ever.'
Then he looked on the Kenites and declaimed his poem. He said: 21
   'Your house was firm, Kain,
   and your nest perched high in the rock.
   But the nest belongs to Beor;   22
   how long will you be Asshur's captive?'
Then he looked on Og and declaimed his poem. He said: 23
   'The Sea-people gather in the north,
   ships from the coasts of Kittim.   24
   They bear down on Asshur, they bear down on Eber;
   he too shall perish for ever.'
Then Balaam rose, left and went home. Balak too went his way.   25

GENERAL INDEX

INDEX OF AUTHORS

INDEX OF SCRIPTURE TEXTS

*The figures following the long dash refer to page numbers.